Pragmatics in
Language Teaching

THE CAMBRIDGE APPLIED LINGUISTICS SERIES

Series editors: Michael H. Long and Jack C. Richards

This series presents the findings of recent work in applied linguistics which are of direct relevance to language teaching and learning and of particular interest to applied linguists, researchers, language teachers, and teacher trainers.

Pragmatics in Language Teaching

Edited by

Kenneth R. Rose
City University of Hong Kong

and

Gabriele Kasper
University of Hawai'i at Manoa

CAMBRIDGE
UNIVERSITY PRESS

PUBLISHED BY THE PRESS SYNDICATE OF THE UNIVERSITY OF CAMBRIDGE
The Pitt Building, Trumpington Street, Cambridge, United Kingdom

CAMBRIDGE UNIVERSITY PRESS
The Edinburgh Building, Cambridge CB2 2RU, UK
40 West 20th Street, New York, NY 10011-4211, USA
10 Stamford Road, Oakleigh, VIC 3166, Australia
Ruiz de Alarcón 13, 28014 Madrid, Spain
Dock House, The Waterfront, Cape Town 8001, South Africa

http://www.cambridge.org

First published 2001

Printed in the United States of America

Typeface Sabon 10½/12 pt.

A catalog record for this book is available from the British Library.

Library of Congress Cataloging-in-Publication Data

Rose, Kenneth R.
  Pragmatics in language teaching/Kenneth R. Rose, Gabriele Kasper.
  p. cm. – (Cambridge applied linguistics)
  Includes bibliographical references and index.
  ISBN 0-521-80379-9 – ISBN 0-521-00858-1 (pb.)
    1. Pragmatics 2. Language and languages – Study and teaching. I. Kasper, Gabriele. II.
  Title. III. Cambridge applied linguistics series.

  P99.4.P72 R67 2001
  306.44–dc21   00-068088

ISBN 0-521-80379-9 hardback
ISBN 0-521-00858-1 paperback

Contents

Contributors

Kathleen Bardovi-Harlig, Indiana University
James Dean Brown, University of Hawai'i at Manoa
Chantal Crozet, Australian National University
Thom Hudson, University of Hawai'i at Manoa
Gabriele Kasper, University of Hawai'i at Manoa
Anthony J. Liddicoat, Griffith University, Australia
Haruko Minegishi Cook, University of Hawai'i at Manoa
Connie Ng Kwai-fun, City University of Hong Kong
Kimberly Niezgoda, Kanazawa Institute of Technology, Japan
John M. Norris, University of Hawai'i at Manoa
Amy Snyder Ohta, University of Washington, Seattle
Kenneth R. Rose, City University of Hong Kong
Carsten Röver, University of Hawai'i at Manoa
Satomi Takahashi, Rikkyo University, Japan
Yumiko Tateyama, University of Hawai'i at Manoa
Dina Rudolph Yoshimi, University of Hawai'i at Manoa

Series editors' preface

Compared with phonology, morphology, and syntax, second language pragmatics, like second language vocabulary, was a relatively neglected area of second language acquisition and applied linguistics until about 15 years ago, but it has seen a veritable explosion of work of late. That work has been both theoretical and empirical, and sometimes difficult even for educated outsiders to come to grips with, in part because it has frequently crossed traditional boundaries of second language acquisition and use. Some researchers have concentrated on unearthing what Hymes once referred to as those "rules of use without which rules of grammar would be useless," some (rather fewer) have focused on how those rules are acquired (or not), and some have attempted to address both aspects. Recently, as this volume demonstrates, the domain has grown to include both the teaching and the testing of second language pragmatics, and has involved additional research cultures and knowledge bases.

Two pioneers and internationally acknowledged experts in this field are Kenneth Rose and Gabriele Kasper. Each has published extensive original empirical research on interlanguage and crosscultural pragmatics, each has written authoritative reviews of the pragmatics literature, each has helped focus the research agenda, each has contributed to our understanding of appropriate qualitative and quantitative research methods for the work at hand, each has taught numerous courses and seminars and supervised graduate student research on pragmatics, and each has lectured on these subjects around the world. Their vast and diverse experience is readily apparent in the lucid and authoritative overview with which they begin this volume, as well as in their subsequent individual contributions.

Unlike any other books on the topic to date, *Pragmatics in Language Teaching* focuses on two crucial, yet still relatively unexplored dimensions of L2 pragmatics: teachability and assessment. Professors Rose and Kasper have assembled a set of truly intriguing studies by some of the leading researchers at work on these issues today. The result is a welcome addition to the Cambridge Applied Linguistics Series, a volume that should be invaluable to researchers, language teachers, language testers, and students of pragmatics everywhere.

Michael H. Long
Jack C. Richards

Preface

To our knowledge, this is the first edited volume devoted solely to class-room research on interlanguage pragmatics, and as such is situated at the interface of second language acquisition, pragmatics, and educational research. The chapters in this collection address a range of issues in the learning of pragmatics and discourse in classroom contexts – both second and foreign language – from a diversity of approaches to teaching and research. Coverage is provided not only for various options in instruction but also for the assessment of pragmatic proficiency, a heretofore largely neglected area. It is our hope that the work reported in this collection will inspire others to further explore issues raised here in their own research, thus guaranteeing that this will not be the last book on this topic.

We would like to extend our sincere appreciation first and foremost to our contributors for undertaking the research reported here, agreeing to include it in our collection, and following through in such a timely and professional manner at each stage of the process. Thanks also to the series editors for their support, two anonymous reviewers for their helpful comments, as well as everyone else we had the pleasure of working with at Cambridge University Press, including Olive Collen, production editor. And a special thanks to David Thorstad, whose expert handling of our multilingual manuscript was nothing short of amazing.

Kenneth R. Rose
Gabriele Kasper

1 *Pragmatics in language teaching*

Gabriele Kasper and Kenneth R. Rose

Introduction

By such milestones as the appearance of the Threshold Level for English (Van Ek, 1975) and Wilkins's Notional Syllabus (1976), communicative language teaching (CLT) has been with us for nearly three decades. A strong theoretical impetus for the development of CLT came from the social sciences and humanities outside language pedagogy. Different notions of communicative competence, proposed by Hymes from the perspective of linguistic anthropology (1971) and by Habermas (1984) from the vantage point of social philosophy, served as guiding constructs for the design of communicative competence as the overall goal of language teaching and assessment. An influential and comprehensive review of communicative competence and related notions was offered by Canale and Swain (1980), who also proposed a widely cited framework of communicative competence for language instruction and testing. While pragmatics does not figure as a term among their three components of communicative competence (grammatical, sociolinguistic, and strategic competence), pragmatic ability is included under "sociolinguistic competence," called "rules of use." Canale (1983) expanded the earlier version of the framework by adding discourse competence as a fourth component. A decade after the original framework had been published, Bachman (1990, pp. 87ff.) suggested a model of communicative ability that not only includes pragmatic competence as one of the two main components of "language competence," parallel to "organizational competence," but subsumes "sociolinguistic competence" and "illocutionary competence" under pragmatic competence. The prominence of pragmatic ability has been maintained in a revision of this model by Bachman and Palmer (1996, pp. 66ff.).

1

Defining pragmatics

What exactly is the communicative ability that has gained such attention in second language pedagogy? Pragmatics has been defined in various ways, reflecting authors' theoretical orientation and audience. A definition that appeals to us, not least for its usefulness for second language pedagogy, has been offered by Crystal (1997, p. 301), who proposes that pragmatics is "the study of language from the point of view of users, especially of the choices they make, the constraints they encounter in using language in social interaction and the effects their use of language has on other participants in the act of communication." In other words, pragmatics is defined as the study of communicative action in its sociocultural context. Communicative action includes not only using speech acts (such as apologizing, complaining, complimenting, and requesting), but also engaging in different types of discourse and participating in speech events of varying length and complexity. Following Leech (1983), this book will focus on pragmatics as interpersonal rhetoric – the way speakers and writers accomplish goals as social actors who do not just need to get things done but must attend to their interpersonal relationships with other participants at the same time.

As a means of mapping out the relevant territory for the study of how people accomplish their goals and attend to interpersonal relationships while using language, Leech (1983) and Thomas (1983) divided pragmatics into two components: pragmalinguistics and sociopragmatics. *Pragmalinguistics* refers to the resources for conveying communicative acts and relational or interpersonal meanings. Such resources include pragmatic strategies such as directness and indirectness, routines, and a large range of linguistic forms which can intensify or soften communicative acts. For one example, compare these two versions of an apology: the terse *Sorry* versus the Wildean *I'm absolutely devastated – could you possibly find it in your heart to forgive me?* In both versions, the speaker chooses from among the available pragmalinguistic resources of English which serve the function of apologizing (which would also include other items, such as *It was my fault* or *I won't let it happen again*), but she indexes a very different attitude and social relationship in each of the apologies (e.g., Fraser, 1981; House & Kasper, 1981a; Brown & Levinson, 1987; Blum-Kulka, House, & Kasper, 1989), which is where sociopragmatics comes into the picture. *Sociopragmatics* has been described by Leech (1983, p. 10) as "the sociological interface of pragmatics," referring to the social perceptions underlying participants' interpretation and performance of communicative action. Speech communities differ in their assessment of speakers' and hearers' social distance and social power, their rights and obligations, and the degree of imposition involved in particular communicative acts (Blum-Kulka &

House, 1989; Olshtain, 1989; Takahashi & Beebe, 1993; Kasper & Rose, 1999, for review). The values of context factors are negotiable; they are subject to change through the dynamics of conversational interaction, as captured in Fraser's (1990) notion of the "conversational contract" and in Myers-Scotton's Markedness Model (1993). As Thomas (1983) points out, although pragmalinguistics is, in a sense, akin to grammar in that it consists of linguistic forms and their respective functions, sociopragmatics is very much about proper social behavior, making it a far more thorny issue to deal with in the classroom – it is one thing to teach people what functions bits of language serve, but it is entirely different to teach people how to behave "properly." Here learners must be made aware of the consequences of making pragmatic choices, but the choice to act a certain way should be theirs alone (Siegal, 1994, 1996).

Pragmatics in language teaching

In many second and foreign language teaching contexts, curricula and materials developed in recent years include strong pragmatic components or even adopt a pragmatic approach as their organizing principle. A number of proposals for instruction in different aspects of pragmatic competence are now based on empirical studies of native speaker (NS) discourse, on both NS and interlanguage material, or on the classic set of comparable interlanguage, L1 and L2 data. Examples of target-based teaching proposals for L2 English are Holmes and Brown (1987) on complimenting, Myers-Scotton and Bernsten (1988) on conversational structure and management, and Bardovi-Harlig, Hartford, Mahan-Taylor, Morgan, and Reynolds (1991) on conversational closings. Proposals based on NS and interlanguage data include the "pedagogic interactional grammar" by Edmondson and House (1981), comprising a large number of speech acts and discourse functions, and Rose's (1994b) recommendation for consciousness-raising activities on requesting. Bouton (1994a) suggests an instructional strategy for improving learners' comprehension of indirect questions, thus far a notable exception in that the proposed instruction is informed by a longitudinal study of learners' implicature comprehension. But with the exception of his study, the research-based recommendations for instruction in pragmatics have not been examined in action, that is, how they are implemented in classrooms and how effective they are for students' learning of the targeted pragmatic feature.

There is now a large and fast-growing literature on interlanguage pragmatics, that is, learners' use and acquisition of L2 pragmatic ability (Kasper & Blum-Kulka, 1993; Kasper & Rose, 1999; Rose, 2000;

Bardovi-Harlig, this volume). Participants in these studies are often foreign language learners, who may have little access to target-language input and even less opportunity for productive L2 use outside the classroom. Second language learners participating in interlanguage pragmatics research often also receive formal instruction. And yet, most of the interlanguage pragmatics research informs about learners' pragmatic ability at a particular point in time without relating it systematically to their learning experience in language classrooms. To date, only one early full-length book publication has addressed the relationship between classroom language learning and pragmatic development in a second language (Wildner-Bassett, 1986). In order to investigate how the learning of L2 pragmatics – both the learning processes and the outcomes – is shaped by instructional context and activities, three major questions require examination: what opportunities for developing L2 pragmatic ability are offered in language classrooms; whether pragmatic ability develops in a classroom setting without instruction in pragmatics; and what effects various approaches to instruction have on pragmatic development. The first and third questions clearly call for classroom research – the resources, processes, and limitations of classroom learning can be explored only through data-based studies in classroom settings. As a new kid on the block, classroom-based interlanguage pragmatics research can profit from the vast literature on educational research generally and second language classroom research specifically (e.g., Chaudron, 1988; Allwright & Bailey, 1991). A review of research on opportunities for pragmatic learning in L2 classrooms that do *not* offer any form for direct teaching in pragmatics reveals both limitations, especially of teacher-fronted teaching, and potentials for pragmatic development over time (Kasper, this volume). Data-based studies on classroom-based learning of L2 pragmatics are the focus of Part II of this book.

Answers to the second question – whether pragmatic ability develops without pedagogical intervention – can be gleaned from the pragmatics and interlanguage pragmatics literature. Adult learners get a considerable amount of L2 pragmatic knowledge for free. This is because some pragmatic knowledge is universal (e.g., Blum-Kulka, 1991; Ochs, 1996), and other aspects may be successfully transferred from the learners' L1. Current theory and research suggest a number of universal features in discourse and pragmatics. Conversational organization through turn taking and sequencing of contributions is a universal property of spoken interactive discourse, much as cultural and contextual implementations may vary. Basic orientations to the effectiveness and social cohesiveness of communicative action, such as the Cooperative Principle (Grice, 1975) and politeness (Brown & Levinson, 1987), regulate communicative action and interaction throughout communities, even though what counts as cooperative and polite and how these principles are implemented in context varies across cultures. Speakers and listeners have the ability to convey pragmatic intent indirectly and infer indirectly conveyed meaning by utilizing cues in the utterance, context information, and various knowledge sources (Gumperz, 1996). The main categories of communicative acts – in Searle's (1976) influential classification, representatives, directives, commissives, expressives, and declarations – are available in any community, as are (according to current evidence) such individual communicative acts as greetings, leave-takings, requests, offers, suggestions, invitations, refusals, apologies, complaints, or expressions of gratitude. Universal pragmatic knowledge includes the expectation that recurrent speech situations are managed by means of conversational routines (Coulmas, 1981a; Nattinger & DeCarrico, 1992) rather than by newly created utterances. It subsumes an implicit understanding that strategies of communicative actions vary according to context (Blum-Kulka, 1991), specifically, along with such factors as social power, social and psychological distance, and the degree of imposition involved in a communicative act, as established in politeness theory (Brown & Levinson, 1987; Brown & Gilman, 1989). The major realization strategies identified for some communicative acts have been found stable across ethnolinguistically distant speech communities. For instance, the speech act set for apologies comprises as its major semantic formulas an explicit apology, an explanation, and an admission or denial of responsibility; minor, more context-dependent strategies include an offer of repair, a promise of forbearance, and an expression of concern for the hearer, all of which can be intensified or mitigated. These strategies have been found to be used in English, French, German, and Hebrew (Olshtain, 1989), Thai (Bergman & Kasper, 1993), and Japanese (Barnlund & Yoshioka, 1990; Maeshiba, Yoshinaga, Kasper, & Ross, 1996). For requests, the major strategies differ according to their level of directness – direct, conventionally indirect, and indirect – together with external and internal modification, and are available to NSs and ESL or EFL learners with such diverse native languages as Chinese (Johnston, Kasper, & Ross, 1998; Rose, 2000), Danish (Færch & Kasper, 1989; Trosborg, 1995), German (House & Kasper, 1987), Hebrew (Blum-Kulka & Olshtain, 1986), Japanese (Hill, 1997), Malay (Piirainen-Marsh, 1995), and Spanish (Rintell & Mitchell, 1989) and to learners of such target languages as German (House & Kasper, 1987), Indonesian (Hassall, 1997), and Norwegian (Svanes, 1992). In their early learning stages, learners may not be able to use such strategies because they have not yet acquired the necessary linguistic means, but when their linguistic knowledge permits it, learners will use the main strategies for requesting without instruction.

Learners may also get very specific pragmalinguistic knowledge for free if there is a corresponding form-function mapping between L1 and L2, and the forms can be used in corresponding L2 contexts with corresponding effects. For instance, the English modal past as in the modal verbs *could* or *would* has formal, functional, and distributional equivalents in other Germanic languages such as Danish and German – the Danish modal past *kunne/ville* and the German subjunctive *könntest* and *würdest*. And, sure enough, Danish and German learners of English transfer ability questions from L1 Danish (*"Kunne/ville du låne mig dine noter?"*) and L1 German (*"Könntest/würdest Du mir Deine Aufzeichnungen leihen?"*) to L2 English ("Could/would you lend me your notes?") (House & Kasper, 1987; Færch & Kasper, 1989), and they do this without the benefit of instruction. Positive transfer can also facilitate learners' task in acquiring sociopragmatic knowledge. When distributions of participants' rights and obligations, their relative social power, and the demands on their resources are equivalent in their original and target community, learners may need to make only small adjustments in their social categorizations (Mir, 1995).

Unfortunately, learners do not always capitalize on the knowledge they already have. It is well known from educational psychology that students do not always transfer available knowledge and strategies to new tasks. This is also true for some aspects of learners' universal or L1-based pragmatic knowledge. L2 learners often tend toward literal interpretation, taking utterances at face value (rather than inferring what is meant from what is said) and underusing context information (Carrell, 1979, 1981). Learners frequently underuse politeness marking in L2 even though they regularly mark their utterances for politeness in L1 (Kasper, 1981). Although highly context-sensitive in selecting pragmatic strategies in their own language, learners may underdifferentiate such context variables as social distance and social power in L2 (Tanaka, 1988; Fukushima, 1990). On the one hand, then, adult learners bring a rich pragmatic knowledge base to the task of acquiring the pragmatics of a second or foreign language – so rich that, in Bialystok's (1993) view, their task (unlike that of L1-acquiring children) is predominantly one of achieving control of processing over already available pragmatic knowledge, for instance, selecting contextually appropriate linguistic forms to express pragmatic intent. Although we believe that this may be an underestimation of the complexity of L2 pragmatic learning – especially when positive pragmatic transfer is no option – Bialystok's position underscores the significant role that existing pragmatic knowledge plays in L2 learning and suggests that language instruction purposefully build on it. On the other hand, learners do not always use what they know. There is thus a clear role for pedagogical intervention, not with the purpose of providing learners with new information but to make them aware of what they know already and encourage them to use their universal or transferable L1 pragmatic knowledge in L2 contexts.

At the same time, ethnolinguistic variation is obviously abundant in pragmatics, confronting learners with new learning tasks. Specific context factors may be regularly attended to in some, but not all, communities. For instance, in comparable contexts, urgency was found to influence the request strategies of German but not of Japanese speakers (Morosawa, 1990). As predicted by politeness theory (Brown & Levinson, 1987; Brown & Gilman, 1989), power relationships, social and psychological distance, and degree of imposition constrain communicative action universally, but actors' assessment of the weight and values of these universal context factors varies substantively from context to context as well as across speech communities (Blum-Kulka & House, 1989). For instance, in a series of studies, Beebe and Takahashi established that social status influenced the performance of face-threatening acts by NSs of Japanese and NSs of American English, but the impact of status on actors' choice of speech act strategies was stronger in the case of the Japanese than the American participants (e.g., Takahashi & Beebe, 1993). Furthermore, certain communicative acts are known in some communities but not in others. For example, in the category of declarations, acts tied to a particular institutional context derive their function from the institution and will not be available outside it. Thus, sustaining and overruling objections presupposes an adversarial legal system and rising to order a type of formal meeting arranged by parliamentary procedures. Performing communicative acts appropriately often involves norms specific to a particular cultural and institutional context, such as supporting a refusal of an adviser's suggestion with appropriate reasons and status-congruent mitigation in the course of an academic advising session (Bardovi-Harlig & Hartford, 1990). Pragmalinguistic and sociopragmatic conventions are tied to the grammatical and lexical structures of particular languages. Thus, ability questions (e.g., "Can you return the videos?") do not seem to be conventionalized as request in Polish (Wierzbicka, 1985), while exclamatory questions (e.g., "What is this beauty!") are conventionalized as complimenting strategy in Egyptian Arabic but not in different varieties of English (see Miles, 1994, for review).

Although learners thus have to learn some new ethnolinguistically specific conventions when acquiring L2 pragmatics, much of the variability in the way that communicative acts are performed lies less in the absolute availability of a pragmatic strategy than in the degree to which a strategy is conventionalized in a speech community. For instance, Freed (1994) identified sixteen functions of questions in informal native English conversation, but for such illocutions as warning, disagreeing, refusing, or criticizing (Sakamoto & Naotsuka, 1982;

Beebe & Takahashi, 1989a, 1989b; Bardovi-Harlig & Hartford, 1990), information questions appear to be more highly conventionalized in Japanese or Indonesian than in English. Crosscultural differences in conventionalization can further be illustrated by pragmatic strategies such as rejecting (rather than accepting or qualifying) compliments (Wolfson, 1989a), complimenting as a request strategy (Holmes & Brown, 1987), complaining through an intermediary (Steinberg Du, 1995), prefacing corrections to a lower-status person by positive remarks (Takahashi & Beebe, 1993), offering a statement of philosophy in refusals (Beebe, Takahashi, & Uliss-Weltz, 1990), explicitly apologizing, explaining and offering repair in apologies (Olshtain & Cohen, 1983; Barnlund & Yoshioka, 1990; Bergman & Kasper, 1993), and selecting different directness levels in requesting (Blum-Kulka & House, 1989; House & Kasper, 1987). In addition to these crosscultural differences, the indexical meaning of speech acts and strategies varies inter- and intraculturally. Whether indirectness is perceived as more or less polite than directness, or whether volubility indexes more or less power, depends on cultural preferences and the context of use (Blum-Kulka, 1987; Tannen, 1993b). In the area of conversational management, active listening – signaling attention and alignment through response tokens – is an interactional practice in many communities, but the structural patterning, response tokens, and their epistemic and interpersonal meanings vary crossculturally (e.g., White, 1989; Ohta, this volume). As Bardovi-Harlig (this volume) demonstrates, many aspects of L2 pragmatics are not acquired without the benefit of instruction, or they are learned more slowly. There is thus a strong indication that instructional intervention may be facilitative to, or even necessary for, the acquisition of L2 pragmatic ability.

How can pragmatics be taught?

The apparent necessity – or, at least, usefulness – of instruction for pragmatic development brings us back to our third question: what are the effects of various approaches to instruction in pragmatics? Given the wide range of instructional contexts, there is not likely to be one approach which is to be preferred over all others in every context. Yet an intriguing issue to examine is whether despite such variation, potentially universal principles of instruction in pragmatics may be identified, in analogy with principles proposed for grammar teaching (e.g., Robinson, in press). At the same time, particular strategies of instructional intervention may prove differentially appropriate for different pragmatic learning targets, student characteristics, and institutional and sociocultural contexts. It is a central goal of this book to take stock of what is known about the effectiveness of instruction in pragmatics to date and illustrate the wide range of research approaches that can usefully be adopted to investigate this issue. To that end, Kasper (this volume) reviews the classroom-based research on the teaching of pragmatics up to the present. Part II includes studies examining learning processes and outcomes of second and foreign language teaching when instructional environments have not been arranged to target particular features of L2 pragmatics. The studies presented in Part III investigate the effects of instruction in a variety of specific pragmatic features and skills, aiming at different target languages and student populations and employing different instructional approaches.

It has often been noted that the content and forms of language teaching are significantly influenced by the content and forms of language testing. Especially in instructional contexts where formal testing is regularly performed, curricular innovations that comprise pragmatics as a learning objective will be ineffective as long as pragmatic ability is not included as a regular and important component of language tests. The models of communicative language ability we referred to initially (Canale & Swain, 1980; Canale, 1983; Bachman, 1990; Bachman & Palmer, 1996) were expressly designed to provide constructs for language instruction *and* assessment, yet tests of pragmatic ability are few and far between. One exception is the Canadian Development of Bilingual Proficiency project (e.g., Harley, Allen, Cummins, & Swain, 1990a), in which tests for grammatical, discourse, and "sociolinguistic" competence in L2 French were developed. Sociolinguistic ability, defined as "the ability to produce and recognize socially appropriate language in context" (Harley, Allen, Cummins, & Swain, 1990b, p. 14), was operationalized as requests, offers, and complaints produced in oral roleplays, the selection of contextually appropriate realizations of speech acts in a multiple-choice format, and written directives in a formal letter and informal notes. But until recently, comprehensive approaches to the assessment of pragmatic abilities in a variety of second languages have been lacking. Two roads have been taken to remedy this problem. One is to examine the sociolinguistic, pragmatic, and discourse properties of existing tests, such as oral proficiency interviews, in order to evaluate how capable these tests are of assessing pragmatic ability. The other approach is to develop principles, instruments, and procedures specifically for pragmatic assessment. The final part of this book illustrates both options for the testing of pragmatic ability.

PART I:
THEORETICAL AND EMPIRICAL
BACKGROUND

The chapters in Part I provide the theoretical and empirical background to the data-based studies which follow. In Chapter 2, Kathleen Bardovi-Harlig discusses how native speakers (NSs) and nonnative speakers (NNSs) differ in their use of pragmatic knowledge in production and comprehension. The production section of her chapter is organized around the four-way distinction utilized in Bardovi-Harlig (1996), namely, culture-specific speech act use, use of semantic formulas, use of linguistic devices, and utterance content. After providing ample evidence from the research literature that NNSs' understanding and use of the pragmatics of the target language often differ considerably from those of NSs, she discusses how these differences have been explained, including input factors, learner expectations, teaching materials, level of proficiency, and washback. The chapter concludes with a summary of evidence of the need for instruction, but Bardovi-Harlig is careful to note that although the evidence indicates divergence of interlanguage pragmatics from target-language pragmatic practices, such differences per se do not constitute a mandate to teach (or facilitate the acquisition of) target-language pragmatics – many other factors need to be considered in determining what, if any, areas need to be targeted for instruction, or how instruction is to be implemented.

Gabriele Kasper begins in Chapter 3 by noting that although pragmatics has played a considerable role in approaches to first and second language classroom research, classroom research has played only a minor role in interlanguage pragmatics thus far. She then reviews the small body of research on pragmatic learning in the second or foreign language classroom, considering both observational studies, which focus on classroom processes and the opportunities they afford for pragmatic learning in authentic instructional contexts (that is, contexts that have not been specifically arranged for research purposes), and interventional studies, which examine learning outcomes subsequent to some form of (often quasi-experimental) treatment. One recurrent outcome of the observational studies is the limited opportunities that teacher-fronted instruction offers for the acquisition of target-language pragmatics. The interventional studies converge on demonstrating that, overall, pragmatic aspects are teachable, and explicit instruction is more effective than implicit teaching. Kasper notes that although the substantive outcomes of the interventional studies are encouraging, the exclusive product focus they adopt is quite limiting because it provides little or no information about how different approaches were implemented, how students participated in the activities, what interactional and cognitive learning strategies they employed, and what stages of pragmatic learning, if any, they progressed through. As a way of moving past these shortcomings, Kasper calls for classroom research on pragmatics that combines process and product perspectives, relating learning outcomes to classroom processes. Such a strategy will include longitudinal observation of classroom discourse as well as explorations of students' and teachers' subjective theories about second language pragmatics and how pragmatic ability can best be developed in an instructional context, enabling us to explain outcomes, control how intervention was implemented, assess and change interventional measures, and afford ongoing exploration of substantive and methodological issues.

2 Evaluating the empirical evidence
Grounds for instruction in pragmatics?

Kathleen Bardovi-Harlig

Introduction

Everyone who works with a second or foreign language, whether learners, teachers, or researchers, knows a funny story about crosscultural pragmatics – or maybe the stories are really not that funny. From the perspective of the speaker, they may be about feeling silly, helpless, or rude; from the perspective of the listener, they may be about feeling confused, insulted, or angry. Anecdotal evidence inspires us to say that we ought to teach, as one of our ESL students said, the "secret rules" of language. Much research has gone into identifying how speakers of various languages realize speech acts, take turns, and use silence, for example, so that what our student called the secret rules are not unknown; and even if our knowledge is incomplete at this stage, could it form the basis of an informed pedagogy? In other words, is there empirical evidence that warrants the development and implementation of a pedagogy of pragmatics in second and foreign language instruction? In this chapter, I will review the empirical evidence that shows that native speakers (NSs) and nonnative speakers (NNSs) of a given target language appear to have different systems of pragmatics, discuss the factors that influence the development of L2 pragmatics systems, and then address the question of whether differences in pragmatics systems warrant instructional treatment.

The evidence

This review adopts a speech act perspective. Although it is not the only way of viewing pragmatics, speech act research has been well represented in crosscultural and interlanguage pragmatics research, and provides a common analytic framework which facilitates comparison across studies. Although most of the research has focused on production, there are additional studies (although many fewer) that have investigated judgment and perception. The interlanguage pragmatics studies have investigated intermediate to advanced learners from a variety of first language backgrounds, and have used a variety of data collection techniques from different sources, including natural conversations, role-plays, and written questionnaires. Even grammatically advanced learners show differences from target-language pragmatic norms. That is to say, a learner of high grammatical proficiency will not necessarily possess concomitant pragmatic competence. It is equally important to note that at least at the higher levels of grammatical proficiency, learners may also evidence a wide range of pragmatic competence. Advanced NNSs are neither uniformly successful, nor uniformly unsuccessful, pragmatically; however, they are more likely to be less successful as a group than NSs on the same task where contextualized reaction data are available (as in the case of authentic conversations and institutional talk).

Production

There are many ways in which learners can differ from NSs in the production of speech acts. Cohen (1996) identifies three areas for such differences: speech acts, semantic formulas, and form. Blum-Kulka (1982) also notes that speech act realizations may deviate on three levels: social acceptability of the utterance, linguistic acceptability of the utterance, or pragmatic acceptability reflected in shifts of illocutionary force. In this chapter, I will divide the differences between learners and NSs into four main categories and then give representative examples of each: NSs and NNSs may use different speech acts, or where the same speech acts are used, these may differ in semantic formula, content, or form (Bardovi-Harlig, 1996).

Choice of speech acts. NNSs may perform different speech acts than NSs in the same contexts, or, alternatively, they may elect not to perform any speech act at all. The best examples of this come from authentic conversations and role-plays where speakers have some flexibility in determining what they will say or do. In authentic academic advising sessions, NSs and NNSs favor different speech acts (Bardovi-Harlig & Hartford, 1993). NSs produce more suggestions than NNSs per advising session, whereas NNSs produce more rejections per advising session than NSs do. The two speech acts seem to serve the same function, that of control. NSs exert control over their course schedules by making suggestions; in contrast, the NNSs control their course schedules through rejections, by blocking the suggestions of their advisers (Bardovi-Harlig & Hartford, 1993). Although both groups of students participate in determining what courses they ultimately take, the resulting feeling of harmony in the interview is perceived (by the advisers) to be noticeably different.

A second example comes from role-play data collected by Cohen and Olshtain (1993). The scenario in this example was designed to elicit an apology. However, in the transcript of one Israeli learner of English, we learn that for at least that one learner of English, the conditions for an apology were not satisfied by the scenario.

(1) Scenario presented to NNS (Cohen & Olshtain, 1993, p. 54)[1]

> You arranged to meet a friend in order to study together for an exam. You arrive half an hour late for the meeting.
>
> Friend (annoyed): I've been waiting at least half an hour for you!
>   You: _____

(2) Transcript of role-play (Cohen & Olshtain, 1993, pp. 54–55)

> Friend: I've been waiting at least half an hour for you!
> Nogah: So what! It's only an – a meeting for – to study.
> Friend: Well. I mean – I was standing here waiting, I could've been sitting in the library studying.
> Nogah: But you're in your house. You can – you can study if you wish. You can do whatever you want.
> Friend: Still pretty annoying – I mean – try and come on time next time.
> Nogah: OK, but don't make such a big deal of it.
> Friend: OK.

In this exchange, we learn that an appointment with another student to study is not regarded as very important by this learner, and that keeping someone waiting at his or her own house is not a very serious offense. Thus, this respondent may feel that her obligation to apologize is very low. This accords with the findings of Bergman and Kasper's (1993) study of perception, discussed in the section on judgment and perception later in this chapter (see also García, 1989).

As we see in the case of the apology role-plays collected by Cohen and Olshtain (1993), learners may not perform the speech act under investigation. They may also perform a different speech act from NSs in the same context. In the context of the academic advising session, NNSs used rejections rather than suggestions, which were used by NSs. Rejections were found to serve the same function as suggestions in the interviews overall, that of controlling the course schedule. The absence of a particular speech act is often salient. This brings us to the discussion of opting out (Bonikowska, 1988). Opting out is the choice of not performing the speech act under investigation and is particularly difficult to investigate in written questionnaires (Rose, 1994a; Rose &

---

1 There is an error in the original report of the scenario which has been corrected here. Readers may also see Cohen (1997b, p. 259) for the correction. I cite the original study to appropriately place Cohen and Olshtain's innovative research design in 1993.

Ono, 1995), but it merits study because it may be an important part of understanding why NSs and NNSs differ in speech act realization (Bonikowska, 1988).

Semantic formulas. A second way in which NSs and NNSs may differ is in the choice of semantic formulas (Hartford & Bardovi-Harlig, 1992; Niki & Tajika, 1994; Bardovi-Harlig, 1996; Murphy & Neu, 1996). Semantic formulas represent the means by which a particular speech act is accomplished in terms of the primary content of an utterance (Fraser, 1981; Olshtain & Cohen, 1983; Beebe, Takahashi, & Uliss-Weltz, 1990). For example, as Olshtain and Cohen (1983) point out, an apology may contain an illocutionary force indicating device (*I'm sorry*), an explanation or account of the situation (e.g., *The bus was late*), an acknowledgment of responsibility (e.g., *It's my fault*), an offer of repair (e.g., *I'll pay for the broken vase*), and/or a promise of forbearance (e.g., *It won't happen again*). Semantic formulas are a superset of specific content which is examined in the following section.

Both NSs and NNSs engaged in authentic advising sessions used more explanations than any other semantic formula when rejecting an adviser's suggestion of a particular course, as in Examples (3)–(5):

Explanations

(3) That's the one that conflicts with what I have to take. [NS]
(4) Yeah, but, the books are, probably the books are in German. [NNS] (from Bardovi-Harlig & Hartford, 1991)

Alternative

(5) Well, I'd kind of thought of taking L541. [NS, DCT (discourse completion task)]
(from Hartford & Bardovi-Harlig, 1992)

However, NSs and NNSs differed in their use of alternatives both in actual advising sessions and in response to DCT scenarios based on the advising sessions (Hartford & Bardovi-Harlig, 1992). In the conversational data, alternatives were the second most frequent semantic formula for NSs, whereas alternatives ranked fourth for NNSs, with avoidance as the second ranked strategy. Verbal avoidance is essentially a strategy which diverts attention from the actual force of the student's contribution as a rejection. Besides hedges (e.g., *I don't know*) identified by Beebe et al. (1990), three additional types of verbal avoidance were identified, all questions in form: postponement, questions asking for the repetition of information, and the request for additional information, illustrated in the following examples (Bardovi-Harlig & Hartford, 1991):

(6) Um . . . Can I decide if next week? I want to think a little bit
more.
[postponement]
[NNS, L1 Chinese]

(7) What was that last course?
[Q requests repetition of information]
[NNS, L1 Spanish]

During the course of the advising sessions NNSs were often encouraged
by the adviser to supply the underrepresented alternative semantic formula as in the following:

(8) NS Adviser in response to NNS, Korean

A: Well what would you take if you didn't take phonetics? Have you
thought of a replacement?
[14 turns]
All right. Well . . . uh . . . well what, do you suggest? I mean,
what you're suggesting is, first you said you want to take phonetics,
but now you say you don't want to take phonetics, so . . . what,
what do you suggest as an alternative?

In a study of complaints, Murphy and Neu (1996, p. 199) also
found a difference in the use of semantic formulas, or what they call
"semantic components." The NSs, fourteen American men, and the
NNSs, fourteen Korean men, all of whom were graduate students,
completed an oral discourse completion task in which they were asked
to assume the role of a student whose assignment was unfairly graded
by his professor. The NSs and NNSs showed relatively high agreement
on three of the four semantic formulas used to realize the complaints.
All of the subjects except one of the NNSs began the complaint with
an explanation of purpose as in Examples (9) and (10).

(9) Uh, Dr. Smith, I just came by to see if I could talk about my
paper. [NS]

(10) Good afternoon, Professor. Uh, I have something to talk
to you about my paper . . . [NNS, L1 Korean]

Respondents also showed relatively high agreement on the use of the
justification and solution formulas. However, NSs and NNSs differed
noticeably on the formula which constitutes the head act. All of the
NSs (14/14) used a complaint, as in Example (11), whereas only three
of the fourteen NNSs did. The majority of the NNSs used a criticism
instead of a complaint, as in Example (12).

(11) I think, uh, maybe it's my opinion. Maybe the grade was a little
low. [NS]

(12) But you just only look at your point of view and, uh, you just
       didn't recognize my point. [NNS, L1 Korean]

However, as Murphy and Neu observe, the use of different semantic
formulas for the head act constitutes a difference in the choice of speech
act rather than in use of semantic formula (a criticism rather than a
complaint), and thus this case seems to provide evidence for use of different speech acts as well.

Content. A third way in which NSs and NNSs may differ is in the
content of their contribution. Whereas a semantic formula names the
type of information given, content refers to the specific information
given by a speaker. Even in cases when NSs and NNSs use the same
semantic formulas, the content that they encode can be strikingly different (Takahashi & Beebe, 1987; Beebe et al., 1990). A case in point
is the content of explanations, a semantic formula found in refusals. In
a comparison of the explanations offered by Americans and NSs of
Japanese using English, Beebe, Takahashi, and Uliss-Weltz (1990) characterized the explanations of the Americans as providing more details
and the explanations of the Japanese as being vague by the American
norm. When refusing an invitation, for example, an American might
say *I have a business lunch that day,* whereas a Japanese speaker might
say *I have something to do.* In a very telling example, Beebe and col-
leagues report that a Japanese speaker of English declined an invitation
by saying *I have to go to a wedding.* The explanation seemed quite def-
inite in its content, and almost led the researchers to reconsider their
characterization of Japanese-English explanations as vague – until they
learned some weeks later that the wedding had been the woman's own!
Thus, when judged by American expectations, the explanation not only
seems vague, but perhaps may even be a violation of Grice's (1975)
maxim of quantity.

In an experiment designed to test differences in the content of explanations in rejections based on the natural data collected from the advising sessions, Hartford and Bardovi-Harlig (1992) gave NSs reasons for
rejecting courses which included several reasons that had been given by
NNS graduate students in their advising sessions, but not in NS sessions. These included reasons such as a course being too difficult, or
too easy, or even telling the adviser that his or her own course was
uninteresting. NSs in the experiment generally avoided using such content and invented other reasons to reject the courses. In contrast, NNSs
used the reasons given in the experiment, reflecting their production in
the actual advising sessions. Another area of difference is content in
compliments. Compliments often reflect cultural values (Manes, 1983).
An ethnographic study of compliments in the Kunming dialect of
Mandarin Chinese conducted by Yuan (1998) shows that the content
of Chinese compliments often differs from that reported for English

speakers in the literature (e.g., Manes, 1983; Holmes, 1988). These topics included the behavior or ability of children, desirable personality traits, and the cleanliness of one's house, and the more widely used compliments on appearance.

Form. The fourth way in which NNS production may differ from the NS norm is in the form of a speech act. A longitudinal study of pragmatic development in the context of the academic advising session found that in early sessions NSs and NNSs differed in what speech acts they produced, whereas in subsequent sessions they produced the same speech acts, but these differed in form (Bardovi-Harlig & Hartford, 1993). Learners often did not use the mitigators used by their NS peers; moreover, they often used aggravators which were never used by NSs. NSs made suggestions as found in (13)–(15).

(13) Perhaps I should also mention that I have an interest in sociolinguistics and would like, if I can, to structure things in such a way that I might do as much sociolinguistics as I can. [NS]
(14) I was thinking of taking sociolinguistics. [NS]
(15) I have an idea for spring. I don't know how it would work out, but . . . [NS]

In contrast, in the NNSs often employed suggestions such as the following:

(16) In the summer I will take language testing. [NNS]
(17) So, I, I just decided on taking the language structure. [NNS]

In an experiment employing a written DCT, NS and NNS respondents were given a scenario in which their adviser had suggested that they take a course in which they were not interested (Hartford & Bardovi-Harlig, 1992). Even when the content of the rejection is held constant by using a DCT, there is a striking difference in the form. The NS rejection in Example (18) exhibits the downgraders *I'm not sure* and *really,* whereas the NNS rejection in (19) exhibits an upgrader, *at all.*

(18) I'm not sure that I'm really interested in the topic. [NS]
(19) I would rather not take this course because the topic doesn't interest me at all. [NNS]

Researchers have also identified the use of routines or "typical expressions" (Hudson, Detmer, & Brown, 1995, p. 50) as a difference between realizations of speech acts by NSs and NNSs (Scarcella, 1979; Takahashi & Beebe, 1987; Cohen & Olshtain, 1993; Wildner-Bassett, 1994; Hudson, Detmer, & Brown, 1995; House, 1996). Routines such as *Could you give me a ride/a lift,* as part of a request, or *How clumsy of me,* as part of an apology, make the speech act or semantic formula immediately recognizable to the hearer, and are used more often by NSs than by NNSs.

In this section I have presented the ways in which NS and NNS speech act realization can differ. However, it is important to note that learners' utterances may exhibit more than one nonnative feature at a time. Nontarget-like semantic formulas may encode nontarget-like content in nontarget-like form. It is also important to note that there may be acquisitional stages in which one feature is more characteristic than another. For example, learners may use the same speech acts preferred by NSs at an earlier stage than acquiring appropriate form (evidencing a so-called U-shaped learning curve). In sum, we have evidence from a variety of sources that learners differ noticeably from identifiable NS norms in at least four areas where the use of speech acts is concerned, producing utterances that reflect the choice of a different speech act, semantic formula, content, or form than those evidenced by NSs.

Judgment and perception

Production studies provide an analysis of differences that are easily observable in L2 speech and written simulations of speech. Perception and judgment studies investigate differences that are no less real, but are somewhat less obvious to an observer. This set of studies is smaller and less cohesive than the production studies; however, it shows that learner judgments and comprehension are often different from those of NSs.

Studies of judgments by learners show how learners may differ from NSs in a number of ways. For example, NNSs may also differentiate more request strategies than NSs, such as identifying seven politeness levels compared to the five levels distinguished by NSs on the same card-sorting task, but at the same time not recognize boundaries between strategies where NSs did (Carrell & Konneker, 1981; Tanaka & Kawade, 1982). A study of the perception of NSs of English and Spanish and Spanish-speaking learners of English revealed differences in perceptions of the degree of imposition involved in a request (Mir, 1995). Learners may also have difficulty identifying the intent of a speech act, as Koike's (1996) study of English-speaking learners of Spanish showed in the case of suggestions. Olshtain and Blum-Kulka (1985) showed that adult learners of Hebrew differ significantly from NS Hebrew respondents to judgment tasks in two areas: tolerance for positive politeness (learners show less tolerance than NSs) and rejection of directness (learners rate directness as less acceptable than NSs). As length of stay increases from 2 years of residence to 2–10 years, and more than 10 years, learners move toward the target-like norm, showing an increase in tolerance for positive politeness and directness. For example, in response to a scenario asking for a loan, an informal optimistic strategy *How about lending me some money* was accepted by

Israelis, but rejected by learners. Israelis also accepted the direct *Lend me the money, please,* which learners also rejected. Bergman and Kasper (1993) conducted a study of learner perceptions related to apologies. A group of thirty Thai speakers of English and thirty NSs of English completed an assessment task in which they were asked to rate severity of offense, obligation to apologize, likelihood of the apology being accepted, and offender's loss of face. The NS and NNS responses similarly exhibited high correlations between obligation to apologize and severity of offense, severity and likelihood of acceptance, severity and face-loss, and obligation and face-loss, leading Bergman and Kasper to conclude that the severity of offense is related to the offender's obligation to apologize (see also Olshtain, 1989). However, NSs and NNSs differed most noticeably on their ratings of the obligation to apologize. Out of twenty scenarios, twelve were rated as higher on obligation by the Americans than by the Thai learners of English. If a speaker does not feel the obligation to perform a particular speech act, it is less likely that she or he will. This may account for some of the opting out, or substitution of one speech act for another, as seen earlier.

In a study of perceptions of politeness in requests, Kitao (1990) found differences in Japanese EFL and ESL learners, with ESL learners more closely approximating the NS norms. The study of perceptions is particularly relevant to the issue of what utterances learners take as input and whether learners notice how their own utterances compare to those of other target-language speakers. Bardovi-Harlig and Dörnyei (1998) investigated this question in a study of the identification and rating of pragmatic infelicities and grammatical errors in response to a videotape with twenty scenarios. In a test of 543 learners and their teachers (N = 53) in two countries (Hungary and the United States), the results showed that EFL learners and their teachers consistently identified and ranked grammatical errors as more serious than pragmatic errors, but that ESL learners and their NS English teachers showed the opposite pattern, ranking pragmatic errors as more serious than grammatical errors. They also reported that learners did not always recognize pragmatically "good" test items. In a study of perception of pragmatic transferability, Takahashi (1996) found that the Japanese EFL learners could not identify the English requests that were functional equivalents of Japanese request strategies. For example, the functionally equivalent English request form for the Japanese *V-shite itadake-nai-deshoo-ka* in a highly imposing request situation is a biclausal form of *Would it be possible to VP.* However, the learners consistently identified its functional equivalent as the monoclausal English request form *Would/Could you (please) VP,* a formula with the same conventionalized form as the Japanese request. Given the observation that NSs of English embed the propositional content of requests in order to mitigate them in high imposition situations, Takahashi concludes that learners' L2 pragmatic competence regarding requests differs considerably from the pragmatic knowledge of NSs of English.

Bouton has conducted a series of studies on the interpretation of implicatures in English by NNSs (1988, 1990, 1992, 1994b). Bouton (1988) tested 436 international students arriving at the University of Illinois using a multiple-choice instrument with thirty-three items, finding that although NSs and NNSs interpreted the same implicature in the same context 75% of the time, that left a full 25% of the time in which different implications were drawn by the NNSs. Bouton (1992) retested thirty of the original subjects four-and-a-half years later and found that the NNSs had improved to the point where twenty items showed no significant difference in interpretation between them and the NSs, whereas only five of the items showed no difference in the previous study. Fifteen of the similarly interpreted items were related to Grice's (1975) maxim of relevance; five of the items involved understated criticism, related to the maxim of quantity. Bouton (1994b) reported on a second longitudinal study run on another group of university students which confirmed the findings of his earlier work – learners performed noticeably better on implicatures whose interpretation is idiosyncratically dependent on the meaning of the utterance in its particular context. Relevance-based implicatures are of this type.

In contrast, learners performed noticeably worse on implicatures based on a formula of some sort, whether structural, semantic, or pragmatic. One implicature of this type is the pope-question implicature, in which a speaker answers a question with a question whose answer is obvious. Pope-questions include examples such as *Does the sun rise in the east?* (for which the answer is "yes"), the well-known *Is the pope Catholic?* for which the category is named (and for which the answer is also "yes"), and *Does a frog have hair?* (for which the answer is "no"). Bouton (1994b) gives the example of two students discussing the likelihood that a teacher will give an exam the day before a school vacation. The teacher has promised to give the exam and has said that no one would be excused from taking it. When one student asks whether the teacher will actually give the exam, the second student responds with *Does the sun come up in the east these days?* (p. 96). Understanding the implicature generated by the pope-question requires that the learner know the answer to the second question (i.e., that the sun does in fact come up in the east), and must also assume that the answer to the first question is the same as the answer to the second question, and just as likely to be true. Without this formula, the learner cannot arrive at the implicature.

Pragmatic comprehension, the comprehension of speech acts and discourse functions, can also be inferred from conversational data, as Kasper

(1984) showed. Conversational data from NS-NNS role-plays reveal that learners may understand phatic contributions as referential, and may also fail to identify the illocutionary force of indirect speech acts. In Example (20) the learner misses an indirect request in the first NS turn, but catches it in the second, after the NS restates the request more directly.

(20)   NS: You're drinking a beer there.
     NNS: Yes.
     NS: Erm er will I might er if you were kind enough to offer
         me one I probably wouldn't say no.
     NNS: Of course of course yes (laughing).

Kasper suggests that learners may rely too heavily on bottom-up processing and have problems activating frames relevant in the given context.[2] Data from academic advising sessions can be interpreted similarly. Advisers often open the directive phase of the advising session (Agar, 1985) with questions such as those in Example (21).

(21)   Okay . . . so you looked through the list of courses, so you
     pretty much know what you want to take?
     Do you have some idea of what you would want to take?
     Do you know what you want to do?
     (Bardovi-Harlig & Hartford, 1996)

The production data indicate that NS student participants interpret these questions as indirect requests for them to suggest a set of courses for the coming semester. In the case of at least some NNS students, the questions may instead be comprehended simply as direct questions to which they provide a literally correct answer, as in Example (22), but do not result in the perlocutionary effect desired by the adviser (Bardovi-Harlig & Hartford, 1990).

(22)   A: Do you know what you want to do?
     S: More or less.
     A: Let's hear it.
     [Pause.]
     A: You've done 530, 31, 43, so you probably want to do 542,
        I bet you . . .
     S: Yes, that's phonological.
     A: Yes, phonology.

From the student's response, it is clear that he has understood the literal meaning of the question, and in fact, later demonstrates that he is familiar with the courses. The student also misses the second prompting from the adviser (*Let's hear it*), perhaps because he may be

2 Other sources of difficulty in pragmatic comprehension may be that learners do not make use of illocutionary force indicating devices (IFIDs) and that they have too little flexibility for shifting the frame if an interlocutor's turn is not consistent with the current frame (Kasper, 1984).

unfamiliar with the expression, or reluctant to tell the adviser what his course selections are.

It is possible to discern what might be considered another type of comprehension from production data, namely, recognition of the function of a speech act apart from its illocutionary force. Wolfson (1989a) argues that learners of English are often not aware that status-equal Americans use compliments as conversation openers. In Wolfson's compliment corpus, learners' responses to compliments show that they recognize their illocutionary force, but not their conversational function of opening a conversation, even in cases such as Example (23) in which the American makes a second attempt (Wolfson, 1989a, p. 230).

(23)   American female student to her Chinese female classmate:
     A: Your blouse is beautiful.
     B: Thank you.
     A: Did you bring it from China?
     B: Yeah.

A similar case may be made for the interpretation of what Boxer (1993) refers to as "indirect complaints," which, like compliments, are frequently used by NSs of English to build rapport. In conversational dyads, NSs favored commiserating responses to NNSs' indirect complaints (e.g., *Oh no*), whereas NNSs favored nonsubstantive responses (e.g., *uh hmn*). The nonsubstantive responses appear to be possible second-pair parts to indirect complaints, but ignore the function of the indirect complaint to achieve further interaction. Although there is no certain way of separating comprehension from production strategies in conversational data, these data do suggest that comprehension and pragmatic assessment may influence at least some of the learner productions discussed in the preceding section. It is further important to investigate perceptions of L2 speech acts addressed to learners. If we expect learners to use speech addressed to them as input, we need to investigate how learners perceive and understand such input.

Factors in determining L2 pragmatic competence

Several explanations for pragmatic differences between learners and NSs have been proposed: availability of input, influence of instruction, proficiency, length of exposure, and transfer. I will examine each of these.

Input

Of particular importance to a discussion of pedagogy and pragmatics is the availability of relevant pragmatic input in academic encounters and in textbooks. Kasper (1997b) and Bardovi-Harlig and Hartford (1996) characterize academic talk (teacher-student talk) as an unequal status encounter, where the speech of the higher-status speaker – the teacher – does not serve as a pragmatically appropriate model for the speech of the learners. Consider the case of the Spanish teacher who (appropriately) says to her students *Dígame* . . . (an imperative form meaning *Tell me . . .*) but who finds it quite impolite when her students say the same thing to her (Silvia Rodriguez, personal communication, 1997). Teacher-fronted talk can be supplemented by additional activities that broaden the range of speech acts and speakers, and that provide a broader range of models and opportunities for learners (Kasper, 1997b). If teacher talk is not intended as a pragmatic model for learners, textbooks with conversations are designed to be models for students, and yet they generally fall short of providing realistic input to learners.

In the title of his 1988 paper ("Language taught for meetings and language used in meetings: Is there anything in common?"), Williams captures the question investigated by a series of comparisons of textbook presentation and authentic language more generally (Scotton & Bernsten, 1988; Billmyer, Jakar, & Lee, 1989; Bardovi-Harlig, Hartford, Mahan-Taylor, Morgan, & Reynolds, 1991; Boxer & Pickering, 1995; Bouton, 1996). As an illustration, consider the results of a survey of textbooks on teaching closings (Bardovi-Harlig et al., 1991). The survey examined the presentation of closings by twenty contemporary ESL textbooks which contained dialogues, and found that only twelve included complete closings in at least one dialogue and that very few did so on a consistent basis. Only one text had several examples of complete closings. Textbooks typically represent conversations as getting only as far as shutting down a topic and occasionally as far as a preclosing. It is often the case that a particular speech act or language function is not represented at all. In other cases, speech acts are represented, but not realistically. For example, Bouton (1996) showed that 80% of the invitations in one ESL textbook used a form of invitation which appeared only 26% of the time in a published corpus on NS invitations. Scotton and Bernsten (1988) cited examples of direction-giving exchanges devoid of grounders and confirmation checks that characterize such exchanges. Boxer and Pickering (1995) found a general lack of so-called indirect complaints in textbooks, and no discussion of the function of the speech act as a social strategy. Boxer and Pickering also point to a lack of information about the interlocutors and the context of the textbook conversations. There are a few newer books which do try to present relevant information to learners (see Boxer & Pickering, 1995; Bardovi-Harlig, 1996), but it is important to recognize that, in general, textbooks cannot be counted on as a reliable source of pragmatic input for classroom language learners.[3]

3 For readers who are interested in improving the state of affairs described in this section, the pedagogy of pragmatics is discussed by Bardovi-Harlig (1992, 1996),

Instruction

In addition to specific types of input available, other aspects of instruction may play a role in perpetuating some of the nontarget-like realization of speech acts. It should be clear that instruction may also increase a learner's movement toward the target-language norm. (See the review by Kasper, this volume, and the papers that follow. See also Bouton, 1994a; House, 1996; Kasper, 1997a.)

Instructional emphasis on L1-L2 correspondences may contribute to learners' inclination to use L1 strategies, but may not itself cause them (Takahashi, 1996). Instructional emphasis on one semantic formula over others, as in the case of *I'm sorry* in apologies (Mir, 1992), may encourage overuse of the formula. In fact, general course organization may contribute to lack of pragmatic focus or opportunities for communication (Cohen, 1997). We may also extend the curricular issue to the question of language assessment: For foreign language learners the success of learning is typically measured by being able to take some grammar-oriented language exam, whereas in second language contexts, even if there are tests to be taken, rewards are also provided by successful communication with NSs. As far as the consequences are concerned, the gap between grammar and pragmatics in EFL samples indicates that emphasis on microlevel grammatical accuracy in the foreign language classroom may be at the expense of macrolevel pragmatic appropriateness (Bardovi-Harlig & Dörnyei, 1998; but see Niezgoda & Röver, this volume). This may change somewhat as tests in pragmatics are developed (Hudson, Detmer, & Brown, 1995; see also the chapters by Brown, Hudson, and Norris, this volume).

Level of proficiency and length of stay

The influence of the level of L2 proficiency on pragmatic competence and performance has not been widely researched (Kasper & Schmidt, 1996). Nor have different stages of pragmatic development been investigated in any detail (but see Schmidt, 1983; Ellis, 1992; Bardovi-Harlig & Hartford, 1993). As Kasper points out, very little work in the acquisition of pragmatics has been done, and none of the published literature includes beginning language learners (Kasper, 1996; Kasper & Schmidt, 1996; Kasper & Rose, 1999).

Bardovi-Harlig et al. (1991), Billmyer (1990a, 1990b), Bouton (1990), Boxer and Pickering (1995), Cohen (1996), Holmes and Brown (1987), Kasper (1997b), and Rose (1994b, 1997), among others.

It appears that proficiency may have little effect on the range of realization strategies that learners use: Both intermediate and advanced learners use the same range of realization strategies used by NSs (Kasper & Schmidt, 1996). Similarly, Takahashi (1996) did not find any proficiency effects on perception of L1 transferability to L2 pragmatics. Other areas are apparently more sensitive to level of proficiency. In a study of refusals made by Japanese ESL learners at two levels of proficiency, Takahashi and Beebe (1987) found that low and high proficiency learners differed in the order and frequency of semantic formulas they used. The lower proficiency learners were also more direct in their refusals than higher-level ESL learners. (Interestingly, proficiency did not make a difference in the EFL group that was studied, presumably because neither level of proficiency in the EFL situation receives enough input.) The use of external modifiers used in L2 Hebrew increases with linguistic proficiency, as does the number of words used (NNSs exceeded NSs of Hebrew on this measure; Blum-Kulka & Olshtain, 1986).

Proficiency may also influence transfer. Advanced learners were found to be better than intermediate learners at identifying contexts in which L1 apology strategies could and could not be used (Maeshiba, Yoshinaga, Kasper, & Ross, 1996). The use of modality markers (downtoners, understaters, hedges, subjectivizers, intensifiers, commitment upgraders, and cajolers) also improves with proficiency (Trosborg, 1987; see House & Kasper, 1981a, for modality markers). Three groups of Danish learners of English (intermediate, lower advanced, and higher advanced) showed a noticeable increase in their usage at each level, more closely corresponding to NSs of English. Japanese learners of English as a second language showed a greater tendency to soften the directness of their refusals than did lower-level Japanese ESL learners, and they also showed a greater level of formality, both of which Takahashi and Beebe (1987) attributed to transfer from Japanese refusals. In a rare study which includes low-level learners, Scarcella (1979) found that when making requests, the low-level students invariably relied on imperatives, whereas higher-level learners showed sensitivity to status, using them only with equal familiars and subordinates. Koike (1996) also found a proficiency effect in the recognition of the intent of speech acts in a study of the perception of Spanish suggestions by English-speaking learners of Spanish. Third- and fourth-year students were significantly better at identifying the intended force of the suggestions than the first- and second-year students, although even the higher group identified the intent only little more than half of the time.

Length of stay is also a factor in pragmatic development. Olshtain and Blum-Kulka (1985) reported an increase in acceptance of positive request strategies and directness by NNSs of Hebrew as their length of stay increased from less than 2 years to more than 10 years. A 1-year longitudinal study of advising-session talk found that NNSs showed an increase in the use of speech acts favored by NSs in the academic context, and they showed a decrease in speech acts not used by NSs. In the same period, however, NNSs did not conform to NSs' use of mitigators and nonuse of aggravators (Bardovi-Harlig & Hartford, 1993). A study of awareness of deviations from the NS norm shows that tutored ESL learners are more sensitive than EFL learners to pragmatic infelicities; that is, learners in the host environment (with daily exposure to the L2, but who received no instruction in pragmatics) identified pragmatic problems more often and ranked them as more serious than did the EFL learners. Within the ESL group, learners at a high level of proficiency showed greater pragmatic awareness than learners at lower proficiency. Bouton (1992, 1994b) also found that ESL learners enrolled at an American university without specific training in pragmatics became increasingly target-like in their interpretation of implicature as length of stay increased up to 3 years. Even shorter lengths of stay might help learners become more target-like, particularly with respect to highly salient conversational functions such as greetings. American learners of Kiswahili who had been to Tanzania showed much more target-like use of multiple turns in lengthy Kiswahili greetings (Omar, 1991, 1992). American university students of French also adjusted their greetings to be more target-like during a semester in France, but theirs became shorter and less frequent (Hoffman-Hicks, 2000).

Grammatical competence may also limit the value of the input to the learner (Bardovi-Harlig, 1999a). For example, tense-mood-aspect morphology is often used in mitigation; both past tense and modals serve as play-downs (House & Kasper, 1981a; Færch & Kasper, 1989). A learner who has not achieved control over prototypical uses of tense-mood-aspect morphology may not be ready to extend the use of those forms to politeness markers. As a case in point, an intermediate ESL student was engaged in a pedagogical task derived from the video scenarios used by Bardovi-Harlig and Dörnyei (1998). In one of the "good" scenarios (no grammatical or pragmatic problems) a student responds to his teacher's invitation *Peter, we need to talk about the class party soon* with *Yeah, if tomorrow is good for you, I could come any time you say.* The learner identified the use of *could* as problematic, explaining that *could* was used for past, but that this sentence was talking about *tomorrow* (Bardovi-Harlig, field notes, 1997). It is clear from earlier work that grammatical competence does not guarantee pragmatic competence (Olshtain & Blum-Kulka, 1985; Bardovi-Harlig & Hartford, 1990), but it is not yet clear to what extent the development of pragmatic competence depends on grammatical competence (House, 1996; Bardovi-Harlig, 1999a).

First language, first culture

The most widely investigated influence on speech act realization is the first language and culture (e.g., Takahashi & Beebe, 1987; Mir, 1992; Bergman & Kasper, 1993; Maeshiba et al., 1996; Takahashi, 1996). The interest in L1 pragmatic influence may reflect the strong link of interlanguage pragmatics research to crosscultural pragmatics research. Pragmatic transfer – defined by Kasper (1997b, p. 119) as "use of L1 pragmatic knowledge to understand or carry out linguistic action in the L2" – may have positive and negative outcomes. Positive transfer results in successful exchanges, whereas negative transfer, resulting from an assumption that L1 and L2 are similar where, in fact, they are not, may result in nonnative use (or avoidance) of speech acts, semantic formulas, or linguistic form. Examples of L1 influence include the case of apology formulas used by Japanese learners of English to express gratitude, and the use of proverbial expressions by Arabic learners in the same context (Bodman & Eisenstein, 1988). Form may also show L1 influence as in the use of *must* in directives by German-speaking learners of English (House & Kasper, 1987). Takahashi (1996) identifies L1 as the primary cause of the patterns identified, and instruction as a secondary influence.

Evaluating the empirical evidence

It is clear from this review of representative studies that the empirical evidence shows that learners who have received no specific instruction in L2 pragmatics have noticeably different L2 pragmatic systems than NSs of the L2. This is true for both production and comprehension. This review is very much like a traditional error analysis. It has concentrated, as error analyses do, on apparent areas of difficulty rather than on learner success, and on problematic areas rather than on the acquisition process (in large measure because that is what is available in the literature). Areas of difficulty have been traditionally interpreted as areas in need of instruction (Ellis, 1994). It is also clear that learners are successful in certain areas of pragmatics. Moreover, every study reviewed here (as well as others) shows strong situational effect: Certain scenarios are harder to negotiate than others. What we know with certainty is that there are differences between L1 and L2 pragmatics. Of the areas of divergence that have been identified, we do not yet know which will cause the most communicative difficulty, offense, humor, or even hurt feelings. Additional studies of conversation and ratings by target-language speakers may help to identify the potentially most disruptive differences (Kasper, 1997a).

Do differences in pragmatic production and interpretation actually warrant pedagogical intervention? Do we need to "fix" every difference? Many of the pedagogical issues are beyond the scope of this chapter, but I would like to address my comments here specifically to the differences in underlying pragmatic systems and their potential causes.[4] What I will assume here is a group of language learners and their teachers who are desirous of improving L2 pragmatics. One of the easiest causes of non-target-like pragmatics to overcome pedagogically is incomplete or misleading input to learners in pedagogical materials. Although improving input to learners is undoubtedly more easily said than done, providing authentic, representative language to learners is a basic responsibility of classroom instruction (Williams, 1988; Scotton & Bernsten, 1989; Bardovi-Harlig et al., 1991; Rose, 1993, 1994b, 1997; Boxer & Pickering, 1995; Bouton, 1996; Kasper, 1997b). Providing opportunities beyond teacher-fronted status-unequal encounters is also indicated for its value in pragmatic input and practice (Kasper, 1997b), as well as for its more general pedagogical benefits.

Another clear area of pedagogical necessity is assisting learners with comprehension. Both comprehension and providing authentic input seems to fall under the heading of "fair play: giving the learners a fighting chance." Not only the comprehension of indirect speech acts and implicature fall under this heading, but also the social interpretations of certain speech acts. A learner may not want to offer compliments or "indirect complaints" herself in a conversation with an NS, but she might want to be able to do her part to respond to attempts to initiate conversations which these speech acts often do (Wolfson, 1989a; Boxer, 1993). If a learner does not recognize the social function of such speech acts, then she cannot hold up her end of the conversation in response to such speech acts when other people use them. Going to the other extreme, the most difficult difference to tackle pedagogically may be the use or nonuse of certain speech acts as a result of cultural (or individual) preferences. (And, in fact, this may be one difference that we decide not to tackle.) Thomas (1983, p. 104) observed that

> correcting pragmatic failure stemming from sociopragmatic miscalculation
> is a far more delicate matter for the language teacher than correcting
> pragmalinguistic failure. Sociopragmatic decisions are social before they
> are linguistic, and while foreign learners are fairly amenable to corrections
> which they regard as linguistic, they are justifiably sensitive about having
> their social (or even political, religious, or moral) judgment called into
> question.

---

4 Clearly an important issue is the identity of the learner population and the learning
   context (Boxer & Pickering, 1995; Kasper, 1997b), both of which involve complex
   pedagogical issues that are not the focus of this chapter.

Thinking about this issue in the terms used in this chapter, consider the case of compliments in American English. In the English-speaking world, Americans are considered to be rather robust givers of compliments. Learners from other cultures who would feel uncomfortable or insincere giving as many compliments as Americans do may nonetheless want to give an occasional compliment. The role of instruction may be to help the learner encode her own values (which again may be culturally determined) into a clear, unambiguous message.[5] Using a commonly recognized compliment formula such as *I (really) like/love NP* or *NP is (really) ADJ* helps relay the message clearly without asking a learner to compromise her values and adopt those of the target culture. Similarly, instruction related to form may also be nonthreatening following Thomas's assessment, since language pedagogy is still generally geared to form.[6] Less clearly a matter of form, and therefore perhaps less "linguistic" than "cultural," is the use of semantic formulas. Consider the case of direct complaints identified by Murphy and Neu (1996). Although most people I know would prefer not to have to lodge a direct complaint at all, especially to a teacher or a supervisor, it is occasionally necessary, as in the case of a student who thinks his paper may have been graded erroneously by his teacher (Murphy & Neu, 1996). Whatever the L1 preference for criticism as a semantic formula in complaints might be, faculty responses to student messages suggest that American faculty are somewhat put off by criticism and would respond better to a direct complaint (Hartford & Bardovi-Harlig, 1996). Learners could be aided by being pointed toward the (culturally) more successful semantic formula.

Taken as a whole, then, the research indicates that learners who receive no particular instruction in pragmatics show divergence in L2 pragmatics in several areas. I have argued that making contextualized, pragmatically appropriate input available to learners from early stages of acquisition onward is the very least that pedagogy should aim to do (see also Bardovi-Harlig et al., 1991; Bardovi-Harlig, 1996). Without input, acquisition cannot take place. I have also argued that we owe it to learners to help them interpret indirect speech acts as in the case of implicature, and the social use of speech acts, as in the case of compliments. Where instructors and researchers differ (not in opposition to each other, but as individuals) is in the determination of the most that

---

5 By instruction I mean any action undertaken by a teacher to facilitate acquisition. This may be as subtle as engineering an input flood or bringing NSs into the classroom as interlocutors, or as direct as explicit instruction. The best means of facilitating the acquisition of pragmatics is another issue that remains to be resolved.

6 The ultimate success of any pedagogy would be subject to acquisitional constraints, as in other areas (Ellis, 1994; Bardovi-Harlig, 1997), and remains to be tested.

pedagogy should aim to accomplish. The adoption of sociocultural rules as one's own in an L2 may have to be an individual decision. Providing the information so that a learner can make that choice is a pedagogical decision. The most appropriate and effective ways to deliver this information and the manner in which learners integrate such information into a developing interlanguage remain empirical questions.

3 Classroom research on interlanguage pragmatics

Gabriele Kasper

Introduction

Pragmatics has played a considerable role in first and second language classroom research, but classroom research has played only a minor role in interlanguage pragmatics thus far. Virtually all of the instruments designed for L2 classroom observation include, or are even entirely based on, pragmatic and discourse categories, for instance, the FLint (Foreign Language Interaction) system (Moskowitz, 1971), the FOCUS (Foci for Observing Communications Used in Settings) system (Fanselow, 1977), the Embryonic Category System (Long, Adams, McLean, & Castaños, 1976), or the COLT (Communicative Orientation in Language Teaching) system (Fröhlich, Spada, & Allen, 1985) (see illustration and discussion of instruments and procedures for classroom research by Allwright, 1988; Chaudron, 1988; van Lier, 1988; Allwright & Bailey, 1991). As a case in point, an early observation schedule such as Moskowitz's FLint (1971) system included such speech-act categories for examining teacher talk as accepting, discussing, referring to, praising, complimenting, confirming, joking, clarifying, summarizing, repeating, asking questions, giving information, lecturing, correcting, giving directions, requesting, criticizing. Perhaps the most well known scheme for the analysis of classroom discourse is Sinclair and Coulthard's (1975), a hierarchically structured model based on Hallidayan systemic linguistics. Less well known in the English speaking world but much used in northern Europe is Ehlich and Rehbein's (1979) model, based on their pattern theory of action. Although the theoretical origin of Ehlich and Rehbein's model and its formal and functional properties differ considerably from Sinclair and Coulthard's, each represents a distinct discourse-pragmatic approach to classroom interaction. Whereas pragmatics has thus figured prominently as a *research tool*, much less attention has been paid to pragmatics as the *object* of classroom research. One of the central issues in second language acquisition research is whether and how instruction influences second language development, yet in comprehensive reviews of research on this topic, reports on the effect of instruction on learners' acquisition of L2 pragmatics are conspicuously absent (e.g., Larsen-Freeman & Long, 1991; Ellis, 1994).

The purpose of this chapter is to review the small body of data-based research on pragmatic learning in the second or foreign language classroom and to propose some guidelines for future research on this topic. Some of the suggestions have been implemented and illustrated by recent studies, reported in subsequent chapters. The questions I will address are: What do we know about actual classroom learning of L2 pragmatics? What issues has research on instruction in L2 pragmatics examined? What theoretical perspectives have been adopted? What research approaches and techniques have been used? And what are the main outcomes of this research?

The studies discussed in this chapter are classroom-based; that is, they investigate pragmatic learning within L2 classroom settings. I distinguish between observational and interventional studies. Observational studies focus primarily on classroom *processes,* either without a view to learning *outcomes* or with learning outcomes being analyzed as emerging in and through classroom interaction. Predominantly, the observed classrooms are *authentic* in the sense of not being specifically arranged for research purposes. Pragmatics may or may not be a planned learning objective in these lessons. Interventional studies, on the other hand, examine the effect of a particular instructional treatment on students' acquisition of the targeted pragmatic feature. Broadly, these studies can be characterized as classroom experiments if we understand *experiment* in a liberal sense, that is, as including not only experimental designs but also quasi-experimental and preexperimental research arrangements in the sense of Larsen-Freeman and Long (1991).

Observational studies

Just like early interlanguage pragmatics research outside the classroom, the first observational studies focused on language use rather than pragmatic development in the classroom setting. These nondevelopmental studies are summarized in Table 1. Initial research on the acquisition of pragmatic ability in L2 classrooms was inspired by constructs of communicative competence as the overall learning and teaching goal of general second and foreign language instruction (e.g., Canale & Swain, 1980). From the first study by Long et al. (1976) until the late 1980s, the overarching question raised by the nondevelopmental observational studies was what opportunities for pragmatic input and conversational practice the language classroom affords. Specifically, studies examined speech acts and discourse functions, discourse organization and management,

TABLE 1. NONDEVELOPMENTAL OBSERVATIONAL STUDIES

Study	Observational goal	Classroom organization/ language	Comparison	Data collection/ analysis
Long et al., 1976	speech acts, discourse functions	lockstep vs. pairs/EFL	lockstep vs. pairs	audio/Bellack, FOCUS, Embryonic Category System
Kasper, 1985	repair	teacher-fronted/EFL	metalinguistic vs. referential phases; non-classroom IL	audio/CA inspired, pattern theory*
House, 1986	discourse markers, strategies	role-play, teacher-fronted/EFL	target talk (role-play) vs. classroom talk	audio/Edmondson & House, 1981
Lörscher, 1986	discourse organization	teacher-fronted/EFL	non-classroom L2	audio/CA inspired
Lörscher & Schulze, 1988	politeness	teacher-fronted/EFL	non-classroom L2	audio/politeness theory
Kasper, 1989a	discourse organization	teacher-fronted/EFL	non-classroom IL	audio/DA
Poole, 1992	language socialization	teacher-fronted/ESL	non-classroom child L2	video, audio/DA
Falsgraf & Majors, 1995	teachers' directives	NR/JFL immersion	English L1, Japanese L1	video, interviews/directness scale, statistical analysis
Hall, 1995a	topic development, management	teacher-fronted/ Spanish FL	NA	video, audio, field notes, interviews/DA
Ohta, 1995, 1997	requests, collaborative learning	teacher-fronted/JFL	teacher-fronted vs. role-play; two different students	video, audio/DA
Lim, 1996	language socialization	teacher-fronted/JFL	NA	audio interviews, questionnaire/DA
He, 1997	identity construction	teacher-fronted/ Chinese supplementary	two different classes and teachers	audio, field notes, interviews/DA

*Ehlich & Rehbein (1979)
Note: CA = conversation analysis, DA = discourse analysis, NA = not applicable, NR = not reported

discourse markers and strategies, repair, and politeness. Such aspects of pragmatics and discourse had been investigated in conversation analysis, and research on speech-act realization and politeness and were seen as central components in L2 learners' discourse and pragmatic competence. Three early studies explored the opportunities for conversational practice offered by different forms of classroom organization or activities. Long et al. (1976) compared the teacher-fronted lockstep format with pair work. House (1986) and Kasper (1985) compared different phases of the same lesson. House's students first conducted a series of open role-plays (called "target talk") and subsequently discussed their role-play performance in a teacher-fronted debriefing session (called "classroom talk"). In my 1985 study, I compared repair patterns as they occurred in a "metalinguistic" lesson phase, devoted to the explanation of new vocabulary, and a "referential" phase, in which a novel was discussed. Both Long et al. (1976) and House (1986) found that the learner-centered pair work and role-plays greatly increased the range of speech acts and discourse functions performed by the students. Even within the teacher-fronted format, I noted that during the referentially oriented discussion phase, repair patterns were more consistent with those in noninstructional conversation than in the metalinguistic vocabulary explanation phase (Kasper, 1985).

Rather than contrasting different formats of classroom organization and activities, other studies in the late 1980s investigated how teacher-fronted classroom interaction fared in comparison to discourse practices outside the classroom. These comparisons demonstrated that teacher-fronted interaction is substantially more restricted in providing pragmatic input and occasion for productive language use. The teacher-fronted format presents shorter and less complex openings and closings, a limited range of discourse markers (Lörscher, 1986; Kasper, 1989a), and little politeness marking (Lörscher & Schulze, 1988). The simplification of discourse organization and management is an immediate consequence of the IRF structure – Initiation (by the teacher)-Response (by a student)-Follow-up (by the teacher) – the basic interactional routine of teacher-fronted teaching (see discussion in Chaudron, 1988, p. 37). This exchange structure strongly favors monopolization of topic management, turn allocation, and third-turn assessment by the teacher (Lörscher, 1986; Ellis, 1990). In addition, the German EFL teachers in Lörscher and Schulze's (1988) study adopted a highly transactional style; that is, they indexed the interpersonal level of social interaction only minimally. Thus students did not receive models of appropriate politeness marking as needed for interaction outside the classroom.

Since the early 1990s, research on pragmatics in second language classrooms has profited from new theoretical perspectives. The earlier studies had focused on the interactional constraints on discourse and communicative action in different instructional and noninstructional contexts. Although this issue remains a concern, research in the 1990s expanded its scope to the sociocultural context of linguistic practices and the participation structures in different activity types. Two approaches in particular, language socialization theory and sociocognitive theory, have informed observational studies on pragmatics in language classrooms. In the definition of its most prominent representative, "Language socialization is the process whereby children and other novices are socialized through language, part of such socialization being a socialization to use language meaningfully, appropriately, and effectively" (Ochs, 1996, p. 408). Because of its dual focus on language use and cultural practices, language socialization is a particularly fruitful perspective on the acquisition of pragmatic ability. Sociocognitive theories of development emphasize the interrelation of social, cognitive, and linguistic development, the collaborative construction of these interrelated knowledge components in social interaction, and their embeddedness in historical, sociocultural, and institutional contexts (Vygotsky, 1978; Wertsch, 1991; Lantolf, 2000). From a sociocognitive point of view, the intra-individually focused notion of communicative competence has to be expanded to the inter-individually oriented concept of interactional competence, as proposed by Joan Kelly Hall in a series of publications (e.g., Hall, 1995a, 1995b; Hall & Verplaeste, 2000).

Second language and bilingual socialization processes have been examined in different instructional contexts, including ESL and JFL (Japanese as a Foreign Language) for adult students, Japanese immersion at preschool and elementary school level, and supplementary L1 instruction for children. This research demonstrates how cultural information is conveyed implicitly through teacher-student interaction and how the teachers' socialization practices are informed by the social and pragmatic norms of the target culture. In the first language socialization study of adult ESL classrooms, Poole (1992) observed a number of recurrent features in the teachers' interactional style: expert-novice convergence (through the teachers' guessing of students' intended meaning, utterance simplification, and jointly constructed responses), attribution of successful task completion to the students (even though the teacher might have carried out most of the task herself), and downplay of the status differential between students and teacher. The teachers thus imported interactional preferences typical of child socialization by white, middle-class American caregivers into their interaction with adult ESL students. The cultural messages conveyed by the teachers in Poole's study, all native speakers of American English, contrast with those in Lim's (1996) investigation of beginning JFL classes taught by native and nonnative speakers of Japanese. The socialization goals pursued by these teachers were to instill in students an appropriately status-congruent mode of interaction, a sense of responsibility for the entire group, and displays of diligence and conformity as desirable classroom behaviors. Lim reports crosscultural conflict between students' and teachers' interactional styles, for instance, between the solidarity style adopted by some of the Japanese-American students in interaction with their teacher and the teacher's expectations of a deference style, appropriate in a Japanese classroom. In a comparative language socialization study, Falsgraf and Majors (1995) specifically examined teachers' directives as indices of teacher-student status relationships. Teacher directives in JFL immersion classes and elementary school classes in Japan were significantly more direct than those in English-medium classes. While the high directness style reflects the teachers' authority and the status differential between teachers and students, it also characterizes the relationship between teachers and young students as close and informal. Yet another classroom setting was observed by He (1997), who examined supplementary courses in Chinese for the children (ages 4 to 8) of Chinese parents residing in the United States. Comparing the interactional styles of two teachers from mainland China, He notes marked differences in the teachers' modes of conveying information, evaluating students' performance, disciplining students, granting or denying permission, and in the participation structures they encourage. As in the previous studies, these teachers socialize their students not just to norms that are generally approved in the target culture but to practices appropriate for classroom interaction. Importantly, He's study also underscores the striking variability between teachers' interactional styles and thus counteracts misguided beliefs of monolithic cultural norms of classroom interaction.

Studies by Hall (1995a) and Ohta (1995, 1997) take up some of the issues raised in the earlier discourse-pragmatically focused investigations as well as in second language classroom research generally and analyze them from a sociocognitive perspective. Based on a yearlong observation of a class in first-year Spanish as a foreign language, Hall (1995a) examined how topic development and management were interactively constructed in teacher-fronted speaking practice. The predominant pattern in this recurrent activity was local lexical chaining; that is, coherence was established through teacher or students repeating parts of the previous utterance. However, the teacher did not orient students to overall communicative goals and even discouraged such orientation. Hence, the discourse displayed local but no global coherence. In the teacher-controlled IRF exchange structure, students were not provided opportunities for developing the interactional, linguistic, and cognitive knowledge of a complexity required in ordinary conversation. Hall expresses concern that "extended participation in such a practice could facilitate the development of L2 interactional *in*competence" (p. 55).

At the same time, she underscores that the pedagogical practice witnessed in the observed lessons is widely accepted among L2 teaching professionals and even praised as good teaching because the teacher used Spanish only and provided an "acquisitionally rich environment" with ample "comprehensible input" and interactional modification. In light of the interaction hypothesis of second language learning (e.g., Long, 1996), the observed practice thus provided students with requisite input to develop formal L2 knowledge. In sociocognitive perspective, however, students were not provided with the opportunity to develop interactional competence. Hall's study throws into relief the importance of second language acquisition (SLA) and educational theory for evaluating classroom practices. Although interaction-based SLA theory and sociocognitive theory agree in the preeminent role they assign to the linguistic environment in L2 learning, they hold conflicting positions about *what* information the learning environment needs to deliver – formal-linguistic versus discourse-pragmatic information – and, consequently, how the learning context needs to be structured in order to develop learners' L2 abilities.

Ohta (1995, 1997) compared how second-year JFL students learned to use polite request strategies in Japanese in teacher-fronted exchanges and role-plays involving two students of different JFL ability. The collaborative interaction between the students created a range of opportunities for using Japanese that was not available in teacher-fronted exchanges and thus provided a greater potential for L2 learning in the Zone of Proximal Development, "the distance between the actual developmental level as determined by independent problem solving and the level of potential development as determined through problem solving under adult guidance or in collaboration with more capable peers" (Vygotsky, 1978, p. 86). Importantly, whereas Vygotsky contended that assisted performance requires a more capable partner, Ohta (1995, 1997) demonstrated that both the stronger and the weaker learner capitalized on their available interactional skills and shifted expert–novice roles during interaction. In other words, and contrary to popular belief, it was not the case that only the weaker learner profited from the activity at the cost of the stronger partner. Also, there was no evidence of participants' picking up each other's errors; rather, they assisted each other in reaching more advanced levels of communicative ability. Ohta's study thus gives us useful pointers for evaluating different forms of small-group work and highlights some advantages of asymmetrical pairing.

Consistent with qualitative-interpretive methodology, the sociocognitive and language socialization studies are based on extensive observation, supplemented by interviews, over extended periods. Their rich database thus allows for grounded analysis (e.g., Strauss & Corbin, 1990), that is, inductive identification and abstraction of culturally significant patterns of interaction. Both the extended observation and the combination of observation and interviews set the language socialization and sociocognitive studies apart from the earlier discourse-pragmatic research, which was often based on a single observation of a particular classroom and did not include an interview component. The sociocognitive studies analyzed interactional learning activities in the Zone of Proximal Development, at a microlevel of L2 learning. But consistent with the discourse-pragmatic investigations in Table 1, the studies cited thus far do not examine L2 pragmatic learning in a macrodevelopmental perspective; that is, they do not examine how learners develop pragmatic ability over time. A (macro)developmental focus is adopted by the next group of observational classroom-based studies, summarized in Table 2.

Following Schiefflin and Ochs's (1986) distinction, the studies listed in Table 2 illustrate *language acquisition* and *language socialization* research. The studies by Rod Ellis (1992), Cohen (1997), and Kanagy and Igarashi (1997) represent well-established approaches within second language acquisition research: longitudinal case studies based on participant and nonparticipant observation and self-study diaries. The first study to trace learners' development of pragmatic ability in a second language classroom was Rod Ellis (1992, 1997). He observed the requests of two beginning ESL learners (aged 10 and 11) for a period of 2 years. He proposed three stages through which learners' ability to produce requests evolves. Early learners' utterances conveyed requestive intent through highly context-dependent, minimalist realizations, expressing the intended reference and illocution but no relational or social goals – for example, *me no blue* for "I don't have a blue crayon," or direct formulaic requests such as *leave it, give me*. In the next stage, requests were mainly performed by means of unanalyzed routines (*can I have; have you got*); illocutionary force was indicated by lexical cues (*please, maybe*). Toward the end of the observation period, the prepackaged routines were gradually unpacked and became increasingly available for productive use. For instance, ability questions as requests were now used as flexible sentence frames, shifting in perspective between speaker ("Can I take book with me?") and hearer focus ("Can you pass me my pencil?"). Relational goals (politeness) were beginning to be overtly marked, albeit with a restricted range of strategies, such as modifying requests externally by giving reasons and internally by the lexical downgrader *please*. These three tentative stages of pragmatic development are congruent with early grammatical development and the important role of formulaic speech in beginners' interlanguage (cf. Ellis, 1994). Over time, the two learners' use of direct requests decreased, while conventionally indirect requests increased, a pattern also found in L1 pragmatic

TABLE 2. DEVELOPMENTAL OBSERVATIONAL STUDIES

Study	Observational goal	Classroom organization/ language	Comparison	Data collection/ analysis
Ellis, 1992	request	mixed/ESL	non-classroom L2	audio/modified CCSARP*
Ohta, 1994	socializing expression of affect	teacher-fronted/JFL	non-classroom L2, different instructors	video, audio, interviews/DA (quantitative and qualitative)
Cohen, 1997	pragmatic ability	teacher-fronted/JFL	pragmatic vs. grammar; prior learning experience	diary/research questions
Kanagy & Igarashi, 1997	interactional routines	child/JFL immersion	different classroom activities	video, audio/JCHAT**
Kanagy, 1999	interactional routines	child/JFL immersion		video, audio/JCHAT
Ohta, 1999	sentence-final particle *ne*	pair work/JFL	non-classroom L2	video, audio/ DA, CA

*Blum-Kulka, House, & Kasper (1989); CCSARP = Crosscultural Speech Act Realization Project
**Japanese CHAT (Codes for Human Analysis of Transcripts, Oshima-Takane & MacWhinney, 1994)

development and cross-sectional interlanguage pragmatic studies (Hassall, 1997; Hill, 1997; Rose, 2000; Kasper & Rose, 1999, for review). Rod Ellis also comments that the learners' range of request strategies achieved at the end of the observation period remained considerably more restricted than that of adult native speakers, suggesting among other possible reasons more limited input opportunities in the classroom setting.

Rod Ellis's study is strongly reminiscent of longitudinal SLA research on learners' development of L2 linguistic or pragmatic ability outside the classroom. Studies on developmental sequences in the acquisition of negation, *wh*-questions, or interrogatives (e.g., Ellis, 1994, for review) have followed the same methodology in that developmental sequences are abstracted from a set of naturalistic, longitudinal data, without much concern for the textual, situational, and interactional context in which the structure in question occurs. Rod Ellis's request study is thus strongly pragmalinguistic in flavor and fits well with mainstream SLA research.

Kanagy and Igarashi (1997) examined English-speaking children's acquisition of pragmatic routines in a JFL immersion kindergarten. A large part of the teacher's utterances and the activities she engaged the students in were managed by formulaic routines, such as greetings, taking attendance, classroom organization, prelunch and end-of-lesson routines, and cleaning up. The study specifically addressed the role of formulaic utterances in L2 learning. Analyses of student–teacher interactions at weeks 4 and 11 revealed that initially children relied strongly on formulaic, elicited patterns, whereas 7 weeks later, they had considerably increased their use of spontaneous, original L2 utterances. This finding agrees with studies of early pragmatic development by ESL and JSL ners of different ages and in different learning environments, such chmidt's (1983) case study of Wes, an adult Japanese immigrant to vaiʻi acquiring English in a naturalistic context, the classroom study od Ellis's two adolescents (Ellis, 1992, 1997) just discussed, and yer's (1992) investigation of the acquisition of sentence-final particle y adult JSL learners. It is also consistent with much-cited SLA classics such as Hakuta (1974) and Wong-Fillmore (1976), all of which attest to the constructive role of routines in L2 learning: Initially unanalyzed routines enable learners to participate in verbal interaction from early on and long before their "creative" L2 competence would permit such participation, and they form the material from which learners eventually abstract elements and structures for original linguistic productions (cf. recent reviews by Kasper, 1995; Weinert, 1995). This view of the function of formulas in language acquisition, both first or second, agrees with cognitive-psychological proposals such as Bialystok's dimension "analysis of knowledge" in her two-dimensional model of language proficiency (e.g., Bialystok, 1993) and Nick Ellis's (1996) emphasis on chunking and sequence learning in language acquisition. The routines examined in Kanagy and Igarashi's (1997) study were part of the children's linguistic environment from day 1, yet the children incorporated them differentially into their own production. Considering what conditions may favor children's productive use of routines, Kanagy and Igarashi propose that "pragmatic needs are a significant factor in the language production process, influencing what types of teacher input emerge as output in the earliest stages of L2 acquisition" (p. 260).

In her more recent study of the same classroom setting, Kanagy (1999) adopts a language socialization perspective to trace the children's increasing participation in the daily interactional routines *aisatsu* (greeting), *shusseki* (attendance), and *jiko-shookai* (personal introduction). These routines differed in their degree of formulaicity, ranging from entirely scripted (attendance) to somewhat flexible (greeting) to quite variable (introduction). Through the teacher's verbal and nonverbal modeling, repetition, praise, corrective feedback, and scaffolding provided by both teacher and peers, the children gradually learned to engage competently in these routines, which required control not only of the linguistic components but also of the appropriate nonverbal conduct. Kanagy points out the dual effect of these socialization strategies:

through the provision of scaffolded help, such as modeling scripts and verbal and nonverbal cues, the teacher socializes the children into interactional competence beyond their initial L2 ability. In doing so the teacher conveys an implicit message that success in kindergarten life involves a set of skills which all can learn by carefully observing and following. (Kanagy, 1999, p. 1489)

Quite a different longitudinal case study that borrowed its methodology from earlier work in SLA is reported by Cohen (1997), who kept a diary during his participation in a semester-long course of first-year accelerated Japanese. This diary investigation is a self-study in the tradition of earlier diary studies in SLA research (e.g., Bailey, 1983; Schmidt & Frota, 1986; Campbell, 1996). Cohen's diary study aimed at describing his progress in acquiring different aspects of pragmatic ability in Japanese and how explicit information about Japanese pragmatics was provided in the classroom. Cohen reports that he acquired some ability to perform such speech acts as requests, expressions of gratitude, and apologies, though not at the ability level he had hoped for. He also provides evidence of sociopragmatic and pragmalinguistic transfer from other languages, transfer avoidance, and the difficulty of achieving control over routine formulas and selecting expressions with the appropriate formality level. One outcome of the study is a remarkable interaction of cultural and learning style factors. As an active learner with a highly interactive learning style, Cohen intended to adhere to North American cultural implementations of the Quantity and Manner maxims, which would have amounted to talking more and being more specific than appropriate in Japanese. However, his low degree of L2 knowledge and control prevented the plan from being implemented, and thus Japanese conversational norms were involuntarily observed. This example of averted sociopragmatic transfer supports Takahashi and Beebe's (1987) hypothesis that (negative) pragmatic transfer and proficiency may be *positively* correlated because pragmatic transfer may be counteracted by low L2 proficiency. Cohen also comments on his reluctance to follow Japanese sociolinguistic rules that seemed "illogical" to him, such as using honorifics when speaking about a higher-status person to an equal- or a lower-status interlocutor (p. 151). This brings to mind Siegal's (1996) study of Anglo-European women learning Japanese in Japan, some of whom decided against adopting normative Japanese female speech styles. Documenting evidence on learners' resistance to L2 ethnolinguistic practices is of great theoretical and practical interest because it forces us to rethink what "communicatively competent in L2" means, questions the rationale for adopting a native-speaker model as a target norm for nonnative speakers (V. Cook, 1999), and sheds light on the interrelation of cultural values, the learner's identity, and L2 learning (Norton, 2000).

The outcomes of Cohen's learning experience highlight the discrepancy between achievement and proficiency, or successful classroom performance according to the syllabus (Cohen placed as the best student of his class), and low ability to use the target language effectively in communication. As Cohen comments, "I had become socialized into the culture of rote mastery learning well enough to succeed at it" (p. 155). Learning experiences in the foreign language classroom such as Cohen's are reflected in Bardovi-Harlig and Dörnyei's (1998) study on the relationship between ESL and EFL learners' grammatical and pragmatic awareness, demonstrating that Hungarian EFL learners' grammatical awareness was superior to that of ESL learners, whereas their pragmatic awareness was much less developed. However, a replication study by Niezgoda and Röver, reported in this volume, suggests that when students are well prepared and highly motivated and teachers are trained in and deliver a communicative approach, high grammatical and pragmatic awareness on the part of FL students may result.

Discourse evidence for this more encouraging scenario comes from Ohta's JFL studies (1994, 1999, 2001, this volume). Ohta (1994) is a longitudinal study of teacher talk in first-year JFL, in which she observed how affective particles were used by three teachers, all female NSs of Japanese. Compared to conversational settings outside the classroom, teachers used a narrower range and lower frequency of affective particles, a finding similar to the use of discourse and politeness markers in EFL classrooms (Lörscher, 1986; Lörscher & Schulze, 1988; Kasper, 1989a). Although the teachers were consistent in their use of particles over the year – that is, they did not change it with students' improving L2 proficiency – there were marked individual differences in their particle use, reflecting teachers' instructional philosophy. Whereas the structurally oriented teacher's particle use diverged most strongly from that in non-instructional conversation, the two communicatively oriented teachers frequently provided assessments marked by the particle *ne*, as in turns 6 and 7 in the exchange below (from Ohta, 1994, p. 318):

1	T:	*Sue-san wa yoku kaimono o shimasu.*
		Sue goes shopping often.
2		*Doko de shimasu ka? Doko de shimasu ka?*
		Where do you shop? Where do you shop?
3		*Depaato de: Suupaa de?*
		At a department store? At the supermarket?
4	Sue:	*Uh, uh:: Bullocks.*
5	T:	*Bullocks! Bullocks de yoku kaimono o shimasu.*
		Bullocks! She often shops at Bullocks.
6 →		*Okanemochi desu ne::. ()*
		You're rich *ne::.*
7 →		*Sue-san wa okanemochi desu ne::.*
		Sue is rich, *ne::.*

The teachers thus modeled the selection and sequential position of affective particles for students consistent with conversational use and provided learning opportunities for the entire class through "legitimate peripheral participation" in the sense of Lave and Wenger (1991).

Turning from affective particles supplied in teachers' input to students' production, Ohta (1999) examines how a first-year student's productive use of *ne* and other third-turn assessments developed over the period of three academic quarters. The student's teacher regularly provided evaluations and comments in the follow-up slot of the IRF routine, in which the student participated peripherally and actively. During the early stages of pair work with different partners, the student and her partner produced question-answer sequences without incorporating any third-turn response. The student's first third-turn responses were expressions of comprehension and comments (*aa soo desu ka*), followed by evaluative assessments such as *mm* and *ii desu ne* to spontaneous, content-specific alignment tokens. This developmental sequence proved robust when several students' performance of third-turn responses was charted longitudinally (Ohta, 2001, this volume).

Although the observational studies consistently demonstrate the benefits of peer activities for pragmatic learning, recent work also suggests that the teacher-fronted Initiation-Response-Follow-up (IRF) routine may provide learning opportunities that have been overlooked thus far. Ohta (2001) suggests that for evaluating the potential for L2 learning in the IRF, the learning target may be a decisive factor. As we have seen, an important feature of conversational ability in Japanese is to act as an active listener and orient to the current speaker's contribution by providing listener responses. In classroom discourse, a prime locus for a listener response is the third turn in the IRF exchange, the follow-up turn. In Ohta's corpus, 97% of the follow-up turns in the IRF routine are taken by the teacher. Since listener responses typically occur in this discourse slot, the students are not provided much opportunity to use listener responses productively during IRF, but they are massively exposed to the teacher's listener responses as peripheral participants. As Ohta (1999, 2001, this volume) demonstrates, it is in peer interaction that students have most occasion to produce listener responses, but their peripheral participation in the IRF routine, supported by the teacher's explicit guidance to use response tokens, enables students to gradually develop their productive use of assessments and alignments in peer activities.

From Ohta (2001), it follows that the IRF exchange warrants closer inspection with a view to different learning targets and its comparability to pragmatic and discourse practices outside the classroom. Another issue that may strongly influence opportunities for pragmatic learning in the IRF is how the routine is implemented by the teacher. Hall (1998) examined more closely how the same teacher as in her 1995a study interacted with four students during IRF-structured speaking practice. She identified qualitatively different patterns of teacher–student interaction. The teacher assigned different interactional status to the students: two students were accorded status as primary players, the other two as supporting staff. To the primary players, the teacher displayed more attention, treated their contributions as knowledgeable and relevant, and gave them more rights to participation. The supporting staff received less teacher attention, and their participatory rights were increasingly curtailed as the semester progressed. Hall suggests that the students' differential participation opportunities in the same teacher-fronted exchange structure may affect their development of interactional ability in Spanish. As she notes, "it was not the IRF exchange per se that limited learning here. Rather, it was both the amount and qualitative nature of the opportunities for participation in the exchange that the teacher made available to each of the students" (p. 308). As Ohta (2001) and Hall (1998) have shown, longitudinal, microanalytic studies of classroom discourse afford insights into classroom processes that have largely escaped previous research and enable us to reevaluate activities and organizational formats for L2 classroom learning.

In conclusion of this review of observational classroom-based research on pragmatic learning, we note that studies have been informed by different theoretical orientations – pedagogically oriented models of discourse-pragmatic competence, second language acquisition theories, language socialization, and sociocognitive theory. These different orientations are reflected in the selection of topics and issues for study, their treatment, methodological choices, and, of course, in the evaluation of outcomes. One recurrent result that transcends such differences is the limitation of teacher-fronted teaching as an interactional format and the benefits of peer interaction in the acquisition of discourse-pragmatic ability. However, recent studies have also demonstrated that different theoretical perspectives help us see old classroom practices in a new light. With the special attention paid to interactional routines and different forms of participation, studies adopting a language socialization and sociocognitive approach emphasize the role of peripheral participation as a stepping-stone to enable learners' assisted and independent performance. They also point out that the IRF routine's high frequency and predictable exchange structure "allow beginning language learners to anticipate how classroom discourse is likely to unfold" (Ohta, 1999, p. 1498), thereby channeling attention and contributing to language socialization.

Interventional studies

Next, I will examine interventional studies of instructed pragmatic learning, summarized in Table 3. Looking at the background sections of these research reports, we find that just like their early observational counterparts, the first interventional studies were grounded in pragmatic theory and research, and, in some cases, in pedagogical approaches. For instance, Wildner-Bassett (1984, 1986) compared the effectiveness of Suggestopedia and an eclectic teaching approach in teaching pragmatic routines ("gambits") to EFL students. House and Kasper's early study (1981b), although using current terminology ("explicit/implicit"), was in fact inspired by the debate about effective grammar teaching in the language teaching community in Germany at the time. For instruction in sociostylistic variation in French, Lyster (1994) adopted from Stern (1992) an approach called *functional-analytic*[1] teaching, which emphasized sociolinguistic variation, context factors, and speech acts.

Together with its pedagogical foundation, Lyster's study is also informed by current SLA and cognitive theory. The French immersion students who participated in his study had to unlearn their pervasive

---

1 *Analytic* in Stern's sense implies rule isolation and form-focused practice. The term thus denotes the exact opposite to what *analytic* means for Wilkins (1976) and Long (e.g., Long & Robinson, 1998), who call Stern's analytic "synthetic." Confused . . . ?

TABLE 3. INTERVENTIONAL STUDIES

Study	Teaching goal	Proficiency	Languages	Research focus	Design	Assessment procedure/ instrument
House & Kasper, 1981b	discourse markers & strategies	adv.	German-EFL	explicit vs. implicit	pretest-posttest, L2 baseline	role-play
Wildner-Bassett, 1984, 1986	pragmatic routines	int.	German-EFL	eclectic vs. Suggestopedia	pretest-posttest, control	role-play
Billmyer, 1990a, 1990b	compliments	high int.	Japanese-ESL	±instruction	pretest-posttest, control, L2 baseline	elicited conversation
Olshtain & Cohen, 1990	apologies	adv.	Hebrew-EFL	teachability	pretest-posttest, L2 baseline	DCT
Lyster, 1994	sociostylistic variation	Grade 8 immersion	English-French FL	±instruction	pretest-posttest, delayed posttest, control, classroom observation	oral production, written production multiple choice
Wildner-Bassett, 1994	pragmatic routines & strategies	beg.	English-German SL	teachability to beginning FL students ±instruction	one group pretest-posttest	questionnaires, role-play
Bouton, 1994a	implicature	adv.	Mixed-ESL	±instruction	pretest-posttest, control	multiple choice
Kubota, 1995	implicature	int.	Japanese-EFL	rule explanation vs. consciousness raising	pretest-posttest, delayed posttest, control	multiple choice, sentence composing
House, 1996	pragmatic fluency	adv.	German-EFL	explicit vs. implicit	pretest-interim posttest, classroom observation, interviews	role-play

Study	Feature	Level	Context	Treatment	Design	Measure
Morrow, 1996	complaints, refusals	int.	Mixed-ESL	teachability/ explicit	pretest-posttest, delayed posttest, L2 baseline	role-play, holistic ratings
Tateyama et al., 1997	pragmatic routines	beg.	English-JFL	explicit vs. implicit	posttest	multimethod
Fukuya, 1998	downgraders (requests)	int.	Mixed-ESL	consciousness raising	one group pretest-posttest	role-play, DCT
Fukuya et al., 1998	sociopragmatics (requests)	high int	Mixed-ESL	focus on form vs. focus on formS	pretest-posttest, control	NS-rated DCT
Pearson, 1998	thanks, apologies, commands, requests	high beg.	English-Spanish FL	metapragmatic discussion vs. additional input	pretest-posttest, delayed posttest	oral & written tasks
Fukuya & Clark, in press	mitigators (requests)	int./adv.	Mixed-ESL	input enhancement vs. explicit	posttest, control	listening comprehension tests, multiple choice

Note: Languages are listed as learners' L1-target language; FL = foreign language; SL = second language.

use of the address form *tu* and replace it by more sociolinguistically sensitive choices between the formal and informal address pronoun. Lyster described their learning task in terms of an information-processing model of skill acquisition, where the initial stages require effortful, controlled production under conscious awareness. In order to restructure their sociolinguistic knowledge and make it available for effective use, Lyster contends that learners have to engage in productive language use rather than just in recognition activities.

Lyster's study is indicative of a change in theoretical orientation seen in interventional research. Although pedagogical theory and practice continue to inform such investigations, there is now a noticeable shift toward engaging SLA theory and research, which in turn is underwritten by psycholinguistics and cognitive psychology in general. The SLA-oriented interventional studies are based on three interrelated hypotheses: Schmidt's noticing hypothesis (Schmidt, e.g., 1993a, 1995), Swain's output hypothesis (Swain, 1996), and Long's interaction hypothesis (Long, 1996). The first two hypotheses relate to different stages in the language learning process. The noticing hypothesis holds that in order for input to be turned into intake and thus made available for further processing, it needs to be registered under awareness.[2] The output hypothesis suggests a number of important acquisitional roles for productive language use: During utterance production, learners may notice gaps in their interlanguage knowledge; output is one way of creating and testing hypotheses about L2; productive language use beyond entirely formulaic speech requires analyzed knowledge that is not called upon in comprehension; and automatization of language representations requires repeated productive use, as any skilled behavior does. In Long's recent formulation, the interaction hypothesis integrates the noticing and output hypotheses. It proposes that "negotiation of meaning, and especially the negotiation work that triggers interactional adjustments by the NS or more competent interlocutor, facilitates acquisition because it connects input, internal learner capacities, particularly selective attention, and output in productive ways" (Long, 1996, pp. 451ff.). Further, according to many, though not all, SLA theorists, in purely meaning-oriented L2 use, learners may not detect relevant input features. Therefore, Sharwood Smith (1993) proposed that in order for noticing to occur, input may have to be made salient through input enhancement, which, so one hopes, will raise the learners' consciousness about the target feature. When and how input may be most beneficially enhanced and, additionally, when and how feedback is best provided, are controversial issues. A volume in this series edited by Doughty and Williams (1998)

---

2 There is considerable controversy about whether or not awareness is required in order to make novel information available for storage in long-term memory. For dissenting views, see Tomlin and Villa (1994) and Truscott (1998).

represents widely differing positions on form-focused instruction. According to the most radical position, "[f]ocus on form involves . . . an occasional shift in attention to linguistic code features – by the teacher and/or one or more students – triggered by perceived problems with comprehension or production" (Long & Robinson, 1998, p. 23). In contrast, the traditional focus on formS isolates the target material from its use in meaningful interaction and usually presents it proactively; that is, its presentation is not elicited by a problem experienced by the learners and thus may not be compatible with the learners' "built-in syllabus."

The SLA literature on the acquisition of morphosyntax now boasts a large number of classroom-based or classroom-oriented studies that engage the hypotheses and concepts sketched in the preceding discussion. In pragmatics, such research is still in the initial stages. One reason may be that it is not always obvious how principles proposed for instruction in grammar might translate to pragmatics. The notion of focus on *form* (FonF) may appear inapplicable to pragmatics because pragmatics is never *only* form. Pragmalinguistic knowledge requires mappings of form, meaning, force, and context, which are sometimes obligatory (as in the case of prepackaged routines) and sometimes not (as in the case of indirectness). Since sociopragmatics refers to the link between action-relevant context factors and communicative action (e.g., deciding whether to request an extension, complain about the neighbor's barking dog) and does not necessarily require any links to specific linguistic forms at all, aligning sociopragmatics with FonF requires even more conceptual acrobatics.

In a first step to extend FonF to pragmatics, it may help to remind ourselves of the following relations: focus on meaning versus focus on form(S), language-in-use versus metalinguistic, and pragmatic versus metapragmatic. The contrast between "focus on meaning" and "focus on form(S)" is paralleled by the opposition between language-in-use and metalinguistic (information) and allows for an analogous distinction between pragmatic action and metapragmatic information. Just as the shift from focus on meaning to a focus on form can be triggered by a grammatical error in the learner's utterance and result in a recast, that is, a (partial) repetition of the learner's utterance with the wrong form corrected, the shift from pragmatic action to metapragmatic comment can be triggered by a contextually inappropriate pragmatic feature. As long as such problems are clearly pragmalinguistic, that is, the learner chooses an inappropriate *form* – a wrong discourse marker, routine formula, or modal verb to index illocutionary force or mitigation, for instance – *and* limited to short utterance segments, such problems may be fairly easy to identify and recast. But if the problem is sociopragmatic, things get murky. One complication is that unlike inappropriate pragmalinguistic choices, which can often be identified within one utterance or turn, sociopragmatically infelicitous selections may be more difficult to locate. The learner may choose a politeness style that is too much to the negative or positive spectrum of politeness, in the ears of the interlocutor or teacher. Styles come as a package of features, distributed over the entire discourse (Cook, this volume). Isolating and repairing a particular feature is thus not an option. Furthermore, in talk-in-interaction, the appearance and sequencing of communicative acts are jointly accomplished. If the learner starts out a complaint about a loud party by commenting to her neighbor that he and his friends seemed to have had a lot of fun the night before, and the neighbor instantly launches into apology, explanation, and a promise of forbearance, the learner will never have to perform anything close to a complaint, yet she has reached her communicative goal successfully. In a teaching sequence about complaining, there is thus no occasion for intervention during the ongoing interaction, even though the learner never did complain. But perhaps the most serious reservation against instant identification and repair of sociopragmatic problems is that such intervention presupposes firm sociopragmatic norms against which communicative action can be assessed – norms which privilege a particular course of communicative action and negatively sanction others. Although such norms strongly constrain ritual communication and (to greater or lesser extent) institutional discourse, less prestructured encounters such as casual conversation present a wide range of allowable, and largely unpredictable, contributions, regulated by a "conversational contract" (Fraser, 1990) that is always subject to renegotiation. What counts as sociopragmatically appropriate is thus guided by social, cultural, and personal preferences and the dynamics of the ongoing interaction. Such preferences and the options and constraints emerging from the interaction itself elude instant repair; they can most adequately be addressed in metapragmatic discussion.

A study by Fukuya, Reeve, Gisi, and Christianson (1998) highlighted the difficulty of adapting strategies developed for instruction in linguistic form to teaching sociopragmatic information. One stumbling block in their study on teaching the sociopragmatics of requesting was to operationalize the distinction between focus on form and focus on formS. Another problem was how a focus on form can be implemented through recasts during ongoing interaction, reflecting the difficulties already discussed. Although recasting of sociopragmatic information is restricted to highly prestructured interactions, it appears more promising to extend the distinction between a focus on form and formS to sociopragmatics. According to Long and Robinson (1998), form- and formS-focused instruction differs not so much in substance – what kinds of metalinguistic information is given – but in the role and contextualization of metalinguistic information in the syllabus and class activities. As long as the metalinguistic information is embedded in purposeful activities, triggered by an actual learner problem, and teachable at the learners' current stage of interlanguage development, the intervention registers as FonF. If this is applied to instruction in pragmatics, we can conclude that it is not the quality of the provided metapragmatic information that describes different teaching strategies in analogy to the FonF–FonFS distinction but the role of metapragmatic information in the syllabus and its relation to practice activities. Metapragmatic comment generated by students' pragmatic action (in authentic contexts, pedagogical tasks, role-plays) or observations would seem quite compatible with FonF. And indeed, without referring to FonF, several of the interventional studies illustrate what might better be termed FonFF in pragmatics – a focus on form and function.

As evident from the column "Research focus" in Table 3, many studies have a component suggesting that the targeted pragmatic feature is described, explained, or discussed – in short, made the object of *metapragmatic* treatment. Metapragmatic *instruction* is often combined with metapragmatic *discussion,* requiring active student participation in a teacher-fronted format or small groups. A number of studies have addressed the efficacy of metapragmatic instruction by comparing it to other teaching strategies, sometimes under the labels "explicit" and "implicit" teaching. Several studies (House & Kasper, 1981b; House, 1996; Tateyama, Kasper, Mui, Tay, & Thananart, 1997; Pearson, 1998; Tateyama, this volume) have compared metapragmatic instruction with input and practice-only conditions. All of these studies (except for Tateyama, this volume, on one measure) found an advantage for explicit metapragmatic teaching. Fukuya and Clark (in press) compared input enhancement and explicit metapragmatic instruction in teaching mitigators to ESL learners. The input enhancement condition presented filmed request scenarios including on-screen captions of the requests, with the mitigators highlighted. For the explicit instruction condition, students received a 6-minute metapragmatic presentation on the use of mitigators in requests prior to watching the same video but without the captions. No treatment differences or differences between treatment and control groups were found, for various reasons discussed in the paper.

Fukuya and Clark (1999) defined *input enhancement* as an implicit instructional technique that does not provide metapragmatic information. By contrast, S. Takahashi proposes a much broader view of input enhancement. In her study on instruction in request strategies to Japanese EFL students (Takahashi, this volume), she distinguished three different degrees and types of input enhancement (Sharwood Smith, 1993): explicit teaching, featuring metapragmatic explanation about form–function relationships of the target structures; form-comparison, in which students compared their own request realizations with those of native speakers; and form-search, in which students identified the target strategies in provided request scenarios. These three input-enhancement varieties were contrasted with a meaning-focused condition, in which students listened to aurally presented request events, read transcripts, and answered comprehension questions. The explicit group learned all four request strategies more successfully than the other three groups. Students in the other three conditions did equally poorly. One possible explanation is that the teacher-delivered metapragmatic explanation was consistent with the instructional style predominant in Japanese college classrooms. Written immediate retrospective reports revealed that the students who successfully provided the target structures attended more to linguistic features in the request strategies, whereas students who supplied more nontarget-like structures noticed more discourse-related features of requesting, such as different supporting moves and presence of apology. The explicitly taught students displayed more attention to request-related linguistic forms than the students in the other conditions. For those students, nontarget request forms which were well rehearsed since their high school days, such as *would you please*, remained cognitively more accessible than the newly taught more complex forms and were thus more available for recall, even when students had noticed the target forms in the input.

Takahashi's findings bear both similarities and differences to research on the effects of different instructional conditions on the acquisition of formal linguistic features. Such studies consistently demonstrate that for many target structures, a focus on meaning alone is not effective (which agrees with Takahashi's results). But different from Takahashi's findings, they also show the effectiveness of such learning conditions as form-comparison and form search (e.g., Ellis, 1995). Future research will have to explore under what conditions inductive techniques may be beneficial in teaching pragmatics.

The interventional studies also raise the issue of what may be an appropriate *length of treatment*: How much time do learners need in order to notice and understand novel pragmatic information, and how much time do they need to make such information available for comprehension and production in spoken interaction and written discourse? What factors may shorten or lengthen the time necessary for pragmatic learning in instructional settings? The studies in Table 3 vary considerably in treatment length, ranging from an entire 14-week semester (House & Kasper, 1981b; House, 1996) and a 5-day intensive course of 40 hours (Wildner-Bassett, 1984, 1986) to 12 hours distributed over 5 weeks (Lyster, 1994) to one-shot treatments of a mere 25 minutes (Tateyama et al., 1997) or 20 minutes (Kubota, 1995). It is encouraging to note that for some instructional targets, even short treatments may prove effective. For instance, Tateyama et al. (1997) demonstrated that both "implicitly" and "explicitly" taught beginning JFL learners profited from 25 minutes of instruction in highly frequent formulaic routines – *sumimasen, arigato, gomen nasai, moshiwake arimasen* – and they even learned, to some extent, how to use these routines context-appropriately. It was not possible to administer delayed posttests, but some of the posttest role-plays had to be conducted a few weeks after the treatment and they indicated that students had retained the routines quite well. This is all the more surprising in that students did not have the opportunity for conversational practice following the treatment; however, they were given worksheets to practice with, and this activity appears to have helped them commit the formulas and their pragmatic functions to memory.

But short treatments can also be quite ineffective. Kubota (1995) replicated Bouton's (1994a) study on instruction in implicature, comparing the effectiveness of consciousness-raising and rule explanation for EFL students in Japan. Although students did show gains on a posttest immediately after receiving a 20-minute treatment in implicature in English, neither the instructed groups nor the controls were able to perform successfully on new implicature items. In other words, it seems that students either remembered the exact implicature examples from the treatment material but did not understand the Gricean maxims and their systematic violations as they underlie different implicature types, or they were unable to apply such recently acquired knowledge to new contexts. There are many differences between Tateyama et al.'s and Kubota's studies that may explain why the short treatments were differentially effective, such as the JFL versus EFL teaching contexts, culturally preferred learning styles, and individual variation in the two student populations. But one difference that stands out is the instructional target. Understanding and using implicature require pertinent cultural, linguistic, and pragmatic knowledge, the ability to access and integrate such knowledge fast and match it with context and textual information. This task is appreciably more complex and cognitively demanding than using a few short routine formulas. Pragmatic learning tasks of such complexity require sustained attended exposure and active collaborative processing of the learning material in order for learners to establish enduring representations that are available for recognition and recall.

The results of Kubota's study also contrast with those of the original study by Bouton (1994a), which demonstrated that "tough" implicatures – those that proved difficult to learn through exposure – can be successfully learned through instruction. A number of important differences between Bouton's and Kubota's studies may account for the variable outcomes. First, unlike the one-shot treatment in Kubota, in Bouton's study, students received six class sessions of instruction in implicature distributed over 6 weeks. Second, the students in Bouton's study had a much higher proficiency in English than those in Kubota's study. Third, the studies were conducted in different learning environments – EFL in Kubota's case versus ESL in Bouton's. In several respects, the second language context put the ESL students at an advantage. As shown in the pretest, they had already mastered some implicature types through exposure alone and were thus able to build on this skill. Through the instruction, they were alerted to implicatures outside the classroom; thus their opportunities for observation and online comprehension were maximized. It was part of the instruction to foster the link between implicature learning inside and outside of the classroom: Students were encouraged to bring examples of implicatures they had encountered into the classroom and make them available for metapragmatic discussion. The ESL learners were thus in a distinctly more favorable learning situation than the EFL students; however, their advantage was not one of exposure alone – recall that the entire motivation for Bouton's study derived from learners *not* acquiring all implicature types through exposure only. The crucial point seems to be that the instruction combined learning opportunities inside and outside the classroom: *inside* the classroom by raising learners' awareness about implicature and improving their comprehension of it, and *outside* the classroom by focusing their attention to implicatures and encouraging them to seek out practice opportunities. Rather short periods of teaching pragmatics can be effective when learning opportunities inside and outside the classroom are combined – and not just for receptive skills such as implicature comprehension but also for productive pragmatic abilities. The treatment in Billmyer's (1990a and b) study on instruction in complimenting lasted 6 hours, as in Bouton's study. Compared to controls, the instructed students improved their complimenting ability on five out of seven measures. Morrow's (1996) research on teaching complaints and refusals to ESL learners demonstrates that after only 3½ hours of instruction, ESL learners improved their performance of these speech acts and maintained their gains at the time of the delayed posttest 6 months after the intervention. This is very good news indeed, considering how often learning effects immediately after treatment prove to be short-lived. The great potential of SL teaching for developing learners' pragmatic ability lies in its capacity to alert and orient learners to pragmatic features encountered outside the classroom, encourage them to try out new pragmatic strategies, reflect on their observations and their own language use, and obtain feedback.

Compared to an SL environment, opportunities for learning L2 pragmatics in FL settings are much more restricted. What kinds of instructional measures may offset at least some of the limitations in FL learning? For complex pragmatic abilities – conversational skills, pragmatic fluency – time on task seems to be decisive. Sustained focused input, both pragmatic and metapragmatic, collaborative practice activities, and metapragmatic reflection appear to provide learners with the input and practice they need for developing most aspects of their pragmatic abilities. Support for this contention comes from interventional studies that provided pragmatic instruction over an entire semester (House & Kasper, 1981b; House, 1996) or a weeklong intensive course (Wildner-Bassett, 1984, 1986) and from the observational JFL studies discussed earlier, notably Ohta's and Kanagy and Igarashi's work. Their studies showed that through sustained input and collaborative practice, students acquired pragmatic routines and the ability to index alignment in interaction. Supported by metapragmatic instruction and discussion, students can make significant gains in pragmatic ability in FL classrooms.

Approaches to research on classroom learning of pragmatics

A glance at the columns "Data collection/analysis" in Tables 1 and 2 and "Design" in Table 3 reveals a striking and consistent methodological difference between the observational and interventional studies reviewed in this chapter. Without exception, the interventional studies feature varieties of a pretest–posttest design. Very few studies include a delayed posttest (commendable exceptions are Lyster, 1994; Kubota, 1995; Morrow, 1996; Pearson, 1998), although this may not be the result of an oversight on the part of the researcher but a consequence of institutional constraints in the research setting (Rose & Ng, this volume; Takahashi, this volume). However, if a treatment does not extend over an entire term or semester, administering it early in the course will often allow the teacher to posttest toward the end of the course. For treatments extending over the entire course, one solution is intermittent testing during the treatment phase (House, 1996; Yoshimi, this volume). Intermittent testing also has the advantage of providing feedback to the researcher that may be used to adjust the treatment in later phases of the course.

Only seven of the seventeen interventional studies include a control group. The rationale for a control group is, of course, to allow the investigator to assess whether posttreatment effects observed in the experimental group(s) are in fact the result of the treatment. In the studies that compare different experimental teaching approaches – implicit versus explicit, for instance – comparison is often made between those approaches, without including a control group that received instruction "as usual," that is, without including any elements of the treatment. Doing without a control group is often logistically mandated, because recruiting yet another class for a study, or dividing one intact class into still more groups, may not be institutionally or administratively possible. For instance, Takahashi (this volume) had four experimental groups; adding a control group would not have been feasible. As long as research is carried out in regular classroom settings, there is little choice but to accommodate institutional constraints and compromise accordingly. Surely, second language researchers would still want to conduct studies on instruction in the less commonly taught languages even if there was just one section of a particular course available, and this section was too small to subdivide. One great benefit of working within actual institutions of language education is that research results can be translated into recommendations for pedagogical practice with more plausibility than results from laboratory studies. Authenticity of the research setting and translatability of research results are thus closely interrelated, and classroom research aiming not only at theoretical insight but also at pedagogical impact is well advised to heed these quality criteria. It is true that the specificity of local classroom settings poses limits to the generalizability of findings from an individual study to other instructional contexts (Chaudron, 1998); however, stable research outcomes across a variety of educational settings do indicate that such findings are generalizable/transferable. A good example is the superior learning effect of explicit over implicit teaching, observed with very few exceptions in the interventional studies. While there is no guarantee that explicit instruction proves universally more effective, the research evidence strongly suggests that for populations comparable to the ones in the reviewed literature – predominantly college students in post-industrial societies – explicit teaching of pragmatics is more conducive to learning. This tentative generalization is supported by a quantitative meta-analysis of seventy-seven types of instruction studies with a predominant focus on grammar, demonstrating a clear advantage for explicit over implicit teaching (Norris & Ortega, 2000).

The downside of research in authentic instructional settings is that classrooms are poor laboratories (an observation verging on tautology). There is no way of controlling the entire gamut of variables that may interact with the "treatment." The large-scale psychometric classroom studies of the 1960s and 1970s (see Chaudron, 1988, for discussion) were abandoned largely because it was impossible to assess how the measured achievements came about, how the treatments ("methods") were implemented, or how students responded to different components of the treatment during different phases of the (quasi) experiments. Although later classroom research inquiring into the effect of pedagogical measures on learning outcomes has been considerably more restricted in focus than the "methods" studies, one methodological problem that the older and more recent studies share is the assumption that learning effects are the results of the treatment as designed, without examining whether the treatment was actually implemented according to plan and whether the control groups, if indeed there were any, did not receive any teaching in the treatment target or followed instructional practices that were part of the treatment. In his review of classroom research on the effect of focus on form, Chaudron (1998) notes that of the twenty-six included studies, "not even half . . . follow up with a discourse analysis of the lessons to ensure that such a focus occurred" (p. 11). Of the seventeen interventional pragmatic studies, only Lyster (1994) and House (1996) performed regular classroom observation. In addition, Lyster also conducted a teachers' workshop prior to the experimental instruction in order to ensure that the participating instructors understood the treatment in detail. But neither House nor Lyster analyzed the classroom observation data systematically and related it to students' posttreatment performance. The interventional pragmatics research thus falls into the category of *product* studies, focusing on learning outcomes without systematically relating such outcomes to observed classroom practices. As has been noted with respect to research into the efficacy of second language teaching approaches in general, the lack of information on classroom processes is problematic (Long, 1984).

In contrast, the majority of the observational studies document classroom interaction in detail, using transcribed audio or video recordings, which are then analyzed according to a specified discourse-pragmatic approach. These studies thus afford insights into classroom processes, with the potential of linking such processes to elements of pragmatic learning: teacher input, occasions for productive performance in collaborative activities, and development of pragmatic ability over time. Although there is a continued need for more observational studies, especially longitudinal studies with a developmental focus, it is also timely to combine interventional with observational research strategies. Process-product-classroom research, already called for by Long (1984), allows researchers to explain learning outcomes, assess and change interventional measures, and check on how an instructional treatment was delivered; it also affords ongoing exploration of substantive, theoretical, and methodological issues.

Among the methodological issues is the role of self-report in classroom research. In ethnographic studies, self-report obtained through interviews is standard procedure. Yet some classroom researchers have voiced skepticism about the usefulness of interviews in connection with discourse-analytical approaches to classroom investigation. Cazden (1986) points out that much of speakers' discourse knowledge is proceduralized into automatic routines and thus is not available to conscious awareness and self-report, a position shared by microanalysts of spoken discourse and supported by Cook's study in this volume. Incidentally, the micro-analysts' view is consistent with Ericsson and Simon's (1993) informa-tion-processing theory on online verbalization, according to which only consciously attended information can be verbalized. At the same time, some components in the planning of nonroutinized communicative action will require speakers' attention, especially in novice language users, and such information is available for verbal report (Cohen, 1996). Finally, one important issue in learning L2 pragmatics is what cultural, social, and personal meanings and functions students and teachers ascribe to communicative practices. In order to explore such subjective theories (Grotjahn, 1991) on pragmatics and their possible changes in the course of development and through experiences inside and outside the classroom, interviews are an appropriate method of data collection.

PART II:
ISSUES IN CLASSROOM-BASED LEARNING
OF PRAGMATICS

The chapters in Part II explore a variety of issues in the classroom learning of different aspects of L2 pragmatics. Rather than examining directly the effects of particular approaches to instruction (discussed in Part III), the focus here is on the incidental acquisition (or nonacquisition) of pragmatics that results from classroom language learning. Chapters 4 and 5 (Niezgoda and Röver, Cook) explore learners' interlanguage pragmatic knowledge as the result of L2 (classroom) learning, but without examining empirically how these learning outcomes relate to classroom processes or specific instructional measures. These studies are thus classroom-oriented rather than classroom-based (Nunan, 1991). Kimberly Niezgoda and Carsten Röver replicated Bardovi-Harlig and Dörnyei's (1998) study on the effects of learning environment and proficiency on learners' awareness of pragmatic and grammatical errors in the target language. The previous study had found that learners in the second language setting had stronger awareness of pragmatic than of grammatical errors, whereas learners in the foreign language setting were more aware of grammatical than of pragmatic errors. For their study, Niezgoda and Röver used the same video-prompted task requiring participants to distinguish grammatical from pragmatics errors, and to rate both for seriousness. Although their ESL sample was generally comparable to that in the original study, their EFL group was markedly different in that it consisted of a highly select group of learners who had gained entrance to an English-language teacher-training program at a prestigious Czech university. Their findings corroborate Bardovi-Harlig and Dörnyei's results in one central respect: The ESL group rated pragmatic errors as more severe than grammatical errors. But Niezgoda and Röver also found substantial differences, particularly that the responses of their EFL group more closely matched Bardovi-Harlig and Dörnyei's ESL group, which suggests that environment may not be the most important factor accounting for learners' pragmatic awareness. They argue that these results provide evidence that pragmatic awareness can indeed be acquired in an FL context. In addition, their findings strongly encourage further observational and interventional research to determine specifically how pragmatics can be taught in an FL classroom.

As has been much emphasized in the interlanguage pragmatics literature, learners' communicative success hinges to a large extent on their ability to express interpersonal meanings with target-language resources. But information about how learners acquire, or fail to acquire, alignment and politeness through classroom learning is scarce. Chapters 5 (by Cook) and 6 (by Ohta) address this issue, both examining learners and teachers of Japanese as a foreign language (JFL) at different sites in the United States. Referring to Gumperz's work on contextualization and inferencing, Haruko Cook investigates JFL learners' ability to assess the politeness of nonnative speakers' use of Japanese in a job interview. She finds a glaring discrepancy between students' inability to identify impolite speech and the instructors' unanimous assessment of politeness and impoliteness in the given context. However, instructors were able to identify only violations of the prescriptive norm (failure to use *masu* style), whereas most of them did not identify such co-occurring politeness features as hedges and contracted forms. This difference between language use and instructors' metapragmatic awareness reflects folklorist views of Japanese, according to which politeness begins and ends with honorifics. In JFL teaching, such a restricted view of politeness is problematic because many politeness features appear to escape students' attention unless such features are made salient in some way and thus become more noticeable. Cook's chapter emphasizes the importance of indexicality for L2 teaching and of language teachers' education in the pragmatics and sociolinguistics of the target language. Continuing the topic of conveying and understanding interpersonal meaning in Japanese, Amy Snyder Ohta reports the results of a longitudinal study of the development of interactional style in adult JFL learners. This multiple case study is innovative in several respects: It examines both teachers' and learners' use of sentence-final *ne* in the FL classroom context and thus makes it possible to assess the learners' opportunities for input and use over the entire observation period. This allows the author to identify not only developments in the frequency and discourse environments where learners use *ne*, but also a pragmatic restructuring of sorts, moving from acknowledgment of the previous speaker's contribution to alignment with the interlocutor. Ohta's study provides much reason for optimism about the potential of FL classrooms for pragmatic learning. Appropriate listening behavior is a subtle discourse practice whose acquisition requires extensive input and occasion for conversational practice. Even though their contact with Japanese was restricted to the classroom, the students were able to acquire culturally appropriate listener abilities over time. But since students' ability to produce assessment and alignment responses evolves gradually over several stages, as Ohta demonstrates, tracing such development requires persistent longitudinal observation.

4 Pragmatic and grammatical awareness

A function of the learning environment?

Kimberly Niezgoda and Carsten Röver

Introduction

A question that has received surprisingly little attention in second language acquisition research is whether learners' pragmatic and grammatical competence in a second language (SL) develop hand in hand or differentially. In other words, if students can produce impeccable conditional clauses, does that also imply that they will be able to order a hamburger? In an exploration of the relationship between pragmatic and grammatical competence, Bardovi-Harlig and Dörnyei (1998) undertook an award-winning study[1] to investigate the effects of environment and language proficiency on learners' metalinguistic assessment of pragmatic and grammatical errors in the target language. They found that learners in an SL setting assessed pragmatic errors as more severe than grammatical errors, whereas learners in a foreign language (FL) setting assessed grammatical errors as more severe than pragmatic errors. This study is a replication of Bardovi-Harlig and Dörnyei (1998), but also investigates whether the environment effect they found is inevitable, or whether a highly select group of exceptional students may be able to overcome it.

Grammatical, pragmatic, and communicative competence

Although Larsen-Freeman and Long (1991, p. 39) assert that "a definitive analysis of communicative competence is just as elusive as was language proficiency," the notion of communicative competence has been a driving force in SL curriculum development, teaching, and – more recently to a smaller extent – testing (Swain, 1985; Wesche, 1987; Alderson, 1988). Definitions of communicative competence tend to include (among other things) at least two components: a code component, which describes a language user's knowledge of syntax, morphology, semantics, lexis, and

---

1 The study received the TESOL award at the 33rd Annual International TESOL Convention, New York.

phonology; and a use component, which describes a language user's ability to use language appropriately for a purpose within a given context. Campbell and Wales (1970) and Hymes (1972) conceptualize communicative competence as the knowledge of rules of grammar, on the one hand, and rules of language use appropriate to a communicative situation, on the other. Based on their conceptualizations, detailed models of communicative competence have been suggested by Canale and Swain (1980, revised by Canale, 1983) and Bachman (1990, revised by Bachman & Palmer, 1996). Both models make a fundamental distinction between competencies for pragmatic aspects of language use and for aspects concerned with linguistic code features.

In their seminal article, Canale and Swain (1980) subsumed under communicative competence three subcompetencies, later extended by Canale (1983) to four:

- grammatical competence, the knowledge of linguistic code features such as morphology, syntax, semantics, phonology
- sociolinguistic competence, the knowledge of contextually appropriate language use
- discourse competence, the knowledge of achieving coherence and cohesion in spoken or written communication
- strategic competence, the knowledge of how to use communication strategies to handle breakdowns in communication and make communication effective

Pragmatic competence is represented in this model as sociolinguistic competence, which Canale (1983, p. 7) described as encompassing both "appropriateness of meaning" and "appropriateness of form." This distinction echoes Leech (1983), with appropriateness of meaning paralleling Leech's sociopragmatic component, which includes an interlocutor's knowledge of pragmatic conventions and the ability to assess situational context and speech intentions. Appropriateness of form resembles Leech's (1983) pragmalinguistic component (and Clark's [1979] conventions of means and form) and concerns the mapping of a linguistic realization of a speech intention to a situation.

The second major influential model, proposed by Bachman (1990) and revised by Bachman and Palmer (1996), considers communicative competence a dynamic system in which world knowledge ("knowledge structures") and language competence feed into strategic competence, which describes the degree to which linguistic intentions are efficiently executed. Strategic competence interacts with psychophysiological mechanisms, which in turn interact with situational context. Grammatical and pragmatic competence are part of Bachman's language competence, which he subdivides into organizational competence and pragmatic competence. Organizational competence concerns a speaker's control of the formal aspects of language and is further subdivided in grammatical competence (vocabulary, syntax, morphology, phonology) and textual competence (cohesion/coherence, rhetorical organization), thereby encompassing Canale's (1983) discourse competence. Pragmatic competence consists of sociolinguistic and illocutionary competence, with the former again paralleling Leech's (1983) sociopragmatic component and the latter corresponding to Leech's concept of a pragmalinguistic component. Although all major definitions of communicative competence recognize grammatical and pragmatic competence as separate components of communicative competence, their empirical validation has proved elusive. An early factor analytic study by Bachman and Palmer (1982a) identified a general factor, which they hypothesize may represent information processing in extended discourse, and two subfactors, one for grammar/pragmatics, the other for sociolinguistics. Although this seems to support Canale and Swain's framework, it is noteworthy that Bachman and Palmer's subtraits for their pragmatics competence were vocabulary, cohesion, and textual organization, and the subtraits for sociolinguistic competence included register, nativeness, and cultural references. Their study did not explicitly focus on speech acts and situational appropriateness, although competence in those areas probably influenced interview ratings.

In a second large-scale factor analysis, Harley, Allen, Cummins, and Swain (1990b) were unable to replicate Bachman and Palmer's (1982a) factor structure, finding instead a general factor and a method factor. However, in direct comparisons of their native speaker and immersion student groups, they found significant differences in grammatical competence, little difference in discourse competence, and significant differences on most measures of sociolinguistic competence, which they operationalized as recognition and production of situationally appropriate speech acts. Other studies have tackled the issue from a more developmental viewpoint and have shown that learners' grammatical competence and pragmatic competence do not necessarily increase hand in hand (cf. Kasper, 2000, for an overview). For example, learners may produce grammatically complex and correct but pragmatically inappropriate utterances (Eisenstein & Bodman, 1986) or use grammatical features, such as modals, in their speech but not to modify the illocutionary force of specific speech acts (Salsbury & Bardovi-Harlig, 2000). Conversely, learners may produce pragmatically appropriate utterances with grammatical errors (Walters, 1980; Eisenstein & Bodman, 1986, 1993). Although these studies indicate that grammatical competence and pragmatic competence are separate and independent components of communicative competence, they do not investigate factors which may accelerate the development of one or the other. One factor that has received attention is the learning setting.

L2 pragmatic competence and setting

Takahashi and Beebe (1987) found a greater degree of proximity to American English norms in the refusals of Japanese ESL students than in those of EFL students. Similarly, Röver (1996) found a strong superiority in the recognition of situationally appropriate routines for German EFL learners with stays in an English-speaking country of as little as 6 weeks as compared to learners who had not spent time in an English-speaking country. House (1996) found a similar tendency for the pragmatic fluency of her German learners of English. Although it seems that the SL situation confers an advantage for the development of pragmatic competence, this does not mean that it is impossible to improve learners' pragmatic competence in the FL setting. House (1996) did just that by means of university-level courses focused on routines taught to advanced German learners of English. She found a positive teaching effect, as did Wildner-Bassett (1984, 1994), for teaching English or German gambits, respectively, in an FL setting. However, House (1996) also found that the teaching effect was not strong enough to override the initial advantage enjoyed by those who had spent time in the target-language culture.

Three longitudinal case studies also shed light on the effect of learning environment on the differential development of pragmatic and grammatical competence. In an early investigation of Schumann's (1978) acculturation model, Schmidt (1983) followed the development of the communicative competence of his native Japanese-speaking participant Wes over the course of 3 years, during which time Wes lived in Honolulu and showed a greater increase in pragmatic competence than in grammatical competence, the latter stagnating early, which Schmidt attributes to Wes's strong motivation for engaging in communication and his broad command of formulaic utterances at the outset of the study. In a similar second language environment study based on diary and interview material, Schmidt and Frota (1986) report on Schmidt's learning of Brazilian Portuguese. The study is focused on Schmidt's acquisition of Portuguese grammar and word usage, but it indicates rapid development of pragmatic competence and the ability to realize communicative intent. However, partially accountable for this process might be Schmidt's conscious quest to seek out input opportunities and keep interactions flowing. A case study from a foreign language situation is Cohen's (1997) self-report of his learning of Japanese in an introductory course at the University of Hawai'i. Cohen focused on the development of his pragmatic ability in Japanese but found himself lagging in pragmatic competence, both in his ability to analyze situations for their appropriacy conditions and in his command of linguistic form to express speech intentions. The focus of the class he attended was strongly on grammar, vocabulary, and writing, with little attention to instruction in pragmatic aspects of Japanese. A comparison between Schmidt's and Cohen's findings highlights the strong effects of the FL environment versus the SL environment. Wes and Schmidt, living in the SL environment, developed in their pragmatic abilities, while Cohen, living in an FL environment and receiving formal instruction, did not. This seems to indicate that it is the environment that promotes pragmatic competence: Wes and Schmidt were highly motivated to increase their pragmatic competence and did; Cohen was also motivated but did not.

What accounts for this differential effect of the FL and SL situation? Bardovi-Harlig and Hartford (1993), Kasper (1996), and Schmidt (1995) argue for an input-based explanation. Pragmatic competence will increase only if there is sufficient input containing enough exemplars of the target feature, if this input is noticed, and if learners can analyze it sufficiently and develop control (Bialystok, 1993). Classrooms tend to be lacking in this type of input because they do not offer the wide array of communicative contexts to which SL learners are exposed outside instructional settings (Kasper, 1997a). Since classrooms often constitute a learner's only exposure to the target language in the FL setting, little pragmatic competence will develop. At the same time, learners are exposed to grammatically rich input in classrooms, often in addition to more or less explicit grammar instruction and assessment focusing on grammar. This leads to a higher awareness of the grammatical properties of language, and eventually to much stronger grammatical than pragmatic development.

The differential effects of the SL setting and the FL setting on the development of pragmatic and grammatical awareness were the focus of a cross-sectional study by Bardovi-Harlig and Dörnyei (1998), which provides the foundation for our research. Their ESL population consisted of 173 learners of intermediate to advanced ESL proficiency recruited from Indiana University's intensive language program, while the EFL population consisted of 370 Hungarian high school and university students who self-assessed their English as roughly low intermediate to advanced.[2] During the study, participants viewed twenty video scenes of brief conversations in English, containing a pragmatic error, a grammatical error, or no error in the final utterance. After each scene, participants indicated whether the final utterance was "appropriate/correct" and, if it was not, how "bad" the "problem" was on a scale from "not bad at all" to "very bad" (Bardovi-Harlig & Dörnyei, 1998, p. 260). Analyses indicated significant differences based

---

2 Bardovi-Harlig and Dörnyei's study also included 28 NS ESL teachers in the United States and 25 Hungarian EFL teachers, as well as a group of 112 Italian EFL teachers, all of whom will be ignored for purposes of this study. Results for these groups were similar to the results found for the learners.

on learning environment, proficiency, and learner versus teacher status. ESL learners found more pragmatic errors and assessed them as significantly more severe than their EFL counterparts. EFL learners showed the opposite tendency: They found more grammatical errors and rated them as significantly more severe than the ESL learners did. Although Bardovi-Harlig and Dörnyei followed Schmidt (1995) in adopting awareness as the underlying construct that explains learners' assessments, we feel that in order to avoid terminological confusion, the construct is more precisely described as learners' perceptions of the importance of grammatical errors relative to pragmatic errors. From these perceptions, inferences can be drawn as to the role of pragmatics and grammar in the learning environment, encouraging learners to notice one over the other in the input and eventually raising or lowering learners' awareness of these input features.

In investigating effects of proficiency level, Bardovi-Harlig and Dörnyei found an increase in error severity rating with proficiency level for both groups, with one major exception: Whereas high-proficiency EFL learners rated grammatical errors as much more severe and pragmatic errors as somewhat more severe than low-proficiency students did, high-proficiency ESL students rated pragmatic errors as somewhat more severe, but rated grammatical errors as significantly *less* severe than lower-proficiency ESL students did. Severity assessments of grammatical errors decreased with proficiency in the SL setting, whereas they increased strongly in the FL setting. The results of this study strongly support the notion that setting is a major variable in the development of pragmatic and grammatical competence: The EFL setting promoted the development of grammatical competence at the expense of pragmatic competence, and the ESL setting produced the opposite effect. However, one study alone does not provide conclusive evidence, as not all FL and SL classes are equal, nor are student ability and motivation. Also, we follow Hatch and Lazaraton (1991) in lamenting the absence of replication studies in the field of SLA. Specifically, we wondered whether the environment effect, which Bardovi-Harlig and Dörnyei found, is invariable or whether certain learner groups can perhaps develop high pragmatic awareness in the FL setting whereas other learner groups fail to do so in the SL setting. We therefore replicated Bardovi-Harlig and Dörnyei's research using the same instrument and procedures but with different learner populations.[3]

3 We are very grateful to Kathleen Bardovi-Harlig and Zoltán Dörnyei for discussing their study with us in detail and granting us permission to use their research instrument.

The study

Our research questions follow Bardovi-Harlig and Dörnyei's in that we are also concerned with ascertaining the degree of learners' pragmatic and grammatical awareness in relation to their learning environment and their proficiency levels, hoping that this will render a clearer picture of the role of the SL setting in the development of pragmatic awareness. Specifically, we address the following questions:

- Does the learning environment influence learners' awareness of pragmatic and grammatical errors?
- Does the learners' proficiency influence their degree of awareness of pragmatic and grammatical errors?

Method

Participants

For administrative and technical reasons, we could not administer standardized proficiency measures to our learners. Therefore, we had to rely on proficiency assessments by their institutions and have no outside standard for comparing the ESL and EFL groups with each other (see Table 1).

ESL LEARNERS IN THE UNITED STATES

Unlike Bardovi-Harlig and Dörnyei's learners at Indiana University, our ESL sample was not preselected on the basis of their scores on standardized tests. Forty-eight L2 learners studying English in a private language school in Honolulu were recruited for this study. No screening for proficiency takes place before admission to the language school. Informal interviews with students indicated that they were attending the school for a variety of reasons, including improving their English-language skills to enhance their careers or university education in their home countries, but also combining the business of learning English with the pleasure of spending an extended period on a tropical island with outstanding surfing beaches. Our students resembled Bardovi-Harlig and Dörnyei's population in their length of residence in Hawai'i, which was 4.7 months on average, compared to 5.3 months' residence in Indiana in Bardovi-Harlig and Dörnyei's group. They also represented a diverse population which included seven languages: Brazilian Portuguese (2), Korean (3), Japanese (25), Chinese (3), Italian (3), Swiss German (8), and Swiss French (4). Like Bardovi-Harlig and Dörnyei, we restricted ourselves to the four upper levels of the students

TABLE 1. BACKGROUND OF THE PARTICIPANTS

| Group | N | Gender | | Age (M) |
		Male	Female	
Czech	124	18	106	21
U.S.	48	12	36	23

enrolled at the school, with level being determined by students' scores on a written and oral placement instrument administered on their first day of instruction and used to assign students to one of twelve groups, ranging from "beginner" to "highly proficient."

EFL LEARNERS IN THE CZECH REPUBLIC

The Czech population consisted of 124 students studying English in the Czech Republic at the university level. The students represented a typical EFL population with limited exposure to the L2 outside of the classroom context. However, these students differed radically from Bardovi-Harlig and Dörnyei's EFL population in that they represented a highly select sample. They had gained admission to the university English program after passing rigorous written and oral entry examinations on the basis of which only 50 out of several hundred applicants (numbers range between 400 and 900) to the program were eventually accepted. All these students were studying to be teachers of English at the primary and lower secondary level and had made English the central part of their career plans. Students received 14 to 20 hours of monolingual English instruction per week for the duration of the program (5 years). In addition, they were expected to interact with teaching staff in English in and out of the classroom. Because students were not separated by proficiency at the outset of the program, we determined proficiency levels by how far students had advanced in the program, which depends on their passing teacher-designed achievement tests assessing their reading, writing, listening, and speaking ability in English.

Instrument

The same videotape and questionnaire as in the original study were used for this replication. The videotape consisted of twenty scenes, eight containing pragmatic errors in the final utterance, eight containing grammatical errors, and four containing correct final utterances. Scenes in the video take place between Anna, Peter, their classmates, and teachers with cross-gender variables eliminated. Anna speaks only with female counterparts, and Peter only with male. Settings are taken from a school environment: classrooms, hallways, and teachers' offices. The actors are Hungarian high-proficiency NNSs of English who have good pronunciation. The only exception is one teacher who is played by an NS of British English. Items within the video were grouped into sets of five with each set containing two ungrammatical items, two pragmatically incorrect items, and one correct item. Items within each group were arranged randomly. The participants first listened to a set of instructions and then watched a scene with a pragmatically infelicitous item. The scene, like all others in the video, was shown twice with a clear indication, a flashing exclamation point on a blue screen, that the upcoming sentence was to be assessed. Students were instructed to first "just watch the scene" and then, after the second showing, to "watch and mark your answer sheet." If the response was "not good," as in the example, learners rated the severity of the error on the scale provided. Participants then viewed dialogues like the following:

The teacher asks Peter to help with the plans for the class trip.

T: OK, so we'll go by bus. Who lives near the bus station? Peter, could you check the bus times for us on the way home tonight?
P: No, I can't tonight. Sorry.

The utterance to be judged appeared in the following format:

> 1. No, I can't tonight.
>   Sorry.

Was the last part appropriate/correct?   Yes   No
If there was a problem, how bad do you think it was?
Not bad at all ____:____:____:____:____:____ Very bad

In completing the task, learners always first judged the appropriateness and/or correctness of the utterance and then rated the severity of the problem. After completion of the replication phase of the study, the questionnaire was run a second time on a subset of both populations to ensure that the original instrument was valid and that participants were in fact recognizing grammatical errors as grammatical and pragmatic errors as pragmatic. Fifteen participants received a brief explanation of the concepts of pragmatic error and grammatical error, and subsequently watched the video and completed the questionnaire with the added task to label each error they identified as either grammatical or pragmatic. The pragmatic and grammatical items were identified correctly with mean scores ranging from .86 to 1.00. Scores, however, for the correct items produced means ranging from .40 to 1.00, probably indicating a rejection bias (L. White, 1989) similar to the one reported by Bardovi-Harlig and Dörnyei (p. 249).

Analysis

In accordance with Bardovi-Harlig and Dörnyei's original study, only fourteen of the twenty items were included in the analysis. For every correctly identified item, students received a score of 1 on an identification scale; for an incorrectly identified item, they received a score of 0. In addition, for items that students correctly identified as inappropriate/incorrect, their rating of the severity of the error was recorded on a severity scale of 0 (not bad at all) to 6 (very bad). If a student did not recognize an inappropriate/incorrect utterance as such, and therefore received an identification score of 0, a severity rating of 0 was assigned retroactively. We think that this is a defensible policy because believing that an utterance is correct is quite similar to considering the utterance "not bad at all." This scoring method is in compliance with the methods used in the original study. Scores were computed on two scales for grammatical and pragmatic items: an error recognition scale, and a severity rating scale. A participant's score on the error recognition scale simply represented the percentage of recognized errors in relation to total errors present for the particular item type. The score on the severity scale was the average of a subject's severity ratings across all items of the particular type.

Results

Question 1: Does environment influence awareness?

This first question was designed to test whether learners would show differential awareness depending on their learning environment.

BETWEEN-GROUP COMPARISONS

Overall, the Czech EFL learners outperformed the ESL learners at error identification and severity rating for both grammatical and pragmatic items (Table 2). Compared to the ESL sample, the Czech sample recog-

TABLE 2. COMPARISON OF ESL AND EFL ERROR IDENTIFICATION AND SEVERITY RATINGS

	Pragmatic		Item type Grammatical		t-value	
	M	SD	M	SD		
U.S. sample (*n* = 48)						
Error identification (%)	57.08	28.88	54.17	27.18	-.62	n.s.
Severity rating	2.40	1.32	1.89	1.14	-2.37	*p* < .05
Czech sample (*n* = 124)						
Error identification (%)	80.16	23.72	84.54	21.16	1.56	n.s.
Severity rating	3.07	1.48	3.08	1.23	.056	n.s.

Note: M = Mean; SD = Standard deviation

nized significantly more grammar errors (84.54% versus 54.17%, $t = 8.795$, $p < 0.01$, $d = 1.266$) and significantly more pragmatic errors (80.16% versus 57.08%, $t = 6.282$, $p < 0.01$, $d = .882$). The Czech samples also rated grammar errors as significantly more severe ($t = 5.813$, $p < 0.01$, $d = 1.005$) and the same tendency held for pragmatic errors ($t = 2.681$, $p < 0.01$, $d = .479$). Both the Czech and U.S. participants in this study have higher error recognition scores than Bardovi-Harlig and Dörnyei's EFL and ESL learners.

IN-GROUP COMPARISONS

ESL students rated pragmatic errors significantly more severely than grammatical ones (Table 2) ($t = 2.37$, $p < .05$, $d = 0.417$), which replicates Bardovi-Harlig and Dörnyei's finding on this question though with a much smaller effect size. Unlike Bardovi-Harlig and Dörnyei's Hungarian EFL group, however, Czech learners did not rate pragmatic and grammatical errors significantly different ($t = 0.056$, $d = .01$, n.s.). Where Bardovi-Harlig and Dörnyei found a strong effect on severity perception in favor of grammar items, in this study there was no effect whatsoever. Thus, although the ESL sample rated pragmatics errors as more severe than grammar errors and the Czech sample did not, the Czech sample noticed a much higher number of both error types and perceived both error types as much more serious than the ESL sample.[4]

Question 2: Does the learners' proficiency level influence their degree of awareness?

ESL and EFL participants were divided into high-proficiency and low-proficiency groups, based in the ESL population on their placement test scores and in the EFL population on the level to which they had progressed in the university English program. To increase the reliability of this admittedly rough proficiency estimate, only the highest- and the lowest-proficiency groups were compared. This is in accordance with Bardovi-Harlig and Dörnyei (1998).

ESL SAMPLE: ERROR RECOGNITION SCORES

In an analysis within proficiency groups, we found that low-proficiency learners recognized significantly more of the pragmatic errors than of the grammatical errors (60% versus 46%, $t = 2.856$, $p < 0.01$, $d = .5$). High-proficiency learners, on the other hand, showed the opposite tendency. They recognized more of the grammatical than of the pragmatic errors, though the difference was not significant, possibly because of the small subsample size (N = 11). An analysis comparing proficiency groups

---

4 In accordance with Bardovi-Harlig and Dörnyei (1998), no separate analysis was conducted for the effect of item type for the whole sample.

TABLE 3. EFFECTS OF PROFICIENCY ON ESL LEARNERS' JUDGMENTS
OF CORRECTNESS

	Pragmatic		Item type Grammatical		t-value	
	M	SD	M	SD		
Low proficiency (n = 31)	.60	.28	.46	.28	-2.86	p < .01
High proficiency (n = 11)	.49	.35	.73	.14	2.05	n.s.

Note: M = Mean; SD = Standard deviation

TABLE 4. EFFECTS OF PROFICIENCY ON ESL LEARNERS' JUDGMENTS
OF SEVERITY

	Pragmatic		Item type Grammatical		t-value	
	M	SD	M	SD		
Low proficiency (n = 31)	2.65	1.29	1.62	1.04	-4.72	p < .01
High proficiency (n = 11)	1.78	1.45	2.68	1.17	1.64	n.s.

Note: M = Mean; SD = Standard deviation

showed that high-proficiency learners recognized significantly more grammar errors than low-proficiency learners did ($t = 4.086$, $p < 0.001$, $d = 1.363$), whereas the difference for recognition of pragmatic errors was not significant (see Table 3).

ESL SAMPLE: ERROR SEVERITY RATINGS

For severity ratings within proficiency groups (Table 4), low-proficiency learners rated pragmatic errors as significantly more severe than grammatical errors ($t = 4.72$, $p < 0.001$, $d = .889$). High-proficiency learners did not differ significantly in their severity ratings for the two error types. In a comparison between proficiency groups, one finds that the high-proficiency learners' severity ratings for grammatical errors were significantly more severe than the low-proficiency learners' ratings ($t = 7.93$, $p < 0.01$, $d = .96$), whereas the difference between severity ratings for pragmatic errors was not significant. To exclude the possibility that the low-proficiency learners had lived longer in Hawai'i, length of residence was compared for the proficiency groups and – as expected – a significantly longer residence for the high-proficiency learners was found compared to the medium- and low-proficiency learners ($F(2,45) = 4.8$,

TABLE 5. EFFECTS OF PROFICIENCY ON EFL LEARNERS' JUDGMENTS
OF CORRECTNESS

	Pragmatic		Item type Grammatical		t-value	
	M	SD	M	SD		
Low proficiency (n = 36)	.78	.24	.66	.24	2.22	p < .05
High proficiency (n = 35)	.86	.22	.98	.06	3.18	p < .05

Note: M = Mean; SD = Standard deviation

$p < 0.05$). In addition, error recognition scores and severity ratings were correlated with length of residence, and the only significant correlation was a mild *negative* correlation ($r = -0.286$, $p < 0.05$) between pragmatic severity rating and length of residence in Hawai'i. It seems that for the ESL sample higher proficiency and a longer stay in the target community meant less awareness of pragmatic errors.

CZECH SAMPLE: ERROR RECOGNITION SCORES

A similar, though less pronounced, difference in grammatical awareness between high- and low-proficiency learners was found in the Czech sample (Table 5). Low-proficiency Czech learners identified significantly more pragmatic than grammatical errors ($t = 2.331$, $p < 0.05$, $d = .5$), while high-proficiency Czech learners found significantly more grammatical than pragmatic errors ($t = 3.178$, $p < 0.01$). An analysis between proficiency groups showed that this difference also holds across groups for grammatical error recognition: high-proficiency Czech learners found significantly more grammatical errors than low-proficiency Czech learners (98% versus 66%, $t = 7.804$, $p < 0.001$), but there was no significant difference for recognition of pragmatic errors.

CZECH SAMPLE: ERROR SEVERITY RATINGS

There were no significant differences in severity ratings within the subsamples (Table 6). A comparison between subsamples showed that high-proficiency Czech learners rated grammatical errors as significantly more severe than low-proficiency Czech learners ($t = 3.495$, $p < .01$, $d = .849$). Czech high- and low-proficiency learners did not differ significantly in their severity rating for pragmatic errors.

The instrument

The reliability of the questionnaire for pragmatic severity ratings and grammatical severity ratings was satisfactory at $\alpha = 0.73$ and $\alpha = 0.79$,

TABLE 6. EFFECTS OF PROFICIENCY ON ESL LEARNERS' JUDGMENTS
OF SEVERITY

	Pragmatic		Item type Grammatical		t-value	
	M	SD	M	SD		
Low proficiency (n = 36)	3.03	1.32	2.43	1.40	-1.88	n.s.
High proficiency (n = 35)	3.33	1.32	3.45	1.03	0.35	n.s.

Note: M = Mean; SD = Standard deviation

respectively. However, separate reliability computations for the Hawaiian ESL and Czech EFL samples indicate that data from the Czech sample are a great deal more reliable than from the ESL sample. Reliability for both, grammatical and pragmatic severity ratings, is a comfortable $\alpha = 0.78$ for the Czech sample, compared to a reliability for grammatical severity ratings of $\alpha = 0.65$ and for pragmatic severity ratings of $\alpha = 0.55$ for the ESL sample. There is a great deal of error variance on both scales in the ESL sample, possibly because of small sample size and more guessing, which indicates that results obtained from the ESL sample must be interpreted with caution.

Discussion

The findings of this study corroborate Bardovi-Harlig and Dörnyei's results in one central respect: As in their study, our ESL group considered pragmatic errors as more severe than grammatical errors. However, we also found intriguing differences, suggesting in contrast to previous studies that environment may not be the most important factor accounting for learners' pragmatic awareness. Because both EFL and ESL learners were aware of pragmatic infelicities, it seems important to discuss the issue of environment, as addressed by the original study.

Environment

In stark contrast to the study by Bardovi-Harlig and Dörnyei, environment had little effect in our study, except for ESL learners' higher pragmatic than grammatical awareness. Our Czech EFL learners were much more similar in their pragmatic awareness to Bardovi-Harlig and Dörnyei's ESL group than to their Hungarian EFL group. As Table 2 shows, their severity ratings for pragmatic errors (3.07) were only somewhat lower than Bardovi-Harlig and Dörnyei's ESL learners' ratings (3.63), and clearly higher than their EFL learners' (2.04). They recognized nearly as many pragmatic errors (80%) as Bardovi-Harlig and Dörnyei's ESL sample (84%) and more than their Hungarian EFL sample (61.9%). However, of the Czech EFL group of 124 learners, only 15 had spent any time in an English-speaking country, and they did not differ significantly in their recognition scores and severity ratings from their fellow students without residency. It seems therefore that contact can account for students' pragmatic awareness in our sample, but contact is not a sufficient generalizable explanation: Surely the ESL population had more contact with English-language speakers than the EFL population. We would argue that the explanation lies in an interaction between exposure to pragmatic and grammatical input and individual learner characteristics, specifically the degree to which learners actively attend to input. The Czech learners differed radically from Bardovi-Harlig and Dörnyei's Hungarian learners in that they had all decided to make English the focus of their careers. This is a highly select sample consisting of students who are – for whatever reason – strongly capable of using the limited input they receive in educational settings to boost their language proficiency. In terms of the noticing hypothesis (Schmidt, 1995), these students' threshold for noticing a linguistic feature, be it grammatical or pragmatic, may be extremely low: Their attention does not have to be drawn; they probably use a great deal of top-down processing and actively search for grammatical rules and pragmatic conventions. No such conclusion can be drawn for Bardovi-Harlig and Dörnyei's Hungarian EFL sample and our Hawaiian ESL students. The Hawaiian ESL learners' reasons for learning English may vary widely, and they entered the language school without proficiency screening. They may or may not engage in active searches of the input for rules and conventions, and their threshold for noticing linguistic features may be much higher although input is more readily available to them. A possible test effect that may have advantaged the Czech group must also be mentioned in this context: All test situations are based on a university setting. The EFL learners operate in such a setting, so they could relate pragmatic items to their daily experience, which may have been more difficult for the ESL learners. It remains an open question as to how EFL learners would have scored if situations in other settings, such as restaurants and stores, had been used, which would have required them to transfer their pragmatic knowledge to the new situation.

A second puzzling finding in our data was the high level of pragmatic awareness of the low-proficiency EFL group. These were learners who had spent only 6 months in the university, where they were immersed in an English-only environment for about 15 hours per week. Previously, they had attended school where no more than 3 to 5 hours a week were devoted to English. Yet their recognition of pragmatic errors was greater than their recognition of grammatical errors and their severity ratings for the former were also higher, but not quite significantly so. Only five of these thirty-six learners had ever set foot in an English-speaking country. This finding could possibly be attributed to a cohort effect reflecting recent changes in primary and secondary FL instruction in the Czech Republic. Until 1990, Russian was the dominant FL and a requirement for all students. In fact, prior to entering the university, high-proficiency students had had at least 6 years of secondary education in Russian and only 2 in English. The exact opposite holds true for low-proficiency students. Since the early 1990s, the two most popular languages in the Czech Republic have been English and German, with a majority of students taking one from age 10 and both from age 15. Low-proficiency students had no Russian-language requirement and were in fact free to choose EFL. The majority of them have studied EFL for at least 8 years. In addition, these students, unlike their high-proficiency counterparts, had access to American and British textbooks, had qualified NS and NNS teachers of EFL, and were exposed to a communicative language teaching approach (A. Lenochova, personal communication, April 18, 1999). If nothing else, this is evidence that pragmatic awareness can indeed be acquired in the FL environment, or more specifically, in the FL classroom. In addition, it strongly encourages further observational and instructional research to determine specifically how pragmatics can be taught in an EFL classroom.

Does proficiency lead to awareness, or does awareness lead to proficiency?

Our last question is clearly of the chicken-and-egg variety, but it is relevant nonetheless because a problem inherent in our samples is the uncontrolled effect of proficiency on participants' pragmatic awareness. Were the Czech EFL students much more proficient than the Hawaiian ESL students and Bardovi-Harlig and Dörnyei's Hungarian students, and (if so) did that lead them to recognize more errors and rate them as more severe? Or did their learning environment with its focus on accuracy and constant feedback, coupled with their determination to make the most of the limited input they receive, lead to their greater awareness of pragmatic and grammatical errors? We would argue that it is pointless to discuss "general proficiency" as if it were an underlying unitary factor that is independent of grammatical and pragmatic awareness. Do the Czech learners have greater awareness because they have greater proficiency, or do they have greater proficiency because they have greater awareness? Arguing from the constructs of communicative competence outlined earlier, both are linked inextricably. The question is, rather, how environment influences the balance of pragmatic and grammatical awareness and – assuming that awareness is a necessary condition for learning – how it affects the balance of pragmatic and grammatical competence. Our research indicates (contra Bardovi-Harlig & Dörnyei) that this effect is possibly much more attributable to an interaction of individual learner characteristics and environment than to the learning environment alone.

Limitations

A methodological problem of our study is the small number of forty-eight ESL students, in particular for the high-proficiency group (eleven students). Also, the low reliability of the test instrument when administered to the ESL sample raises concerns. Both problems limit the generalizability of findings based on this sample, but since we mostly focused in our discussion on the EFL sample, these limitations should have little impact. The main limitation in our study, as in Bardovi-Harlig and Dörnyei's, is the absence of any production data. In terms of models of communicative competence, we have primarily tapped our participants' pragmatic competence – their ability to recognize the essential environment variables that influence pragmalinguistic choices. We simply do not know how they would perform in an English-speaking environment and outside a school setting. In a similar vein, we cannot predict to what extent students (particularly our EFL sample) will be able to transfer their pragmatic knowledge to settings other than educational institutions. Whether the EFL students would perform as well in attempting to interact appropriately with a bus driver, a customs officer, or a salesclerk remains undetermined. Furthermore, it is impossible to deduce and predict developmental trajectories from cross-sectional comparisons. Only true longitudinal studies or time-series designs can render insight into how learners' pragmatic awareness develops under different conditions and for different learners.

Future research

As Kasper and Schmidt (1996) have pointed out, developmental research is sorely needed in interlanguage pragmatics to identify common learning paths and the development of the balance between grammatical and pragmatic abilities. At the same time, our research shows the intriguing possibility that individual learner factors might play a fundamental role in the development of grammatical and pragmatic awareness. The isolation of these factors and the comparison of their effect and interaction with a given environment in the course of learners' acquisition of pragmatic competence are important and challenging research tasks for the future.

5 Why can't learners of JFL distinguish polite from impolite speech styles?

Haruko Minegishi Cook

Introduction: The indexical nature of language

Although language is a symbolic system to describe objects in the world, it is also a major tool by which we communicate who we are, what we are doing, and how we feel toward addressees and the events around us. The former is referred to as the *referential function of language*, and the latter its *indexical function*. According to Peirce (1955), there are three kinds of signs: symbols, icons, and indexes. Of these three, indexes are signs that indicate contextual information. For example, dark clouds index rain, and smoke indexes fire. Lyons (1977, p. 106) defines *indexicality* as "some known or assumed connexion between a sign A and its significatum C such that the occurrence of A can be held to imply the presence or existence of C." As we can see, language is full of expressions which point to the existence of particular aspects of the social context in which they are used. For example, pronouns such as *I* and *you* index the current speaker and the current addressee, respectively, in the speech context.[1] Spatial expressions such as *here* and *there* index a place close to the speaker and a place close to the addressee, respectively, in the speech context. Indexes are interpreted only in the current speech context. This property of linguistic expressions is called *indexicality* (Silverstein, 1976; Lyons, 1977; Ochs 1988; Duranti, 1997). Indexes are not limited to pronouns and spatial and temporal expressions in language. Researchers working on theories of situated meaning consider most linguistic features as indexical expressions, for they are interpreted in speech contexts (e.g., Duranti & Goodwin, 1992; Gumperz & Levinson, 1996).

I thank Gabriele Kasper and Diana Eades for their helpful comments. A shorter version of this chapter was presented at the SLRF Conference held in Hawai'i, October 1998, and at the Annual Conference of the American Association for Applied Linguistics held in Stamford, Connecticut, March 1999.

1 Personal pronouns, temporal expressions, and spatial expressions are also referred to as *deixis* (Fillmore, 1976; Levinson, 1983).

Since indexes are interpreted in context, they contextualize the referential component of an utterance. Gumperz (1982a, 1992, 1996) proposes a subclass of indexes, which are called "contextualization cues." Contextualization cues are defined as "constellations of surface features of message form . . . by which speakers signal and listeners interpret what the activity is, how semantic content is to be understood and *how* each sentence relates to what precedes or follows" (1982a, p. 131, emphasis in original). Although some indexes such as personal pronouns point to visually available contexts or contexts directly referred to in the preceding talk, contexts of contextualization cues are ambiguous (Gumperz, 1996). Prosody, paralinguistic signs, code choice, and choice of lexical forms or formulaic expressions serve as contextualization cues.

The following examples provide some illustrations of contextualization cues in both English and Japanese.

(1) In a taped elementary school classroom session, the teacher told a student to read. The student responded, "I don't wanna read." The teacher got annoyed and said, "All right, then, sit down" (Gumperz, 1982a, p. 147).

In this example, the student said *I don't wanna read* with a rising intonation, which serves as a contextualization cue. Gumperz states that when the tape was played, some interpreted the student's utterance as a refusal, but others, in particular black informants, interpreted it as a request for encouragement. Rising intonation in this particular context is interpreted in two contrasting ways. This example illustrates that there are different interpretive conventions held by different social groups even when the members of the different groups speak the same language. In example (2), which is a summary of a passage from Gumperz (1982a, p. 168), a tone grouping and an accent placement function as contextualization cues and different interpretive conventions lead to cross-talk.

(2) In London, a West Indian bus driver announced 'Exact change please' as passengers were getting on the bus. When he saw some passengers did not have the exact amount or had no money ready, he announced it again. But this time he said it with extra loudness, high pitch, and falling intonation on both *change* and *please* and placed a pause before *please*. The driver's announcement was perceived as rude by British passengers.

For British and American English speakers, falling tone indicates definiteness and finality in contrast to rising tone, which indicates tentativeness. Thus, falling tone on the word *change* and *please* sounds demanding and rude. Furthermore, setting off *please* highlights the directness. For West Indians, however, tone group units are smaller and constrained syntactically rather than semantically. In addition, the nucleus placement within a tone group is on the last content word of that group. Thus, the falling tone on the two words does not index definiteness and finality but is rather the consequence of the tone grouping. For these reasons, the driver's utterance is not interpreted as being rude by West Indians. As we can see, a particular variant of English is signaled on three different grammatical levels, namely, phonological, morphological, and lexical. Members of a social group have expectations about what pronunciations normally go together with what morphological or lexical options. These co-occurring features signal how the referential message should be framed, what the activities are, how the speaker feels toward the addressee, and/or the topic of the talk among other things. Such expectations are part of a native speaker's (NS) overall communicative competence.

A contextualization cue is a powerful tool for sense making in social interaction. While in English prosody serves as a major contextualization cue, languages such as Japanese are rich in morphological contextualization cues, which include honorifics and sentence-final particles. For example, a referential expression of gratitude used by a lower-status person in a formal situation to a higher-status person can be rude if it lacks proper honorific expressions, as example (3) illustrates.

(3) *Tetsudatte kurete doomo arigatoo*
helping giving (me) very thank
"Thank you very much for helping me"

Although this utterance conveys gratitude in the referential message, it is quite rude if the addressee is higher in status and/or the speech context is formal, for the utterance lacks appropriate honorific morphology. The gerundive verb *kurete* (giving [me]) should be an honorific one, *kudasatte,* to exalt the addressee, and the *doomo arigatoo* (thank you very much) should be a more polite version with the polite verb, *gozaru,* and the addressee honorific suffix, *-masu,* as in *doomo arigatoo gozaimasu.* These examples show that, in social interaction, how an utterance is said is more important than what is said. In the case of Japanese, since pragmatic information is largely encoded in the morphology, it is more salient and accountable. NSs of Japanese readily judge the utterance in (3) as rude in the above-mentioned context, contrary to what the referential message conveys.

For second and foreign language learners, learning how to interpret and use contextualization cues is extremely difficult. Gumperz (1996, p. 383) explains the reason why they are difficult to learn, noting that

because of the complexity of the inferential processes involved and their inherent ambiguity, contextualization cues are not readily learned, and certainly not through direct instruction, so that . . . second-language speakers may have good functional control of the grammar and lexicon of their new language but may contextualize their talk by relying on the rhetorical strategies of their first language. Contextualization conventions are acquired through primary socialization in family or friendship circles or intensive communicative co-operation in a finite range of institutionalized environments.

By their nature, then, contextualization cues are also difficult to teach explicitly in a classroom. What makes it even more difficult to teach them is that contextualization cues often co-occur to produce certain social meaning. In Gumperz's words (1996, p. 383):

As relational signs – not readily amenable to decontextualized treatment – contextualization cues signal by making salient certain lexical strings within the context of grammatical rules. Foregrounding, moreover, does not rest on any one single cue. Rather assessments build on co-occurrence judgments that simultaneously evaluate clusters of cues to generate hypothesis-like tentative – i.e., valid for the moment – assessments that draw on typified knowledge and are subject to constant change as the interaction progresses.

I will illustrate by using natural data how a collocation of contextualization cues foregrounds particular social aspects of interaction. Example (4), which comes from Okamoto's data (1998, p. 144), is an exchange between a salesclerk and a customer.

(4) At a women's clothes section of the department store in Osaka: A female customer asks a sales woman who was talking with another customer.

> C: *Kore no ookii no nai?*
>   "Don't you have this in a larger size?"
> S: *Hai shooshoo o-machi-itadakemasu ka.*
>   "Yes, could you please wait for a moment?"

In Japanese department stores, salesclerks are expected to serve customers in a very polite manner, and customers are entitled to receive such a service. The speakers in (4) know this norm and choose appropriate collocations of contextualization cues. The salesclerk uses *hai* (yes) and *shooshoo* (a moment), which are the more formal versions of *un* and *chotto*. The store clerk also uses both addressee and referent honorifics on the verb. The honorific prefix *o-* on the verb stem *machi* (wait) and auxiliary verb *itadaku* (receive) are both referent honorific form and the addressee honorific *masu* form is suffixed on the verb *itadaku* as in *itadakemasu*. A collocation of these linguistic features indexes formality, which is normally expected in the speech of a salesclerk in a department store (except for the food section in the basement, where salesclerks prefer to be more forceful and create less distance from customers in speech). The customer in (4), on the other hand, does not use any honorifics. Her utterance ends with the plain form (nonhonorific counterpart of the *masu* form) *nai* (does not exist) and also includes *kore* (this), which is a less formal version of *kochira* (this). These co-occurring features index informality, which is normative in customers' speech to a salesclerk.

In order to speak and interpret utterances appropriately, interlocutors need to know what social role they play in a given speech event and what is the normative expectation of that role in society. They further need to know that certain linguistic features collocate in a certain speech style or register (pragmalinguistic knowledge) and that a particular co-occurrence structure is linked to certain social roles and situations (sociopragmatic knowledge). Since any inferencing processes are as complex as demonstrated here, nonnative listeners are faced with an enormous task of interpreting native speech. They must have the linguistic, sociolinguistic, pragmatic, and discoursal knowledge of the linguistic features in question, sociocultural knowledge pertinent to the speech event, and the ability to draw on these knowledge sources and match them with the input (including contextual information) in the high-speed parallel processing fashion required by the online processing of oral input. For foreign language learners, learning this inferencing process is a far greater task than for second language learners. As pointed out by Gumperz (1996), NSs acquire contextualization conventions primarily through socialization processes in the family, among friends, and in institutional environments. When language is used as a resource for dealing with social life, language is a means of communication but not an object of inspection. Typically foreign language learners are restricted to the classroom, an environment with limited input and occasion for practice. This is also an environment in which language tends to be treated as an object, and the classroom organization is teacher-fronted (Kasper 1997a, this volume). Thus, we can presume that the opportunities for language socialization are very limited in the foreign language classroom. To learn to communicate in an appropriate manner in the target language, foreign language learners need to distinguish different speech styles and the social meaning associated with each style. Apparently, it is difficult to learn contextualization conventions in a foreign language classroom, in particular when learners have little positive transfer from L1 to rely on.

Are students of Japanese as a foreign language (JFL) able to distinguish polite from impolite speech styles? What factors influence their success or failure in recognizing such stylistic differences? Can learners of JFL notice co-occurring linguistic features of a particular speech style and associate the style to certain social situations, in particular, when the content of a message and the speech style are in conflict? One of the ways to test the learners' ability to understand the social meaning of an utterance is to see whether they notice the social meaning in such an instance. Does instruction in pragmatic features help learners notice them? If so, what type of instruction is most beneficial? To my knowledge, there has been no study on foreign language learners' comprehension of appropriate speech styles. This chapter examines second-year American JFL students' pragmatic judgment of a polite speech style (application for a job) after two and a half semesters of typical foreign language instruction at the university level.

The study

As a part of a regular midterm exam given to 201 level Japanese classes at the University of Hawai'i at Manoa during the fall semester of 1997, students were given a listening comprehension test. Its results are the basis of this study.[2]

Participants

A total of 120 students in 12 sections taught by 8 instructors participated in this study.[3] According to the instructors' subjective reports, 7 sections were average classes, 3 were below average, and 2 were above average. Thus, overall, the students who participated in this study were average students taking Japanese at the University of Hawai'i. Students who pass Japanese 102 with a grade of C or above are placed at the level of Japanese 201. Almost all the students who participated in this study were NSs of English. Only 0.9% were NSs of other languages: Chinese, Korean, Laotian, and Filipino.[4] In addition, 0.6% of the students reported that they currently lived with or lived for a substantial length of time with an NS of Japanese, and 0.4% lived in Japan or Okinawa for more than a year. Fifty-four percent were female students, and 46% were male.

Eight instructors participated in the study, out of which seven were female and one was male. Their ages ranged from the 30s to the early 50s. Half of them were NSs of Japanese, who were raised in Japan and

2 This midterm exam question was not initially designed for this study. It was created by three or four instructors who taught the course and not by the researcher.
3 In the fall semester of 1997, a total of 248 students were enrolled in Japanese 201. About half the students who took Japanese 201 participated in this study.
4 Student information from three sections was lacking. However, since the makeup of these classes in general does not vary in any significant way, that missing information would probably not affect the overall nature of the whole pool of student participants.

received their B.A. from a Japanese university, and the other half were nonnative speakers (NNSs) who were considered to be near-native speakers of Japanese and had experience living in Japan for more than a year. All eight instructors held a master's degree from the University of Hawai'i. Seven of them held the degree from the East Asian Language Department, and one from the Department of English as a Second Language. Two instructors were also doctoral students in the East Asian Language Department and were concurrently taking courses in interlanguage pragmatics and/or second language acquisition. One instructor had been teaching Japanese for 20 years, three for more than 10 years, and four for less than 10 years. All eight of the instructors were interviewed by the researcher after the results of the midterm exam were given to the students.

Material

In the question that is the focus of this study, students are given a help-wanted ad of a clothing company called Pineapple Republic that is seeking an English-Japanese bilingual clerk. The four qualifications required for this job are to speak polite Japanese, to be able to work during weekends and evenings, to be able to use Excel, and to have knowledge of Japanese fashion trends. Students then hear three short audiotaped self-introductory speeches in Japanese given by three applicants applying for this job. Each applicant's speech is played three times. They are asked to choose the most appropriate applicant and write in English the reason why they made that choice.

The appropriateness of the applicants' speech should be judged by students according to what they say (referential content of the message) and how they say it (pragmatic meaning). In this question, as I elaborate below, one of the speakers' (Applicant A) speech was problematic in that the referential content of the message did not match the pragmatic meaning indexed by co-occurring linguistic features. On the level of the referential message, Applicant A states that she is very good at Japanese, but a collocation of features that serve as a contextualization cue indicates that her speech style is too informal for the occasion. Thus it implies that her Japanese is not good enough. Can JFL students notice the inappropriate speech style, indexed by a collocation of the linguistic features, that is in conflict with that of the referential content? If they do, can they make a pragmatic judgment similar to that of NSs? In this sense, this exam question offers a good opportunity to investigate JFL students' ability to focus on social meaning indexed by co-occurring features. The following are the texts that were read to the students three times.

Three applicants' speech texts: Each applicant's speech consists of a self-introduction, a reason for application, statements of qualifications, and a closing. In the following examples, the *masu* form is marked by a single underline, the plain form by a dotted underline, and the particle *yo* and the contracted forms by a double underline.

APPLICANT A

Introduction

1. *Watashi no namae wa Susan Suzuki desu. Sue to yonde kudasai.*
   My name is Susan Suzuki. Please call me Sue.

Reason for application

2. *Mae ni Crazy Shirts de shigoto o shite imashita.*
   I used to work in Crazy Shirts.

Statements of qualifications

3. *Nihongo wa watashi wa totemo yoku dekimasu yo. Daigaku de ninen benkyoo shita kara.*
   I am very good at Japanese *yo* because I studied in university.

4. *Sore kara senmon wa kompuuta da kara, Excel wa tsukaemasu yo.*
   And since my major is computer, I can use Excel *yo*.

5. *Shuumatsu mo yoru mo shigoto daijoobu.*
   It's OK to work on weekends and evenings.

6. *E, to fasshion wa KIKU terebi o yoku miteru n[5] da kara, Nihonjin ga donna fasshion ga suki ka yoku shitteru yo.*
   Uh, as for fashion, because I often watch KIKU TV [Japanese TV], I know well what kind of fashion Japanese people like.

Closing

7. *Ja, doozo yoroshiku.*
   Well, please treat me well.

8. *Henji mattemasu.*
   I am waiting for your reply.

APPLICANT B

Introduction

1. *Watashi wa Jim Thomas to mooshimasu.*
   I am called Jim Thomas.

Reason for application

2. *Hawai'i Daigaku no gakusei na node, ima shuumatsu to yoru no shigoto o sagashite imasu.*
   Since I am a student at the University of Hawai'i, I am looking for a job during evenings and weekends.

---

5 *n* is a contracted form of the nominalizer *no*. In speech, *n* occurs even when the context is rather formal. For this reason, *n* is not included in Table 3.

3. *Choodo Pineapple Republic no shigoto ga ii n ja nai ka to omotte
kono teepu o tsukutte <u>imasu</u>.*
I am making this tape thinking that the Pineapple Republic work
is just right for me.

Statements of qualifications
4. *Nihongo wa haha ga Nihonjin de, Nihon ni ninen hodo sunde
<u>imashita</u> kara, hanasete, yomete, <u>kakemasu</u>.*
Since my mother is Japanese and I lived in Japan for 2 years,
I can speak, read, and write Japanese.
5. *Kompuuta wa amari suki ja nai n <u>desu</u> ga, Excel wa <u>tsukaemasu</u>.*
I do not like computers much, but I can use Excel.
6. *Boku no shumi wa amari nai n <u>desu</u> ga, tokidoki gitaa o
<u>hikimasu</u>.*
I do not have many hobbies, but I sometimes play the guitar.

Closing
7. *Doozo yoroshiku onegai <u>shimasu</u>.*
I request you to please treat me well.

APPLICANT C
Introduction
1. *Watashi no namae wa Keiko Grant <u>desu</u>. Kono natsu McKinley
kookoo o sotsugyoo <u>shimashita</u>.*
My name is Keiko Grant. I graduated from McKinley High
School this summer.

Reason for application
2. *Watashi wa fasshion ga daisuki <u>desu</u>.*
I like fashion very much.
3. *Pineapple Republic de yoku kaimono o <u>shimasu</u>.*
I often shop at Pineapple Republic.
4. *Mae kara, konna mise de shigoto ga shite mitai to omotte
<u>imashita</u>.*
I think that I have been wanting to work in such a store
for a while.

Statements of qualifications
5. *Nihongo wa kodomo no toki ni zutto Nihon ni sunde ita node
<u>hanasemasu</u>.*
I can speak Japanese because I lived in Japan when I was a child.
6. *Yomu no wa kantan na mono nara yomeru n <u>desu</u> ga, shimbun
to ka wa chotto . . .*
I can read simple things but newspaper is a little [difficult].

7. *Excel wa mada heta na n desu ga, nan toka tsukaemasu.*
   I am still not good at Excel, but I can manage it.
8. *Gambatte sugu joozu ni naritai to omoimasu.*
   I think that I will try to improve my skill soon.
9. *Watashi wa oboeru no ga hayai n desu.*
   I can learn fast.

Closing
10. *Doozo yoroshiku onegai itashimasu.*
    I request you to please treat me well.

TABLE 1. SELF-REPORTED QUALIFICATIONS OF THE THREE APPLICANTS

Qualifications	Applicant A (female)	Applicant B (male)	Applicant C (female)
1. Speak polite Japanese	speak well	able to write, speak, and read	able to speak but can't read newspaper
2. Work during weekends and evenings	yes	yes	——
3. Use computer program Excel	yes	yes (but does not like computers much)	yes (but not skillful)
4. Have knowledge of Japanese fashion trends	yes	——	interest in fashion

Table 1 shows the three applicants' self-reported qualifications (the referential content of the message). According to the referential content of the message that the three provide, Applicant A qualifies in all respects. In contrast, Applicants B and C impart information that can be interpreted negatively in applying for the job. Applicant B mentions that he does not like computers much, and Applicant C states that her Japanese and computer skills are not so good. In addition, Applicants B and C do not indicate whether or not they have the required qualifications 4 and 2, respectively. Thus, in terms of what they say (referential content of the message), it is clear that Applicant A is the best choice.

The appropriate way of presenting oneself in applying for a job in Japanese is constituted by the presence and absence of various co-occurring linguistic and nonlinguistic features. Since the speech was on audio-recorded tapes in this study, we consider only linguistic features. I call the features that are positively evaluated in this social context

TABLE 2. POSITIVE PRAGMATIC FEATURES

	Applicant A (female)	*Applicant B (male)*	*Applicant C (female)*
formal form (*masu* form)	inconsistent use of *masu* 6 *masu* forms (5 plain forms)	consistent use of *masu*	consistent use of *masu*
appropriate hedges	no	yes	yes
fixed expression	yes	yes	yes
appropriate honorific	no	yes	yes

TABLE 3. NEGATIVE PRAGMATIC FEATURES

	Applicant A (female)	*Applicant B (male)*	*Applicant C (female)*
informal form (plain form in the main clause)	5	0	0
final particle	*yo* 3	0	0
contracted form	*teru* 2	*teru* 0	*teru* 0
	temasu 1	*temasu* 0	*temasu* 0

"positive features" and those that are negatively evaluated, "negative features." Tables 2 and 3 list the characteristics of the three applicants' speech with respect to the linguistic features that convey social meaning. The positive features include the use of the formal form (*masu* form), which is marked by the morpheme -*masu* on the sentence-final verbal or *desu* as a copula, appropriate fixed expressions, hedges, and honorifics, and the negative features include the plain form on the sentence-final verbal, the final particles such as *yo,* and certain contracted forms, all of which make the speech too informal.[6]

Both Applicants B and C consistently use the formal *masu* form, but Applicant A uses the informal form (the plain form) five out of eleven times on the verbal ending. Although the other two applicants consistently use the positive pragmatic features, Applicant A does not use two of them. Furthermore, Applicant A uses all the negative pragmatic features when the others do not use them at all. A qualitative comparison of the three applicants' speech further reveals how Applicant A's speech is inappropriate. In the sections of statements of qualifications and closing, Applicant A's speech becomes problematic. In social contexts such as a

6 Here the *kara* clause is counted as a main clause, for it functions more like a main clause because its degree of subordination is not deep.

taped speech for a job application in which a consistent mannered self-presentation (acting in role on stage) is required, the *masu* form (the formal form) on the sentence-final verbal indexes the display of a good self-presentation (Cook, 1999). Thus the use of the *masu* form is considered the norm in this social context, and the use of the plain form gives an impression that the speaker is too informal, for he or she does not present himself or herself properly. Applicants B and C consistently use the *masu* form in the sentence-final position whereas Applicant A uses the plain form (indicated by a dotted line in the speech text) five times.

In Japanese society, a display of humble attitude is valued, in particular in unequal power encounters. A lower-status person is expected to sound hesitant, indirect, and apologetic even when, from a Westerner's point of view, he or she has no obvious reason to do so (Mizutani & Mizutani, 1978). An assertion of one's strong qualification thus needs to be modified in Japanese with a hedge or indirectness even when one applies for a job. We see a clear contrast between Applicant A and Applicants B and C in terms of assertive force. Both Applicants B and C do not assert that they are good at Japanese, but, by stating that they lived in Japan and/or have a Japanese mother, they imply that they are good in Japanese. Applicant C mentions that she is not skillful in using Excel but will try to improve, which humbles her own ability but gives a positive future perspective. Humbling one's own ability is an appropriate hedge in applying for a job in Japanese as long as one provides a positive attitude for future improvement. Another way to hedge one's assertion in Japanese is the use of the verb *to omou* (to think that). The expression *to omou* softens the speaker's position by indicating that what is said is his or her point of view (Locastro & Netsu, 1997). Both Applicants B and C use this hedge, whereas Applicant A does not. Applicant B uses it when he states his reason for applying in line 3 (*Choodo Pineapple Republic no shigoto ga ii n ja nai ka to omotte* [I am making this tape thinking that the Pineapple Republic work is just right for me]). Applicant C uses this hedge when she states her reason for application and her positive outlook for skill improvement in line 4 (*Mae kara, konna mise de shigoto ga shite mitai to omotte imashita* [I think that I have been wanting to work in such a store for a while]) and in line 8 (*Gambatte sugu joozu ni naritai to omoimasu,* [I think that I will try to improve my skill soon]).

However, both Applicants B and C also use expressions that give rather a negative impression as well. B states in line 5 that *Kompuuta wa amari suki ja nai n desu ga* (I do not like computers much), and C expresses in line 6 that *shimbun to ka wa chotto* (newspaper is a little [difficult]). Applicant C subtly makes this statement by omitting the word *difficult*. When the job qualifications specify knowledge of Japanese fashion trends, Applicant B does not indicate such knowledge, and Applicant C only mentions that she likes fashion in general. In contrast, Applicant A directly asserts all qualifications required for the position. She asserts her good Japanese language proficiency and her ability to use Excel, both of which she acquired at school. She also states her knowledge about Japanese fashion trends. She asserts her qualifications without an appropriate hedge but with the assertive final-particle *yo*. She states in line 3 that *Nihongo wa watashi wa totemo yoku dekimasu yo* (I am very good at Japanese *yo*), in line 4 that *Excel wa tsukaemasu yo* (I can use Excel *yo*), and in line 6 that *Nihonjin ga donna fasshion ga suki ka yoku shitteru yo* (I know well what fashion Japanese people like *yo*). Note that the other applicants do not use the particle *yo* at all. By the particle *yo*, the speaker asserts himself or herself by drawing the addressee's attention to the speaker's words (Cook, 1991). The particle *yo* can be polite if it occurs with an utterance which humbles the speaker. For example, when it occurs with a refusal of a compliment, it emphasizes the speaker's humble attitude. Hence *yo* is polite in this instance. When *yo* occurs with an assertion, however, it reinforces the assertive attitude of the speaker. For this reason, its use is rude in this context. Thus, the assertions of Applicant A are judged by NSs as severely inappropriate.

In a formal context, certain contracted forms sound too informal. One of them is the form *-teru* or *-temasu*, which is formed by deleting [*i*] from the progressive/stative construction, *-te iru* (verbal gerund form *-te* + verb *to be* in the plain form) or *-te imasu* (verbal gerund form *-te* + verb *to be* in the *masu* form). Applicant A uses the progressive/stative construction four times in her speech. She chooses the contracted form *teru* (in line 6) twice and *temasu* (in line 8) once. In contrast, both Applicants B and C consistently use the more formal noncontracted form *-te imasu*.

In Japanese, the use of appropriate fixed expressions is very important, particularly in formal situations. It is customary to end a message that asks the addressee's favor with a fixed expression such as *doozo yoroshiku* (Please treat me well) or a more polite version, *doozo yoroshiku onegaishimasu* (I request you to please treat me well). All the applicants use one of the versions of this fixed expression; Applicant A uses the shortest version, *doozo yoroshiku*, Applicant B uses the more polite *doozo yoroshiku onegai shimasu*, and Applicant C, the most polite version with the dishonorific expression (i.e., humbling the speaker), *itashimasu* (do). Furthermore, if an applicant refers to the prospective employer's action or belongings, or mentions his or her action in relation to the prospective employer, he or she is expected to use honorifics (and dishonorifics) to exalt the prospective employer's action or belonging and humble his or her own action or belongings. When she says that *Henji mattemasu* (I'm waiting for your reply),

Applicant A neither exalts the prospective employer's reply with the honorific prefix *o-* as in *o-henji* (honorable reply) nor does she humble her own action of waiting with the humble form *o-machi shite orimasu* (I am humbly waiting). In addition, she uses the informal, contracted form, *temasu*.

In sum, Applicant A's speech is far more pragmatically inappropriate than the others because of a lack of appropriate collocations of features. As indicated by the instructors' comments, Applicant A's inappropriate speech style weighs far greater than her self-reported good qualifications.

Procedure

In the listening comprehension task, students were instructed that they were to take the role of the bilingual manager of Pineapple Republic and that they would write a report in English to their supervisor as to who they thought to be the best applicant for the job and why that decision was made. They were given a help-wanted ad which lists the four qualifications for the job. After listening to the taped self-introduction of the three applicants three times, they selected who they thought to be the most qualified applicant and wrote in English their justification for their selection. Ten points were allocated to this question. Since this was a listening comprehension task, regardless of which applicant was selected, if their reasons for selection matched the content of the tape, the students were given points. Thus, the students who selected Applicant A did not lose all the points. They were given full points if their justifications for selection matched the content of the recording.

In order to shed light on possible sources for the students' assessments, eight of the instructors whose students participated in the test were interviewed after the test results were obtained and returned to the students. The instructors were interviewed in the researcher's office. The interview was conducted in Japanese with instructors who are NSs of Japanese and in English with instructors who are NNSs of Japanese. They were asked the following six questions:

1. Were you surprised that the majority of students chose Applicant A?
2. Why do you think that the majority of students chose Applicant A or did not choose Applicant C?
3. Do you teach pragmatic functions in class?
4. If you do, how do you teach them?
5. Do your students ask about the pragmatic functions of the forms involved?

6. How do you rate this class (these classes) – is it an average or a better-than-average class?

Since the interviews were conducted more like a conversation in a friendly atmosphere, the six questions were used as a guideline. Some instructors provided more information than others. The length of the interviews varied from 15 minutes to 30 minutes. Interviews were tape-recorded. The researcher listened to the tapes and took notes. The analysis of the interviews was made based on the notes.

Results

Recognition of speech styles

As shown in Table 4, out of 120, an overwhelming 97 students (80.8%) chose Applicant A as the most desirable applicant for the job, 17 (14.2%) chose Applicant C, and 6 (5%) chose Applicant B. It became clear from the students' explanations that the main reason for choosing Applicant A was that, according to the referential content of the three applicants' speech, she satisfied all the qualifications.

Table 5 categorizes the ninety-seven students who chose Applicant A into three groups. Group 1 consists of sixty-eight students who evaluated positively Applicant A's Japanese skill. Out of them, sixty students specifically mentioned that Applicant A is very good at Japanese, which is a literal translation of her self-reported statement (*Nihongo wa watashi wa totemo yoku dekimasu yo*). The fact that these students commented that A is very good at Japanese and that they did not offer any negative comment on her speech style suggests that they focused only on the referential content and that they did not notice A's impolite manner of speech. One of the students even commented that A's manner of speaking was very polite. Another eight students positively commented on A's Japanese. Their comments, such as "A displays politeness," "A learned polite Japanese," and "A's Japanese sounds very good," again indicate that they failed to notice A's inappropriate manner of speaking. Thus, apparently, sixty-eight students in Group 1 did not notice the pragmatic meaning indexed by the linguistic features listed in Tables 2 and 3. Group 2 consists of twenty-three students who did not specifically mention Applicant A's good Japanese skill. They either stated that Applicant A can speak Japanese or that she studied Japanese for 2 years in college. It is not clear whether they noticed Applicant A's inappropriate speech style. If they did, they certainly could not judge it as a crucially negative factor for applying for a job. Group 3 consists of six students who negatively evaluated Applicant A's Japanese skill or style but still chose her as the most suitable applicant because of the

TABLE 4. DISTRIBUTION OF STUDENTS' CHOICES

Applicant A	Applicant B	Applicant C	Total
97	6	17	120
80.8%	5.0%	14.2%	100%

TABLE 5. REASONS FOR CHOOSING APPLICANT A

1. Positive evaluation of A's Japanese skill	68
(A is very good at Japanese = 60)	
(other positive comments = 8)	
2. No mention of A's good Japanese skill	23
3. Negative evaluation of A's Japanese skill	6
Total	97

other qualifications. This indicates that they do not understand that in applying for a job in Japanese, an inappropriate speech style is problematic even when the other qualifications are good.

Factors in student choices

All the instructors negatively evaluated Applicant A's speech based on her inappropriate use of the pragmatic features listed in Tables 2 and 3 rather than the referential content. As a part of their communicative competence, we assume that these co-occurring features are simultaneously accessible to the instructors. The data of the present study suggest that these features are not accessible to the majority of the students in an online comprehension task. The sixty-eight students in Group 1 in Table 5 apparently did not notice Applicant A's inappropriate speech style. The twenty-three students in Group 2 may or may not have noticed A's inappropriate speech style. If they did not, they did not have access to the pragmatic functions of the co-occurring features either. Even if they did, they lacked sociopragmatic knowledge (i.e., knowledge that links the speech style to a certain social situation). Or it is possible that the students in Groups 1 and 2 misunderstood what it was that they were supposed to judge. The six students in Group 3 certainly did not have sociopragmatic knowledge that in applying for a job in Japanese, the informal speech style is unacceptable no matter how good the other qualifications are. The judgments made by the students in Groups 2 and 3 may be the result of a negative transfer from L1 culture in which self-assertion in applying for a job is valued, sounding sure of oneself is a very important asset, and what counts more is what is said rather than how it is said. The fact that at least half the students failed to notice the pragmatic meaning in the listening comprehension test suggests that average students at the 201 level focus on the referential content of the message and barely pay attention to the pragmatic meaning indexed by collocations of linguistic features. This raises the question of the effects of instruction.

The effects of instruction

How (and to what extent) were the co-occurring pragmatic features that constitute an appropriate formal speech style for a job application taught in the class? According to the interviews, none of the eight instructors expected this outcome at all. They were unanimously surprised. For them, it was obvious that Applicant A's speech style was definitely impolite for applying for a job. In the instructors' words, Applicant A was "out of the question." In their judgment, Applicant C was the most suitable for the position, and Applicant A was by far the worst. They thought that most students would choose either Applicant B or Applicant C.[7] The instructors assumed that since students learned by the 201 level the pragmatic functions of the *masu* and plain forms, they would notice A's use of the plain form and could judge it impolite in this context. Six instructors mentioned that the reason why the majority of students chose Applicant A was that they focused on the referential content and that they could not pay attention to the speech style. One instructor reported that after the exam, she read the same texts twice to the students. This time she told them to pay attention to the forms. After hearing the texts twice, some students figured out why Applicant A's speech was impolite. This suggests that when students are specifically instructed to pay attention to the pragmatic function, they may recall what was taught in class. After the exam, one of the NS instructors was told by her students that Applicant A sounded enthusiastic. This comment concurs with that of two NNS instructors, who grew up in Hawai'i. They speculated that Applicant A was chosen by many students because her voice quality sounded enthusiastic and convincing. When I (as an NS of Japanese) listened to the tape, Applicant A did not sound enthusiastic at all. It seems that the voice quality of Applicant A gave an impression to some local students that she was enthusiastic. Enthusiasm may be one of the factors that contributed to the choice of Applicant A.

Among the pragmatic features listed in Tables 2 and 3, the only one that was recognized by all instructors as a factor responsible for A's impolite speech style is her use of the plain form in the main clause predicate. The distinction between the *masu* and plain forms is perhaps

---

7 In this question, even if students chose Applicant A or Applicant B, if their reason for that choice was well argued, they received full or partial points.

TABLE 6. INSTRUCTIONAL METHODS OF THE *MASU* AND PLAIN FORMS

Instructor	Were masu/*plain* forms taught in 201 class?	What activities were used to teach them?	Did students ask about the functions of these forms?
1	no (assumed to be learned previously)	role-plays	yes (better students)
2	no	—	yes
3	yes	role-plays, conversation drills	no
4	yes (often)	role-plays	yes (better students)
5	no (assumed to be learned previously)	—	yes (a few)
6	yes	skits, dialogue	yes
7	no (assumed to be learned previously)	—	no
8	yes	role-plays	yes

the most salient because all the final verbs in the main clause have to be morphologically marked by either the *masu* or the plain form. Table 6 summarizes the instructors' treatment of the *masu* and plain forms in their classrooms.

The instructors teach the functions of these forms in role-plays and conversation drills. In fact, prototypical uses of these forms are first introduced in the textbook at the 101 level and mentioned throughout the textbook whenever relevant conversations appear.[8] For this reason, the instructors assumed that students would be able to notice any use of the plain form and judge it as inappropriate for a formal occasion such as applying for a job. Furthermore, six instructors reported that their students asked about the appropriate use of the *masu* and plain forms in class, especially when they created a skit or performed a role-play. Two reported that better students asked questions on these forms. This indicates that some students are consciously aware of this distinction when they have time to think about it but may not notice it in an online listening comprehension task. Furthermore, in reality, the situation is more complicated than a simple dichotomy of the two forms. Not all instances of the plain form mark the informal speech style. The contrast between the two forms is made only when they appear on the verbal in the main clause. Typically, in a subordinate clause the plain

8 The textbook used in this course was *Situational and Functional Japanese* published by Tsukuba University, Japan.

form occurs and it does not contrast with the *masu* form in the pragmatic function. For example, Applicant C states *Mae kara, konna mise de shigoto ga shite mitai to omotte imashita* (I think that I have been wanting to work in such a store for a while). In this utterance, the word *mitai* (want to try) is in the plain form, which is embedded in the quotation *to omotte imashita* (have been thinking that). Because it is in the embedded clause, this use of the plain form does not index informality. Furthermore, whether the plain form is contrasted with the *masu* form depends on a degree of subordination. For example, two clauses that denote a cause, the *node* and *kara* clauses, differ with respect to social meaning when they occur with the plain form. In the *node* clause the plain form does not necessarily index informality, but in a *kara* clause the plain form does index informality. In this sense, it is more like an independent clause. For this reason, in formal speech, the use of the *masu* form in a *kara* clause is more appropriate. Applicant A's speech contains three *kara* clauses and each takes the plain form, which sounds too informal. In contrast, Applicant C uses a *node* clause (*zutto Nihon ni sunde ita node*). The verb *ita* (was) is in the plain form, but because it is in the *node* clause, it does not index informality. In an online comprehension task, it must be difficult for students to differentiate a plain form in the embedded clause from that in the main clause and to assign a different pragmatic meaning to each.

Only Instructor 8 noticed pragmatic features other than the *masu* and plain forms which contributed to A's impolite speech style. She pointed out that the use of the particle *yo* was extremely impolite in this context and that a lack of hedges in A's speech further contributed to her impoliteness. She mentioned that she came to realize inappropriate pragmatic features while she was administering the midterm exam. She reported that she did not explain the function of the particle *yo* explicitly in class, except for correcting its wrong use by the students. The interviews with the instructor revealed that although students were taught at some point in their Japanese study that the particle *yo* is an assertive particle, generally no explicit instruction was given that its use is inappropriate in asserting one's qualification in a social context such as applying for a job. Furthermore, no instruction was given with respect to the function of hedges in formal social situations in Japanese society. In addition, Instructor 8 commented that during the midterm planning session, the members of the midterm exam committee did not even discuss why Applicant A's speech was pragmatically inappropriate because the inappropriateness was obvious to them.[9] The instructors' reports on their classroom instruction suggest that other than the

---

9 The midterm exam was created by a committee consisting of three to four instructors who taught Japanese 201 during the fall semester of 1997.

sentence-final *masu* and plain forms, the functions of most of the pragmatic markers listed in Tables 2 and 3 are more or less inaccessible to the instructors' awareness. This is perhaps because these pragmatic markers as contextualization cues have different indexical functions in different social contexts. They have, in Gumperz's words (1996, p. 383), "inherent ambiguity." NSs learned them in their socialization process as a means of real-life communication. Hence, these features are not brought to the conscious attention of the instructors or of their students. A question that suggests itself is whether Instructor 8's more explicit awareness of pragmatic features had an impact on her students' performance on the exam.

Looking at the twelve sections (i.e., classes) of Japanese instruction, we see that the results of Section 1 were markedly different from those of the rest. In this section, out of ten students only two chose Applicant A while six chose Applicant C and two chose Applicant B. Furthermore, five students who chose Applicant B or C noted that Applicant A's speech style was neither polite nor humble. In other words, half the class clearly noticed and was able to judge Applicant A's inappropriate use of the pragmatic markers. This section was taught by Instructor 8, who, when necessary, gave explicit instruction on both the functions of *masu* and plain forms and the final particles. Instructor 8 also taught another section (Section 2), in which five students out of seven (71%) chose Applicant A. According to her self-report, she taught both sections in the same method and manner. Thus, the better performance of Section 1 cannot be attributed to the instructor's teaching method. The difference between the two sections was that whereas Section 2 was an average class, Section 1 consisted of many exceptionally highly motivated students. According to Instructor 8, many students in Section 1 were interested in Japanese culture and had a strong desire to visit Japan or work with Japanese people. Interest in other cultures, societies, and their members is a part of integrative motivation (Clément, Dörnyei, & Noels, 1994). A comparison of the results of Sections 1 and 2 suggests that students who have a high integrative motivation notice pragmatic functions that are taught.

Discussion and conclusion

In this study, contrary to the instructors' expectation, 80.8% of the students chose Applicant A, who was regarded by the instructors as by far the worst applicant because of her impolite speech style. Among the ninety-seven students who chose Applicant A, sixty-eight did not notice her impolite speech style and gave it a positive evaluation; twenty-three students either did not notice A's inappropriateness or could not judge it as such. Only six students noticed her inappropriate speech style but could not judge it as a crucially negative factor. Only 14.2% of all the students chose Applicant C, who was considered the most desirable applicant by the instructors.

Recent classroom research on interlanguage pragmatics has found that, in general, teaching pragmatics is beneficial to second and foreign language learners (Kasper, 1997a; Kasper & Rose, 1999). So far, these findings are made largely in the areas of speech acts (Beebe & Takanashi, 1989a, 1989b; Billmyer, 1990a, 1990b; Olshtain & Cohen, 1990; Morrow, 1996;), pragmatic routines and strategies (Wildner-Bassett, 1994; House 1996; Tateyama, Kasper, Mui, Tay, & Thanamart, 1997), and conversational implicatures (Bouton, 1994a; Kubota, 1995). If teaching pragmatics is beneficial, we would expect that the teaching of contextualization cues should not be an exception. Knowledge of inferential processes is indispensable in developing performance-based teaching and testing materials. Explicit instruction in many of the contextualization cues, however, is extremely difficult in a foreign language classroom for several reasons. First, NSs learn inferential processes through primary socialization, in which language is used as a means of communication rather than an object of inspection. Second, since these processes are typically unconscious, NSs have little awareness of how they arrived at their interpretation and what linguistic forms are involved in these processes, so even NS instructors are often not consciously aware of their pragmatic functions. Third, contextualization cues as indexes are inherently ambiguous as to which aspects of context are foregrounded. Finally, a collocation of contextualization cues often foregrounds certain social information, such as speech styles being indexed by co-occurring cues. These difficulties, however, can be overcome by the enhancement of instructors' pragmatic, sociolinguistic, and discoursal knowledge of the target language and culture. In other words, in order to teach inferential processes effectively in a foreign language classroom, the instructor needs to analyze the social context of the teaching materials and fully understand pragmatic functions of linguistic forms and what exactly constitutes a "framing" (Tannen, 1993a) or expectation structure that surrounds an utterance.

Some contextualization cues are more noticeable than others. For example, the functions of the *masu* and plain forms in this study were more readily available to the consciousness of the instructors than the others as a marker of a speech style. They are also clearly explained in the textbook. This study has demonstrated that at the 201 level explicit instruction of one contextualization cue was not sufficient for the majority of the students to notice and judge an impolite speech style during a comprehension task. To teach an appropriate speech style for a given speech event, it is necessary to teach students a range of co-occurring contextualization cues that constitute that speech style.

Furthermore, it is important to instruct students to pay attention to the relationship between linguistic form, its social meaning, and the social context in which that particular meaning is foregrounded, for one of the instructors' reports suggests that only when students are told to pay attention to these forms may they recognize their social meanings.

This study suggests that there may be a relationship between intrinsic motivation and an ability to understand the social meaning of contextualization cues. More studies are needed to determine the role of motivation in conversational inferencing. Furthermore, a discrepancy was found between the instructors' expectations and the students' performance in terms of the comprehension of pragmatic meanings. What the instructors considered obvious was not obvious to the students at all, which suggests that it is important for instructors to have knowledge of linguistic, pragmatic, discoursal and cultural structures of the target language as well as those of the students' native language and evaluate what needs to be explicitly taught in class.

This study, however, has limitations. Since initially the midterm exam was created for the exam per se and was not designed for the research project, it was not possible to obtain more detailed information concerning the students' choices. For this reason, it is difficult to determine exactly why students made their choices, but it certainly raises the following questions, which need to be investigated fully in future research. First, why, on a listening comprehension task, don't average JFL students notice a pragmatic feature which has been taught to them? Is the reason cognitive or sociocultural? In other words, is the failure to notice and judge the function of a pragmatic feature the result of cognitive salience of the referential content of the message? Or is it the result of negative transfer from the students' L1 culture? It is feasible that most students chose Applicant A because they considered her direct manner of speaking as a positive characteristic in the Hawai'i context. The name of the store, Pineapple Republic, which appeared in the midterm exam closely resembles Banana Republic, which sells young people's clothes in Hawai'i as well as in the rest of the United States. Thus, it is plausible that the students assumed that the Pineapple Republic was an American company operating in Hawai'i. The exam also stated that Pineapple Republic was seeking a bilingual store clerk. For these reasons, the students may have thought that A's speech is appropriate from the expected interactional norm in such stores in Hawai'i which values a close relationship between the customer and the store clerk. However, the instructors apparently expected the Japanese social norm to be used. In future exam questions similar to this one, a setting should be clearly stated so that the appropriate social norm is apparent to both the instructors and the students. Second, in what ways is an integrative motivation helpful in noticing pragmatic features that have been taught? In order to answer this question, it is necessary to obtain much more detailed information from the students about why they are learning Japanese. Future studies should include questionnaires that investigate JFL students' attitude toward Japanese people, sociocultural knowledge about Japan, and interest in the Japanese language. Third, the present study suggests that in order to understand the pragmatic meaning of a speech style, JFL students need to know a wider range of co-occurring linguistic forms and their pragmatic functions which constitute various speech registers as well as their specific cultural norms of interpretation. Is the full range of co-occurring features teachable in a JFL class? If so, what is the relative effect of different instructional approaches? Unlike a speech act, which is readily accessible to the instructor's consciousness, a range of co-occurring features such as those discussed in this study is more subtle and often beyond the consciousness of average NSs. In this sense, it is more difficult to bring it to the instructor's attention. And finally, will the results of the exam significantly improve if students are specifically instructed to pay attention to how the applicants speak? If so, making students notice at least one pragmatic feature that is explicitly taught out of the several that constitute a particular speech style helps them judge appropriateness.

6 A longitudinal study of the development of expression of alignment in Japanese as a foreign language

Amy Snyder Ohta

Introduction

Foreign language curricula have traditionally focused on the grammar, sound system, and vocabulary of the target language, but with the advent of communicative language teaching, time has increasingly been devoted to activities which promote the ability to accomplish tasks in the target language, and to interact appropriately in different situations. Pedagogy texts encourage teachers to provide learners with authentic listening and speaking opportunities, and to teach them how to use the language for natural interactional processes, such as repair (Hadley, 1993; Lee & VanPatten, 1995). Little work has investigated, however, how participation in communicative classrooms relates to the development of learners' interactional competence. This chapter attempts to fill this gap by examining how two adult learners of Japanese as a foreign language (JFL) develop the ability to use listener responses in Japanese, in particular expressions of acknowledgment and alignment. Facility with these is an important area of pragmatic competence in Japanese, where such expressions occur considerably more frequently than in English (Maynard, 1989; Strauss, 1995). The study draws on longitudinal data from a corpus of Japanese classroom interaction (Ohta, 2000b) which allows observation of how interactional style develops over time. Findings show the variability of the developmental pace of the two learners, but suggest that they follow a similar developmental sequence moving from expressions of acknowledgment to alignment. The results help in understanding pragmatic development in the FL classroom, and the role that the activities of the classroom setting and intervention of the teacher play in developmental processes.

Expressions of acknowledgment and alignment in Japanese

The role of the listener is important in both American and Japanese conversation. Listeners use a range of strategies to show attention and empathy, including confirmation questions, assessments, repair initiations, anticipatory responses, and the back-channel responses called *aizuchi* in Japanese. Japanese speakers are highly verbal listeners who frequently use verbal expressions to show listenership (Maynard, 1989). These verbal listener responses may be considered as falling along a continuum from acknowledgment to alignment (Strauss, 1995). In Strauss's system of classification, continuers fall toward the acknowledgment of the continuum, while assessments generally show alignment. Strauss suggests that agreement tokens fall in the middle of the continuum because they may function as either continuers or assessments.

Japanese listeners frequently use these items to express alignment with their interlocutors. Strauss's study, which compared conversations of people who experienced the 1994 Northridge Earthquake in southern California, found that Japanese interlocutors were more prone to express alignment and to utter assessments than either their Korean or American counterparts. This does not mean that the American or Korean pairs were less sympathetic or less interested, but that the interactive style of the Japanese differed in the extent to which verbal expressions of alignment were used. Strauss provides the following excerpt of Japanese conversation as an example:

1 10   Ai: *maa rosanzerusu mo sou iu- na: nanchiundaroo ibento*
             no ooi tte iu ka: warui imi de
             Well, Los Angeles has been, what shall I say? Eventful,
             in a bad sense.
→ 2   Hide: *ho:nto ni ne shizen to no tata- ne tatakai desu yo ne*
             It's true *ne*. It's like a strug- *ne* struggle against nature *ne*
→ 3   Ai: *ne soo desu nee*
             ne. Exactly *nee*
   4   Hide: *Demo amerika no:, seifu toka:. sono: amerikajin kanari*
             borantia seishin ga aru shi: Kanari hayaku hukyuu
             hayakatta desho
             But the American government, or well, the American people
             have a pretty good volunteer spirit, and the damage repair
             was pretty fast, right?
→ 5   Ai: *Hayakatta shi*
             (It) was fast, and
→ 6   Hide: *Nee boku ga bikkuri shita no wa taioo ga hayai na: to*
             omotte. seifu nanka mo. n nihon no taioo ni kuraberu to ne?
             Nee what surprised me was, I thought that their reaction
             was fast, and the (American) government's too, compared to
             Japan's reaction *ne*?

→ 7   Ai: *Hayai desu yo ne*
                 It was fast, *ne?*
   8   Hide: *Mattaku yuushuu. ii desu yo ne*
                 Completely excellent. (They are) good *ne*
   9   Ai: *Ee. nihon wa nanka yosan kimeru toka itte [yuujuufudan*
                 desu yo ne.
                 Yeah. As far as Japan is concerned, (they) say something
                 like they have to budget the costs and they can't make
                 a [decision *ne*
→ 10   Hide: [*Nnneee*
                 [*Nnneee*

(From Strauss's [1995] #19; emphasis added)

In the first two lines, Ai assesses life in Los Angeles, as eventful in a negative sense. Note in line 2 how Hide aligns with Ai. He both agrees in the beginning of his turn with *ho:nto ni ne* (it's true, isn't it), and then upgrades her assessment. In line 3, Ai agrees with Hide's upgrade. *Ne* plays an important role in the aligning expressions of both Hide and Ai. This particle is a critical element of assessment and alignment in Japanese. Hide continues in line 4, praising American volunteerism in yet another assessment, with which Ai aligns in line 5. Ai repeats the adjective Hide used, and does her own upgrade using the particle *shi* (moreover). Next, we see how expressions of alignment can be piled one on top of another, as in line 6, Hide aligns with Ai by saying *nee*. Just as Ai concurred with Hide's upgrade earlier, in line 6 Hide expresses alignment with Ai's expression of alignment, saying *nee*, which alone functions to express alignment. This excerpt shows repeated use of assessment and alignment through line 10, where Hide provides a final expression of alignment, *Nnneee*. Through this conversation, Hide and Ai, who had never met before this encounter, show a remarkable level of alignment. This is constructed with repeated use of *ne*-marked aligning expressions.

The particle *ne* is a key component of any conversational interaction in Japanese (Maynard, 1989; Cook, 1992). Cook (1992) has defined *ne* as a marker of affective common ground. The shared affect in Strauss's example attests to the power of Cook's description of *ne*. *Ne* derives its affective power through its epistemological characteristics of marking shared information. Kamio (1990, 1997) notes how *ne* marks information that is accessible to both interlocutors. One common example of this is routine greetings in Japanese, which often refer to the weather. Figure 1 shows a typical greeting sequence, where the fact of the hot day is the information shared by the interlocutors. The particle *ne* marks both initial and aligning assessments in this common expression of greeting, and works to construct an agreement in feeling even as it marks joint access to an experience.

Atsui desu	*ne:*	(It's hot, isn't it?)
Soo desu	*ne:*	(It is, isn't it?)

Figure 1 Use of ne *in indexing joint access to information and alignment.*

The frequency of these expressions in ordinary conversation underscores their importance for the learner of Japanese as a second or foreign language. Foreign learners must learn to use *ne* appropriately if they are to interact in Japanese in a socially appropriate way (Yoshimi, 1999). The intricacy of Japanese listener responses and the use of *ne* in these responses as a tool for showing alignment combine to make appropriate listening behavior difficult for learners to acquire (Sawyer, 1992; Ohta, 1994; Siegal, 1996; Yoshimi, 1999). Matsuda (1988), who studied beginning learners of Japanese residing in Japan, found that 80% of the learners did not use any sort of listener response. Regarding the use of *ne*, Sawyer's (1992) participants, Americans studying in Japan, were slow to use *ne*-marked expressions of alignment. Yoshimi (1999) found errors in using *ne* to be common. Learners of Japanese may also suffer a disadvantage compared to Japanese children in terms of the availability of these resources in their learning environments. Whereas interaction with children is rich in the use of *ne*, and the particle, in turn, is acquired by children very early (Clancy, 1985), studies of interaction between Japanese native speakers and learners have found that native speaker use of *ne* is reduced as compared to native-native conversation. In addition, studies of beginning Japanese L2 classrooms have found *ne* to occur in recurrent classroom routines, but with a frequency much lower than in ordinary conversation (Ohta, 1993, 1994). Whether or not the Japanese L2 classroom can play a positive role in shaping learners' interactional style, therefore, remains to be seen.

This chapter builds on previous studies in three ways. First, the learners whose development was examined in previous research were studying abroad in Japan. Development of listener responses among classroom foreign language learners of Japanese has not been examined. In fact, classroom learners have been shown to be sensitive to pragmatic information conveyed through classroom discourse (Ohta, 1997, 2000b). Questions remain, however, regarding the formal and informal opportunities the classroom provides for the learning of pragmatic information and how interactional style develops when it is not the focus of instruction. Second, this study has a longitudinal, developmental focus, which allows for the observation of pragmatic development over time. Third, Strauss's (1995) suggestion that listener responses fall along a continuum from acknowledgment to alignment provides a framework which may prove helpful in understanding learner development. Perhaps students who still experience difficulty with aligning expressions may have a useful command of certain expressions of acknowledgment. In order to express alignment, the listener must first understand the interlocutor's talk, and then select an appropriate expression that is congruent with the tenor of that talk. In contrast, acknowledgment responses are more of a "one size fits all" response that can be used to show comprehension or receipt of information more generally. This study will provide further insight into how interactional competence develops in classroom learners of Japanese.

The study

Data

Longitudinal data were collected over 1 academic year, following two students, Candace and Rob (all names used are pseudonyms), as they proceeded through a large university Japanese language program. These data are part of a larger study which followed seven students, four first-year and three second-year, through the academic year (Ohta, 2001). The two students whose development we will examine here, Candace and Rob, were first-year students in the same class for 2 of the 3 quarters,[1] making their data sets particularly relevant for comparison of developmental processes, since their learning environments were similar. Classes were video- and audiotaped two to three times per quarter over the year,[2] with the students wearing clip-on microphones to obtain a record of their interactions in both teacher-fronted and pair or group interactions. Five 50-minute class periods, distributed over the year, were transcribed and analyzed, as shown in Table 1.

Candace and Rob were in the same class in the fall quarter and had the same teacher for fall and winter quarters; they had different teachers in the spring quarter. Transcription conventions used in this chapter are shown in the Appendix. As much as possible, colloquial English has been used for the translations of the Japanese utterances. When this was not possible, abbreviations are used in the English gloss to show Japanese grammatical markers. These are listed with the transcription conventions.

---

1 In the United States, colleges and universities are on either a semester (two-term) system or a quarter (three-term) system. A quarter consists of 10 weeks of instruction, with a 1-week final exam period.

2 As Table 1 indicates, the 4/21 data are the latest available for Rob. Rob's tape recorder failed when data were collected in his class in May.

TABLE 1. DATES OF DATA COLLECTION

Name	Dates					
Candace	11/27		1/24	2/28	4/24	5/22
Rob	11/27	12/2	1/24	2/28	4/21	

Analysis

The data were analyzed from a conversation analytic perspective. Conversation analysis has attracted attention recently as a tool for SLA research (Markee, 1995, 2000). Through this process, expressions of acknowledgment and alignment produced by teachers, the targeted students, and their classmates were examined. Classroom interaction is structured differently from ordinary conversation, not only in its turn-taking conventions, but also in interactional structure, which has been shown to be dominated by a three-turn Initiation-Response-Follow-up (IRF) sequence (Sinclair & Coulthard, 1975; Ohta, 1993, 1994; Markee, 2000). Particular attention was paid to the follow-up turn of this sequence, since previous analysis of Japanese classroom discourse has found that teachers tend to use expressions of alignment in this location (Ohta, 1993, 1994); acknowledgment expressions have also been found to occur in this sequential location (Ohta, 1999). Development by the targeted students of the use of the third turn of the IRF, therefore, was a focus of analysis.

Results: Listener responses used in the classroom

Analysis of the teachers' use of listener responses showed that a range of listener responses from acknowledgment to alignment occurred throughout the academic year. The expressions that occurred are illustrated in Table 2. Students had broad exposure to the listener-response expressions shown in Table 2 through the teachers' use of these expressions when interacting with the students (Ohta, 2001). In the following example, one of the teachers uses the informal acknowledgment expression *mm* (uh huh) as well as *aa soo desu ka* (oh really):

2 1 T: *Paulson-san, terebi o mimasu ka?*
          Mr. Paulson, do you watch television?
   2 P: *Hai mimasu*
          Yes, I do.
→ 3 T: *Mm donna terebi o mimasu ka?*
          Uh huh what kinds of programs do you watch

TABLE 2. EXPRESSIONS OF ACKNOWLEDGMENT AND ALIGNMENT USED
FREQUENTLY BY TEACHERS

Acknowledgment		Alignment	
Japanese	English translation	*Japanese*	English translation
Un, mm	"uh huh"	*Soo desu ne*	"It is, isn't it"
Hai, ee	"yes"	*Ii desu ne*	"nice," "great," "good"
Aa soo desu ka	"I see," "Oh really"	_____ *desu ne*	"that's _____ isn't it"
Soo desu ka	"Oh really"		

```
    4  P:   Um Oprah (.) o mimasu
            Um I watch (.) Oprah
 → 5  T:    Aa: soo desu ka?
            Oh, is that so
```

(Yasuda, 11/27)

The expression of alignment used most frequently by the teachers was *ii desu ne*, which, as Table 2 shows, serves the dual function of giving praise and of commenting on the content of a learner's utterance. Teachers used other expressions of alignment as well, such as *zannen desu ne* (that's too bad), and other assessments tailored to the content of student talk:

```
 3  1  T:   Unagi o tabemasu ka?
            Do you eat eel?
    2  S1:  Iie tabemasen
            No, I don't
    3  T:   Tabemasen (.) jya S2-san unagi o tabemasu ka?
            You don't (.) well, do you eat eel, S2?
    4  S2:  Hai tabemasu
            Yes, I do.
 → 5  T:    Tabemasu (.) oishii desu ne:.
            You do (.) It's good ne:.
```

(Yasuda, 11/27)

Teachers also guided students in the use of listener responses, prompting students to use the expressions *aa soo desu ka* (oh really), and to use aligning assessments during a greeting routine involving talk about the weather. When this routine occurred, it was used at the very beginning of class time:

```
 4  1  T:   Hai jya hajimema:su (.) ohayoo gozaima:::su
            OK let's begin (.) good morning.
    2  Ss:  Ohayoo gozaimasu
            Good morning
```

3   T: *Kyoo wa iya na tenki desu ne:*
          The weather is unpleasant today *ne*:
4   Ss: *Soo desu ne:*
          It is *ne*:
→ 5   T: *Iya:: soo desu ne::*
          Unpleasant it is *ne*::

(Yasuda, 11/24)

In this example, the students readily respond with the aligning assessment *soo desu ne*. When the students failed to do so, teachers would prompt them to provide the assessment. Teachers also guided students in using confirmation questions and other expressions of alignment. These examples of how teachers used listener responses are typical of the data under examination here, and likely occurred throughout the academic year. In this way, whether they participated peripherally as the teacher interacted with others, or more directly as the interlocutors of the teacher, a range of listener-response expressions as well as guidance in the use of these expressions was available to Candace and Rob in their day-to-day classroom experience.

Compared to listener response use in ordinary conversation (Maynard, 1989; Horiguchi, 1990), the range of expressions used in these classrooms is limited both in range and in frequency. Unlike participants in ordinary conversation, these beginning classroom learners did not tell stories, or give lengthy descriptions of experience, but made much shorter contributions. In ordinary conversation, native-speaking interlocutors often take turns made up of multiple turn-constructional units (TCUs). A TCU is the minimum unit of a turn that can stand alone, and may consist of a word, phrase, or sentence. In the classroom corpus examined here, student turns were generally made up of only one TCU. This has ramifications for teacher use of listener-response expressions, since the use of shorter turns decreases opportunity for use of listener responses.

The learners' development

Results of the analysis show that both Candace and Rob develop the ability to use expressions of acknowledgment, with Candace also beginning to use *ne*-marked expressions of alignment. In the fall (11/27), neither Candace nor Rob use the follow-up turn of the IRF sequence for Japanese expressions of acknowledgment or alignment. Of Candace's 20 opportunities to use the follow-up turn in pair-work interaction, she does not take the turn in 14 cases; the few follow-up turns she does take are used for laughter (3), or acknowledgment expressions in English (3). Rob's use of the language is strikingly similar, although the students were never paired with one another in the data examined. Rob also has 20 potential follow-up turns, 11 of which are not used; like Candace, he also laughs (6), and expresses acknowledgment in English (1). He also uses the follow-up turn for repair of a partner's error (1), and does an acknowledgment response in Japanese, using the word *hai* (yes/OK) once. The following excerpt shows this lack of listener responses when Rob and his pair-work partner do an interview activity in Japanese:

5 1 R: *Uh:* (..) *supotsu wa: itt- iya-* (.) *supo:tsu wa:: shimasu* (.) *ka.*
    Uh: (..) sports TOP itt- iya- (.) do you do sports?
  2 S: *Iie shimasen*
    No I don't
  3 R: *Uh biru wa nomimasu* (..)[*ka?*
    Do you drink beer?
  4 S: [*Nomimasu* (.) *yomimasu* (.) *uh hai^ yomimasu*[3]
    [drink (.) read (.) uh yes I read
  5 R: *hahahaha Benkyoo shimasu* (..) *ka?*
    Hahahaha Do you (.) study?
  6 S: *Uh hai benkyoo shimasu,*
    Uh yes I study,
  7 R: *Uh:* (.) *eiga* (.) *imasu* (.) *ekimasu*
    Uh: (.) do you (.) go to (.) movies
  8 S: *Iie ikimasen*
    No I don't
  9 R: *Niuuyooku Timesu o – Shiatoru taimusu yomimasu?*
    Do you read the *New York Times* – the *Seattle Times*?
 10 S: *Uh hai yomimasu*
    Uh yes I do.

                (Rob, 11/27)

Expressions of acknowledgment are not scripted in this activity, and the students don't use them, but simply run through questions and answer in a sort of "interrogation" style. At this level, although they have already been introduced to the expression *Aa soo desu ka*, students do not use it. Candace's performance at this point is quite similar to Rob's:

6 1 S: *Supo:tsu o shimasu ka?*
    Do you do sports?
  2 C: *Hai^* (.) *hai shimasu*
    Yes (.) yes I do.
  3 S: (.)
  4 C: *B- Biiru:.* (.) *biiru: o:* (.) *nomimasu ka:?*
    Do you (.) drink (.) beer?
  5 S: *Iie nomimasen.*
    No I don't.

---

3 Note the similar pronunciation of *nomimasu* (drink) and *yomimasu* (read) in Japanese.

    6 (.)
    7 C: *Nihongo: benkyoo shimasu ka?*
            Do you study Japanese?
    8 S: *Hai shimasu*
            Yes I do.
    9 C: Hehehe

                                        (Candace, 11/27)

In this class, listener-response expressions were almost completely con-
fined to learner conversation in English, which occurred when learners
were trying to figure out how to proceed, or when asking each other
questions about Japanese vocabulary or grammar. Candace's and Rob's
way of using Japanese during peer interaction, however, gradually
changes as the year proceeds. In the January data, an important sign of
change is the students' growing flexibility in the use of the follow-up
turn when doing pair work in Japanese. Although learners hardly utilized the follow-up turn in the earliest data set, in the January data they
begin to use the turn for repetition of their partner's response, for
acknowledgment responses in English, or for repair of a partner's error.
Confusion of acknowledgment and alignment expressions also
emerges. Rob conflates the aligning expression *soo desu ne* and the
acknowledgment *Aa soo desu ka*. Yoshimi (1999) found errors with
soo desu ne to be quite common in a small group of learners who had
studied Japanese in their home country (from 1 to 3.5 years), and had
little experience in Japan (from 1 to 3 months). In Yoshimi's interview
data involving these learners, *soo desu ne* was used inappropriately
31% of the time. Therefore, it is not realistic to expect Rob to use the
expression with a high degree of accuracy only 4 months into his career
as a Japanese learner. Rather, Rob's error is evidence of his progress in
using listener responses and increased flexibility as a listener, even
though his use of *soo desu ne* is inappropriate here. In the following
excerpt from Rob's 1/24 class, Rob works to show acknowledgment,
misusing *soo desu ne* for *Aa soo desu ka* (line 6), and using a confirmation question (line 8). Neither is done appropriately, but his use of the
follow-up turn as a place to show responsiveness to his interlocutor during interaction in Japanese is a big step forward as compared to earlier
data.

    7 1 S: *Kyoo nani o shimashita ka?*
                What did you do today?
       2 R: *Paati ga arimasu.*
                There is a party.
       3 S: *Aa: soo desu ka?*
                Oh really?
       4 R: *Kinoo nani o shimashita ka?*
                What did you do yesterday?

```
  5  S:  (.) Nemasu
          (.) I sleep
→ 6  R:  Aa: soo desu ne:. Nanji goro nemasu ka?
          Yes that's right. What time do you go to sleep?
  7  S:  Sanji goro desu
          At around three
→ 8  R:  Sanji goro desu? ((sounds surprised))
          At around three?
```

(Rob, 1/24)

Developmental changes in the interaction include Rob's partner, who uses *Aa soo desu ka* appropriately in line 3, giving Rob the opportunity to experience his partner's use of this expression.

Candace also shows development from November through January, using *Aa soo desu ka* appropriately in the 1/24 class, but not yet using it consistently. Candace never confuses *Aa soo desu ka* with *soo desu ne*. Candace uses *soo desu ne* only as a hedge, not as an expression of alignment. This may account for why she does not confuse the two expressions.

```
8  1  C:  Kinoo: nani o shimashita ka:?
          What did you do yesterday?
   2  S:  Um: benkyoo (.) shimashita^.
          Um: I (.) studied.
→  3  C:  Ah:: soo desu ka?
          Oh really?
   4  S:  Mm (..) Uh kinoo nan nani o shimashita (.) ka?
          Mm (..) Uh wha- what did you do (.) yesterday?
   5  C:  Nihongo o benkyoo o shimashita:,
          I studied Japanese.
   6  S:  Hai
          Yes
→  7  C:  Uh: to: uh: sentaku o shimashita ka:[ (.) shimashita
          Uh and I studied Japanese Q        [ (.) I studied Japanese.
   8  S:  [Ah soo desu ka?
          [Oh really?
```

(Candace, 1/24)

Candace uses *Aa soo desu ka* appropriately in line 3. She also responds appropriately to her partner's use of the minimal expression of acknowledgment *hai* in line 6 by adding further information about what she did the previous day. Candace's partner appropriately responds to this added information with *Aa soo desu ka* in line 8. Not only do Candace and Rob begin to use the follow-up turn more flexibly to try out different expressions, but development is also evident in the interactional style of their pair-work episodes as a whole, as their pair-work interlocutors also increase their use of these expressions.

In the 2/28 class, both students continue using *Aa soo desu ka*, now using it appropriately and spontaneously. In addition, both make better use of the third turn of the IRF sequence as a place to show interest in and understanding of their interlocutor's contributions. In the following excerpt from Candace's class, Candace's increase in responsiveness is evident. She not only uses *Aa soo desu ka* in line 9, but in line 3, she says *Aah*, acknowledging her partner's response, and repeats her partner's response in line 5. In line 6, when the partner self-corrects, Candace repeats that correction in line 7.

9   1   C: *Donna:: donna:: shatsu shatsu o um motte imasu ka?*
             What sort of what sort of shirts shirts do you have?
    2   S: *E::h takusan (.) uh aka:i*
             E::h a lot of (.) uh re:d
→   3   C: *Aah*
             Oh
    4   S: *Akai*
             Red
→   5   C: [*Akai? a^*[
             [Red? A^[
    6   S: [*Aoi*   [*aoi::*
             [Blue   [blue
→   7   C: *Aoi? A::h*
             Blue? O::h
    8   S: *Uh shatsu (.) T-shatsu o mot- uh motte imasu.*
             Uh shirts (.) I have T-shirts.
→   9   C: *Ah soo desu ka?*
             Oh really

                                             (Candace, 2/28)

Candace is becoming more flexible in her use of listener responses. Rob's development is less dramatic, but he shows an increase in responsiveness, using *hai* to acknowledge completion of a partner's answer, shown below in line 5, as well as using repetition in response to his partner's answer:

10 1   R: *Fujin fuku uriba*
             The women's clothing department
    2   S: *Fujin? OK. Fujin fuku uriba:: (.) ga arimasu.*
             Women's? OK. The women's clothing department (.) is there.
    3   R: *Uriba*
             Department
    4   S: *Uriba:: (.) ga arimasu.*
             Department (.) is there.
    5   R: *Hai.*
             Yes.

                                               (Rob, 2/28)

Rob also uses *Aa soo desu ka* appropriately, and does not misuse *soo desu ne*.

In the spring quarter, Rob and Candace are in different classes, with different teachers. Both show a dramatic increase in appropriate use of listener-response expressions. Rob uses *Aa soo desu ka* nineteen times in the 4/21 class, in contrast to having used it only three times in the 2/28 class. He also attempts to use *ne* in a responsive way, but misuses the particle, again saying *soo desu ne*, an assessment, in a context where *Aa soo desu ka*, an expression of acknowledgment, would have been appropriate. Candace increases use of the acknowledgment expressions *aah, hai,* and *mm* in the 4/24 class. Most striking about these April classes is Candace's spontaneous use of *ne*-marked expressions of alignment which show appreciation of or empathy with her partner's response. In the next example, Candace and her partner work on a sentence-connecting activity. Candace's partner, S, shows empathy with the difficulty Candace has had putting together a complex sentence. In line 1, Candace expresses understanding of the teacher's explanation (not shown), and, in line 2, her partner sympathetically responds with an assessment aligning with the emotional tenor of Candace's experience.

11 1 C: *Hai. Wakarimasu.*
          Yes. I understand.
→ 2 S: (.) *Taihen desu ne*
          (.) That's difficult *ne*
   3 C: ((Laughs))
   4 S: *(Tanaka-san) wa nihonjin de (nihongo) no sensei desu.*
          (Ms. Tanaka) is Japanese and is a (Japanese language) teacher.
→ 5 C: *Nn ii desu ne.*
          Oh that's good.

(Candace, 4/24)

In line 4, Candace's partner links two sentences of her own. Candace, then, uses an assessment to compliment her partner's performance in line 5. Here both Candace's partner and Candace use spontaneous assessments that are appropriately responsive to their interlocutors. In fact, Candace uses *ne*-marked alignment expressions six times in the 4/24 class, all without prompting from the teacher or guidance from instructional materials. Earlier in the same class, Candace used *taihen desu ne* (how difficult/arduous) in private speech (self-addressed speech), commenting on the difficulty of a grammar problem. Later, after a partner's English assessment ("This is hard"), Candace responds in Japanese with *taihen desu ne*, appropriately showing alignment with the feelings expressed by her partner. She also uses *ii desu ne* two other times in addition to that shown in the excerpt above. In contrast, Rob does not yet show any use of spontaneous assessments. And, although he consistently expresses acknowledgment using *Aa soo desu ka*, Rob uses fewer types of acknowledgment expressions than Candace does. Table 3 summarizes their progress as of the last data collected.

TABLE 3. PROGRESS BY THE END OF THE ACADEMIC YEAR IN USE OF A RANGE
OF LISTENER RESPONSES

	Un/Mm/hai	*Aa soo desu ka*	*Soo desu ne*	*~desu ne*
Rob	Uses *hai* occasionally	Uses spontaneously	misuses for *Aa soo desu ka*	Uses only when scripted
Candace	Uses all three	Uses spontaneously	Uses as a hedge, not as a listener response	Uses spontaneously

From acknowledgment to alignment: Proposing a developmental sequence

Candace's and Rob's development, though different in pace, appears to follow a similar developmental sequence, that may apply to other beginning language learners as well. A common sequence that accounts for both Candace's and Rob's data is proposed in Table 4. Both Candace and Rob begin at Stage 1 in the fall quarter (11/27 data). In early winter (1/24 data), Candace and Rob have both moved into Stage 2. A month later (2/28), both students are in Stage 3. Two months later, Rob (4/21) is in Stage 4, using acknowledgment expressions with facility. He does not use any alignment expressions, but none were scripted for use in the activities, and the teacher also did not prompt students to use them. Candace (4/24) has moved to Stage 5 at this point, using two alignment expressions, *ii desu ne* and *taihen desu ne*, appropriately and spontaneously. A month later (5/22), Candace remains at Stage 5, but uses a slightly broader range of alignment expressions, adding *zannen desu ne*. Here, at Stage 5, Candace has acquired the ability to show alignment with her interlocutor in Japanese within the limits of her vocabulary, using the affective particle *ne* appropriately for this purpose. She is, however, still fairly limited, in that she does not use a very broad range of vocabulary, but sticks to particular expressions. In the present data, Rob develops through Stage 4, and Candace through Stage 5.

Suggestion of a developmental sequence is not meant to obscure individual differences. Different students will develop at different rates. In addition, Candace and Rob show that different learners may be sensitive to different sorts of expressions. Rob's misuse of *soo desu ne* shows his awareness of this expression's potential as a listener-response expression; Candace, however, does not use *soo desu ka* for this function. Rob does not show awareness of minimal response expressions beyond the formal expression *hai*, whereas Candace also uses the more

TABLE 4. PROPOSED DEVELOPMENTAL SEQUENCE IN ALIGNMENT EXPRESSIONS
FOR JFL LEARNERS

Stage 1	Students ask and answer preformulated questions. There is no use of expressions of acknowledgment or alignment, in English or in Japanese, unless scripted. The follow-up turn of the IRF sequence is left unused, with speakers moving immediately, or after a pause, to a new initiation.
Stage 2	Students begin to use the follow-up turn for expressions of acknowledgment, such as repetition of Japanese words and laughter. Use of Japanese minimal expressions of acknowledgment such as *hai* are rare. Alignment expressions are used only where scripted.
Stage 3	Students begin to use *Aa soo desu ka* to show acknowledgment, particularly when prompted by the teacher, but occasional spontaneous use also emerges. Occasional use of the Japanese minimal response *hai* continues. Alignment expressions are used where scripted, and on a limited basis when prompted by the teacher.
Stage 4	Students use *Aa soo desu ka* with facility, beginning to use minimal expressions of acknowledgment beyond *hai*, such as *mm* and *un*, on occasion. Alignment expressions appear when prompted by the teacher.
Stage 5	Spontaneous use of a limited range of Japanese expressions of alignment emerges. Minimal response expressions occur more frequently. Expressions of alignment are limited to those commonly used by the teacher, with little to no creative expansion.
Stage 6	Students use a range of expressions of acknowledgment appropriately. Alignment expressions are used spontaneously, with greater lexical variety tailored to conversational content.

informal expressions *un* and *mm*. There is variability both in the rate of development and in the range of expressions each is working to acquire. Any developmental sequence proposed needs to be understood as a flexible construct; in addition, this proposed sequence should be revised based on examination of the development of other learners.

Socialization of interactional style in the classroom

Over the academic year, these learners develop not only as speakers but also as listeners. Candace's and Rob's growth in interactional competence is evidence of the power of peripheral participation (Lave & Wenger, 1991) in interactional routines (Peters & Boggs, 1986; Ohta, 1999, 2001) in the socialization of interactional style. In teacher-fronted settings, learner opportunity to use the follow-up turn – the primary sequential location acknowledgment and aligning expressions in this setting – rarely occurs, since the third turn is almost always taken by the teacher (Ohta, 1993, 1994). Each student does, however, have access to peripheral participation as an addressee or an auditor. In these roles, students are privy to the teacher's use of these expressions. Learners have many opportunities to observe the teacher interacting as a listener with other students in situations where he or she may be invited to orally participate at any time, and it has been shown that learners are active in these contexts (Ohta, 2000b, 2001). And, teachers often add a third-turn follow-up expression when they have students address one another in front of the class (Ohta, 1993, 1994). Learners are also exposed to these expressions in instructional materials which script their use in pair activities. Scripting allows learners to use listener responses earlier than they would emerge spontaneously, arguably raising learner awareness of these types of utterances. Teacher prompting also may increase both the use of and learner awareness of these expressions.

The power of both peripheral and direct participation is evident in the development of Rob and Candace. Rob and Candace had similar interactive experiences in Japanese class in terms of teacher–learner interaction. Another area of peripheral participation occurs in the peer learning context, where the learners, as speakers, experience the listener responses of their peer interlocutors. In this context, there are striking differences in the frequency with which expressions of acknowledgment and alignment are used by Candace's and Rob's peer partners. For example, in the 4/24 classes, whereas both Candace and her peer partners use *ne*-marked expressions of alignment, neither Rob nor Rob's partners do so. Throughout the year, Candace's partners consistently use listener responses more frequently and with more variety than do Rob's partners. This finding has implications for Rob's and Candace's development. Language socialization processes rely on speech accommodation – the accommodation of interlocutors' ways of speaking to one another. Although this accommodation prototypically involves the "novice" moving toward norms established by the "expert," socialization processes operate among peers as well. Learners may accommodate each other's interactional styles by using or avoiding use of expressions of alignment. Candace may, in fact, be accommodating her interlocutor's conversational style, or vice versa, and the same may be true of Rob and his peer interlocutors. Research on first language acquisition has shown the socializing power of interaction in shaping how language learners develop interactional competence (Schieffelin & Ochs, 1986). Educators across the curriculum agree on the power of peer learning (Tharp & Gallimore, 1988; Gall, 1992; Herrenkohl & Guerra, 1997). Peers provide strong role models for one another as interlocutors work to accommodate the interactive styles of their peers.

Along with differences in how Candace's and Rob's partners used listener-response expressions, there are other important differences between the peer learning settings in which Candace and Rob participate. In Candace's case, time and time again Candace and her peers use Japanese not only to do the assigned tasks, but to move *beyond* what is assigned. They use pair-activity time to its fullest, using every minute of the time allotted, and using Japanese for as wide a variety of functions as they are able to. Rob and his partners, on the other hand, do the assigned tasks, but rarely push beyond what is strictly required. They tend to stop doing tasks as soon as they are complete, falling silent or using additional time as their own personal free time. These differences are also evident in Candace's and Rob's use of English with peers during learning tasks. Candace and her partners persist in using Japanese, even though this restricts the range of what they are able to talk about. English is used rarely, and mainly to access help or when they not sure what they are supposed to be doing. In contrast, Rob and his partners use English to talk about a variety of things, and to chat when finished with assigned tasks.

The teachers did not assign learners to partners in any of the classes analyzed here. It is possible that when learners are free to work with whomever they like, they may seek out others with similar goals and interests, or with similar levels of investment in the classroom language learning process. The general similarity of the pair partners to one another in this study contrasts with previous studies of pair work in a Japanese language class where the teacher managed the pairings, and where learners were paired with partners of a range of Japanese language strengths and weaknesses (Ohta, 1995, 1997, 2000a, in press). Symmetry of ability may bode well for high achievers, for highly motivated students, or for students who find classroom activities particularly engaging. For students who have less of a stake in using Japanese, who are less interested in classroom activities, or who are less motivated language learners, it is possible that being paired with a similar classmate may be less productive. Differences in Rob's interactions, in fact, are evident when comparing how he performs with different partners who show different levels of investment in the task at hand. This is something that remains to be examined in a future study. However, studies of asymmetrical pairings in a Japanese language class (Ohta, 1995, 1997, 2000a, in press) found that both the more and the less proficient learners benefited from peer language learning activity. Further studies are needed, however, to examine how peer interactional processes in foreign language classes are affected by the choice of a peer partner, and to provide further insight into how interlocutor choice may affect not only grammatical development (Ohta, 2000a, in press), but pragmatic development as well. The choice may not be a trivial one, but may have an impact on classroom language acquisition processes. As for the present study, it is clear that learners do acquire listener-response expressions, and that they move from expressions of acknowledgment to alignment, and develop at different rates. These results not only show the sensitivity of learners to the pragmatic information available in the interactional environments of their classrooms, but also show the potential of the Japanese language classroom as a place where learners work to acquire an interactional style that will serve them well as a foundation for further growth as they move outside the classroom and begin to interact with native speakers at home or abroad.

Appendix: Transcription conventions

[	Indicates overlap with portion in the next turn that is similarly bracketed.
[[	Indicates overlap with portion in the next turn that is similarly bracketed. Used when the single bracket is used in the previous line/turn so that there will not be confusion regarding what brackets correspond to.
(	line to be discussed in the text
___	Portion of special note to the current analysis is underlined.
CAPS	Small caps in the discourse are used to show the speaker's emphasis.
?	rising intonation
,	slight rise in intonation
.	falling intonation
(( ))	comments enclosed in double parentheses
:	elongation of a syllable
(.)	brief pause
(#)	timed pause
-	false start
T:	The teacher in the particular excerpt; the identity of "T" may differ across excerpts.
S1:, S2:	unidentified student
INT	Japanese interrogative marker *ka*
TOP	Japanese topic marker *wa*

PART III:
THE EFFECTS OF INSTRUCTION
IN PRAGMATICS

Compared to areas such as grammar, lexis, or phonology, the effects of instruction on interlanguage pragmatic development have been explored far less. As Kasper (this volume) points out, the research that has been done to date does indicate that pragmatic development, though observed to occur in second language classrooms without instruction, can be facilitated by instruction, particularly when that instruction is of an explicit nature. Part III consists of five chapters examining the effect of different instructional approaches on specific aspects of L2 pragmatics. In Chapter 7, Anthony Liddicoat and Chantal Crozet investigate the effects of instruction given to Australian university students of French as a foreign language on the acquisition of one target interactional practice, namely, responding to a question about the weekend. Previous research indicates that although the question "Did you have a good weekend?" is a phatic, ritualized greeting which requires little or no elaboration in the response for Australians, for French speakers the question is not phatic and often elicits a lengthy response replete with lively descriptions to which the listener is expected to carefully attend. The potential for misunderstanding, frustration, and negative stereotyping that these differences present has been well attested. In their study, Liddicoat and Crozet used role-plays in a pretest/posttest design with an intervening four-phase instructional treatment consisting of awareness raising, narrative reconstruction, production, and feedback. They found that after instruction, learners did more closely approximate French norms, in terms of both particular language features and content. A delayed posttest conducted 1 year later showed that only the content appeared to have been retained. Their study shows, then, that interactional norms can be taught and acquired in an FL context but that without sustained occasion for conversational practice in the target language, gains made during instruction may be difficult to maintain.

In Chapter 8, Kenneth Rose and Connie Ng report the results of a study which compared the effects of inductive and deductive approaches to the teaching of English compliments and compliment responses to university-level learners of English in Hong Kong. There were three

121

groups in all – a deductive group, an inductive group, and a control group. Both treatment groups received instruction in the target speech acts, but while the deductive group was provided with metapragmatic information through explicit instruction before engaging in practice activities, the inductive group engaged in pragmatic analysis activities in which they were expected to arrive at the relevant generalizations themselves. Three measures of learner performance were administered in a pretest/posttest design: a self-assessment task, a discourse completion task (DCT), and a metapragmatic assessment task. The DCT and metapragmatic assessment task were also administered to native speakers of English and native speakers of Cantonese. Results were mixed, indicating no effect for instruction on learner confidence or metapragmatic assessment of appropriate compliment responses. However, the results from the DCT showed a marked increase in the use of compliment formulas by both treatment groups, with no similar increase for the control group. Results for compliment responses revealed a positive effect only for the deductive group, indicating that although inductive and deductive instruction may both lead to gains in pragmalinguistic proficiency, only the latter may be effective for developing sociopragmatic proficiency.

In Chapter 9, Satomi Takahashi examines the effects of input enhancement on the development of English request strategies by Japanese EFL learners at a Japanese university using four input conditions, namely, explicit teaching, form-comparison, form-search, and meaning-focused conditions. These four conditions differ from each other in degrees of input enhancement, with the explicit teaching condition manifesting the highest degree of input enhancement and the meaning-focused condition the least. Takahashi addresses two issues, first, whether the degrees of input enhancement affect the learning of request strategies, and second, whether learner confidence in formulating request strategies is influenced by the types of input conditions. A pretest/posttest design was adopted, using an open-ended DCT with a measure of the subjects' confidence in selecting their request forms. Written immediate retrospective self-report data were also collected in order to gain information about the subjects' conscious decisions during their request performance. The results indicated that the degrees of input enhancement influenced the acquisition of request forms, explicit teaching having the strongest impact, followed by form-comparison, form-search, and meaning-focused. The explicit instruction helped the learners both develop their pragmatic competence and enhance their confidence in performance to a greater extent than the three implicit conditions, and the self-report data also showed that the form-search and the meaning-focused conditions equally failed to draw the learners' attention to the target forms in the input. These findings lend support to Schmidt's (1993a,

1995, 1998) Noticing Hypothesis, which claims that linguistic forms can serve as intake for learning only if the learners actually notice them.

In Chapter 10, Yumiko Tateyama presents the findings from her study on the effects of explicit and implicit instruction in the use of attention getters, expressions of gratitude, and apologies to beginning students of Japanese as a foreign language (JFL). Each group received treatments four times over an 8-week period, with the treatment for the explicit group including explicit metapragmatic information, whereas that for the implicit group withheld it. Participants engaged in role-play and multiple-choice tasks as well as two different forms of self-report. The results show that there was no statistically significant difference between the two groups in the multiple-choice and role-play tasks. However, close examination of the errors in the multiple-choice tasks indicates that the participants in the explicit group were more successful in choosing the correct answers in items which required higher formality of the linguistic expressions. It seems that these participants benefited from explicit teaching on how the degree of indebtedness in thanking situations, the severity of offense in the apology contexts, and such factors as age, social status, and in-group/out-group distinction intricately influence the choice of routine formulas, which suggests that some aspects of interlanguage pragmatics are teachable to beginners before they develop analyzed second language knowledge.

In Chapter 11, Dina Yoshimi discusses the results of a study of instructional approaches to facilitate development in the comprehension and production of discourse markers in JFL. Three times per week over 16 weeks, a group of high-intermediate learners of JFL received instruction which consisted of a read-discuss-retell format designed to raise the learners' awareness of the existence and location of discourse markers in both spoken and written discourse, and to increase their understanding of the organizing, interactional, and expressive functions of these linguistic items. Three additional data collection sessions, in which learners were asked to tell a personal narrative and then retell a text they had not retold in class, were also held. Yoshimi expected that in the context of the retelling learners would notice where they had difficulty communicating their meaning, and focus their attention on these areas for improvement, but despite the explicit instructional focus on discourse markers, the extensive NS input, and the structured opportunities for learner production, learner use of the target discourse markers in extended turns at talk was extremely limited in a number of ways. Yoshimi argues that discourse markers in Japanese may constitute a domain of pragmatic competence that is particularly resistant to the effects of consciousness-raising, but she also considers the possibility that these results are due to an inadequacy in the realization of the experimental instructional approach.

The chapters in this section rely heavily on instruments such as questionnaires and pretests/posttests, as well as a range of materials used in instructional treatments. Although we recognize the value of including as much of this material as possible – both for better understanding the studies, and for facilitating the efforts of those interested in replicating work reported here or carrying out similar work – because of space limitations, we were not able to do this. However, we encourage interested readers to contact authors of individual chapters to obtain further information on the materials used in their studies.

7 Acquiring French interactional norms through instruction

Anthony J. Liddicoat and Chantal Crozet

Introduction

The emergence of intercultural competence in language teaching (Kramsch, 1993, 1995; Lustig & Koester, 1993; Byram & Zarate, 1994; Crozet, Liddicoat, & Lo Bianco, 1999) has led to a need to focus on a second language as a vehicle for communication in cultural contexts, and this in turn implies that an important goal for language learning is developing an understanding of *appropriate* communication in the target language (Zarate, 1986; Buttjes & Byram, 1990; Kramsch, 1995; Tickoo, 1995; Fantini, 1997; Liddicoat, 1997b). Consequently, language teaching now needs to be seen more in the context of intercultural communication, with the aim of preparing learners to communicate outside their own cultural boundaries (Bolten, 1993; Crozet, 1996; Liddicoat, 1997b; Liddicoat & Crozet, 1997; Liddicoat, Crozet, Jansen, & Schmidt, 1997; Crozet & Liddicoat, 1999; Crozet et al., 1999). In such a perspective, pragmatic and discoursal practices become an integral part of language learning from early on because they play a central role in intercultural communication, and mismatches between them have been identified as a key factor in communication breakdowns. Many studies have shown that culturally based differences about what is expected during communication can be a significant cause of crosscultural communication difficulties (Gumperz, Judd, & Roberts, 1979; Wierzbicka, 1985, 1991; Kotthoff & Auer, 1987; Gudykunst & Kim, 1992). These expectations may be linked to differences in the realization of particular speech acts, or they may be linked to broader, and often more diffuse, issues of discourse organization and conversational style. Thomas (1983, 1984) has shown that when speakers do not share the same cultural background, sociopragmatic failure is more likely, resulting largely from a lack of shared resources for understanding what a particular contribution is *doing* at a particular place in talk.

Gumperz (1982a, 1982b) has demonstrated that the misuse by second language speakers of aspects of the surface forms of utterances, including routine formulas which may signal relevant interpretive frames, can

125

often lead to misunderstandings. These surface forms of language, or contextualization cues, are fundamentally implicated in the context-bound process of interpreting what is happening in a conversation and how one should respond. Differences in discourse organization and conversational style can have important consequences for the second language speaker. If a second language speaker does not have "native-like" command of conversational management, she or he is less likely to create a favorable impression with interlocutors (Gumperz et al., 1979; Marriott, 1990; Bilbow & Yeung, 1998). Tannen (1984a, 1984b, 1986) has argued that differences in conversational style are linked to problems and misunderstandings in both intracultural and intercultural interactions. Such differences are often small and subtle; however, the consequences for interaction and interpretation of such small and subtle differences may be quite large (Erickson, 1975; Gumperz et al., 1979; Erickson & Shultz, 1982; Béal, 1990, 1992). Norms of interaction on which communication in the target-language culture are based are, therefore, an important component of language learning viewed as a culturally and socially contexted phenomenon. This presents a particular problem for both the language learner and the language teacher. Wolfson (1989b) has argued that interactional norms that underlie talk are not consciously available to speakers. Given this unconsciousness of the patterned nature of interaction in one's first language, the challenge faced by the language learner in attempting to acquire the appropriate use of a new language is doubly difficult in that both the starting point and the finishing point are in some sense hidden. Learners need to be assisted in noticing these differences (Schmidt, 1993b).

When it comes to the discoursal features of language which can be called *interactional norms*, the problems of noticing are compounded. For example, Schegloff (1986) has demonstrated that in telephone openings the question "How are you?" normally receives a default "OK"-type answer. However, when such an answer is not produced, it is not interpreted as wrong, but rather as doing something different. The "OK" response indicates "nothing special happening," whereas some other answer indicates that "something special is happening," that is, that the speaker is communicating something beyond the normal access ritual function of these utterances. As such, where expectations about a question such as this are not shared by all participants in the interaction, the different frames of interpretation may not reveal themselves through the interaction itself. In the context of foreign language learning, where the chances for noticing a difference between the target language's culturally based patterns of interaction and those of one's first language are limited, the possibilities of noticing such differences are inevitably low. In these cases, students need to have their attention focused through instruction on elements of interaction which are salient and which vary between the target-language culture and the first language culture (Crozet, 1996; Crozet & Liddicoat, 1998). This chapter seeks to determine whether discoursal rules relating to different degrees of ritualization between the two languages can be taught and learned within the context of the foreign language classroom.

Method

Participants

The main participants for this study were a group of ten second-year university-level French students in the *ab initio* stream, studying in Australia. These students had completed 1 year of study of French, beginning at tertiary level. In addition, a follow-up study was conducted a year later with an inevitably reduced number of students (six). In Australia, French is typically studied as a foreign language and students have little or no contact with French language and culture outside of the classroom. In particular, students have very little opportunity for interacting with native speakers (NSs) of French other than their teachers.

Procedure

This study is based on three samplings of students' performance in a role-play task based on the question *"T'as passé un bon week-end?"* The role-plays were performed by dyads of students and were videotaped. The videos were then transcribed noting both verbal and nonverbal elements in the interaction. Data were collected in order to assess students' performance on this task prior to instruction, immediately after instruction (at the completion of week 10 of the module), and approximately 1 year after having completed instruction. The data, therefore, allowed for an overview of the starting point for learning and the impact of teaching, but also for retention. The question of retention was of interest because these students had not received additional instruction in an intercultural framework after the completion of the module they undertook in their second year of study. Role-plays were chosen for data collection because they enabled a corpus of reasonably comparable spoken language texts to be collected from the participants. Although such role-plays are not ideal for the study of interaction (cf. Liddicoat, 1997a), collecting spontaneous data for such a project would have been impossible. In the foreign language context in which these data were collected, the students did not interact spontaneously in French outside the classroom. The context for the use of French, then, was pedagogical and, within this context, open role-plays that specified the initial situation but did not prescribe conversational outcomes (Kasper & Dahl, 1991) had been used both as practice activities and as assessment tasks and were often videotaped. Thus, the role-plays were representative of the ways in which these students used French. The role-play dialogues varied considerably in content but at the same time provided data suitable for comparison.

Case study: Did you have a good weekend?

The cultural context

The starting point for this investigation was a unit of teaching which focused on the question *"T'as passé un bon week-end?"* This question was chosen because previous research (Béal, 1992) had demonstrated that it presented substantial crosscultural difficulties between speakers of French and speakers of Australian English. The issue here is not so much a question and its particular answer, but rather the cultural and interactional role of "identical" sequences of talk in two languages. Different roles between languages lead to different uses of language. Béal's study showed that even highly proficient users of language, with in-country experience, had not acquired the discourse style and content differences found in their second language and the lack of such acquisition was a significant cause of intercultural communication breakdown.

Béal has described two very different patterns of conversation with quite different norms for content, sequencing, and interactional style. When Australian and French people interact, these differences lead to frustration for the participants. Béal demonstrates that the differences between the two speech communities are not random, but rather are based on cultural understandings of the question "Did you have a good weekend?" and its purpose in the interaction. In Australian English, this question is generally initiates a ritualistic exchange which forms a part of a greeting sequence on Mondays. It is a formulaic question, followed by formulaic answer, and is typically reciprocated. For example:

Extract 1 (from Béal, 1992, p. 28)

1 Woman: Did you have a pleasant weekend?
2   Man: I did. What about you?
3 Woman: I did too.
4   Man: What did *you* do?
5 Woman: We went to a birthday dinner on Saturday and a barbecue on Sunday.
6   Man: Food food food . . .
7 Woman: Yes, we ate our way through most of the weekend.

This sequence is very simple in its structure. The response indicates something generally positive about the weekend, without going into too much detail. The sequence is potentially finished at line 3, and many exchanges about the weekend in Australian conversations end at this point. These sequences are extended only if they are followed by additional questions, such as that in line 4, and, as Béal notes, the further talk is usually made up of brief descriptions of predictable types of weekend activities rather than specific details of particular weekend events. The usual form of the "Did you have a good weekend?" question in Australian English is that of a greeting ritual and the talk found in such sequences very closely reflects the "How are you?" sequence also found in English-language openings (Schegloff, 1968, 1986). In the French cultural context, however, the question is not ritualized. The question functions to initiate a topic and the expectation is that talk on the topic will be generated by the question. The resulting talk is quite long.

Extract 2 (from Béal, 1992, pp. 32–35)

```
 1  Woman:  Le weekend a été bon?
 2    Man:  Très bon, très bon. ((under his breath)): très bon... On a fait
            du train.
 3     W:   Du train?
 4     M:   Du petit train à vapeur, qui se ballade
            [Dans les Dandenongs
 5     W:   [Ah, dans les Dandenongs, oui c'est sympa ça!
 6     M:   Une bonne partie de... le retour on s'est retrouvé entre deux
            wagons, sur le marche-pied ((short laugh)).
 7     W:   Tellement y avait de monde?
 8     M:   Tellement y avait de monde.
 9     W:   Mais c'est fou! [le dimanche soir?
10     M:   [?????????????
11     W:   Parce que c'était dimanche soir?
12     M:   Mmm
13     W:   ((short laugh.)) A l'extérieur, en rappel?
14     M:   Oui, oui! Ça... y a la plate-forme entre les deux wagons, on...
15     W:   /Oh ben, Marc ((his son)) a dû adorer ça!
16     M:   Oui, sauf que... il avait des charmilles dans les yeux alors i(l)
            i(l) voit i(l) voyait plus
17     W:   Ah oui alors là c'est moins bon... [:] Bien bien...
18     M:   Et vous ça (a) été bien?
19     W:   Oui, assez calme... Nous avons été au cinéma hier après-midi,
20     M:   /Oui, Denis ((= W's friend)) m'a dit.
21     W:   Voir un truc complètement dingue, mais en fait je crois qu'il
            faut le voir quand même. Mais j'irais pas deux fois, hein! [:]
            on était avec Robert ((colleague of both)).
22     M:   [Ah oui, Robert m'la dit
23     W:   [Melissa ((Robert's wife)) avait refusé de venir
24     M:   [Robert m'l'a dit qu'c'était...
25     W:   [Je crois qu'elle a bien fait! ((laugh))
26     M:   Il m'a présenté ça comme une version modifiée de
            'La Grande Bouffe'.
27     W:   Très modifiée... très modifiée... oui ((under her breath)):
            complètement dingue...
```

Translation (as literal as possible)

1 Woman: Was your weekend nice?
2 Man: Very nice, very nice. ((under his breath)): very nice . . .
          We took a ride on a train.
3 W: A train?
4 M: That little steam train, the one that snakes [through the
        Dandenongs
5 W: [Ah, in the *Dandenongs*! Yes! It's a lot of fun, that!
6 M: For quite a bit of the . . . on the way back, we ended up
        in between two carriages, on the stepladder! ((short laugh))
7 W: Because it was so crowded?
8 M: Because it was so crowded.
9 W: How crazy! [on Sunday afternoon?
10 M: [????????????
11 W: Because it was Sunday afternoon?
12 M: Mmm.
13 W: ((short laugh)). Right on the edge, virtually abseiling!
14 M: Yes yes! That . . . there's a platform between the carriages, we
15 W: /In that case, Marc ((his son)) must have loved it!
16 M: Yes, except he . . . he got coal dust in his eyes, so he . . . he
        couldn't see!
17 W: Ah yes, well then, talk about some fun! [:] Well well . . .
18 M: And what about you, was it good?
19 W: Yes, rather quiet . . . we went to the movies yesterday afternoon
20 M: /Yes Denis ((W's friend)) told me.
21 W: To see something really sick, but in fact, I think it was worth
        seeing all the same. But I wouldn't go again, that's for sure!
        We were with Robert ((colleague of both)).
22 M: [Ah yes, Robert told me
23 W: [Melissa, ((Robert's wife)) refused to come along
24 M: [Robert told me that it was
25 W: [I think she had the right impulse! ((laughs))
26 M: The way he told me, he said it was some variation on
        La Grande Bouffe.
27 W: Some variation, some variation indeed! Yes . . . ((under her
        breath)): really sick . . .

In Extract 2, the question leads to a long discussion, which breaks off
at the end of the transcription when M redirects the talk to another
coworker. The question is, therefore, not reciprocated. The discussion
is quite detailed and the contrast with the more ritualized Australian
version is very marked. The answer immediately following the question
is not simply a vague positive comment about the weekend, as in the
Australian example in Extract 1, but also immediately volunteers an
activity. In addition, the talk about the weekend is designed as specific
talk about a specific occasion between specific interlocutors. This is particularly apparent in the amount of contextual information included in
parentheses in the transcription. Béal summarizes the essential differences

TABLE 1. DIFFERENCES BETWEEN FRENCH AND ANGLO-AUSTRALIAN SPEAKERS
IN ANSWERING THE QUESTION "DID YOU HAVE A GOOD WEEKEND?"

Australian	*French*
Ask the question of everybody. It is a conversational routine for Australian people (on Monday mornings). The answer is generally short, friendly, and reciprocal.	You don't have to ask the question of everyone. It is not part of French conversational routine on Monday mornings.
Be positive without being enthusiastic.	If the question is asked, expect to receive a detailed answer.
Mention typical weekend activities.	Be sincere, give your opinion on what you did on the weekend. Describe your feelings, including negative ones.
Give facts rather than opinions.	Be entertaining or lively in your descriptions. Dramatize what you have done.
Say only what is useful and interesting for the hearer.	Show you know the people and places the other mentions. Talk about your family and friends.
Use a conversational style which shows care for the other: • Don't interrupt the person who is talking. • Listen attentively. Wait until the person who is talking stops speaking completely to say what you want to say.	Use a conversational style which shows you are interested in what the other is saying: • Repeat and add to what the person is saying. • Interrupt the person who is talking. • Overlap each other when talking.

as shown in Table 1. The impression one gains from these differences is that the typical French interaction which results from the question "Did you have a good weekend?" is longer, more developed, and more animated than its Australian equivalent.

In noting these differences, it needs to be emphasized that it is not impossible for the question "Did you have a good weekend?" to become a topic of conversation in Australian English, but this is not the default interactional practice. Topical talk at this point implies a marked departure from the expected course of action and changes the social interaction from a "greeting on Monday" to claiming a particular relationship between the participants. In most cases, the question "Did you have a good weekend?" does not emerge as a topic for talk unless it receives a second question about the weekend, such as "What did you do?" or even a repeating of the question itself. These second questions indicate a willingness on the part of the recipient to attend to a telling about the events of the weekend. Making a telling about the weekend a relevant next activity after the question "Did you have a good weekend?" requires negotiation in the Australian context. In the French context, however, a relevant next activity is not negotiated, for the question itself indicates a willingness to attend to the telling.

It is clear from Béal's (1992) study that the cultural norms and understandings which underpin this event often are not acquired, even by nonnative speakers who are highly competent in the language of their interlocutors. In the foreign language context, where there are fewer opportunities for exposure to the target language and its culture, such culturally specific behaviors are impossible to pick up from input. Therefore, we decided to determine whether such aspects of language-in-use could be taught in the classroom. Béal's study suggests that in the situation we are investigating, speakers who do not have access to the norms of the target language and culture negatively transfer the rules of their own culture. The situation, then, is one in which a ritual exists in one of the languages which does not have a counterpart in the other (cf. Kerbrat-Orecchioni, 1993). Whether a contribution is ritualized has implications for the ways in which the language is used. Ritualized and nonritualized utterances are treated differently in interaction.

The starting point, then, for this study was to investigate how students who had received instruction about the question "Did you have a good weekend?" as socially and culturally contextualized language use responded to this question. The resulting dialogues were definitely of the "Australian" type already discussed as Extract 3 shows.

Extract 3

1 Anne: *T'as passé un bon weekend,*
2 Beth: *Uhm pas grand-chose j'ai- je suis allée chez ma- mon Amie (   )*
         parce que c'était nécessaire.
3 Anne: *Ah bon?*
4 Beth: *Oui oui. et vous- et tu?*
5 Anne: *Uhm je vais à Questacom avec mes (.) mes petites sœurs. Nous*
         avons passé quatre heures.
6 Beth: *Oui h. [ah hah hah hah]*
7 Anne: *[hah hah hah hah] elles ont aimé beaucoup.*
8 Beth: *Oui c'est beaucoup à faire.*

Translation (as literal as possible)

1 A: Did you have a good weekend?
2 B: Uhm not a lot I- I went to m- my friend (   ) because it was necessary.
3 A: Really?
4 B: Yes yes. And you- and you?

TABLE 2. FEATURES OF PERFORMANCE IN ROLE-PLAYS WITHOUT INSTRUCTION

		Dyads									
		A		B		C		D		E	
		S1	S2	S3	S4	S5	S6	S7	S8	S9	S10
Content	question leads directly to talk on topic	✗	✗	✗	✗	✗	✗	✗	✗	✗	✗
	detail	✗	✗	✗	✗	✗	✗	✗	✗	✗	✗
	opinions/feelings	✗	✗	✗	✗	✗	✗	✗	✗	✗	✗
	lively/dramatic	✗	✗	✗	✗	✗	✗	✗	✗	✗	✗
	knowing	✗	✗	✗	✗	✗	✗	✗	✗	✗	✗
Form	feedback	✓	✗	✗	✗	✓	✗	✗	✓	✗	✗
	repetition	✗	✗	✗	✗	✗	✗	✗	✗	✗	✗
	overlap	✗	✗	✗	✗	✗	✗	✗	✗	?	✗

Note: ✓ = feature present, ✗ = feature absent, ? = ambiguous result

5 A: Uhm I go to Questacom with my (.) my little sisters. We spent
   four hours.
6 B: Yes h[ah hah hah hah]
7 A: [hah hah hah hah] they liked a lot.
8 B: Yes there's a lot to do.

In this extract it is clear that the sequences involved are simple formulaic utterances, although slightly more expanded than the example given in Extract 1. The structure is reciprocated and the talk does not generate extended talk on the topic. The answer *pas grand-chose* at line 2 echoes the very common formula "Not bad" found in this context in Australian English. The question-answer sequence is briefly expanded by the *ah bon?/oui oui* sequence and then moves immediately to a reciprocal question. These features were evident in all of the dialogues recorded. In all cases, the utterances were short, there was little elaboration, and the weekend was not pursued as a first conversational topic but rather as a prelude to the first topic.

If we examine these conversations in terms of Béal's (1992) description of French conversations, we can see that there is almost no similarity between the performance of students who had not received any teaching about the cultural context of "Did you have a good weekend?" and French NS behaviors (see Table 2). Table 2 reflects students' performance according to the main differences between French and Australian interactions presented in Table 1. These features have been divided into two broad groups: those relating to the content of talk and those relating to the form of talk. Of the content features, moving directly to topical talk is of central importance, because if the conversation does not move to topical talk, there may be no opportunities to deploy the other features which demonstrate engagement. The formal features included in Table 2 are those which Béal cites as important for displaying involvement in the talk. Most of the features can be considered examples of "high-involvement style" (Tannen, 1984a). Table 2 shows that the talk produced by the students does not have any of the content characteristics which would be expected in this speech event in the French cultural context, indicating that these students are operating with a different set of cultural norms. Some students did provide feedback topics, particularly assessments with a sequence-closing function (cf. Crozet & Liddicoat, 1998), as in Extract 4.

Extract 4

1 Debbie: *Et vous, =quest-ce que vous avez fait?*
2   Chris: *Et vous? Ma femme et moi, nous sommes restés à Canberra.*
         Nous u:hm (.)
3 Debbie: *Oh d'accord.*

Translation (as literal as possible)

1 Debbie: And you, =what did you do?
2   Chris: And you? My wife and I stayed in Canberra. We u:hm (.)
3 Debbie: Oh OK.

This extract represents the minimal form of the exchange consisting of a question-answer pair, followed by a sequence-closing third turn. This use reflects Australian sequential patterns. Although it appears that Chris may not have finished his contribution at this point, Debbie is orienting to Chris's turn as complete, as it would be according to Australian norms. Chris makes no further attempt to talk about his weekend beyond this turn, and the sequence is effectively closed by Debbie's *oh d'accord*.

Teaching approach

The following class activity describes the format which was used to teach the task we entitled "Did you have a good weekend?" The presentation in the next section is meant to represent one possible template for teaching cultural norms in a foreign language. The task "Did you have a good weekend?" was taught as part of a module on spoken language and culture which ran over a 13-week period. In this module, learners were taught norms of interaction in French as well as other features of spoken French. The activity described aimed at getting learners to understand and practice the different cultural norms French and Australian people use to answer the question "Did you have a good weekend?" It was also used as an example to show how negative stereotyping often stems from misunderstanding crosscultural differences in human communication. The activity was divided into four phases according to the methodology developed in Crozet (1996): awareness-raising phase, experimentation phase, production phase, and feedback phase.

Awareness-raising phase

STEP 1

Learners worked in pairs using the target language. They were asked to identify a short list of stereotypes they held, or noticed others holding, about French and/or Australian people. The teacher provided the new vocabulary. Learners typically identified negative stereotypes about the two cultures such as "French people speak too much, they are too personal" or "Australians are laid-back, too indirect." The teacher then suggested that stereotyping often stems from misunderstanding the different cultural norms speakers use in different countries to communicate with each other. As an illustration of this suggestion, the teacher proposed the study of the answer to the simple question "Did you have a good weekend?" in French and Anglo-Australian cultures.

STEP 2

The teacher asked the class to give examples of typical answers to the question "Did you have a good weekend?" in an Australian context; then the teacher and students worked out what the equivalent answers could be in French. The aim of this activity was to show learners that the answer to the question "Did you have a good weekend?" could not be so easily translated from one language to another without knowing the appropriate cultural norms speakers in the two cultures used in providing answers. Next the teacher read out to the class extracts from Béal's (1992) research in which both French people and Australians explain their frustrations with the different ways both cultures use to answer the question "Did you have a good weekend?" The first extract (from Béal, 1992, p. 206), in which an Australian comments on the French, was read in English, the learners' first language:

[A]nd they start giving other people's names, and I mean, we don't particularly want to know all these things and yes . . . they tend to do that. Yeah . . . they do that in . . . what could you say . . . 'How was your weekend?' you know normally you say, 'Oh good . . .', . . . wouldn't know who they're talking about, you know, they tend to do that sometimes, but, that's all right, I mean, you know, that's fine . . . They they'll probably go into a lot more detail and, you know, like tell you where they went, and how their kids liked it, what their wife thought about it, whereas . . . whereas you'll find with an Australian, even though they have got time . . . they still won't . . . you . . . they still won't come out with it all, you know, they'll just say 'Oh yes. We had a good time . . .' and perhaps they'll tell you where they went and that's it. Whereas the French, they'll tend to tell you what . . . er . . . what they had to eat, and it it was nice and, you know.

The second extract (from Béal, 1992, pp. 206–207), in which a French person comments on Australians, was read aloud in French:

Oui, ben oui, je me suis rendu compte que c'est vraiment des formules de politesse! (petit rire de dérision). A la limite si on vous pose la question, c'est qu'on veut vous dire 'Bonjour. Comment ça va?', en fait ils attendent pas la réponse. Si on pose cette question en français, c'est qu'on s'y intéresse, parce qu'autrement on dirait, 'Bonjour, comment ça va?' c'est tout. Bon, mais si effectivement on demande, 'Alors, vous avez passé un bon week-end?' Ça va... bon, ça encourage à dire: 'Qu'est-ce que tu as fait?'... alors que ici (en Australie), à la limite, non c'est bon, 'How was your weekend?' mais c'est bon, 'Bonjour, comment ça va?' et puis on écoute pas. Ou si, effectivement, si on développe, bon à la limite, ils en attendaient pas autant! (petit rire)... moi je suis resté toujours avec mon réflexe français, j'ai pas changé, si on me demande comment... comment était le week-end, je vais dire ce que j'ai fait pendant mon week-end.

Translation (as literal as possible)

Well, yeah, I realize that it's only about being polite (derisive laughter). To an extent, if someone asks you the question, it's because they want to say to you "Hi. How are you?"; in fact they are not waiting for an answer. If you ask this question in French, it's because you are interested, because otherwise you would say, "Hi, how are you?" that's all. Yeah, but if you actually ask, "So, did you have a good weekend?" It's going . . . well, it encourages one to say: "What did you do?" . . . whereas here (in Australia), to an extent, no well it's, "How was your weekend?" but well it's, "Hi, how are you?" and then they don't listen. Or else if actually, if you go on, well to an extent, they were not expecting that much! (short laughter) . . . I, I've kept my French habit, I have not changed, if someone asks me how . . . how was the weekend, I am going to say what I did on the weekend.

The aim of Step 2 was to make the problem of crosscultural communication a concrete issue. After the reading of the extracts, learners were asked to comment on their responses to them, their thoughts, and their feelings.

STEP 3

The teacher explained that for Australian people the answer to the question "Did you have a good weekend?" functions mostly as a conversational routine on Monday mornings, often as a way to make contact. The expected answer is short, friendly, and reciprocal. For French people, the answer to the same question is not part of the Monday morning first-contact strategy. It is a genuine question which requires a detailed answer. Learners were given the list of the six differing rules (see Table 1), which they read and discussed in pairs. The teacher also showed on a transparency a transcription of a typical French answer to the question "Did you have a good weekend?" as well as a transcription of a typical Australian answer. Both transcriptions were authentic data taken from Béal's (1992) research.

Experimentation phase

After having been presented with the different cultural norms used by French and Australians speakers to answer the question "Did you have a good weekend?" learners engaged in a multimedia task based on an unscripted videotaped conversation between two NSs of French. In this task learners had to reconstruct the correct sequence of a conversation in which NSs displayed norms of interaction appropriate to the context. They were also invited to recognize the norms of interaction which had been brought to their attention during the awareness-raising phase. The conversation had been cut into nine segments which were placed in a random order. The user of the task had to listen to each piece, understand the segment narrative, and then try to reconstruct the original conversation. The students submitted for assessment a short string of characters representing the order of the video segments for assessment.

Production phase

After the multimedia task, learners enacted role-plays of a conversation about a fictitious weekend using the appropriate French norms of interaction. Learners were reminded to integrate in their role-plays features of spoken grammar, familiar vocabulary, and French gestures where appropriate. The role-plays were performed in front of the whole class and filmed.

Feedback phase

During the production phase, the whole class watched the role-plays performed by the learners. After each role-play, a group discussion was held in which the class commented on the appropriateness of the performance in terms of norms of interactions, body language, and other features of spoken language which had been taught. The performers of the role-plays were also invited to comment on how they felt about "acting French." The discussions brought up questions such as: "Should we be speaking like the French?" or "What if we don't like the way the French talk about themselves?" The teacher at this point suggested that learners needed to distinguish between what they had to know to understand French culture and the behavior that could be expected of them in that culture. The discussion led to the understanding that learning to speak in a foreign language is not a matter of simply

TABLE 3. FEATURES OF PERFORMANCE IN POSTINSTRUCTION ROLE-PLAYS

		Dyads									
		A		B		C		D		E	
		S1	S2	S3	S4	S5	S6	S7	S8	S9	S10
Content	question leads directly to talk on topic	✓	✓	✓	✓	✓	✓	✓	✓	✓	✓
	detail	✓	✓	✓	✓	✓	✓	✓	✓	✓	✓
	opinions/feelings	✓	✓	?	✗	✓	✓	✓	✓	✗	✓
	lively/dramatic	✓	✓	✓	✓	?	✓	✓	✓	✓	?
	knowing	?	✗	✓	✓	✓	✓	?	✓	✓	✓
Form	feedback	✓	✓	✓	✓	✓	✓	✓	✓	✓	✓
	repetition	✗	✓	✓	✓	✗	✗	?	✓	✓	✓
	overlap	✗	✗	✓	✓	✗	✗	✗	✗	✗	?

Note: ✓ = feature present, ✗ = feature absent, ? = ambiguous result

adopting foreign norms of behavior, but about finding an acceptable accommodation between one's first culture and the target culture.

Results and discussion

Language use after instruction

The results of the role-plays conducted immediately after teaching evidenced some variability in the language use of the students. This can be seen in Table 3, which shows that students performed well in those aspects of language use which affected the direct content of the talk in which they were engaged; that is, they integrated into their talk elements which were consistent with a nonformulaic interpretation of the question. As such, we can argue that students in these dyads had developed an awareness of a system which was more like the cultural expectations of the target-language group than their own cultural group. These features can be seen in Extract 5.

Extract 5

1   Amy: *Eh salut Angela, salut. Le week-end a été bon?*
2   Angela: *Ah oui en fait le weekend a été vraiment fantastique=ma mère m'a rendu visite*
3   Amy: *oui ta mère. Est-ce que c'est ça j'ai pensé qu'elle était à Sydney en ce moment.*
4   Angela: *Oh non non elle est rentrée à minuit donc euh nous avons passé le week-end ensemble e[uh euh nous avons=*

```
5   Amy:    [bien
6   Angela: =euh vu deux films puis alors nous avons visité le musée
            des beaux arts.
7   Amy:    Oh là là quel jour.
8           (.)
9   Amy:    J'ai- j'ai été euh là aussi avec ma sœur elle éta[it-
10  Angela: [Oui oui
11  Amy:    Samedi matin.
12  Angela: Tu as été là samedi?
13  Amy:    Oui.
14  Angela: Quel dommage j'étais là dimanche.
            ((Continues for 68 more lines))
```

Translation (as literal as possible)

```
1   Amy:    Eh hi Angela, hi. The weekend was good?
2   Angela: Ah yes the weekend was really fantastic=my mother visited me
3   Amy:    Yes your mother. Is that it I thought she was in Sydney
            at the moment.
4   Angela: Oh no no she got back at midnight so euh we spent the week-
            end together e[uh euh we=
5   Amy:    [well
6   Angela: =euh saw two films then we visited the art gallery.
7   Amy:    Oh, my, what a day.
8           (.)
9   Amy:    I w- I was euh there too with my sister.  she wa[s-
10  Angela: [yes yes
11  Amy:    Saturday morning.
12  Angela: You were there Saturday?
13  Amy:    Yes.
14  Angela: What a pity I was there Sunday.
```

Extract 5 clearly differs from Extract 3 in length, and this difference stems primarily from the fact that the weekend has become the topic of talk in this conversation. As such, this conversation has moved away from the status of formulaic.

The only content-related dimension which was not observed in all of the data was the expression of opinions or feelings, the dimension of interaction perhaps most distant from typical Australian norms of interaction. In the standard ritual utterance in the Australian context, elements such as detail, liveliness, and displays of knowing the personal background of one's coparticipant are found, although they tend to be related to close social relationships. However, unsolicited expressions of opinion and, more commonly, feelings are not typical and mark a more abrupt departure from the Australian norm in this situation (Béal, 1992). It would appear that for the other three factors, the interactional task facing the Australian learner of French is to move behaviors associated with very close relationships into a wider social context, whereas with expressing opinions or feelings it is more a case of producing a new type of behavior in a context where this is not typically done. Nonetheless, the responses of participants in the role-plays indicated that, for the majority, introducing such behavior was not problematic.

As for those features of interaction which pertain to form, the results are more mixed. The use of feedback tokens was a feature of all interactions, and this would appear to be a consistent feature in the students' talk in French. Such tokens indicate an involvement of the recipient in the ongoing talk and indicate that interactants are actively constructing their recipiency (Crozet & Liddicoat, 1998).

Extract 6

1 Vera: *Ah non y'a y'a des euh menus spéciaux pour les enfants.*
2 Jane: *Ah.*
3 Vera: *Oui et moi j'ai mangé tout ce que je pouvais manger. Oh.*
4 Jane: *phh ça c'est une bonne idée.*
5 Vera: *Ouais.*
6 Jane: *Tout ce que tu pouvais manger,*
7 Vera: *Ouais.*
8 Jane: *C'est bien.*

Translation (as literal as possible)

1 Vera: Ah no, there are there are special menus for children.
2 Jane: Ah.
3 Vera: Yes and I ate everything I could eat. Oh.
4 Jane: phh that's a good idea.
5 Vera: Yeah.
6 Jane: Everything you could eat,
7 Vera: Yeah.
8 Jane: That's good.

In Extract 6, both Jane and Vera produce feedback tokens and, in fact, this whole sequence is based primarily on such responsive elements. At line 2, Jane produces a receipt token *ah* in response to Vera's telling about the special menus, indicating that the prior message has been heard and understood (cf. Crozet & Liddicoat, 1998). Then Vera continues with her telling at line 3, prompting a more elaborated evaluative response from Jane, which Vera accepts with *ouais*, again acknowledging hearing and understanding. At line 6, Jane produces a repetition which links back to Vera's prior telling, which again receives a feedback token *ouais*. Finally, the sequence which begins at line 2 is closed by Jane's assessment at line 8, with a clear demonstration of Jane's stance toward the talk under way.

Although feedback is used appropriately to show participation in all of the conversations, the range of tokens used is quite limited – in fact, Extract 6 is unusual in the degree of sophistication with which feedback is produced. The majority of tokens produced are acknowledgment tokens which demonstrate hearing and understanding a message, but do not take a stance toward the prior talk (Crozet & Liddicoat, 1998). There is very little in most of the role-plays which could be termed affiliation, indicating that participants in these interactions are not expressing a high level of involvement in the talk. This itself is interesting, given that speakers were instructed to produce lively, dramatic tellings of their weekends. In fact, Jane's acknowledgment token *ah* in line 2 could potentially be seen as a withholding of greater affiliation with the speaker and her current topic of talk (Crozet & Liddicoat, 1998). As such, although NSs are using feedback tokens in appropriate positions in their interactions, they are employing a restricted set of these and are deploying them in a socially restricted way.

Repetition, which is itself a form of feedback, is employed reasonably consistently by the participants in these dialogues. The types of repetitions used in the role-plays were of two basic kinds: simple repetition, and repetition with paradigmatic modification.

Extract 7

1 Janine: *Oh oui y'avait cinq cavaliers par équipe et chaque équipe*
  a dû participer dans les dix jeux.
2 Kay: *Les dix jeu:x.*
3 Janine: *On était là toute la journée.*

Translation (as literal as possible)

1 Janine: Oh yes there were five riders in a team and each team had to
  participate in ten games.
2 Kay: Ten ga:mes.
3 Janine: We were there all day.

In Extract 7, Kay produces a simple repetition, reproducing word for word a constituent of the prior talk. Almost all of the repetitions found in the corpus are of this type, usually consisting of two or three lexical items. In a very few cases, however, participants produced repetitions which involved appropriate substitution of elements such as first and second person pronouns, as in Extract 8.

Extract 8

1 Vera: *J'ai fait du pati[nage sur glace*
2 Jane: [*Oh t'as fait du patinage sur glace* [*oh*
3 Vera: [*oui j'ai- je suis tombé plus[ieurs fois*
4 Jane: [*oh (   ) oh là là*

Translation (as literal as possible)

1 Vera: I went ice sk[ating
2 Jane: [oh you went ice skating [oh
3 Vera: [yes I- I- fell sever[al times
4 Jane: [oh (   ) oh là là

In the first line of Extract 8, Vera produces the statement *J'ai fait du patinage sur glace* in the first person, which is repeated by Jane with the appropriate change of person as *Oh t'as fait du patinage sur glace*. This form of repetition would appear to be cognitively more complex in that rather than simple imitation of the incoming talk, it involves an operation on that talk. This complexity could explain the relative infrequency of these sorts of repetitions in the data. In one case, such a repetition would be appropriate but the repetition is reproduced without the appropriate changes, as in Extract 9, where the repetition of *j'ai pleuré* is not appropriate.

Extract 9

1 Fran: *...mais l'enterrement était bel ah j'ai pleuré j'ai pleuré.*
2 Gill: *Ah j'ai pleuré.*

Translation (as literal as possible)

1 Fran: . . . but the burial was beautiful ah I cried I cried.
2 Gill: Ah I cried.

Overlapping talk causes more problems for the participants, with many dyads having little or no overlapping talk. Cognitively, this is again a difficult task because it means moving from processing utterances to making predictions about the likely trajectory of the utterance so far, and monitoring and anticipating likely possible completions in the talk. Nonetheless, there were examples of overlapping talk in the data, although mostly of short duration. Repetition in overlap thus seems to be the most difficult element. Again, this would appear to be a question of cognitive difficulty, as the recipient needs to not only produce the utterance, but also predict the trajectory of the talk currently under way. The example in Extract 8, where Jane both completes an utterance and modifies it for appropriate person reference, therefore, represents a particularly complex linguistic action.

Language use 1 year after instruction

Table 4 shows that after a year, these learners produced content which was similar to that produced immediately after instruction, but features of form had changed and more closely resembled the language behavior found before instruction. The maintenance of the content in more French-like ways is quite interesting as it indicates that students were producing role-plays with reference to French cultural understandings of this speech event. It indicates that in these role-plays, the learners were no longer interpreting the question as a greeting ritual, but rather as a topically oriented question. As such, the instruction students received about the cultural context of the question "Did you have a good weekend?"

TABLE 4. FEATURES OF PERFORMANCE IN ROLE-PLAYS AFTER 1 YEAR

		Dyads					
		A		B		C	
		S1	S2	S3	S4	S5	S6
Content	question leads directly to talk on topic	✓	✓	✓	✓	✓	✓
	detail	✓	✓	✓	✓	✓	✓
	opinions/feelings	✓	✓	?	✗	✓	✓
	lively/dramatic	✓	✓	✓	✓	?	✓
	knowing	?	✗	✓	✓	✓	✓
Form	feedback	✓	✓	✓	✓	✓	✓
	repetition	✗	✗	✗	✗	✗	✗
	overlap	✗	✗	✗	✗	✗	✗

Note: ✓ = feature present, ✗ = feature absent, ? = ambiguous result

appears to have affected their perception of the nature of this question and assisted them in developing a new and continuing frame of reference for the talk. The shift back to preinstruction use of the formal elements in this talk may be explained in terms of a change of instruction in later study of French in which interactive features of language were no longer emphasized because of a focus on sentence and word-level phenomena.

Conclusion

This study has shown that interactional norms can be acquired even within the confines of a short-term program. After instruction which focused on the cultural role of two "equivalent" utterances in the first language and in the target language, students showed differences in the ways in which they constructed their talk. However, it does not appear that all elements of discourse were equally "learned" as the outcome of instruction. In particular, elements which related to content of talk appear to have been more easily learned and integrated into target language interaction than elements which are related to the language form. Perhaps these more macrolevel aspects of cultural variability are more amenable to instruction because the impact of noticing can be more readily integrated into talk. It could be argued that these cultural elements are more amenable to conscious control; that is, speakers have greater control over aspects of language use such as topic selection and information content than they do over aspects of language form. Formal aspects of language seem to be more conditioned by the development of automaticity, and some areas – such as affiliative overlap – may require high levels of proficiency to enable the necessary monitoring of talk to occur. This study has shown that consciousness-raising about conversational style and content can lead to changes in learners' language and that conversational style is amenable to teaching in a language classroom. Although the study has focused on a single speech event (the use of the question "Did you have a good weekend?"), the real issue here is the recognition that what may appear to be identical utterances in two languages may actually have very different pragmatic and cultural meanings, and that this in turn affects the way in which language is used in such events. Awareness of differences like these is critical for language learners, particularly in their interaction with NSs of the target language.

8 Inductive and deductive teaching of compliments and compliment responses

Kenneth R. Rose and Connie Ng Kwai-fun

Introduction

This chapter reports the results of a study on the effects of inductive and deductive approaches to instruction in pragmatics, with the target features being compliments and compliment responses. The literature on these speech acts – along with that on requests and apologies – is among the richest in crosscultural and interlanguage pragmatics, offering coverage of both pragmalinguistics and sociopragmatics. Compliments and compliment responses were also among the first speech acts to be targeted for empirically informed teaching of pragmatics (Holmes & Brown, 1987), as well as for the study of the effects of instruction in interlanguage pragmatics (Billmyer, 1990a, 1990b). The current study incorporates aspects of each of these lines of inquiry, but adds several elements, namely, the two instructional approaches and the foreign language context.

Background

We will not provide a detailed survey of the literature on the effects of instruction in pragmatics, or on issues such as explicit and implicit learning, both of which receive comprehensive coverage in Bardovi-Harlig (this volume) and Kasper (this volume). We will, however, discuss in brief some of the relevant literature on compliments and compliment responses, the effects of instruction in compliments and compliment responses, and inductive and deductive approaches to teaching.

Research on compliments is largely traced back to the work of Nessa Wolfson and Joan Manes (Wolfson & Manes, 1980; Manes & Wolfson, 1981; Wolfson, 1981a, 1981b, 1983, 1984, 1988, 1989a; Manes, 1983), which provided the first comprehensive description of the formulaicity

This study was made possible by a grant from the City University of Hong Kong (SRG 7000816), for which the authors express their thanks.

145

of compliments in American English. They found that a narrow range of syntactic formulas accounted for the majority of observed compliments, with, as Manes and Wolfson (1981) report, the overwhelming majority (97.2%) of their corpus of 686 naturally occurring compliments falling into one of the following nine syntactic formulas:

1. NP {is, looks} (really) ADJ (PP)
2. I (really) {like, love} NP
3. PRO is (really) (a) (ADJ) NP
4. You V (a) (really) ADJ NP
5. You V (NP) (really) ADV (PP)
6. You have (a) (really) ADJ NP
7. What (a) (ADJ) NP!
8. ADJ (NP)!
9. Isn't NP ADJ!

Although this rather restricted range of formulas came as a surprise to Manes and Wolfson, even more striking was the distribution: the top three syntactic formulas accounted for some 85% of all compliments, with the first formula weighing in at a hefty 53.6%. Later research supported these findings, and extended them to other varieties of English (e.g., Holmes, 1986). The nine syntactic formulas described by Manes and Wolfson provide a useful, if not comprehensive, overview of the pragmalinguistic resources available for complimenting in American English. The significance of this for language teaching has been amply noted in work by Holmes and Brown (1987). In fact, we can hardly imagine a more fitting example of what Thomas (1983) considers the potential for teaching pragmalinguistics as an extension of grammar – these nine syntactic formulas lend themselves very well to instruction as routine formulas which could easily be incorporated into language teaching materials as are other types of sentence patterns.

Compliment responses, beginning with the pioneering work of Pomerantz (1978, 1984) and continuing with researchers such as Herbert (1986, 1989), have also been the object of considerable research. An excellent study on compliments and compliment responses conducted by Miles (1994) provides a useful synthesis of existing categories for compliment responses which was the starting point for this study. These categories include acceptance (e.g., *Thanks*), agreement (e.g., *I like it, too*), disagreement (e.g., *No, it's not really that nice*), self-praise avoidance (e.g., *Anyone can do this*), return compliment (e.g., *You look good, too*), and comment history (e.g., *My mother gave it to me*). We return to compliment response categories later.

An interesting issue in compliment response research – as with any area of pragmatics – is that of potential differences across cultures. In the case of compliment responses, several studies which have found a preference for rejecting compliments in Chinese contexts are relevant for this study because this preference would appear to run counter to the prevailing view of the American preference of accepting compliments.[1] For example, in a study of the compliment responses of native speakers (NSs) of American English and NSs of Mandarin Chinese, Chen (1993) found an overwhelming preference for rejection for the latter (95.73%), while the former employed this option far less frequently (12.7%). And the putative preference for acceptance applies not only to Americans. In a study comparing the compliment responses of NSs of British English, NSs of Cantonese, and Cantonese-speaking learners of English, Loh (1993) found a similar (but less pronounced) trend to Chen, albeit with slightly different categories. She found that NSs Cantonese preferred nonacceptance of one sort or another more frequently than acceptance (59% versus 41%), which contrasted with both the NSs of English and the nonnative speakers (NNSs) of English as well, who preferred acceptance at 57% and 65%, respectively. Research on another "Asian" language – in this case Korean – has yielded similar findings: Yoon's (1991) study found distributions of what she called direct agreement versus indirect modesty strategies to be virtual mirror images for Americans and Koreans. However, we hasten to point out that more research is needed before any conclusions can be reached concerning cultural preferences for compliment responses, and not all existing studies have found a preference for rejection among "Asians." For example, in a study of compliments and compliment responses in Mandarin Chinese, Ye (1995) found a pattern for compliment responses more similar to that often found for Americans, with her participants opting to reject compliments only 13.5% of the time, preferring instead to accept or accept with amendment a total of 71.6% of the time. And in a cross-sectional study of the pragmatic development in English of primary school children in Hong Kong, Rose (2000) found that the Cantonese-speaking group from which baseline data were elicited preferred acceptance to rejection by a margin of 51.82% to 25.3%. It appears, then, that there is conflicting evidence on "Asian" preferences for compliment responses, with several studies indicating some degree of preference for compliment rejection. However, it is fair to say that the evidence for rejection as a preferred "Asian" compliment response strategy is far from unassailable.

The issue of consciousness in second language acquisition (SLA) has long been an area of attention and controversy, perhaps represented best by the polar opposites of certain elements of Krashen's (1982, 1985)

---

1 Both views, of course, could be accused of oversimplification and stereotyping – face-to-face interaction in any language is likely to yield a more complex range of responses than simple acceptance or rejection.

Monitor Model and Schmidt's (1990, 1992, 1993a, 1993b, 1994, 1995, 1998) Noticing Hypothesis. While acknowledging the centrality of this issue in much SLA research, we also note the view that two of the primary constructs invoked in this debate – namely, implicit and explicit learning – are perhaps not what they appear to be (see, e.g., Robinson, 1997). Given that we were not interested in addressing the issue of learning per se, but rather the effects of particular approaches to instruction, we thought it appropriate to characterize this study as such. We realize that this skirts the issue of the nature of learning, but we feel our approach is appropriate at this time. Having acknowledged the controversy over consciousness, however, we hasten to point out that the induction–deduction opposition is also not without its own problems. Although we later discuss in detail the instructional treatments employed in this study, we will take a moment to review Decoo's (1996) articulate and reasoned treatment of this topic. Decoo discusses at length the range of possibilities in the induction–deduction opposition, noting that, like any dichotomy, this opposition actually represents a continuum. Decoo elaborates five modalities on this continuum, from actual deduction to "subconscious" induction on unstructured material. The modalities relevant for the instructional treatments employed in this study are Decoo's (1996, p. 97) Modalities A and B, which he describes as follows:

Modality A – Actual deduction: The grammatical rule or pattern is explicitly stated at the beginning of the learning process and the students move into the applications of this (examples and exercises).

Modality B – Conscious induction as guided discovery: The students first encounter various examples, often sentences, sometimes embedded in a text. The 'conscious discovery' of the grammar is then directed by the teacher: on the basis of examples he [sic] normally asks a few key-questions and the students are led to discover and formulate the rule.

Although Decoo's descriptions of these modalities of induction and deduction clearly involve the teaching and learning of grammar, we can think of no reason why these principles cannot be applied to other areas of language teaching and learning such as pragmatics. We have, in fact, done precisely that in our study: Our deductive treatment is essentially an application of Decoo's Modality A, while the inductive treatment represents his Modality B (more on this later).

Research questions

As noted earlier, Billmyer (1990a, 1990b) was among the first to study the effects of instruction in compliments, finding that although there was an advantage for the instructed group, her participants were able to learn how to compliment in American English with or without instruction. Because they were students at an American university, it appears that Billmyer's learners benefited from the acquisition-rich ESL environment in which they lived, a feature which Kasper (this volume) notes appears to have been a key factor in a number of studies on the effects of instruction in pragmatics. An interesting question, then, is whether results similar to those obtained in SL environments would obtain in an FL context. Billmyer's study also represented only one instructional treatment, and so did not address the issue of differential effects for more than one type of instruction. With this in mind, the research questions for this study centered on the effects of inductive and deductive approaches to teaching pragmatics in an acquisition-poor context, namely:

Do learners benefit from instruction in compliments and compliment responses in a foreign language context?

Are there differential effects of instruction for inductive and deductive approaches to the teaching of compliments and compliment responses in a foreign language context?

Participants

All participants in this study were undergraduate students, participating as members of intact classes, making this a sample of convenience. The two treatment groups and the control group were first-year students in the Faculty of Business at the City University of Hong Kong. They thus share basic demographic characteristics, such as L1, age, and field of study. These groups completed all three of the data collection instruments: a self-assessment questionnaire (SAQ), a written discourse completion questionnaire (DCT), and a metapragmatic assessment questionnaire (MAQ), all of which are described in the next section. Baseline data for both English and Cantonese were also collected from additional participant groups. Participants for the English data were undergraduate students enrolled in first-year composition courses at the University of Illinois at Urbana-Champaign. Two separate intact classes completed two of the three data collection instruments, one completing the MAQ, the other completing the DCT. Another two groups of third-year undergraduates in the Faculty of Business at City University also completed the same two instruments in Cantonese, again with one group for each questionnaire. Table 1 shows the relevant characteristics of the various participant groups. As the table shows, the control group, the two treatment groups, and the two U.S. groups were comparable in terms of age, but the two Cantonese groups – being third-year students – were considerably older. Inasmuch as age affects choice of compliment

TABLE 1. GROUP DEMOGRAPHICS

	Group						
	Control	Deductive	Inductive	U.S. meta	Cant MA	U.S. DCT	Cant DCT
N	12	16	16	15	15	14	15
Female	8	10	8	8	5	7	7
Male	4	6	8	7	10	7	8
Mean age	19.58	19.75	19.38	19.43	21.73	18.93	22.13
SD	0.67	1.18	0.50	1.45	1.22	1.00	0.83

Note: Cant = Cantonese

and compliment response strategies, comparisons between the Cantonese groups and the other groups will have to be treated with caution. Perhaps more important, the gender ratio differs across groups as well. There is a relatively even mix of females and males in four of the seven groups (i.e., the inductive group, the two U.S. groups, and the Cantonese DCT group), but there are significantly more females in two groups (the control and deductive groups), and significantly more males in one (the Cantonese MA group). Research has indicated that gender is an important variable in the use of compliments and compliment responses, so the gender disparity across groups will have to be taken into consideration in interpreting results.

Data collection

As already noted, data were collected using three instruments: the SAQ, MAQ, and DCT. All three questionnaires incorporated the same eighteen compliment scenarios (see the Appendix for the scenarios). These scenarios were derived from a preliminary questionnaire administered to fifteen Cantonese-speaking, first-year undergraduate students in Hong Kong, none of whom were participants in the actual study. The preliminary questionnaire involved a type of exemplar generation (Groves, 1996; Ostrom & Gannon, 1996) in which participants were given a sheet of paper illustrating a compliment (in Cantonese) and asked to list the most recent compliments they had made, received, or witnessed. The sheet provided a numbered list of ten blanks to be completed. Participants were given the option of writing the actual utterance (e.g., *I like that dress*) or describing the scenario (e.g., *I told my friend that I liked her dress*). This procedure yielded a pool of scenarios for use in the three questionnaires. The eighteen scenarios which were included on the three questionnaires were selected based on the following principles: First, the most frequently recurring scenarios (or composites thereof) were chosen; second, scenarios incorporating a range of interlocutors from two contexts (family and school) were chosen; and third,

TABLE 2. QUESTIONNAIRE SCENARIO ATTRIBUTES

Item	Setting	Speaker, hearer	Compliment topic
1	Family	Student = brother	Appearance (new suit)
2	Family	Student < mother	Act (cooked meal)
3	School	Teacher > student	Character-ability (computers)
4	Family	Grandfather > student	Possession (new telephone)
5	School	Student > tutee	Appearance (look smart)
6	School	Student = classmate	Act (in-class speech)
7	School	Teacher > student	Act (term paper)
8	Family	Mother > student	Appearance (look smart)
9	School	Student > tutee	Possession (pencil case)
10	Family	Brother = student	Character-ability (good swimmer)
11	Family	Grandmother > student	Character-ability (play piano)
12	Family	Student < grandmother	Possession (new handbag)
13	School	Teacher > student	Possession (new backpack)
14	Family	Student = sister	Possession (new ring)
15	School	Classmate = student	Character-ability (good singer)
16	Family	Student < father	Appearance (look smart)
17	School	Student > tutee	Act (exam results)
18	School	Student = classmate	Appearance (new haircut)

a range of the most frequently occurring compliment topics based on work such as Manes and Wolfson was represented. Table 2 displays the attributes of the scenarios. As the table shows, there were eighteen scenarios on the questionnaires, with the two contexts of family and school evenly represented. In addition to the student as participant, there were a total of nine additional participants: grandmother, grandfather, mother, father, sister, brother, teacher, classmate, and tutee. Listed along with the participants for each scenario is a tentative indication of the status relations between the two. However, because the instruction in compliments and compliment responses was not to include any information on how the realization of these speech acts may be effected by contextual variables (in fact, little research has addressed this issue), we did not find it necessary to conduct metapragmatic assessment in scenario development to determine how participants viewed status relations in these scenarios, nor did we conduct analyses based on status. Instead, we focused simply on providing a range of contexts in which compliments might occur, which the preliminary questionnaire successfully provided. So although Table 2 does list status relationships for each of the scenarios, these were not validated through metapragmatic assessment and must be considered preliminary. An additional issue we needed to address was the use of English in Hong Kong – given the fact that English is used in very restricted domains by university students in Hong Kong (i.e., education and interaction with non-Chinese, see, e.g., Pennington, 1994), we had to either restrict the scenarios to those domains or create another context in which the scenarios were to take place. We chose the latter, setting the questionnaire scenarios in an English-speaking context, and instructed participants to indicate how they might behave in that context as international students. Although there are obvious problems with this approach, it does overcome for the moment the inherent difficulty of collecting data in a foreign language setting. We now address each of the three questionnaires.

The SAQ format as used in this study was developed by Hudson, Detmer, and Brown (1992, 1995) for the assessment of pragmatic proficiency. This questionnaire presents a number of scenarios involving potential language use, and requires participants to indicate what they believe to be the level of their ability to respond appropriately in those contexts. Essentially, then, the SAQ measures participants' level of self-confidence in their own pragmatic abilities. Given that instruction may have a facilitating or debilitating effect on confidence in language ability, we felt that the SAQ might serve as an interesting pretest/posttest indicator of self-confidence. We also would like to note that Hudson, Detmer, and Brown (1995) found, interestingly enough, that learners' self-ratings on their SAQ correlated highly with NS ratings of their speech-act performance, indicating that the SAQ might reasonably serve as a useful rough estimate of pragmatic proficiency, although certainly not as the basis of any high-stakes decisions. The SAQ was the first of the three questionnaires to be administered. Following are some sample items from the SAQ:

Situation 1: Alex (one of the sons) is a business major. He has an interview today for a part-time job with a large investment company, so he is wearing his best suit. You compliment him on his appearance.

Rating: I think what I would say in this situation would be

very   1 – 2 – 3 – 4 – 5   completely
unsatisfactory   appropriate

Situation 2: You have just finished having dinner at home that was prepared by Mrs. White (the mother). You compliment her on the meal.

Rating: I think what I would say in this situation would be

very   1 – 2 – 3 – 4 – 5   completely
unsatisfactory   appropriate

The MAQ presented the same eighteen scenarios as the SAQ, this time requiring participants to rank-order four possible responses from the most (1) to least (4) appropriate. The potential responses to each of the items represented the three major compliment response strategy categories, that is, acceptance, deflection, and rejection, with the possibility of opting out included as a fourth option. We realize that compliment response strategies are not mutually exclusive; that is, they can co-occur in any number of combinations (as we shall see later in the DCT data). However, for the many possible combinations of compliment response strategies to each be represented as items in a given scenario would produce an unwieldy questionnaire, to say the least. Although our approach is something of an oversimplification, it still produces useful information in terms of general preferences from among the main strategies available. Because the MAQ contains possible responses to compliments for each of the scenarios, it was administered last during both the pretest and the posttest phases – that is, after the DCT – in order to avoid potential instrument effects. Here are some sample items from the MAQ:

Situation 1: Alex (one of the sons) is a business major. He has an interview today for a part-time job with a large investment company, so he is wearing his best suit.

You: "Wow, Alex, you look really great."

Alex: _____   (a)   "Do you really think so?"
               _____   (b)   No response
               _____   (c)   "Thanks – I have a big interview today."
               _____   (d)   "My mother helped me pick out this suit."

Situation 2: You have just finished having dinner at home that was prepared by Mrs. White (the mother).

You: "That was really delicious, Mrs. White."

Mrs. White: _____   (a)   No response
                 _____   (b)   "I thought that the chicken was too dry."
                 _____   (c)   "Thanks – I'm glad you liked it."
                 _____   (d)   "Sue helped quite a bit, you know."

The DCT used in this study also incorporated the same eighteen scenarios that appeared on the SAQ and MAQ, and was modeled essentially on the ubiquitous discourse-completion-task (DCT) format (see, e.g., Blum-Kulka, House, & Kasper, 1989), with one exception: Although the majority of written elicitation tasks require participants to provide one turn, the one used in this study required participants to provide both the compliment and the compliment response for each of the scenarios. Following are sample items from the DCT:

Situation 1: Alex (one of the sons) is a business major. He has an interview today for a part-time job with a large investment company, so he is wearing his best suit. What would you say to compliment him on his appearance? How do you think he would respond?

You: _____
          _____
          _____

Alex: _____

_____

_____

Situation 2: You have just finished having dinner at home that was prepared by Mrs. White (the mother). What would you say to compliment her on the meal? How do you think she would respond?

You: _____

_____

_____

Mrs. White: _____

_____

_____

For the pretest, each of the instruments was administered at 1-week intervals prior to the beginning of instruction (weeks 2, 3, and 4 of the semester); for the posttest, plans were made to follow the same procedure as in the pretest (i.e., administer the questionnaires at 1-week intervals), but because of a high degree of absenteeism, it became necessary to postpone administration of all three questionnaires to be completed in one sitting 4 weeks after instructional treatment had been completed (week 14 of the semester). This was obviously not ideal, but there was nothing that could be done to prevent it. A delayed posttest was initially planned, but had to be abandoned because the students were no longer in intact classes during the semester following the treatment period, thus making it impossible to administer the questionnaires a final time in any controlled fashion.

The fact that all three instruments used in this study were written questionnaires merits some discussion. As in much classroom-based research – in pragmatics as well as other areas of second language acquisition – it is often not feasible to measure instructional effects other than through the use of written questionnaires (or other instruments) designed for that purpose. Although in some cases it may be possible to observe learners interacting in the target language (as was the case with Billmyer, 1990a, 1990b), a foreign language context generally does not afford such possibilities. Use of written instruments, then, appears to be inevitable. We would like to make clear, however, that we are fully aware of the limitations of questionnaires, particularly regarding the sort of information they yield. It is crucial to understand that questionnaires are indirect measures – that is, the data resulting from responses to questionnaires are not the result of direct observation, but instead are mediated, most obviously by respondents but also by a host of other potential variables. Furthermore, because of the impossibility of fully specifying all of the relevant contextual information present in the real world, questionnaires are subject to at least some level of reductionism. At best they offer underspecified (and static) coverage of social contexts, and so must be viewed as lacking in this regard. It must also be recognized that questionnaires are inherently artificial. As Babbie (1998, p. 274) points out, questionnaires "cannot measure social action; they can only collect self-reports of recalled past action or of prospective or hypothetical action." We cannot emphasize too much the importance of this point, particularly given the fact that pragmaticians have often appealed to the questionnaires they use as measures of linguistic action. For example, many researchers using DCTs have worked under the (often implicit) assumption that the data they yield are (or can be) representative of what people actually say or do in face-to-face interaction, just as those who have criticized discourse completion as a viable data collection procedure have done so on the assertion that it is not representative of actual language use. Both the advocates and critics of DCTs miss the point entirely. Questionnaires do not directly measure social (or linguistic) action, so they can neither be expected to do so nor criticized for not doing so. The questionnaires used in this study, then, do not provide information concerning how any of the participants (NSs included) would actually use or respond to compliments in face-to-face interaction, but they can provide information on their knowledge and attitudes regarding the use of compliments and compliment responses, and as such can be used as a measure of changes in knowledge and attitudes that might be the result of instruction.

Treatments

Three intact classes took part in this study, each of which was randomly assigned to two experimental groups and one control group. The control group received no treatment, but completed all three questionnaires during the same time periods as the experimental groups. Each experimental group received instruction in compliments and compliment responses that consisted of six lessons lasting for approximately 30 minutes each. Instruction began in week 5 of the semester, and continued through week 10. Content for both instructed groups was identical, and was based on findings from the literature on compliments and compliment responses. The topics for each of the six lessons were as follows: Cantonese compliments; Cantonese compliment responses; English compliments 1; English compliments 2; English compliment responses; and comparing Cantonese and English compliments and compliment responses. All instruction was carried out by the second coauthor, who also taught the main course.

The rationale for beginning first with L1 pragmatics is discussed in Rose (1994b), who argues that such an approach makes pragmatic concepts more accessible to learners. The instruction included film segments containing compliment exchanges drawn from a corpus of film speech acts compiled by Rose (1997), who notes that film is capable of providing both the target language for detailed discussion and analysis, and the rich contextual detail useful for such analyses. Both groups followed essentially the same procedure, with one exception. The inductive group (Decoo's Modality B) was not provided with any metapragmatic information, but rather was exposed only to the film segments and additional examples, and provided with questions to guide their own discovery of pragmatic patterns or generalizations. The deductive group, on the other hand, was provided with metapragmatic information prior to carrying out analyses of compliment and compliment response data. So, for example, during the first lesson on English compliments, the deductive group viewed a brief film segment to introduce the topic and then received a handout and brief lecture on Manes and Wolfson's nine syntactic formulas *before* completing a worksheet requiring them to identify the syntactic formula of additional compliments taken from the film corpus and construct compliments of their own using the various formulas. The inductive group also watched the film segment, but was required to complete a worksheet on the form of English compliments without the benefit of the explicit pragmalinguistic information supplied to the deductive group. For the inductive group, brief posttask summary discussions were held, but the instructor did not provide explicit pragmatic information at this (or any other) time. All lessons were audiotaped, and these audiotapes were reviewed for the purpose of verifying that the instructional treatment was provided as intended.

Results

Self-assessment

Table 3 displays the pretest and posttest results of the SAQ for the Cantonese-English groups, the only three groups to complete the SAQ. Participants were asked to rate their ability to respond appropriately in a given scenario on a scale of 1 to 5, with 1 being the lowest and 5 the highest. There were eighteen items, producing a maximum score of ninety points. As the table shows, the pretest scores indicate a rather high degree of confidence in the ability to use English appropriately: Group averages range from a low of 57.56 for the inductive group to a high of 66.08 for the control group, which is equivalent to from 3.19 to 3.67 on a 5-point scale. One-way ANOVA results indicate that these scores were significantly different ($F = 4.727$, $df = 2$, $p = .014$), with post hoc tests showing, as expected, that the difference can be accounted for by the disparity in the scores of the control and inductive groups. There

TABLE 3. SAQ PRETEST AND POSTTEST SCORES BY GROUP (MAX = 90)

		Control	Deductive	Inductive
		Group		
Pretest	Mean	66.08	60.06	57.56
	SD	9.45	6.03	6.78
Posttest	Mean	64.00	63.56	60.06
	SD	7.20	7.30	10.75

is considerably more variation in the control group on the pretest, while the variation is roughly equivalent for the two treatment groups. On the posttest, the control group continued to rate their ability higher than the treatment groups, but their self-ratings decreased by 2.08 points as the treatment groups' self-ratings increased, with the greatest gain (3.50 points) made by the deductive group. Although it might appear that the instruction had a positive impact on the self-confidence of the treatment groups, the results are merely suggestive: Repeated-measures, one-way ANOVA examining both within and between-subjects effects indicated that there were no significant within-subjects effects, that is, no significant pretest/posttest differences within each group. However, there was a significant group effect ($F = 3.854$, $df = 2$, $p = .029$), with post hoc analyses once again indicating that the group effect can be accounted for by the drop in the control group posttest scores and the rise in the inductive group posttest scores. The lack of within-subjects effects indicates that the group effect is more the result of this drop in the control group self-ratings and the slight rise in the ratings of the inductive group, not to any instructional effects. Essentially, the inductive group's pretest scores, which were significantly lower than those of the control group, had by the posttest come up to a comparable level.

Metapragmatic assessment

On the MAQ, participants were asked to rank-order four possible responses to a compliment given in a particular scenario, and these responses consisted of the three major compliment response strategies – accept, reject, and deflect – along with the option of saying nothing at all, that is, opting out. The data which this instrument yields can be analyzed in two ways. The first is to treat the MAQ essentially as a compliment-response test. Table 4 displays the results of the MAQ as test scores, with one point given for each correct response, yielding a maximum of eighteen points. An obvious issue here is just what counts as a "correct" response. One way to determine correctness is to simply consider the response of the majority of NSs the "correct" response,

TABLE 4. MAQ PRETEST AND POSTTEST SCORES BY GROUP (MAX = 18)

		Group			
		Control	*Deductive*	*Inductive*	*U.S.*
Pretest	Mean	13.92	12.25	11.94	17.47
	SD	4.81	3.26	4.43	0.92
Posttest	Mean	13.33	12.06	13.50	—
	SD	5.25	4.37	4.95	—

which is what was done here. While there are potential problems with this approach – namely, that it implies that acceptance is the correct compliment response in American English on all occasions and in all contexts – the fact that the U.S. group scored near perfect (17.47), with little variation (0.92), suggests that this approach is warranted for this data set. We do not mean to trivialize contextual variation in compliment responses, nor do we doubt that American compliment responses in face-to-face interaction are likely to be more complex than simple acceptance implies; rather, we would argue that such results point to the possibility that acceptance may be some sort of idealized norm for compliment responses in American English.[2] Looking at the pretest scores, we again see that scores are relatively high, ranging from 11.94 for the inductive group to 13.92 for the control group, which represents from 66.33% to 77.33%. We also see that, as with the SAQ, there is an advantage for the control group, with the inductive group once again pulling up the rear. Unlike the MAQ pretest scores, however, one-way ANOVA results indicate that these differences are not significant. The variation is fairly uniform across groups, and is considerably higher than that for the U.S. group, indicating that there was far less agreement among the Cant-En groups concerning the appropriate response to compliments in these scenarios. Table 4 also reveals that the posttest scores for both the control and the deductive groups dropped slightly, while those of the inductive group increased marginally. This slight advantage for the inductive group on the MAQ is once again merely suggestive: Results of a repeated-measures, one-way ANOVA examining differences both within and between subjects were not significant.

2 We would like to make clear that we are not arguing that second or foreign language learners be forced to adopt NS norms (of whatever variety). It is our position that learners be made aware of the pragmalinguistics resources available and the likely sociopragmatic consequences of each so that they can then make their own informed choices (for more on this, see Rose, 1994b, 1999). In the context of this study, the instructional treatment was based on data from studies on American English, so we would argue that using that variety as a point of comparison is an appropriate means of assessing the effects of instruction.

TABLE 5. MAQ PRETEST RANKINGS BY GROUP (FOUR-POINT SCALE)

		Group				
		Control	*Deductive*	*Inductive*	*U.S.*	*Cant*
Accept	Mean	1.37	1.43	1.47	1.03	1.79
	SD	0.46	0.31	0.38	0.05	0.45
Deflect	Mean	2.15	2.18	2.23	2.34	2.24
	SD	0.23	0.23	0.22	0.33	0.31
Reject	Mean	2.72	2.54	2.47	2.89	2.25
	SD	0.24	0.37	0.28	0.18	0.38
No response	Mean	3.76	3.85	3.83	3.73	3.72
	SD	0.35	0.24	0.22	0.49	0.48

The second way to analyze the MAQ data is to examine the actual rankings of the four options across groups, and how these may have changed over time. Table 5 displays the mean rankings of the four compliment response strategies on the pretest for the three Cant-En groups, as well as the rankings for the U.S. group and the Cantonese group, who completed the MAQ once. In this case, a lower score reflects a more-preferred strategy, with the most-preferred strategy receiving a score of 1 and the least-preferred strategy receiving a score of 4. What is immediately apparent from the pretest scores displayed in Table 5 is that although exact rankings of the compliment response strategy preference differ across groups, the rank order of the strategies is identical across all five groups, with acceptance being ranked first, followed by deflection, then rejection, with opting out last. Examining the average rankings for each strategy reveals some interesting similarities and differences. Acceptance is ranked highest by the U.S. group, next by the Cant-En groups, and lowest by the Cantonese group – but still the preferred strategy overall – forming a rather obvious cline. The gap between deflection and rejection is similar for the U.S. and Cant-En groups, but much closer for the Cantonese group. Opting out receives similar low rankings across groups. It is also worth noting that the variation is not uniform across groups – the significantly lower standard deviation in acceptance for the U.S. groups indicates a higher level of agreement than was found for the other groups. The situation is similar, but less pronounced, for rejection. Turning to the Cant-En posttest scores, which are displayed in Table 6, we see that differences across groups between the pretest and posttest were marginal. As might be expected, a repeated-measures MANOVA examining both within and between-subjects effects for the four strategies did not produce significant results.

TABLE 6. MAQ POSTTEST RANKINGS BY GROUP (FOUR-POINT SCALE)

		Group		
		Control	*Deductive*	*Inductive*
Accept	Mean	1.36	1.44	1.36
	SD	0.43	0.39	0.42
Deflect	Mean	2.05	2.07	2.16
	SD	0.35	0.28	0.22
Reject	Mean	2.66	2.63	2.57
	SD	0.39	0.40	0.45
No response	Mean	3.93	3.85	3.92
	SD	0.11	0.27	0.13

Discourse completion

We now consider the results from the DCT, which consisted of a series of open questions in which participants were asked to supply compliments and compliment responses for the same eighteen scenarios that appeared on the SAQ and MAQ. We remind readers that although we are discussing the DCT last, it was in fact administered second – after the SAQ – so as to minimize the instrument effects from the MAQ, which provided potential compliment responses as items for each scenario and so was administered last. Both the SAQ and the MAQ consist of closed questions which produce easily quantifiable data without the need for subjective coding. Such data are more amenable to statistical analysis than data resulting from open questions, which require subjective coding, thus making the process of analysis more complex. The difficulty associated with the use of open questions is a much-discussed issue in the survey research literature, and there is often a considerable amount of skepticism expressed concerning their value. Although we will not review this literature here (but see Kasper & Rose, in press), we will recount the position of Fowler (1993, pp. 56–57), who argues that

> with no interviewer present to probe incomplete answers for clarity and for meeting consistent question objectives, the answers [to open questions] will not be comparable across respondents, and they will be difficult to code. If such answers are useful at all, it usually is when they are treated as anecdotal material, not as measures.

We believe that this is perhaps an extreme view, but we are in complete agreement concerning the use of answers to open questions as measures: This should be done with caution, if at all. And although we believe that answers to open questions are perhaps above the level of anecdote, we hasten to add that coding of responses to open questions must be rigorous and consistent, and that any statistical analyses conducted with such data must be carefully considered. We will address each of these issues as we discuss the DCT results.

As Fowler points out, open questions are difficult to code. For the analysis of the English DCT responses in this study, all data were coded independently by both coauthors using the following procedure: A subset of both compliments and compliment responses from each of the four groups completing the English DCT was coded independently, and interrater correlations were obtained. Initial values for interrater reliability were less than ideal ($r < .75$), so this process was completed three times with different subsets of responses each time until an acceptable level of agreement was reached ($r > .90$). Once this threshold was reached, all data were then coded independently, and interrater correlations were again high ($r > .90$). The final step in the process was to eliminate the remaining coding discrepancies. This was done on an item-by-item basis through consensus coding. Although this procedure does not eliminate the difficulties of coding open questions – rather, it is perhaps a good illustration of the time-consuming and laborious process involved in the subjective coding of open questions – it does go a long way toward ensuring a more reliable result. However, this by no means removes the messiness associated with such data produced by open questions once they have been coded, which will become more clear as we proceed.

The coding schemes applied in the initial analysis of the DCT data were based on the compliments and compliment response literature discussed earlier. We will briefly review these now. For compliments, Manes and Wolfson's nine syntactic formulas formed the core of the scheme. We found it necessary to add the following four compliment categories: question (e.g., *Where did you buy that phone?*), encourage (e.g., *Keep up the good work*), noncompliment (e.g., *You seem to have an important meeting today*), and opt out. Altogether, then, the coding scheme for compliments consisted of a total of thirteen categories. For compliment responses, the data were coded according to the six categories used in Miles (1994) – acceptance (e.g., *Thanks*), agreement (e.g., *I like it, too*), disagreement (*No, it's not really that nice*), self-praise avoidance (e.g., *Anyone can do this*), return compliment (e.g., *You look good, too*), and comment history (e.g., *My mother gave it to me*) – with the addition of the following five categories: make offer (e.g., *You can have it if you like*), continued effort (e.g., *I will keep doing my best*), answer question (e.g., *I bought it last week*), nonverbal response (e.g., a participant indicating in writing that he or she would simply smile in response), other (e.g., *You're welcome*), and opt out. Thus, there were a total of twelve compliment response categories.

As already noted, the type of data produced through the use of open questions differs in nature from that produced by closed questions. The data produced by the DCT in this study are a good illustration of just how complex responses to open questions can be, and the steps that can be necessary to make some sense of them. One particular problem with the speech acts examined in this study is that they often consist of multiple responses; that is, for both compliments and compliment responses more than one strategy can be used in answer to a particular question. This results in a rather dizzying array of possible combinations, many of which did occur. Thus, although approximately 65% of compliments consisted of a single occurrence of one of the Manes and Wolfson's top three syntactic formulas, most of the remaining compliments involved the use of one of the nine syntactic formulas plus another strategy, yielding more than forty unique combinations of the twelve compliment strategies. For compliment responses, the situation was much the same: Approximately 75% of responses consisted of single occurrences of one compliment response strategy, but there were again an additional forty or so unique combinations of strategies which comprised the remaining responses. Many of these combinations occurred infrequently (in fact, many occurred only once), thus presenting problems for statistical analyses as well – as is generally the case with the analysis of categorical data, categories which yield small numbers pose the problem of empty cells, which threatens to invalidate the statistical procedures used (see Rose & Ono, 1995, for further discussion of the analysis of categorical data produced by DCTs). Clearly, some degree of data reduction was necessary to help make sense of these responses, which we undertook. The resulting categories will be discussed later as the results for each speech act are presented. Before moving on to these results, however, we first will address the issue of research design and statistical analysis.

The design for this study, as noted earlier, is a mixed design, that is, one which examines potential changes within subjects over time, as well as across groups of subjects receiving different treatments. The examination of changes over time necessitates the use of repeated measures, and with that the associated statistical procedures. A design of this sort is fairly common in SLA research, but studies which utilize mixed designs generally involve interval data, which permits the use of tests such as repeated-measures (M)ANOVA, as illustrated with the SAQ and MAQ in this study. However, mixed-design studies in SLA which make use of categorical variables are not so common. In fact, in discussing mixed designs, Hatch and Lazaraton (1991, p. 518) note their complexity and point out that they "were unable to find examples of repeated-measures categorical modeling in the applied linguistics literature." The use of a repeated-measures mixed design with categorical data

TABLE 7. DCT PRETEST COMPLIMENTS BY GROUP

		Group		
		Control (%)	Deductive (%)	Inductive (%)
Strategy	Manes and Wolfson 1–3	37.96	43.75	38.19
	Manes and Wolfson 4–9	22.69	14.24	15.63
	Other compliments	05.56	11.11	8.33
	(Formula +) Q	21.30	15.63	25.00
	Formula + x	7.41	9.03	8.68
	Other	5.09	6.25	4.17
	Total	N = 216	N = 288	N = 288
	$\chi^2 = 19.481$	p = .035		

generally calls for log linear, categorical modeling, which represents a substantial investment in time and resources – particularly for the sort of multiple-response data produced by the DCT in this study – and is so complex and so rarely used that there is generally not a procedure for it in the standard, commercially available statistical software packages such as SPSS or SAS. An analysis of categorical data that is both multiple response and repeated measures would require programming designed specifically for this analysis – a costly and time-consuming proposition. Given the fact that the results for the MAQ and SAQ did not reveal any instructional effects, and that the conditions for pretest/posttest comparison were less than ideal because of the unexpected significant differences on the pretests across groups, we felt it best not to pursue the most powerful procedure and rely instead on less powerful statistical analyses (discussed later in this section). This is clearly a problem that will require more attention in future research, and ours is an interim solution, but one which we would argue is appropriate in this case. We now discuss the DCT findings.

Starting first with compliments, Table 7 displays the results for the pretest using the reduced categories alluded to above. The original thirteen coding categories for compliments, which yielded more than forty unique combinations of compliment strategies, were reduced to the six categories which appear in Table 7. These consist of two groupings of the Manes and Wolfson syntactic formulas (formulas 1–3, and 4–9), two categories which combined one of these formulas with either a question or some other element, a category for compliments which did not conform to Manes and Wolfson's nine formulas, and a category for noncompliments. As the table shows, results of a chi-square analysis indicated that the distribution of compliment strategies on the pretest is not independent of group; that is, there were significant differences

TABLE 8. DCT POSTTEST COMPLIMENTS BY GROUP

		Group		
		Control (%)	Deductive (%)	Inductive (%)
Strategy	Manes and Wolfson 1–3	43.52	52.08	42.36
	Manes and Wolfson 4–9	12.50	21.18	27.78
	Other compliments	11.57	9.03	9.72
	(Formula +) Q	20.83	9.38	12.85
	Formula + x	7.41	4.86	2.08
	Other	4.17	3.47	5.21
	Total	N = 216	N = 288	N = 288
	$\chi^2 = 38.694$	p = .000		

in strategy choice according to group, which means that, as with the MAQ and SAQ, there were pretest differences which would complicate any pretest/posttest comparisons. And it appears that once again the inductive group lags a bit behind, this time in terms of their use of Manes and Wolfson's nine formulas. If we add the first two categories to derive the overall frequency of Manes and Wolfson's nine formulas, we find 60.65% for the control group, 57.99% for the deductive group, and 53.82% for the inductive group. The inductive group also makes greatest use of the (Formula +) Q strategy (25%). We note that all three groups fall short of Manes and Wolfson's distribution discussed earlier, that is, 97.2% of all compliments utilizing the nine formulas, with the top three accounting for 85%. Moving to the results for the posttest, which appear in Table 8, it appears that the control group's choice of strategy has changed little, with an actual decrease of 4.63% in the use of Manes and Wolfson's formulas. On the other hand, the treatment groups evidence a marked increase in the use of the formulas, with the greatest gain going to the inductive group (16.32% versus 15.27%), although the deductive group is highest overall. The totals for the nine formulas on the posttest are 56.02% for the control group, 73.26% for the deductive group, and 70.14% for the inductive group. As the table shows, results of a chi-square analysis indicated that once again choice of strategy is not independent of group, and this time the chi-square value was considerably larger. It would appear, then, that the instructional treatment targeted at familiarizing learners with the nine compliment formulas – that is, the pragmalinguistic aspect of compliments – did have an impact, and that impact was roughly the same for both treatment groups. This could indicate, then, that for the purposes of teaching pragmalinguistics, there is not much to distinguish deductive from inductive approaches. It is also worth noting that the posttest distribu-

TABLE 9. DCT TREATMENT GROUP POSTTEST AND U.S. COMPLIMENTS BY GROUP

		Group		
		Control (%)	Deductive (%)	U.S. (%)
Strategy	Manes and Wolfson 1–3	52.08	42.36	47.20
	Manes and Wolfson 4–9	21.18	27.78	23.80
	Other compliments	9.03	9.72	4.80
	(Formula +) Q	9.38	12.85	19.40
	Formula + x	4.86	2.08	3.60
	Other	3.47	5.21	1.20
	Total	N = 288	N = 288	N = 252

TABLE 10. DCT PRETEST COMPLIMENT RESPONSES BY GROUP

		Group		
		Control (%)	Deductive (%)	Inductive (%)
Strategy	Accept	58.33	69.44	59.38
	Reject/deflect	15.74	8.33	11.46
	Accept/reject	11.11	1076	16.67
	Answer	6.94	7.64	9.72
	Other	7.87	3.82	2.78
	Total	N = 216	N = 288	N = 288
	X^2 = 22.728	p = .004		

tion of compliment strategies for the treatment groups resembles more closely that of the U.S. group, as can be seen in Table 9. Given the rather elementary statistical analyses used here, however, these results must be considered preliminary, but surely worthy of further inquiry.

Moving on to the compliment responses, Table 10 displays the results of the DCT pretest. As with compliments, it was necessary to do a bit of data reduction with compliment responses as well. Recall that the twelve categories employed in the coding of compliment responses yielded a total of more than forty combinations, many occurring very infrequently. These initial twelve strategies were reduced to the following five: accept, reject/deflect, accept/reject, answer, and other. As noted earlier, single-strategy compliment responses constituted approximately 75% of all data, leaving the remaining 25% to be reclassified according to the five categories which appear in the table. This process was largely unproblematic, except for cases in which a main strategy appeared with an additional element that was coded as "other." Data meeting these

TABLE 11. DCT POSTTEST COMPLIMENT RESPONSES BY GROUP

		Group		
		Control (%)	Deductive (%)	Inductive (%)
Strategy	Accept	63.43	80.56	63.89
	Reject/deflect	11.11	2.43	17.71
	Accept/reject	17.13	9.72	5.90
	Answer	5.09	5.21	9.72
	Other	3.24	2.08	2.78
	Total	N = 216	N = 288	N = 288
$\chi^2 = 61.549$	$p = .000$			

criteria were coded as the main category, in effect disregarding the "other" element. As Table 10 indicates, the most frequent compliment response strategy for all three groups was acceptance, with the deductive group evidencing the greatest use of this strategy by some 10%. The deductive group also evidences the lowest use of strategies involving any element of rejection. The distribution of strategies for the control and inductive groups differs slightly, but is largely the same. As shown in Table 10, results of a chi-square analysis of the pretest compliment response data indicated that strategy choice was not independent of group, and this is likely due to the markedly different preferences of the deductive group. Once again, then, unexpected pretest differences complicate matters. Moving to the posttest, we can see from Table 11 that an increase across the board in the use of acceptance, with the deductive group showing a considerably greater gain (11.12%) over the other groups. Responses involving some form of rejection remained constant for the control group, but decreased slightly for the inductive group. As shown in Table 11, results of a chi-square analysis indicated that strategy choice on the posttest, as on the pretest, was not independent of group, this time producing a far greater chi-square value. Table 12 indicates that the distribution of compliment response strategies for the deductive group most closely resembles that for the U.S. group, while the increased use of rejection/deflection by the inductive group on the posttest further distances them from the U.S. distribution. It would appear, then, that the inductive instruction had a potentially negative impact on compliment response strategies, while deductive instruction may have been facilitative of development. So, unlike pragmalinguistics, where both approaches to instruction appear to have had a similarly positive impact, deductive instruction appears to have the edge over inductive instruction where sociopragmatics is concerned.

TABLE 12. DCT POSTTEST AND U.S. COMPLIMENT RESPONSES BY GROUP

		Group			
		Control (%)	*Deductive (%)*	*Inductive (%)*	*U.S. (%)*
Strategy	*Accept*	63.43	80.56	63.89	79.40
	Reject/deflect	11.11	2.43	17.71	0.00
	Accept/reject	17.13	9.72	5.90	20.60
	Answer	5.09	5.21	9.72	0.00
	Other	3.24	2.08	2.78	0.00
	Total	N = 216	N = 288	N = 288	N = 252

Conclusion

This study set out to answer two questions. The first question concerned whether learners benefited from instruction in compliments and compliment responses in a foreign language context; the second sought to determine whether there were differential effects of inductive and deductive approaches to the teaching of compliments and compliment responses in a foreign language context. Although we would have to conclude from the SAQ and the MAQ results that the answer to the first question would be negative (thus rendering the second question moot), it appears that the results from the DCT offer some evidence that instruction was effective. Particularly, the marked increase in the use of Manes and Wolfson's nine compliment formulas – the main content of two lessons – by both treatment groups, with no similar increase for the control group, indicates that both types of instruction had a similarly positive effect. In response to the second question, however, the DCT results for compliment responses revealed a positive effect only for the deductive group, indicating that although inductive and deductive instruction may both lead to gains in pragmalinguistic proficiency (more on this later), only the latter may be effective for developing sociopragmatic proficiency. It could even be argued that the inductive instruction actually had a negative impact on sociopragmatic development, perhaps by raising difficult issues without providing unambiguous solutions; that is, it may be necessary to provide explicitly the kind of information necessary for learners to develop sociopragmatic proficiency in the target language: Simply raising these issues and allowing learners time to reflect – even in "guided discovery" activities – could create more confusion than comprehension. We hasten to note here that the comparable gains for the two treatment groups in terms of pragmalinguistics may be the result of the highly formulaic nature of American English compliments, thus making them an easy object for any sort of instruction. It is not clear whether both approaches would have yielded the same results for other, less straight-forward areas of pragmalinguistics. Studies demonstrating the advantages of explicit instruction (see, e.g., Kasper, this volume; Takahashi, this volume) would appear to indicate otherwise.

There are a number of potential problems with this study that require caution in making claims of any kind. The learners who took part were clearly quite advanced – as indicated by rather high pretest scores – so it is not clear whether similar results would be obtained with less advanced learners. An issue related to the high pretest scores is that of cultural preferences for compliment responses, that is, given the fact that existing research is divided on whether there is an "Asian" preference for rejecting, there was reason going into the study to assume that differences might obtain in compliment response patterns, particularly across the two L1 groups. However, our results indicate that the putative "Asian" preference for rejection has perhaps been overstated, and it may even be the case that the high pretest scores were not related to proficiency but were rather the result of positive transfer. That, of course, is an empirical question. There is also the issue of gender disparity across groups, and although it may be tempting to attribute the inductive group's tendency to lag behind the other groups to the latter two groups' predominantly female makeup, we note that the two female-dominant groups did not perform uniformly across tasks. It is also worth recalling that it was the inductive group – which was equally male and female – that evidenced the greatest gain on the SAQ posttest and on the DCT posttest for compliments. Further research is needed here as well. Another rather unexpected problem we encountered was the differences in pretest results for all three questionnaires; that is, in a study of this kind, one normally expects to find no significant differences across groups on the pretest – which establishes an equal starting point for all participant groups – allowing for more robust comparisons to be made on any posttest differences. Needless to say, significant pretest differences serve to complicate matters considerably. However, given the similar demographics across the control and treatment groups, there was no reason to expect such striking pretest differences. In sum, then, this study has provided some evidence, albeit tentative, that instruction in pragmatics can make a difference in a foreign language context, but that a deductive approach may yield better results for both pragmalinguistics and sociopragmatics. The tentative nature of any conclusions reached here, however, causes us to look forward to future research aimed at addressing these issues.

Appendix: Questionnaire scenarios

1. Alex (one of the sons) is a business major. He has an interview today for a part-time job with a large investment company, so he is wearing his best suit. You compliment him on his appearance.
2. You have just finished having dinner at home that was prepared by Mrs. White (the mother). You compliment her on the meal.
3. You are at the university, and class has just ended. Your teacher overhears you answering your classmate's questions about how to use the computer. She tells you that you are good with computers.
4. You just bought a new mobile phone. When you get home, no one is there but Mr. Bush (the grandfather). He sees your new phone and says it looks like a good phone.
5. It's Sunday afternoon, and you go to Jeff's (your student) house to help him study math. He is dressed in his best clothes because he just got home from church. You compliment him on his appearance.
6. You are at the university, and class has just ended. Your classmate gave a good presentation in class, and you compliment her or him on it.
7. You are at the university, and your teacher has handed back the paper that you wrote 2 weeks ago. As you are getting ready to leave, your teacher tells you that your paper was very good.
8. You have to give an important presentation in class today, so you are wearing your best outfit. Before you leave the house, Mrs. White (the mother) tells you that you look very smart.
9. You go to Jeff's (your student) house to help him study math. You notice that he has a new pencil case, and you tell him that you like it.
10. You and Alex (one of the sons) go to the university swimming pool together to swim. After you finish, Alex compliments you on your swimming.
11. While you are practicing the piano at home, Mrs. Bush (the grandmother) hears you and compliments you on your piano playing.
12. Mrs. White and her mother, Mrs. Bush, have just returned from shopping. Mrs. Bush (the grandmother) bought a new handbag, and you tell her you think it's nice.
13. You are at university, and class has just finished. While you are putting your books away, your teacher notices your new backpack and says that she or he likes it.
14. Sue (the daughter) went shopping and bought some jewelry. You see that she is wearing a new ring, and you tell her that you think it's pretty.

15. On the weekend, you go to sing karaoke with some of your class-mates. After you sing a song, one of your classmates compliments you on your singing.

16. Mr. White (the father) has an important meeting today, so he is wearing his best suit. Before he leaves to go to work, you compliment him on his appearance.

17. You go to Jeff's (your student) house to help him with math. He tells you that he got an "A" on his last math exam, and you compliment him for doing so well.

18. You go to the university after going to the hair salon, and one of your classmates compliments you on your new haircut.

9 The role of input enhancement in developing pragmatic competence

Satomi Takahashi

Introduction

Input enhancement in second language acquisition (SLA) has been addressed in studies of form-focused instruction at morphosyntactic levels, known as Focus on Form (FonF) research (e.g., White, Spada, Lightbown & Ranta, 1991; Carroll, Swain & Roberge, 1992; Fotos, 1993; Spada & Lightbown, 1993; Trahey & White, 1993; see Doughty & Williams, 1998; Long & Robinson, 1998, for an overview). Following Sharwood Smith's (1991, 1993) definition of input enhancement, researchers experimentally manipulated instructional input on L2 structures in various ways: some form of corrective feedback with or without metalinguistic information (e.g., Doughty & Varela, 1998), visual enhancement (textual modification) with the use of bold or italic face (e.g., Alanen, 1995; Jourdenais, Ota, Stauffer, Boyson, & Doughty, 1995; J. White, 1998), and task manipulation directing learners to notice and attend to target structures (e.g., Hulstijn, 1989; Robinson, 1996; Williams & Evans, 1998). All of these studies provided evidence that high levels of attention-drawing activities, as represented by presenting metalinguistic information and corrective feedback, are more helpful for learners in gaining the mastery of target-language structures than simple exposure to positive evidence. These findings thus provide the basis for theoretical verification of Schmidt's (1993a, 1995, 1998) Noticing Hypothesis, which states that conscious noticing is the necessary and sufficient condition for converting input to intake. In contrast to the rich array of input enhancement research into morphosyntactic features, there have been considerably fewer studies specifically focusing on the role of input enhancement in developing L2 pragmatic competence. An increasing number of interlanguage pragmatics (ILP) researchers have become interested in exploring whether L2 pragmatic features can be acquired without any instructional intervention; however, the total volume of research in this area is well below that for

Part of this paper was presented at the Third Pacific Second Language Research Forum, March 26–29, 1998, Tokyo.

mainstream SLA. A few ILP studies have examined the efficacy of certain instructional methods (e.g., Wildner-Bassett, 1984, 1994) and tried to address the issue of teachability (e.g., Olshtain & Cohen, 1990), but these have failed to answer directly the question of how the nature of input enhancement influences the development of L2 pragmatic competence. This chapter examines how differential degrees of input enhancement affect the acquisition of L2 request strategies in instructed settings, and in so doing tests the hypothesis that some forms of input enhancement can facilitate L2 acquisition at the pragmatic level as well.

Background

The limited number of ILP studies on input enhancement can be categorized into two groups according to the nature of enhancement to be compared: instruction providing metapragmatic information versus no instruction, and instruction providing metapragmatic information versus instruction providing no metapragmatic information (see Kasper, 1997a; Kasper & Rose, 1999, for reviews). The studies in the first category (e.g., Billmyer, 1990a, 1990b; Kubota, 1995) showed a greater degree of effectiveness for metapragmatic instruction over no instruction. Billmyer (1990a, 1990b) found that Japanese ESL learners in the instructed group produced a greater number of compliments and appropriate responses to the American partners' compliments than those in the noninstructed group. Kubota (1995) found a similar tendency in the implicature ability of Japanese EFL learners: Learners receiving either deductive or inductive input enhancement outperformed learners in the unenhanced condition, with some advantage for the inductive group. No participants, however, could achieve the expected generalizations from the treatment when encountering new items. In the second category of pragmatic input enhancement studies, House (1996) and Tateyama, Kasper, Mui, Tay, and Thananart (1997) evidenced the superior effect of explicit metapragmatic instruction (the "explicit group") to instruction without providing such metapragmatic information (the "implicit group"). In House (1996), for instance, the advanced English learners of German in the explicit group outperformed the implicit group in making requests in the areas of gambits, discourse strategies, and speech acts. Tateyama et al. (1997) also substantiated the effectiveness of metapragmatic instruction. They focused on the learning of the Japanese multipurpose routine formula *sumimasen* by beginning-level JFL learners. The explicit group participants, who engaged in various explicit metapragmatic activities, evidenced superior performance in the target routine formula to that of the implicit group.

These studies all demonstrated that the target pragmatic features were most effectively learned when they were taught explicitly with some form of input enhancement techniques. Explicit pedagogical intervention is thus considered one of the ways in which learners can most efficiently develop their pragmatic competence in L2. The present study belongs to the second category (i.e., instruction providing metapragmatic information versus instruction providing no metapragmatic information), and examines the effects of differential degrees of input enhancement to determine whether such findings are replicated in the context of Japanese EFL learners learning English request strategies.

Target request strategies

Takahashi (1996) examined the transferability of five Japanese indirect request strategies to corresponding English contexts manifesting two levels of imposition. It was assumed that an L1 request strategy would be more transferable if it were perceived as more appropriate and its target-language equivalent were perceived to manifest the same degree of contextual appropriateness. One of the major findings was that Japanese EFL learners could not identify the English requests that were real functional equivalents of the Japanese request strategies. For example, the functionally equivalent English request form for the Japanese request V-*shite itadake-nai-deshoo-ka* (uttered in a relatively high imposition context) was the biclausal request form "Would it be possible to VP?" The learners, however, could not establish such functional equivalence between these L1 and L2 forms. They in fact contended that a monoclausal English request form "Would/Could you VP?" should be used in the situations where biclausal forms, such as the "Would it be possible to VP?" are more appropriate as request forms. This finding suggests that the Japanese EFL learners lacked the L2 pragmalinguistic knowledge that an English request can be mitigated to a greater extent by making it syntactically more complex by embedding it within another clause. This study focuses on some of these biclausal English request forms as the target strategies for input enhancement.

Input conditions

In this study, input was enhanced by classroom tasks which were intended to lead the learners to focus on the target strategies in one way or another. Four input conditions were set up: explicit teaching, form-comparison, form-search, and meaning-focused conditions. These four conditions differed from each other in degrees of input enhancement, with the explicit teaching condition manifesting the highest degree of input enhancement and the meaning-focused condition revealing the least.[1] The explicit teaching condition (hereafter, ET) was a teacher-fronted instructional setting, where metapragmatic information on the form-function relationship of the target request strategies was provided. In the form-comparison condition (hereafter, FC), learners were instructed to compare their own request strategies with those provided by native-English-speaking requesters in the corresponding situations. The learners in the form-search condition (hereafter, FS) were asked to find any "native(like) usage" in the input containing the target request strategies. In the meaning-focused condition (hereafter, MF), the learners were simply required to listen and read the input and answer comprehension questions. The ET condition was deductive in nature, whereas the remaining three conditions were implicit and inductive in nature without providing any metapragmatic information.

Research questions and hypotheses

The following research questions were addressed:

1. Does the degree of input enhancement affect the learning of target request strategies?
2. Is the learner's confidence in formulating his or her request strategies influenced by the type of input condition?

The previous studies on form-focused instructional effects at the morphosyntactic and pragmatic levels provided a sufficient basis for the following hypotheses:

Hypothesis 1: The ET condition will be the most effective of the four conditions.
Hypothesis 2: Of the three implicit input enhancement conditions, the FC will provide the most efficient learning outcomes, followed by the FS and MF conditions in this order.
Hypothesis 3: The learner's confidence in formulating request expressions after the treatment will be the highest for the ET condition, followed by the FC, FS, and MF in this order.

Hypothesis 2 was motivated by Ellis's (1995) claim that intake is enhanced when learners compare what they have noticed in the input with what they currently produce in their own output. This learning process was exactly realized in the task imposed on the learners in the FC condition.

---

1 Please note that *input enhancement* does not generally refer to explicit instruction, but in this chapter the term is used to refer to all four input conditions.

Method

Participants

The participants were 138 Japanese college students, the majority of whom were male. They were all science majors (freshmen or sophomores) with a mean age of 19.3 years (SD = 1.1). They had received formal classroom instruction in English for 7 to 10 years in Japan. None of them had stayed in English-speaking countries beyond 2 weeks. The participants made up four intact general English classes, taught by the researcher, which were randomly assigned to the four input conditions: ET, FC, FS, and MF.[2] In an effort to determine equivalence of the four groups in terms of their English proficiency, I administered Form One of the Secondary Level English Proficiency Test (SLEP).[3] The results of one-way ANOVA performed on the SLEP raw scores indicated that there was no significant difference in L2 proficiency among the four groups ($F(3, 100) = 2.472$, $p = .0661$). Data from some participants had to be excluded from the analysis because some were absent from the treatment sessions, failed to take the posttest, and/or provided incomplete answers in the pretest and/or the posttest. A few participants in the FC condition also used one of the target request forms in the pretest. Accordingly, the analysis was actually carried out with data from 107 learners: 27 for the ET, 25 for the FC, 24 for the FS, and 31 for the MF.

Design

A quasi-experimental, pretest/posttest design was adopted.[4] Because of the large sample size, discourse completion tests (DCTs) were employed to elicit the main data in the pretest and posttest sessions. In the posttest, the participants' immediate written retrospection was also elicited. The follow-up written retrospection data were collected from the participants in the FC, FS, and MF conditions after the posttest.

Selection of the situations and the target request strategies

The situations in Takahashi (1995, 1996) were adopted as the target situations to be assessed in the pretest/posttest, but only one type was included: situations in which English NSs supplied (through DCTs)

---

2 Data were collected from the ET, FS, and MF groups during the second semester of 1996, and data were collected for the FC group in the following semester.

3 Because the main task in the treatment sessions was reading the role-play transcripts, only the reading section was used.

4 Since participants were available during the 4-month semester period only, administration of a delayed posttest was not possible.

biclausal forms as the appropriate request strategies. This involved "Appointment" (APO) and "Paper Due" (PAD) situations, which manifested a relatively high degree of requestive imposition. Two more situations, "Makeup Exam" (MAE) and "Feedback" (FEB), were also included as the target situations in order to increase the study's reliability. These two situations were not directly tested in Takahashi (1995, 1996), but were found to be close to APO and PAD in terms of the degree of requestive imposition. Furthermore, it was confirmed informally with several English NSs that biclausal request forms were among the most appropriate forms in these two situations as well.

The four target request situations are described as follows:

APO: You have an appointment with Professor H, whose seminar you are now taking, at 10:30 a.m. tomorrow. You are supposed to talk with him about a topic for the term paper for his seminar. However, you suddenly need to go to the dentist around the same time tomorrow. It is very hard to change the appointment with the dentist: you cannot take any other time slot for treatment and you are now feeling a great deal of pain. So, you really want to go to the dentist tomorrow. You know that Professor H is a very busy person, and, in fact, you had a hard time getting an appointment with him, but you have decided to ask Professor H to change the appointment.

PAD: You are now writing a term paper for your sociology course. You have been making the utmost effort to write this paper by staying up late every night. But you cannot proceed with this paper as you had expected because you also must prepare for the final exams for your other courses. The paper is due tomorrow; but it seems that you need a few more days to complete this paper. You know that professors have to submit grade reports as soon as possible and that it takes a while to evaluate a paper, but you have decided to ask Professor B to extend the due date for the paper anyway.

MAE: Since you had a bad cold, you could not take a final exam for the English grammar course. At your university, professors are required to submit students' grades as soon as final exams are over; and thus they hesitate to give their students makeup exams. But you want to take a makeup exam for the course because you have an excuse: You could not take it due to your bad health, so you have decided to ask Professor E (in charge of the course) to give you a makeup exam for the course.

FEB: You are now thinking of submitting your paper for publication in *Student Bulletin*. This paper was written for the Japanese history course offered by Professor S last semester. For this purpose, you had already made a lot of revisions. You really want Professor S to read your revised paper again, to check the revised portions and to give you more detailed comments. Professor S is very busy this semester because he has a lot of classes to teach. But you would really like to submit your revised paper for *Student Bulletin*, so you have decided to ask Professor S to read your revised paper again.

The input situations for the treatment sessions have to satisfy the following two conditions. First, they are sufficiently comparable to APO,

TABLE 1. TARGET REQUEST FORMS USED IN THE TREATMENT SESSIONS

Request forms	Treatment situations
I was wondering if you could VP.	VIO: Participant Codes D, F
Do you think you could VP?	QUS: Participant Code E
Is it possible to VP?	QUS: Participant Code C
If you could/can VP.	VIO: Participant Code G
	QUS: Participant Codes E, H

Note: VIO = "Violin" situation, QUS = "Questionnaire" situation

PAD, MAE, and FEB in terms of the situational variables: The request is made to a higher-status hearer, and the requester is not so familiar with the requestee, as seen in the relationship between a professor and his student in the four target situations. Second, the learners are exposed to input which is controllable but sufficiently close to authentic discourse. Authenticity should be emphasized here so that the findings of this study would be expandable to noticing L2 request strategies in natural discourse. In view of these two points, I chose the two request situations in Takahashi (1987) for the input situations: the "Violin" (VIO) and "Questionnaire" (QUS) situations (VIO = "The student asks his older neighbor to stop her daughter's violin practice at night"; QUS = "The student asks his older neighbor to fill out the questionnaire and return it as soon as possible").[5] In Takahashi (1987), these two situations were used to elicit L1 English requests through role-plays, which were recorded and transcribed. Only the biclausal request forms which were observed both in the NS DCT data and in the NS-NS role-play data were selected. Those forms are listed in the left-most column in Table 1.[6] They were in fact among the request forms most frequently provided by the NS participants in APO and PAD in the DCTs. Moreover, Japanese EFL learners at the college level are supposed to be familiar with those forms. Consequently, as the input base for the treatment sessions, three NS-NS role-play dyads for VIO and three for QUS were used, each of which contained at least one of the request forms in Table 1.

5 There were significant differences among the six request situations (APO, PAD, MAE, FEB, VIO, QUS) in terms of the degrees of requestive imposition: $F(5, 265)=78.208$, $p < .0001$. However, APO, PAD, MAE, and FEB showed imposition equal to or higher than VIO and QUS. It was concluded that inclusion of VIO and QUS as the treatment situations, which shared the biclausal request forms with the four target situations, was justifiable.

6 It was decided to include the form "If you could VP" in this study because it is essentially biclausal.

Pretest and posttest

The pretest DCTs contained twelve situations, four of which were the target request situations (APO, PAD, MAE, and FEB). The remaining eight situations were distracters, consisting of one chastisement, one apology, two refusals, three requests, and one praise (status low to high, or status equals). Situational descriptions were given in English. The participants were asked to provide appropriate request expressions for each situation, and to rate their confidence in selecting their request expression on a 5-point rating scale (1 = not confident at all; 5 = completely confident). The posttest was intended to assess the participants' ability to provide appropriate request expressions for the four target situations only. For each situation, the DCT was provided, followed by the confidence rating scale (the same format as the pretest). The following four questions were then presented to elicit the participants' self-reports on the process of selecting the request expressions provided in the DCT:

1. What made you think that a particular expression was the most appropriate? Please write down the process of your decision making in as much detail as possible.
2. Which language were you relying on in making your decision: Japanese or English?
3. Do you think you would definitely use the expression you selected when you actually face your conversation partner?
4. Do you anticipate any difficulty expressing yourself in English in this task?

The participants were asked to carry out the written retrospection (in Japanese) immediately after providing the request expression in each situation. In both pretest and posttests, the situations were counterbalanced across the participants, and both tests were conducted in class without setting a time limit. In order to eliminate the pretest effect on the treatment, the pretest was administered 1 month prior to the treatment, and the posttest was conducted 1 week after the treatment.

Treatment materials and procedures

The treatment sessions were offered over 4 weeks (90 minutes per week) and were carried out in general English classes. For all four input conditions, the treatment was first given to the target request forms in VIO (Session 1) and then to those in QUS (Session 2). Before the main task was presented in each treatment session, participants in all four groups engaged in the following two warm-up tasks: listening to the input role-play for VIO or QUS while reading the transcripts, and writing a summary of the situation (in Japanese) by focusing on the contextual features, in particular, the relationship between the interlocutors.

For the ET group, two types of treatment materials were prepared for each session. One was handouts in which detailed metapragmatic information on the target request forms was provided, and the other was a composition exercise packet, in which Japanese–English translation exercises using the target request forms were provided. The target request forms were explained using the handouts for about 1 hour for each session. Care was taken to refer to the actual use of the target request forms in the discourse (role-plays) and their function in the particular requester–requestee relationship (i.e., the status low to high, the large social distance). The explanation was followed by 30-minute composition exercises in each session.

FC participants first filled out the open-ended DCTs for VIO and QUS in English. Following this, they received three types of materials for the VIO and QUS sessions: the three transcripts of the NS-NS role-plays for L1 English, the DCTs which they had previously filled out, and the instruction sheet for the task. For each session, the participants were required to compare their own English request expressions (in the DCTs) with those supplied by the NSs (in their role-plays) in the corresponding situation and to discover any differences in request realization patterns. It should be noted here that the FC participants supplied exclusively monoclausal request forms in their DCTs for VIO and QUS (e.g., "Would/Could you VP?"). The task in each session took about 1.5 class hours.

The FS group received three types of material in each session: three NS-NS role-play transcripts for VIO and three such transcripts for QUS, one NS-NNS (the Japanese learners of English) role-play transcript for VIO and one such transcript for QUS (collected in Takahashi and DuFon, 1989), and the instruction sheet for the tasks for this group (Task A and B). In Task A, the participants were instructed to compare the NS requesters' English in the VIO transcripts (or QUS transcripts) with the NNS requester's English in the same situation. They were then asked to list the NS expressions which differed from the NNS English expressions. Note that the NNS requesters exclusively used the monoclausal request forms ("Would/Will you VP?" for VIO and "I want you to VP" for QUS), which were predominantly used by the participants in the present study in the pretest. The participants in this group were then more likely to be able to project their own use of request forms onto the NNS requests in Takahashi and DuFon (1989). Task B was a distracter task in which the participants were asked to look through the

English expressions made by the requestees in the transcripts for VIO (or QUS) and list any expressions which were distinctively native English of which they thought they had no command at all. The participants completed the tasks for each session in about 1.5 class hours.

The MF group participants were required to undertake a focus-on-meaning task in each session. A packet of comprehension questions for each of the six NS-NS role-play transcripts for VIO (three) and QUS (three) was prepared. Each packet contained six to eight comprehension questions, including the questions directly addressing the content of the requests. The participants were asked to carefully read the role-play transcripts for the VIO and QUS and then to answer each question in English. They completed the task for each session in about 1.5 class hours. For the FC, FS, and MF groups, no feedback on the target request forms was provided until the participants completed the follow-up questionnaires.

Follow-up activities

Follow-up questionnaires were used to elicit information on whether the participants in the FC, FS, and MF conditions actually noticed the target request forms in the role-play transcripts. The questionnaires were administered 1 week after the posttest, followed by the explanations of the function of the target request forms.

Data analysis

For each target situation, the number of participants who provided the target request forms in the posttest was compared with that of the participants who supplied nontarget request forms. The significance of the difference in frequency counts was determined through chi-square analysis ($\alpha = .05$). With regard to the confidence rates, a two-way repeated-measures ANOVA was performed, the dependent variable being the confidence rates and the independent variables the test types (two levels, a within-subjects factor) and the input conditions (four levels, a between-subjects factor, $\alpha = .05$). In addition, a one-way ANCOVA with the pretest confidence rates as a covariate was performed to explore differences in the posttest confidence attainment ($\alpha = .05$). The findings were further examined using the self-report data obtained in the posttest and the follow-up data gathered after the posttest.

TABLE 2. REQUEST FORMS PROVIDED IN THE PRETEST

Request forms	Frequency			
	APO	PAD	MAE	FEB
Preparatory questions	48 (45%)	39 (38%)	36 (34%)	27 (27%)
Mood derivables with *please*	29 (27%)	48 (46%)	46 (43%)	21 (21%)
Want statements	9 (8.5%)	10 (10%)	12 (11%)	12 (12%)
Hints	8 (7.5%)	1(1%)	2 (2%)	0 (0%)
Others	13 (12%)	5 (5%)	11 (10%)	40 (40%)
Total	107 (100%)	103 (100%)	107(100%)	100(100%)

Note: APO = "Appointment" situation, PAD = "Paper Due" situation, MAE = "Makeup Exam" situation, FEB = "Feedback" situation

Results and discussion

Quantitative aspects of the effects of input enhancement

The L2 request realization data were coded by two raters (the researcher and another linguist) based on the types of request strategies established in Takahashi (1995). The interrater reliability (percentage of agreement) reached .97. As indicated in Table 2, the results of the pretest showed that none of the 107 participants employed target biclausal request forms for any of the input conditions. The great majority of participants favored either preparatory questions (e.g., "Would you change the appointment?") or mood derivables with *please* (e.g., "Please change the appointment").[7] The same tendency was also observed in the request forms provided in the treatment task sessions (for the VIO and QUS situations) in the FC condition.[8]

With respect to the posttest results (see Table 3), for all four situations the target request forms were provided by the ET participants to a greater extent than any of the remaining three input conditions, and (except for MAE) a significantly smaller number of ET participants provided nontarget forms ($\chi^2 = 7.26$, $df = 1$, $p < .01$ for APO; $\chi^2 = 12$, $df = 1$, $p < .001$ for PAD; $\chi^2 = 5.04$, $df = 1$, $p < .05$ for FEB).[9] In contrast, the FC, FS, and MF participants provided more nontarget forms than target forms in all four situations. The nonexplicit teaching groups

7 See the Appendix for the definition of each request strategy.

8 The following request types were observed: Preparatory questions (VIO = 60%; QUS = 32%); Mood derivables with *please* (VIO = 36%; QUS = 44%); Want statements (VIO = 0%; QUS = 8%); Hints (VIO = 0%; QUS = 4%); and Others (VIO = 4%; QUS = 12%).

9 When the degree of freedom was less than 1, Yate's Correction was applied (Hatch & Lazaraton, 1991, p. 404).

TABLE 3. FREQUENCY OF REQUEST FORMS IN THE POSTTEST

Situations	Conditions	Target forms	Nontarget forms
APO	Explicit teaching (ET)	21	6
	Form-comparison (FC)	8	17
	Form-search (FS)	0	24
	Meaning-focused (MF)	1	30
PAD	Explicit teaching (ET)	23	4
	Form-comparison (FC)	6	19
	Form-search (FS)	0	22
	Meaning-focused (MF)	1	28
MAE	Explicit teaching (ET)	18	8
	Form-comparison (FC)	6	19
	Form-search (FS)	0	24
	Meaning-focused (MF)	0	32
FEB	Explicit teaching (ET)	18	6
	Form-comparison (FC)	6	19
	Form-search (FS)	0	22
	Meaning-focused (MF)	0	29

Note: APO = "Appointment" situation, PAD = "Paper Due" situation, MAE = "Makeup Exam" situation, FEB = "Feedback" situation

also provided more nontarget forms than the ET group. More precisely, the differences in frequency counts for the nontarget forms were: significant between ET and FC in the three situations except MAE ($\chi^2 = 4.35$, $df = 1$, $p < .05$ for APO; $\chi^2 = 8.52$, $df = 1$, $p < .01$ for PAD; $\chi^2 = 5.76$, $df = 1$, $p < .05$ for FEB); significant between ET and FS in all the situations ($\chi^2 = 9.63$, $df = 1$, $p < .01$ for APO; $\chi^2 = 11.12$, $df = 1$, $p < .001$ for PAD; $\chi^2 = 7.03$, $df = 1$, $p < .01$ for MAE; $\chi^2 = 8.04$, $df = 1$, $p < .01$ for FEB); and significant between ET and MF in all the situations ($\chi^2 = 14.69$, $df = 1$, $p < .001$ for APO; $\chi^2 = 16.53$, $df = 1$, $p < .001$ for PAD; $\chi^2 = 13.23$, $df = 1$, $p < .001$ for MAE; $\chi^2 = 13.83$, $df = 1$, $p < .001$ for FEB). However, there were no significant differences among the FC, FS, and MF conditions in terms of the number of nontarget forms for any of the situations.

Closer examination of the realization patterns for the target forms revealed that the participants who provided the targets tended predominantly to use the "I wonder if you could VP" form for all four request situations (see Table 4).[10] A possible explanation for this could

10 However, the difference in frequency counts between "I wonder if" and the other target forms was not statistically significant, except for APO ($\chi^2 = 8.04$, $df = 1$, $p < .01$). (In computing the chi-square for "I wonder if" for FEB, I included the combined form of "I wonder if" + want statement.)

TABLE 4. TARGET REQUEST FORMS PROVIDED IN THE POSTTEST

	Frequency											
	APO			PAD			MAE			FEB		
Request forms	ET	FC/MF	TL	ET	FC/MF	TL	ET	FC	TL	ET	FC	TL
"I wonder if"	17 (81%)	5 (71%)	22 (79%)	18 (78%)	2 (29%)	20 (67%)	14 (78%)	3 (50%)	17 (71%)	10 (56%)	1 (16%)	11 (46%)
"would it be possible"	3 (14%)	1 (14%)	4 (14%)	2 (9%)	4 (57%)	6 (20%)	3 (16%)	2 (33%)	5 (21%)	2 (11%)	2 (33%)	4 (17%)
"Do you think"	0 (0%)	0 (0%)	0 (0%)	2 (9%)	1 (14%)	3 (10%)	1 (5%)	0 (0%)	1 (4%)	4 (22%)	1 (16%)	5 (21%)
"if you could"	0 (0%)	0 (0%)	0 (0%)	1 (4%)	0 (0%)	1 (3%)	0 (0%)	1 (17%)	1 (4%)	0 (0%)	1 (16%)	1 (4%)
"would it be possible" + want statement	1 (5%)	0 (0%)	1 (3.5%)	0 (0%)	0 (0%)	0 (0%)	0 (0%)	0 (0%)	0 (0%)	0 (0%)	0 (0%)	0 (0%)
"would it be possible" + mood derivables with *please*	0 (0%)	1 (14%)	1 (3.5%)	0 (0%)	0 (0%)	0 (0%)	0 (0%)	0 (0%)	0 (0%)	0 (0%)	0 (0%)	0 (0%)
"I wonder if" + want statement	0 (0%)	0 (0%)	0 (0%)	0 (0%)	0 (0%)	0 (0%)	0 (0%)	0 (0%)	0 (0%)	2 (11%)	1 (16%)	3 (12%)
Total	21 (100%)	7 (100%)	28 (100%)	23 (100%)	7 (100%)	30 (100%)	18 (100%)	6 (100%)	24 (100%)	18 (100%)	6 (100%)	24 (100%)

Note: APO = "Appointment" situation, PAD = "Paper Due" situation, MAE = "Makeup Exam" situation, FEB = "Feedback" situation, ET = Explicit teaching, FC = Form-comparison, MF = Meaning-focused, TL = total

TABLE 5. NONTARGET REQUEST FORMS PROVIDED IN THE POSTTEST

	Frequency			
Request forms	APO	PAD	MAE	FEB
Preparatory questions	43 (56%)	41 (56%)	36 (43%)	18 (24%)
Mood derivables with *please*	17 (22%)	23 (32%)	33 (40%)	9 (12%)
Want statements	7 (9%)	3 (4%)	6 (7%)	21 (28%)
Want statements + mood derivables with *please*	0 (0%)	2 (3%)	3 (4%)	8 (10%)
Want statements + preparatory questions	0 (0%)	0 (0%)	1 (1%)	9 (12%)
Others	10 (13%)	4 (5%)	4 (5%)	11 (14%)
Total	77 (100%)	73 (100%)	83 (100%)	76 (100%)

Note: APO = "Appointment" situation, PAD = "Paper Due" situation, MAE = "Makeup Exam" situation, FEB = "Feedback" situation

be that the input frequency of "I wonder if" surpassed the other target forms, and, accordingly, was focused on more in the treatment session for the ET group. No change was found for the realization patterns of the nontarget forms supplied after the treatment. As was the case for the pretest, the great majority of participants who could not supply the target forms relied on the use of either the preparatory questions or the mood derivables with "please" (see Table 5).[11]

With regard to the confidence rates, for each of the four situations, the higher-order interaction effects were found to be significant, demonstrating that the factors of test type and input condition jointly influenced the learners' confidence in supplying a request form (see Tables 6, 7, 8, and 9, and Figures 1, 2, 3, and 4). A one-way repeated-measures ANOVA was further performed as a planned comparison between the pretest and posttest confidence for each condition. For all the four request situations, the ET and MF participants significantly increased their confidence in the posttest: $F(1, 26) = 7.581$, $p < .05$ for ET in APO; $F(1,30) = 15.424$, $p < .001$ for MF in APO; $F(1, 26) = 35.124$, $p < .0001$ for ET in PAD; $F(1, 28) = 6.943$, $p < .05$ for MF in PAD; $F(1, 25) = 24.628$, $p < .0001$ for ET in MAE; $F(1, 31) = 10.416$, $p < .01$ for MF in MAE; $F(1, 23) = 43.346$, $p < .0001$ for ET in FEB; $F(1, 28) = 23.930$, $p < .0001$ for MF in FEB. In contrast, the FS participants actually decreased their confidence in the posttest for APO. However, the difference in confidence rates between the pretest and the posttest for APO was not significant.

11 Not all of the nontarget forms here should be regarded as inappropriate forms for the situations. Some participants employed, for instance, the form of "I'm happy if you could VP." These are acceptable but are not simply the "target" in this study.

TABLE 6. RESULTS OF TWO-WAY REPEATED-MEASURES ANOVA: EFFECTS OF INSTRUCTIONAL CONDITIONS AND TEST TYPES ON CONFIDENCE FOR THE "APPOINTMENT" SITUATION

Source	SS	df	MS	F
Conditions	9.604	3	3.201	3.262*
Participant (group)	101.097	103	.982	
Tests	4.673	1	4.673	11.443***
Tests x conditions	6.718	3	2.239	5.484**
Tests x participant (group)	42.058	103	.408	

Note: $*p < .05, **p < .01, ***p < .001$

Explicit teaching – pretest: mean = 1.815, SD = .681; posttest: mean = 2.407, SD = 1.010
Form-comparison – pretest: mean = 2.400, SD = .764; posttest: mean = 2.600, SD = .707
Form-search – pretest: mean = 2.792, SD = 1.021; posttest: mean = 2.542, SD = .779
Meaning-focused – pretest: mean = 2.258, SD = .773; posttest: mean = 2.903, SD = .870

TABLE 7. RESULTS OF TWO-WAY REPEATED-MEASURES ANOVA: EFFECTS OF INSTRUCTIONAL CONDITIONS AND TEST TYPES ON CONFIDENCE FOR THE "PAPER DUE" SITUATION

Source	SS	df	MS	F
Conditions	11.159	3	3.720	3.883*
Participant (group)	94.822	99	.958	
Tests	13.672	1	13.672	33.091***
Tests x conditions	7.913	3	2.638	6.384**
Tests x participant (group)	40.903	99	.413	

Note: $*p < .05, **p < .001, ***p < .0001$

Explicit teaching – pretest: mean = 1.556, SD = .847; posttest: mean = 2.741, SD = .859
Form-comparison – pretest: mean = 2.360, SD = .638; posttest: mean = 2.640, SD = .757
Form-search – pretest: mean = 2.545, SD = .912; posttest: mean = 2.773, SD = .752
Meaning-focused – pretest: mean = 2.552, SD = .827; posttest: mean = 2.931, SD = .961

TABLE 8. RESULTS OF TWO-WAY REPEATED-MEASURES ANOVA: EFFECTS OF INSTRUCTIONAL CONDITIONS AND TEST TYPES ON CONFIDENCE FOR THE "MAKEUP EXAM" SITUATION

Source	SS	df	MS	F
Conditions	5.746	3	1.915	2.102
Participant (group)	93.834	103	.911	
Tests	10.475	1	10.475	26.500**
Tests x conditions	3.517	3	1.172	2.966*
Tests x participant (group)	40.716	103	.395	

Note: $^*p < .05$, $^{**}p < .0001$

Explicit teaching – pretest: mean = 1.923, SD = .935; posttest: mean = 2.808, SD = .895
Form-comparison – pretest: mean = 2.480, SD = .770; posttest: mean = 2.720, SD = .678
Form-search – pretest: mean = 2.708, SD = .859; posttest: mean = 2.958, SD = .908
Meaning-focused – pretest: mean = 2.469, SD = .718; posttest: mean = 2.875, SD = .707

TABLE 9. RESULTS OF TWO-WAY REPEATED-MEASURES ANOVA: EFFECTS OF INSTRUCTIONAL CONDITIONS AND TEST TYPES ON CONFIDENCE FOR THE "FEEDBACK" SITUATION

Source	SS	df	MS	F
Conditions	7.895	3	2.632	2.879*
Participant (group)	87.760	96	.914	
Tests	27.474	1	27.474	82.571**
Tests x conditions	3.433	3	1.144	3.439*
Tests x participant (group)	31.942	96	.333	

Note: $^*p < .05$, $^{**}p < .0001$

Explicit teaching – pretest: mean = 1.542, SD = .721; posttest: mean = 2.708, SD = .690
Form-comparison – pretest: mean = 2.120, SD = .781; posttest: mean = 2.800, SD = .707
Form-search – pretest: mean = 2.500, SD = .859; posttest: mean = 2.909, SD = .921
Meaning-focused – pretest: mean = 2.103, SD = .817; posttest: mean = 2.828, SD = .805

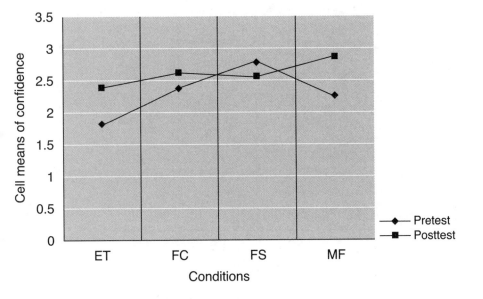

Figure 1 Effect of condition x test for the "Appointment" situation.

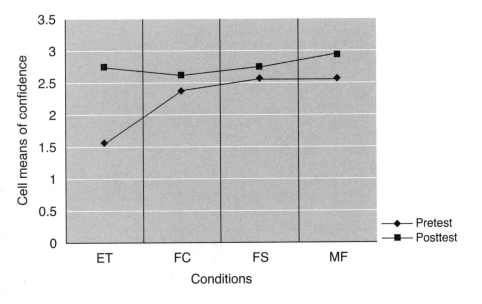

Figure 2 Effect of condition x test for the "Paper Due" situation.

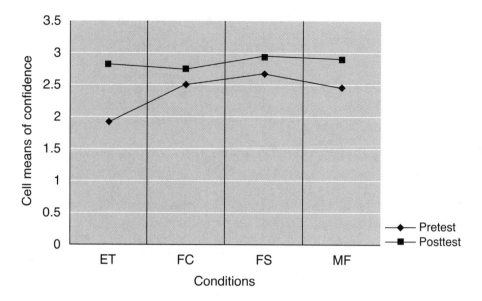

Figure 3 Effect of condition x test for the "Makeup Exam" situation.

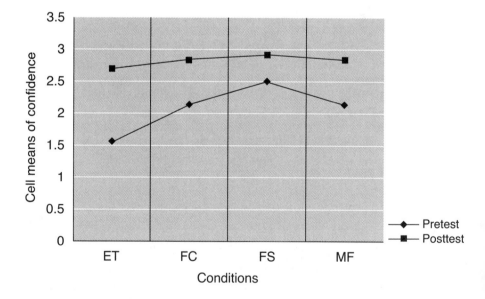

Figure 4 Effect of condition x test for the "Feedback" situation.

The results from a one-way ANCOVA with the pretest confidence rates as a covariate, however, demonstrated that there were no significant differences among the four input conditions in terms of the attained posttest confidence. Furthermore, the posttest means for the four situations in all the input conditions were below 3.0 (out of 5.0). In view of this, then, it can be claimed that none of the input conditions here could make the participants formulate their request expressions with *substantial* confidence.

The findings of the quantitative analysis can be summarized as follows:

1. The ET condition resulted in greater use of the target forms than the FC, FS, and MF conditions. This was observed across all four of the request situations. This finding confirmed Hypothesis 1.
2. The learners in the FC condition provided more target request forms than the learners in the FS and MF conditions. However, this tendency could not be described as pronounced in the light of the relatively large number of nontarget forms supplied by the FC participants in the posttest. In fact, there was no significant difference in the frequency counts of the nontargets provided in the implicit enhancement conditions across the four situations. Hence, we could not argue that the conditions for implicit input enhancement enabled the learners to learn the target request forms, nor could we conclusively claim that the FC provided the most efficient learning outcomes. This finding did not confirm Hypothesis 2.
3. The learners' confidence in formulating request expressions was affected by the levels of input enhancement. On the whole, the learners in the ET and MF conditions showed a greater degree of increase in their confidence. Hence, we could not argue that the outcome of confidence increase was realized by ET > FC > FS > MF in this order. Hypothesis 3, then, was not confirmed. However, it should also be noted that the ultimate level of confidence was not sufficiently high and did not vary among the four input conditions. Thus, it cannot be claimed that the learners in a particular input condition gained significantly higher confidence after the treatment; even the learners who provided the targets in the posttest felt less confident in their task performance.

At this point, there are at least three questions, which cannot be answered through quantitative analysis: Did the ET participants really master the choice of request forms? Why did the FC, FS, and MF participants fail to provide the target forms? Why did the ET and MF participants increase their confidence substantially, as compared to the learners in the remaining two conditions? These questions will be examined through the qualitative analysis in the next section.

Qualitative aspects of the effects of input enhancement

The written immediate retrospective reports collected in the posttest were analyzed for each condition in each request situation. Specifically, the contents of the self-reports were categorized according to whether the participants provided target or nontarget request forms. Those reports showed that learners mentioned either of the following two types of features in their self-report: discourse features only (such as the order of request-related components), and both linguistic features and discourse features, including request forms (see Table 10). Interestingly, a certain correspondence was observable between these self-report contents and the learners' real request performance. The participants who succeeded in providing the target request forms predominantly referred to linguistic features in formulating their request expressions, exemplified as follows:

Enshuu ni atta "I wonder if" *no koubun wo tsukai, tsutae tai youten nomi wo kaita.* ("I used the form 'I wonder if,' which was presented in the classroom exercises, and mentioned only the important point which I wanted to convey to the partner.") (MAE situation: ET condition)

Koko dewa, "I was wondering" *no hyougen no kawari ni,* "Is it possible" *no hyougen wo shiyou shite mita. Gimon-bun ni shite, yori enkyokuteki na kanji wo dasou to shita tame de ari, katei-hou wa yahari shiyou shita.* ("In this situation, I used the form 'Is it possible,' instead of the form 'I was wondering.' This was because I tried to convey a greater degree of indirectness by adopting a question form. And I relied on the subjunctive mood as well.") (PAD situation: FC condition)

Jikan wo henkou shite kure masen ka toiu tokoro wa, jibun no shitteiru "would you" *wo tsukatta.* ("I used the form 'would you,' which I am most familiar with, when I wanted to convey my wish to reschedule the appointment.") (APO situation: FS condition)

In contrast, the learners who provided nontarget forms were more likely to refer only to discourse features as follows:

Kono mae no enshuu de "native" *ga hyougen shite ita youni, saisho ni youkyuu wo dasu no dewa naku, mazu riyuu wo nobete itte, sorekara youkyuu wo dasu toiu keishiki ni shite mita.* ("As the native speaker did in the role-play, I tried to make the request after explaining my current situation rather than before.") (APO situation: FS condition)

TABLE 10. SUMMARY OF SELF-REPORTS

		Target form (posttest)				Nontarget form (posttest)			
Situation	*Report contents*	ET	FC	FS	MF	ET	FC	FS	MF
APO	Including discourse features only	1	1	0	1	1	10	11	15
				Total	3			Total	37
	Including discourse + linguistic features Reference to:								
	Request forms	17	5	0	0	2	5	3	5
	Other linguistic features	0	0	0	0	0	1	6	1
	Both	1	2	0	0	0	0	2	5
	Other	2	0	0	0	3	1	2	4
				Total	27			Total	40
PAD	Including discourse features only	5	0	0	1	0	9	11	20
				Total	6			Total	40
	Including discourse + linguistic features Reference to:								
	Request forms	14	6	0	0	1	8	5	4
	Other linguistic features	0	0	0	0	1	0	1	1
	Both	1	0	0	0	0	2	3	3
	Other	3	0	0	0	2	0	2	0
				Total	24			Total	33
MAE	Including discourse features only	6	0	0	0	0	10	12	22
				Total	6			Total	44
	Including discourse + linguistic features Reference to:								
	Request forms	9	4	0	0	3	7	3	7
	Other linguistic features	0	0	0	0	4	0	3	0
	Both	2	1	0	0	1	2	3	2
	Other	1	1	0	0	0	0	3	1
				Total	18			Total	39
FEB	Including discourse features only	2	0	0	1	0	9	11	18
				Total	3			Total	38
	Including discourse + linguistic features Reference to:								
	Request forms	12	6	0	0	5	7	4	7
	Other linguistic features	1	0	0	0	0	2	3	2
	Both	2	0	0	0	1	0	1	1
	Other	1	0	0	0	0	1	3	1
				Total	22			Total	38

Note: APO = "Appointment," PAD = "Paper Due," MAE = "Makeup Exam," FEB = "Feedback," ET = Explicit teaching, FC = Form-comparison, FS = Form-search, MF = Meaning-focused

Jijou wo kichin to hanasa nakereba, donna ni onegai shite mo aite no kyooju mo wakatte wa kure nai darou to omotta. ("I thought that the professor would not comply with my repeated requests unless I honestly explained the reason why I could not make the deadline.") (PAD situation: MF condition)

A 2 × 2 chi-square procedure confirmed the observed tendency (χ^2 = 11.792, df = 1, $p < .001$ for APO; χ^2 = 9.068, df = 1, $p < .01$ for PAD; χ^2 = 4.807, df = 1, $p < .05$ for MAE; χ^2 = 9.758 , df = 1, $p < .01$ for FEB). These self-report findings then provide us with a basis for addressing the three questions at the end of the preceding section.

In order to examine the level of mastery by the ET participants, I will focus here on the self-reports by those ET participants who provided the target forms and mentioned the linguistic features in their retrospection. They reported that the request forms taught in class (in particular, "I was wondering if you could VP") should be used because they succeed in conveying the appropriate degree of politeness in light of the requester–requestee relationship (i.e., low to high). In view of this, it appears that they were able to generalize what they learned in the treatment session to new comparable situations. However, some of them also referred to (and actually wrote down in the DCT) the form "I would like you to VP." According to them, their high school English teachers emphasized that the modal *would* manifests a greater degree of politeness, and thus they judged that the forms containing this modal should be added to increase the overall politeness.[12] This suggests that the ET learners' competence in realizing appropriate request forms is not stable enough at the end of the 4-week period of metapragmatic instruction and may not achieve a real change in knowledge (Sharwood Smith, 1991; Jourdenais et al., 1995). At the same time, the instruction the learners received in their high school English classes is still operative and plays a relatively influential role in the learners' restructuring process. Because a delayed posttest was not administered, I cannot comment on the lasting effect of the explicit metapragmatic instruction here. However, in view of the instability of their competence and the still insufficient degree of confidence in the posttest (mean = 2.407 for APO; mean = 2.741 for PAD; mean = 2.808 for MAE; mean = 2.708 for FEB), their superiority in performance to the FC, FS, and MF learners might be short-lived (see Kubota, 1995).

As the self-report data indicated (Table 10), for all the request situations, discourse features alone were mentioned to a greater extent by the FC, FS, and MF participants who failed to provide the target forms.

---

12 These self-reports were surprising to me, because I emphasized in the treatment session that the "I would like you to VP" form should be avoided when a low-status person asks a high-status person to do something.

Those participants in fact reported that their focus was concentrated on the best sequence of the utterances involved in request realization. For example, they were preoccupied with determining which component should come first in the discourse: apologetic expression, request expression, reason or excuse, and so on. Furthermore, the majority of them considered the formulation of a good explanation (of why they cannot comply with the request) to be the most important factor in obtaining the requestees' compliance. This observation provides us with some insight into how those participants perceive the notion of politeness. To them, an appropriate degree of politeness is realized as a result of conveying their sincerity in the form of elaborating the explanation (reason/excuse) in a relevant order of related utterances. It appears that they do not regard the request forms as the crucial factors in linguistic politeness. This might be because their monoclausal forms have already been validated by their high school English teachers as the appropriate forms. This again suggests the great influence of prior instruction, which strengthened the false form-function mappings (Takahashi, 1996).

There were, of course, some participants who did refer to the request forms (monoclausal) in their self-reports, but did not mention the function of the forms in the discourse at all. They just reported that "Please VP" or "Would/Will you VP?" should be used because this coincided with instruction provided by their high school English teachers. Moreover, they were rather preoccupied with the relevant choice of words which appeared in the NS transcripts in the treatment. The only exceptions were a relatively small number of FC participants who provided the target forms. They referred to the treatment sessions and stressed the use of syntactically complex forms (i.e., the target biclausal forms) in the target situations. But there was still a tendency for those successful learners to show an interest in discourse features, that is, how to present justifications for the target requesting to obtain the requestee's compliance.

On the whole, then, the FC, FS, and MF participants failed to provide the target forms because they paid more attention to the discourse features than the request forms, and the politeness manifested in their monoclausal request forms was already assured. Another possible explanation would be that the treatment input itself was insufficient (Schmidt & Frota, 1986; Hulstijn, 1989; Trahey & White, 1993; Alanen, 1995; Williams & Evans, 1998) and thus failed to trigger the restructuring of pragmatic knowledge. This implies that it would be difficult to learn the appropriate request forms in natural discourse, where the frequency of such forms might be relatively low. In any case, it is apparent that the treatment was not sufficient for the learners in the implicit enhancement conditions. At the same time, we may surmise that those learners attended more to the discourse-level features in the treatment tasks. Was this really happening? This question will be addressed through analysis of the treatment tasks and the follow-up questionnaires.

The analyses of the treatment tasks lead us to what the participants in the FC and FS conditions noticed and attended to in the treatment input (role-play transcripts). With regard to the FC conditions, we need first to recall the nature of the treatment task. The task required the participants to "notice the gap" (Schmidt & Frota, 1986) between the NS request forms and their own corresponding L2 forms. Because of the nature of this task, almost all of the FC participants referred to the NS target forms in some way. But precisely speaking, their primary focus was placed on *parts* of the target request forms, not the entire forms and their functions. Specifically, the comparison task performed by the FC learners revealed five points as to their focus in the input. First, the majority of the participants pointed out that the NSs used a lot of subjunctive clauses and the words *would/could, wonder,* and *maybe.* According to them, those clauses and words softened the entire requestive imposition. Second, some participants referred to the NS form "Do you think you could VP?" as the form they did not use, but they simultaneously pointed out that this particular form is purely interrogative and not a request, as taught in their high school English classes. Such a perception might have contributed to their failure to understand that L2 form-function relationships are, in reality, context-dependent. Third, some FC participants showed their interest in the frequent NS use of discourse lubricants (e.g., *you know, um,* and silence). Fourth, the great majority of the participants in this condition pointed out that the contents of the request (in particular, justifications for requesting) were greatly different from theirs. Fifth, almost half of the participants mentioned that the NS requests were, on the whole, longer and more elaborate than theirs.

With regard to the FS participants, their "native usage" search task using the NS-NNS role-play transcripts (Task A) was the basis for detecting their focus in the treatment input. Five points were observed as a result of the analysis of their task. First, eleven participants (out of twenty-four) listed one of the target forms, "I was wondering if you'd VP," but three of them concentrated their interest more on the collo-quial phrasing *you'd* rather than the function of the entire sentence. Second, the other target forms such as "Is it possible to VP?" or "Do you think you could VP?" were not listed at all because they were already familiar with those forms themselves, though they did not seem to know that these forms can simultaneously function as requests (see Schmidt, 1990). Third, the participants were more likely to point out that NS English sounds more polite (or indirect) than NNS English. Fourth, as in the case of the FC learners, the participants in the FS condition showed their interest in colloquial and idiomatic expressions (words or phrases), including some discourse lubricants (e.g., *you know, goodness*). Fifth, they were more likely to focus on the content of the explanation (reasons/excuses) for the request and/or its place in the entire discourse developed by the requesters. This fifth point was also the noticing feature shared with the FC participants. In sum, almost half of the FS participants did notice one of the target request forms, but priority in their focus was actually given to the other linguistic and discourse features in the input.

For both FC and FS participants, attention was more likely to be directed to linguistic features other than the target request forms, only parts of the target forms when they noticed them, and some discourse-level features, in particular, the ways of justifying their requests as surmised earlier. The target "sentences" and their functions thus could not be successfully incorporated into their L2 pragmalinguistic knowledge, leading the participants in these two conditions to fail to provide the target request forms. Schmidt (1993b) argues that simple exposure to appropriate input is unlikely to be sufficient for acquisition of L2 pragmatic knowledge because the specific linguistic realizations are sometimes opaque to learners and the relevant contextual factors to be noticed may be defined differently or may not be salient enough for the learner (see Hulstijn, 1989; Doughty, 1991; Sharwood Smith, 1991; Alanen, 1995; Williams & Evans, 1998, for the saliency issue). In the FC and FS conditions, the participants were not simply exposed to the target input; the input was manipulated so that the participants could focus on the targets. However, the observations from the treatment tasks given earlier in this section substantiate arguments made by Schmidt and others.

For the FS condition, we also need to note the following point in addition to the saliency of target structures: Some forms of feedback from an NS counterpart in an interaction could also govern the learner's attention to the target form-function relationship. In the present study, the NS interlocutor in the NS-NNS role-plays in Takahashi and DuFon (1989) did not give any negative feedback to the NNS's monoclausal request forms. This was probably because the NS understood the NNS's intention despite her inappropriate request. But this led the FS participants to judge that such monoclausal request forms are still effective.

The results from the follow-up questionnaires provided direct answers to the question of whether the learners in the implicit enhancement conditions noticed the target forms during the treatment. As indicated in Table 11, on the whole, some learners did notice the target forms. This was particularly remarkable for the FC (24 participants out of the 25) and FS (11 participants out of the 24). The observed tendency for the FC group is understandable because of the nature of the treatment task.

TABLE 11. RESULTS OF FOLLOW-UP TASK

	Conditions		
Features of noticing	FC	FS	MF
Noticed targets + realized appropriate use + realized possible use in posttest → used forms in posttest	8 (32%)	0 (0%)	1 (3%)
Noticed targets + realized appropriate use + realized possible use in posttest → *did not* use forms in posttest	10 (40%)	1 (4%)	3 (10%)
Noticed targets + realized appropriate use → *did not* realize possible use in posttest	3 (12%)	1 (4%)	0 (0%)
Noticed targets → *did not* realize appropriate use	3 (12%)	9 (38%)	3 (10%)
Did not notice targets	1 (4%)	13 (54%)	24 (77%)

Note: FC = Form-comparison, FS = Form-search, MF = Meaning-focused

As for the MF participants, 77% of them did not notice the targets at all. Of particular interest is the comment from one of the MF participants on why she did not provide the target in the posttest: "I noticed the form when reading the transcripts; but when I was asked to write down a request [in the posttest], the first form I came up with in my mind was 'Could you please'" (translation mine). This again clearly indicates the relatively strong effect of their prior knowledge. In contrast, the participant in the MF condition who successfully provided the target form in the posttest reported that he noticed the target request form, its functional meaning, and the contextual features relevant to this form. He was thus able to transfer his acquired knowledge to the new situations. It could be argued, then, that some learners may consciously attend to target form-function relationships even if input is implicit/inductive in nature (see Alanen, 1995; Robinson, 1997). This further suggests the possible effects of individual differences arising from one's motivation and aptitude on learning pragmatic features (see Schmidt, 1993b; Tomlin & Villa, 1994; Alanen, 1995; Robinson, 1997; Williams & Evans, 1998).

A new question arises here as to why several learners in the implicit enhancement conditions did not actually supply the target forms in the posttest although they noticed the target forms in the treatment input and even realized the appropriate use of the forms. This may be because there were perceived differences in the degrees of imposition between the treatment situations (VIO/QUS) and the experimental situations

(APO, PAD, MAE, FEB). Some of the participants realized the possible use of the forms in the posttest, but they might have been unsure whether the request forms they noticed could be used equally appropriately in situations manifesting a slightly different degree of requestive imposition. This interpretation might be particularly plausible in view of the still relatively low confidence rates at the time of the posttest. The findings from the follow-up questionnaires, then, suggest two points. First, L2 learners may not be able fully to transfer their implicitly learned L2 pragmalinguistic features to new contexts, regardless of the degrees of input enhancement. Second, the levels of noticing differ from one learner to another (Sharwood Smith, 1991; Schmidt, 1993b; Robinson, 1997; see also VanPatten, 1994). Some participants noticed both the target form itself and its appropriate function in the discourse, while some others noticed only the target form in the input without exploring its functional meaning.

In all four request situations, the ET participants substantially increased their confidence in supplying the target forms in the posttest. This is understandable because they were explicitly taught what the appropriate request forms are. The MF participants also increased their confidence in the posttest, but possibly for a reason different from that of the ET learners. It seems that they felt confident in the posttest because they thought they could gain mastery over more reasonable discourse structures (e.g., the relevant sequence of request-related components) and could provide the monoclausal request forms which they perceived to be appropriate. In contrast, the FC and FS participants failed to increase their confidence substantially after the treatment in three out of the four situations. In the treatment training sessions, they were asked to make comparisons between the NS request usage and their own corresponding usage (for FC) or to point out NS usage distinctive from that of the NNS (for FS). These tasks might have led them to think that they were expected to master nativelike English during the training. In the posttest, therefore, they might have needed to show that they could not substantially increase their confidence because they judged that they had not yet attained an NS-level command as expected.

Conclusion

The findings of the present study replicated the major findings of the previous studies on input enhancement; that is, the target pragmatic features were found to be most effectively learned when they were under the condition in which a relatively high degree of input enhancement was realized with explicit metapragmatic information. Thus, we could claim that providing metapragmatic information on the target features is most likely to advance the learners' L2 pragmatic competence. However, the degree of attainment of L2 pragmatic competence under the explicit enhancement condition (along with its lasting effect) was questionable, suggesting some limitation to teaching pragmatic features in classroom settings (Kasper, 1997a). The results obtained for the three implicit enhancement conditions also motivate us to explore further the role of input enhancement in developing both linguistic and pragmatic competence in L2. Previous FonF studies (e.g., Lightbown & Spada, 1990; White, Spada, Lightbown & Ranta, 1991; Spada & Lightbown, 1993) have shown that meaning-focused communicative instruction was less effective than form-focused communicative instruction. The meaning-focused input condition in the present study (MF) was, in fact, found to be less effective than explicit instruction. However, the consciousness-raising tasks carried out in the FC and FS conditions were also found to be less effective. In particular, the task for the FC condition was set up so that the learners had a chance to notice the gap between NS request realization patterns and their own interlanguage realization patterns. In other words, the degree of input enhancement for the FC group was intended to be much higher than that for the FS condition (Ellis, 1995), but some of the participants were unable to restructure new form-function mappings in the L2, and the majority of them failed to generalize a new form-function relationship to a new context. This all suggests that L2 pragmatic competence cannot be enhanced with positive evidence alone. But before making such a strong claim, the effects of some other implicit input enhancement conditions, such as those adopting techniques of auto-input (House, 1996) or recasting (Doughty & Varela, 1998), need to be investigated. As Schmidt (1993b) argues, learning requires awareness at the time of learning of target features, and this may be substantiated by this study also, particularly in light of the performance of the ET participants. At the same time, the performance of those participants in the implicit enhancement conditions who failed to provide the targets makes us realize that simple noticing and attention to target pragmatic features in the input do not lead to learning (Schmidt, 1993b; Tomlin & Villa, 1994; Alanen, 1995; Leeman, Arteagoitia, Fridman, & Doughty, 1995). This becomes quite obvious when there are features in the input which are more central concerns to learners, such as ways of justifying requests. As Swain (1996, 1998) and Swain and Lapkin (1995) claim, the output of target features may also contribute to increasing the chances of learners' noticing them, and thus to the development of their pragmatic competence in L2. This is an issue which merits further research.

Appendix: Category of "request strategies" (from Takahashi, 1995)

(S = Speaker, H = Hearer, A = Act/Action)

1. Mood derivables: The speaker states a direct, imperative request to the hearer (e.g., V-*shite kudasai*, "please VP").
2. Performatives: The speaker explicitly indicates the illocutionary force by using a performative verb (*negau*, "ask," e.g., V-*te kudasaru yoo onegai shimasu*, "I ask you to VP").
3. Obligation (expectation) statements: The speaker states that the hearer is under some obligation to perform the desired action (e.g., V-*beki desu*, "You should VP").
4. Want statements: The speaker states his or her want or wish that the hearer will perform the desired action (e.g., V-*shite itadaki tai no desu ga*, "I would like you to VP").
5. Preparatory questions (without mitigated forms): The speaker asks a question concerning the hearer's will, willingness, ability, or possibility to perform the desired action (e.g., V-*shite kudasai mase-n ka*, "Will you VP?"/V-*shite itadake mase-n ka*, "Would you VP?").
6. Suggestion questions: The speaker asks a question concerning a reason why the hearer will or will not perform the desired action (e.g., V-*shite wa doo desu ka*, "How about/Why don't you VP?").
7. Permission questions: The speaker asks if the hearer grants permission for the speaker to have his or her request fulfilled (e.g., V-*shite mo ii desu ka*, "May/Can I VP?").
8. Mitigated-preparatory questions: The speaker asks a question concerning preparatory conditions or a permission question by embedding it within another clause (e.g., V-*suru koto deki mase-n [deshoo] ka*, "Do you think that you can VP/Would it be possible to VP?").
9. Mitigated-preparatory statements: The speaker states a preparatory condition by embedding it within another clause (e.g., -*ka doo ka to omoi mashi te*, "I was wondering if you could VP").
10. Mitigated-want statements (including a reduced form): The speaker states his or her want or wish that the hearer will perform the action in hypothetical situations (e.g., V-*shite kudasaru to arigatai no desu ga*, "I would appreciate it if you would VP"/V-*shite itadakere ba*, "If you would/could VP").
11. Nonconventional (Hints).

10 Explicit and implicit teaching of pragmatic routines

Japanese sumimasen

Yumiko Tateyama

Introduction

The majority of available research on the effects of instruction in pragmatics has focused on learners beyond a beginning level of proficiency (e.g., House & Kasper, 1981b; Billmyer, 1990a, 1990b; Olshtain & Cohen, 1990; Bouton, 1994a; Kubota, 1995; House, 1996), with only two studies to date examining whether pragmatics is teachable to beginners. Wildner-Bassett (1994) found that beginning learners of German improved considerably in their ability to use routine formulas after having received instruction. Tateyama, Kasper, Mui, Tay, and Thananart (1997) – which served as the pilot for the current study – examined the effects of instruction in pragmatics with beginning learners of Japanese at the University of Hawai'i. Students were divided into two groups, and received either implicit or explicit instruction in use of the Japanese pragmatic routine *sumimasen* and related expressions, which are commonly used for getting attention, apologizing, and expressing gratitude. Results showed that the explicit group outperformed the implicit group on a multiple-choice test as well as in role-plays rated by native speakers (NSs) of Japanese. The difference was especially notable in rather complicated situations, where the explicit group benefited more from the teacher's explanation of the use of the routine expressions under study. Although the treatment was provided only once during the 50-minute class period, the effectiveness of the instruction was obvious. In addition to role-plays and the multiple-choice test, students' verbal reports about their performance on role-plays provided valuable information about how they planned and executed speech acts in the target language. Although limited, the work by Wildner-Bassett and Tateyama et al. appears to indicate that pragmatics is teachable to beginning learners, which should be encouraging to language instructors – particularly in foreign language settings, where learners do not have as many opportunities to interact with NSs of the target language as in the

I am deeply indebted to David E. Ashworth, Haruko Minegishi Cook, and Gabriele Kasper for their insightful comments and suggestions throughout this study.

second language (L2) setting and the role of instruction becomes more important. The current study further explores issues raised in Tateyama et al. by examining the effectiveness of longer treatment periods on improving pragmatic ability in a second language.

Pedagogical perspectives

This study was motivated by encounters I have experienced with learners of Japanese who incorrectly use the Japanese routine expression *arigatoo* (thank you) to express gratitude when an NS of Japanese would normally use *sumimasen*. Several researchers (e.g., Eisenstein & Bodman, 1993; Ikoma, 1993) have noted that Japanese learners of English tend to incorrectly use the English expression *I'm sorry* to express gratitude when an NS of English would say *Thank you*. This seems to be negative pragmalinguistic transfer from Japanese *sumimasen*, which is often used in thanking situations. Studies which have examined the use of Japanese formulaic expressions for conveying gratitude and apologies (e.g., Coulmas, 1981b; Ikoma, 1993; Kumatoridani, 1994; Miyake, 1994a, 1994b; Ogawa, 1995) indicate that Japanese often use a quasi-apologetic expression such as *sumimasen* in thanking situations to acknowledge their indebtedness toward the interlocutor. For instance, Coulmas (1981b) explains that once a Japanese person receives an act of kindness, she or he feels obliged to repay it, which leads to the use of *sumimasen* (literally "not finished"). On the other hand, American learners of Japanese tend to express gratitude in most situations with *arigatoo* instead of *sumimasen*, which appears to be negative pragmalinguistic transfer of English *thank you*. These instances of negative pragmatic transfer are good examples of divergent form-function mappings that often distinguish NSs and learners (Kasper 1997a). When an NS of Japanese selects the linguistic means to express gratitude, various factors come into play, such as age, status, and the distinction between in-group and out-group. Nakane (1970) and Lebra (1976) pointed out that Japanese are group conscious and normally identify themselves in relation to others, placing themselves in what Nakane (1970) calls a "frame," which can be a locality or an institution that binds a set of individuals into one group. Those who are inside a frame are called "in-group" members in contrast to "out-group" members, who are outside. Inside every frame, relationships are generally vertical. Japanese usually speak formally to out-group members as well as to in-group members who have higher status. When they interact with in-group members with whom they do not have such vertical relationships, Japanese speak informally. It seems that learners of Japanese who consistently use *arigatoo* to express gratitude have probably not received instruction on how such cultural practices inform the choice of linguistic strategies for thanking and apologizing.

Olshtain and Cohen (1990) observe that EFL textbooks treat speech acts rather simplistically, and it seems that this is the case for Japanese textbooks as well. For instance, Coulmas (1981b, p. 82) points out that *sumimasen* as an expression of gratitude is virtually absent from Japanese textbooks, noting that "[i]n Japanese textbooks *'arigato'* is usually described as the most general and commonly used gratitude expression." After examining several popular Japanese textbooks used in U.S. colleges, I found that most textbooks did not offer explicit information regarding when to use expressions such as *gomen nasai* (I'm sorry), or *mooshiwake arimasen* (I'm terribly sorry) in addition to *sumimasen*. It would seem advantageous to introduce such basic expressions and their uses early on in the teaching of Japanese, but this does not appear to be a common practice. To compensate for this gap, the current study examines approaches in the teaching of these routine expressions to beginning JFL learners.

Research questions

This study investigates the following questions:

1. What are the effects of explicit and implicit instruction in the use of the routine Japanese formula *sumimasen* on beginning JFL learners? Is explicit instruction more effective than implicit instruction?
2. What is the relative effect of long-term treatment as compared to short-term treatment?
3. What is the relative effectiveness of various data elicitation measures (i.e., role-plays, multiple-choice tests, and verbal reports) for the study of the effects of instruction in pragmatics?

Method

Participants

The participants for this study were students enrolled in Japanese 102 (second semester beginning Japanese) at the University of Hawai'i at Manoa.[1] Because of institutional constraints, it was not possible to assign students randomly to the implicit or explicit groups, thus making

1 Japanese 102 is offered for those who have successfully completed Japanese 101, a course for absolute beginners. The class meets 50 minutes a day, 5 days a week throughout the semester. Those who have completed Japanese 102 are generally in the novice-high to intermediate-low range in the ACTFL oral proficiency interview scale.

it necessary to work with intact groups. Two classes taught by the same instructor (the author) participated in the study. The class taught during the fall semester of 1996 served as the explicit group (hereafter, Explicit), while the one taught during the spring semester of 1997 served as the implicit group (hereafter, Implicit). There were 13 students (9 male, 4 female) in Explicit and 14 students (10 male, 4 female) in Implicit.[2] The average age was 19.9 for Explicit and 19.4 for Implicit. All students were NSs of English, except for one Chinese student in Explicit and one Korean student in Implicit. Since both students had been in Hawai'i for more than 6 years at the time this research was conducted and they were advanced learners of English, they were not excluded from this study.

Teaching objectives

The material to be learned consisted of three functions of the routine formula *sumimasen*: getting attention, apologizing, and expressing gratitude.[3] Other formulas fulfilling these functions were also emphasized: the attention-getters *anoo, chotto (sumimasen)*; the apology routines *gomen (nasai), mooshiwake arimasen/gozaimasen*; and the thanking expressions *mooshiwake arimasen/gozaimasen* (focusing on indebtedness), *arigatoo (gozaimasu)* (focusing on appreciation), and *doomo (sumimasen/arigatoo)*. Students were to learn the forms, discourse functions, illocutionary forces, and politeness values of these routines, as well as the context factors constraining their use.

Instruction

Over an 8-week period, each group was given four treatments lasting approximately 20 minutes each. Instruction for the explicit group included the provision of explanations on the use of *sumimasen* and other similar routine expressions mentioned earlier, as well as the viewing of short video extracts from the Japanese television programs *Standard Japanese Course* (Japanese Broacasting Corporation, 1991) and *Yasashii Nihongo* [Easy Japanese] (Japanese Broacasting Corporation, 1996) containing the target features, and the use of handouts which illustrated

---

2 The participants were randomly assigned numbers from Ex1 through Ex13 for the explicit group and Im1 through Im14 for the implicit group. One of the female participants in Implicit (Im5) withdrew from the course in mid-semester, leaving a total of 13 students in Implicit when the study was completed. Im5 participated in the study until the third treatment was administered.

3 Although it is worth exploring how other functions of *sumimasen* listed in Ide (1998) are acquired by learners of Japanese, the current study is limited to the most commonly used functions (i.e., expressing gratitude and apologies as well as getting attention) because the participants are beginning learners of Japanese, and presenting too many functions of the same expression simultaneously may cause confusion for learners.

and explained the differences in usage of the routine formulas according to social contexts. During the initial treatment, students first discussed different functions of *sumimasen*. The second treatment focused on the use of *sumimasen* as an expression of apology, in contrast to *gomen* (*nasai*) and *mooshiwake arimasen/gozaimasen*, while the third treatment focused on the use of *sumimasen* as a means to express gratitude, in contrast to *arigatoo* (*gozaimasu*), *mooshiwake arimasen/gozaimasen*. In the fourth treatment, the instructor briefly summarized the proper use of *sumimasen* and other related routine formulas according to different contexts, and students watched several video clips from Japanese TV dramas which included the pragmatic routines under study. The implicit group did not engage in any of the explicit metapragmatic activities. Instead, during each treatment, the same video clips that were shown to the explicit group once were shown to this group twice. Before watching the video clips, the students were prompted to pay attention to any formulaic expressions they might hear. This was intended to focus the students' attention on pragmatic routines and to minimize the possibility that they would pay more attention to other interesting aspects of the video clips.

Assessment instruments and procedures

Before the first treatment was given, the participants were asked to fill out a background questionnaire which included items on students' motivation and goals for learning Japanese. At the end of each treatment, the students were asked to write a one-paragraph narrative on what they had learned from the lesson. In addition, worksheets on the use of routine formulas consisting of discourse completion tests (DCTs) were provided after each treatment to both groups so that the students could review what they had learned during the treatments and prepare for role-plays and multiple-choice tests (MCTs). The answer keys for these worksheets were provided a few days later.

About 1 week after the first and fourth treatments were given, each student participated in a set of four short role-play scenarios carried out individually with an NS of Japanese. Immediately after the role-plays, each participant was asked to complete a ten-item MCT on routine formulas.[4] When the MCT was completed, each participant responded to a

4 The four scenarios for the first set of role-plays and the ten items for the first MCT were modified versions of the pilot study. The scenarios for the second set of role-plays and the ten items for the second MCT were newly developed by the author and pilot-tested with another group of students. In order to prevent a practice effect, the role-play situations and the MCT items after the first and the fourth treatments were different but all situations required the use of the routine expressions under study. Furthermore, the situations in the second role-play set incorporated the new structures that the learners learned in the course.

questionnaire on the MCT probing for self-assessment, item difficulty, and reasons for choosing particular responses. Following this, there was a structured interview with each student, probing into role-play performance, assessment of the received instruction, and exploration of an alternative way of teaching pragmatics. The role-plays were tape-recorded and later rated by two NS instructors of Japanese using holistic ratings (5-point Likert scales). The rating scale was from 1 (awful) to 5 (wonderful), and "wonderful" referred to a nativelike performance. Raters were allowed to assign points in-between scale degrees (e.g., 2.5, 3.5) when they had difficulty deciding. Both raters listened to the students' role-play performance in each scenario, rated the performance, and offered brief comments or justification on their choice. After scenarios 1 through 4 were rated, the raters were asked to rate the participants' overall performance. Both multiple-choice and role-play tasks were chosen to assess the learners' pragmatic competence because, as Kasper and Blum-Kulka (1993, p. 61) point out, MCTs serve to elicit knowledge displays without making demands on learners' fluency or interactional skills, whereas role-plays assess the ability to compute contextual factors and assemble relevant linguistic material in a highly automatized fashion. Because role-plays make more cognitive demands on learners' comprehension and production systems, they are useful in examining learners' ability to instantaneously incorporate sociopragmatic and pragmalinguistic knowledge in interaction.

Data analysis

The data collected for this study were analyzed both quantitatively and qualitatively. The rating scores for role-plays were tallied and the mean scores for each role-play were compared between the explicit and implicit groups, as well as between the first set of role-plays administered after the first treatment, and the second set of role-plays given after the fourth treatment. The answers for MCTs were also tallied, and the differences between the two groups as well as the first and the second MCTs were compared. Repeated-measures ANOVA was used to see whether there were any statistically significant differences between the groups for role-plays and MCTs. In addition, the correlation between the role-play performances and the MCTs was examined.

Both the role-play performances and the retrospective interviews were tape-recorded and later transcribed. These were qualitatively examined, particularly in regard to the learners' planning and thought processes as well as strategies they employed. The raters' comments were also tape-recorded, transcribed, and examined in terms of the factors which affected their decisions of high or low rating scores.

TABLE 1. MCT SCORES

Students	MCT 1 scores	MCT 2 scores	Students	MCT 1 scores	MCT 2 scores
Ex1	5	8	Im1	9	5
Ex2	9	9	Im2	8	7
Ex3	8	7	Im3	8	6
Ex4	8	9	Im4	7	6
Ex5	7	8	Im5	6	NA
Ex6	8	7	Im6	7	7
Ex7	7	6	Im7	6	6
Ex8	7	9	Im8	7	5
Ex9	7	9	Im9	7	7
Ex10	7	5	Im10	6	6
Ex11	7	8	Im11	8	7
Ex12	8	8	Im12	7	6
Ex13	8	8	Im13	8	10
			Im14	9	6
Mean	7.38	7.77	Mean	7.36	6.46
SD	0.96	1.23	SD	1.01	1.27

TABLE 2. ANALYSIS OF VARIANCE: MCTs

Source of variation	SS	df	MS	F	p
Group	1.65	1	1.65	1.63	.214
Time	.03	1	.03	.12	.736
Group by time	.43	1	.43	1.68	.207

Results and discussion

Multiple-choice tests

As shown in Table 1, there was almost no difference (only .02 points) in the students' mean scores in the first MCT between the two groups (Explicit: 7.38, Implicit: 7.36). In the second MCT, Explicit (7.77) did slightly better than Implicit (6.46), with a 1.31 point difference, but a repeated-measures ANOVA showed no statistically significant difference between the groups (Table 2). It is interesting to note that while the mean score for Explicit slightly increased from the first MCT (7.38) to the second MCT (7.77), there was a decrease for Implicit from 7.36 in the first MCT to 6.46 in the second MCT (Figure 1), although the difference was not statistically significant.

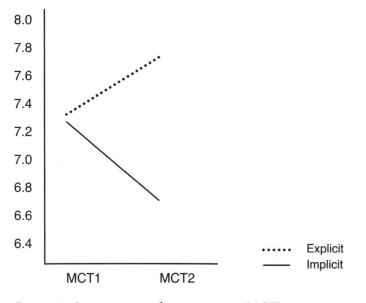

Figure 1 Comparison of mean scores (MCT).

The students generally based their expression selection on the formality of the situation, on the relationship and social status of interlocutors, on age differences, and on the degree of indebtedness and degree of damage. As shown in Table 3, both groups did well when the context was familiar to them; however, Explicit performed better in items which required higher formality, and involved indebtedness and severity of offense. For instance, in Question 2 (teacher washes a coffee pot), eleven of thirteen students in Explicit chose the correct answer (*doomo sumimasen*). In contrast, in Implicit, six of fourteen students chose *doomo arigatoo*, which is inappropriate when used to one's senior. The students who chose *doomo arigatoo* rather than the other two alternatives did so because they (Im6, Im7, Im9, and Im10) believed that *doomo arigatoo* is a more formal, polite way of expressing gratitude. Im13, who also chose *doomo arigatoo*, explained the reason for choosing this expression as follows: "I chose A because I am thanking the teacher for washing the coffee pot. B (*doomo sumimasen deshita*) is apologizing for the trouble they went through to wash it and C (*doomo*) is rude." This comment clearly indicates that Im13 had no knowledge about using the apologetic expression *doomo sumimasen* in a thanking situation.

TABLE 3. THE FIRST MCT RESPONSES

	A		B		C	
	Explicit	Implicit	Explicit	Implicit	Explicit	Implicit
Q1 (B=Answer)	0	0	13	14	0	0
Q2 (B=Answer)	2	6	11	8	0	0
Q3 (C=Answer)	0	7	1	3	12	4
Q4 (A=Answer)	2	9	11	4	0	1
Q5 (A=Answer)	13	13	0	1	0	0
Q6 (A=Answer)	9	14	0	0	4	0
Q7 (A=Answer)	13	14	0	0	0	0
Q8 (C=Answer)	0	1	3	9	10	4
Q9 (A=Answer)	4	9	3	3	6	2
Q10 (A=Answer)	9	12	4	2	0	0

Question 3 (breaking the teacher's video camera) also clearly differentiates the two groups. Twelve students in Explicit chose *mooshiwake arimasen,* which is the most sincere, formal apology. In contrast, seven students in Implicit chose *gomen nasai,* which is usually used toward one's equal or a lower-status person. Interestingly, most of the students who chose *gomen nasai* as the answer indicated that they thought it was the best way to say they were sorry. Furthermore, in Question 8 (receiving a nice gift from a senior colleague) ten students in Explicit chose the most appropriate response, *doomo sumimasen, arigatoo gozaimasu* to indicate indebtedness and appreciation at the same time, but only four students in Implicit chose this expression. The majority of the students in Implicit chose *doomo arigatoo gozaimasu.*

The fact that Explicit students chose the correct answers more successfully than Implicit students seems to demonstrate that explicit teaching contributed to raising their consciousness on proper use of the routine expressions under study. However, in some situations, such as Questions 4 (leaving the teacher's office after going over questions during office hours) and 9 (a friend cleans the kitchen after the party), the overuse of *sumimasen* by Explicit students was observed.

TABLE 4. THE SECOND MCT RESPONSES

	A		B		C	
	Explicit	*Implicit*	*Explicit*	*Implicit*	*Explicit*	*Implicit*
Q1 (B=Answer)	0	0	13	13	0	0
Q2 (A=Answer)	12	13	1	0	0	0
Q3 (B=Answer)	1	1	9	7	3	5
Q4 (A=Answer)	13	11	0	2	0	0
Q5 (B=Answer)	1	5	8	7	4	1
Q6 (B=Answer)	6	7	7	6	0	0
Q7 (A=Answer)	11	10	2	2	0	1
Q8 (C=Answer)	1	2	0	0	12	11
Q9 (C=Answer)	1	0	6	11	7	2
Q10 (B=Answer)	3	4	10	3	1	6

The results of the second MCT responses (Table 4) show a similar tendency as in the first MCT: Some situations (e.g., 1, 2, 4, 7, and 8) were easier to understand, so the majority of students in both groups chose the correct answers. In Question 5 (stepping on a middle-aged businessman's toes), eight of thirteen students in Explicit chose *sumimasen,* which is the most appropriate response, whereas in Implicit seven of thirteen students chose the same response but the remaining five students chose *gomen nasai.* Surprisingly, four students (Im3, Im8, Im11, and Im12) of these five were the same students who chose *gomen nasai* in Question 3 (breaking the teacher's video camera) in the first MCT. As for the reasons for choosing *gomen nasai,* Im8 and Im11 commented that they wanted to apologize. Im12 stated that he had been taught to use *gomen nasai* to apologize by his mother, who spoke Japanese to him. Im3, another participant who chose *gomen nasai* in the same question, commented as follows: "I picked A but now I look at it, I should've picked B because he's older." This comment seems to indicate that even without explicit instruction, learners are capable of figuring out pragmatic rules of the target language to a certain degree. The fact that Im1, Im6, and Im9 – all of whom chose *gomen nasai* in

Question 3 of the first MCT – successfully chose *sumimasen* in Question 5 of the second MCT may support this claim. With more time and practice, Im3 might be able to select the proper routine expression. However, for some students explicit explanations seem necessary, as indicated in Question 10 (going through a narrow path where junior high students are chatting). Although the majority of Explicit students chose *chotto, gomen nasai,* four learners in Implicit chose *chotto,* three chose *chotto, gomen nasai,* and six chose *chotto, sumimasen.* Of those who chose *chotto, sumimasen* in Implicit, two (Im10 and Im14) did so because they wanted to be polite to total strangers. The rest (Im3, Im7, Im8, and Im12) indicated that they chose *chotto, sumimasen* because they wanted to excuse themselves. Im12 commented as follows: "You must say 'Excuse me' and not 'Sorry,'" indicating that she had established incorrect translation equivalents between the Japanese and English routine formulas. For these learners, *gomen nasai* seems to be the sole expression that should be used to apologize. These students could have had a better understanding of these routine formulas if they had received explicit instruction.

As mentioned in the first MCT, the overuse of polite expressions by Explicit students was also observed in the second MCT. For instance, in Question 5 (stepping on a middle-aged businessman's toes), although only one participant in Implicit (Im2) chose *mooshiwake gozaimasen* (which might be too polite in this context), four students (Ex1, Ex6, Ex7, Ex11) in Explicit did so. As reasons for choosing this expression, all these students mentioned that the interlocutor is older and of higher status. It seems that some learners in the Explicit group have become overly cautious in choosing the correct routine expression, and, as a result, they were unnecessarily polite in some situations.

In sum, although no statistically significant effects from instruction were observed, it seems the explicit instruction was effective in enabling learners to select the appropriate expression in items which require higher formality, indebtedness, and severity of offense. However, the fact that learners exposed to explicit instruction became overly polite in some situations suggests that an explicit emphasis on contextually appropriate routines may result in teaching-induced pragmatic hyper-correction. This issue, which has not been noted in the literature before, merits further investigation.

Role-plays

Table 5 shows the overall ratings of the two groups in the two sets of role-plays, referred to as Role-play 1 and Role-play 2. Contrary to the results obtained in the pilot study, in which explicit group learners received higher ratings than those in the implicit group, in the current

TABLE 5. ROLE-PLAY OVERALL RATING SCORES

Students	Role-play 1 overall ratings	Role-play 2 overall ratings	Students	Role-play 1 overall ratings	Role-play 2 overall ratings
Ex1	1.5	2.75	Im1	2	2
Ex2	2.5	2.25	Im2	2.5	2.5
Ex3	4	3.25	Im3	3.75	3.75
Ex4	2.5	2.25	Im4	2.5	2.75
Ex5	3.5	4	Im5	3.5	NA
Ex6	2.5	2.5	Im6	3.5	4.5
Ex7	1.5	1.75	Im7	3	3.5
Ex8	4.25	2.25	Im8	3.75	4
Ex9	3.5	2.75	Im9	3	4.25
Ex10	3.5	3	Im10	2.25	2
Ex11	3	4	Im11	2.5	2.75
Ex12	3.5	3.25	Im12	4.25	3.75
Ex13	2.5	2.5	Im13	4.5	3.75
			Im14	3	4
Mean	2.94	2.81	Mean	3.14	3.35
SD	0.87	0.68	SD	0.76	0.84

TABLE 6. MEAN RATING SCORES FOR EACH SITUATION (ROLE-PLAYS 1 AND 2)

	Explicit		Implicit	
	Role-play 1	Role-play 2	Role-play 1	Role-play 2
Situation 1	2.5	3.19	3.29	3.67
Situation 2	2.53	2.54	2.91	3.25
Situation 3	2.86	2.77	3.2	3.31
Situation 4	3.03	2.73	3.37	3.33
Overall	2.94	2.81	3.14	3.35

TABLE 7. ANALYSIS OF VARIANCE: ROLE-PLAY TASKS

Source of variation	SS	df	MS	F	p
Group	4.92	1	4.92	3.55	.072
Time	1.23	1	1.23	1.11	.302
Group by time	6.23	1	6.23	1.68	.026

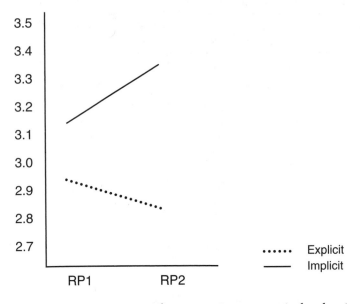

Figure 2 Comparison of mean rating scores (role-plays).

study Implicit received slightly better ratings than Explicit (2.94 versus 3.14 for Role-play 1; 2.81 versus 3.35 for Role-play 2). It is interesting to note that while the mean rating score for Explicit slightly decreased from Role-play 1 (2.94) to Role-play 2 (2.81), there was a slight increase for Implicit from 3.14 in Role-play 1 to 3.35 in Role-play 2 (Figure 2). This is in contrast to the result of the MCTs in which Explicit slightly increased the scores while Implict slightly decreased the scores as shown in Figure 1. Comparing the rating results of each scenario in Role-play 1 and Role-play 2 also yielded similar results: Implicit students received higher ratings than Explicit students (Table 6). However, the differences between the groups were not statistically significant when compared by a repeated-measures ANOVA, as seen in Table 7.

Although no significant group differences resulted from the treatments, some students were rated considerably higher on the second role-plays. For instance, Ex1's ratings in the first role-plays ranged from 1 to 1.75, but for the second role-plays she received ratings of 2.5 and 4. Scores for Ex11 also increased, this time from 2.5 and 3 in the first role-plays to 3.25 and 4 in the second role-plays. Although not as dramatic as Ex1's or Ex11's, Ex5's ratings also increased from 3 and 3.5 to 3.25 and 4.

Some students in Implicit were also rated higher in the second role-plays. For example, Im6's ratings in the first role-plays were 2.5 and 4, but his ratings in the second role-plays increased to 4 and 4.5. Another student, Im9, also had an increase from 2.75 and 3.75 to 3 and 4.25. The increase of these students' rating scores might be the result of the effectiveness of the instruction, but it could also be the result of chance fluctuation. This may be also explained in terms of the auto-input hypothesis (Sharwood Smith, 1988). Confronting one's own output during the retrospective interview after the first role-plays and rigorously examining it with the interviewer might have served as helpful input to the students (cf. House, 1996).[5]

One student (Ex8) received considerably lower ratings in the second role-plays. His ratings in the first role-plays ranged from 3.5 to 4.25, but in the second role-plays they were 1.25 and 3.75. In fact, Ex8's overall ratings dropped from 4.25 to 2.25, as shown in Table 5. His comments on scenario 3 (asking a teacher for permission to leave early) in Role-play 2, for which he received a score of 1.25, illustrate that he had fairly good knowledge about the use of routine expressions, as well as how status differences affect the choice of the proper form: "Obviously I have to be most polite because this is my professor, my superior. I had a hard time saying 'I had a headache and a fever due to cold.' But I know I had to use the most polite forms." Vocabulary and structural problems were the main reasons for his low rating score by the two raters. Ex8 also had considerable difficulty with online processing when engaged in the role-play, as indicated by his comments regarding alternative responses considered in scenario 3:

I considered *mooshiwake arimasen*, but then I realized that I wasn't exactly late, so I didn't need to use it. The first thing I thought about was *sumimasen*, and then I was kind of hesitant between the two, so I picked something between the two: *ano sumimasen*. When I said *doomo arigatoo* at the end, I thought about other options as well: *doomo sumimasen* because I'm kind of indebted to the professor.

When asked why he chose *doomo arigatoo* over *doomo sumimasen*, Ex8 said, "That was a spur-of-the-moment decision. Now the more I think about it, *doomo sumimasen* might have been more appropriate." These comments show that even when the learner has acquired fairly good knowledge about the pragmatic rules of the target language, applying those rules in an actual communicative situation is far more demanding.

Low ratings were given when students did not express gratitude or apologize or when they used the wrong formulas to convey these illocutionary forces. Even when students' productions were pragmalinguistically and sociopragmatically appropriate, dysfluent delivery and

5 During the verbal report session, the participants listened to their audiotaped role-plays before they commented on their performances.

pronunciation errors resulted in low ratings. These findings coincide with what was revealed in the pilot study. In addition, both raters in the current study pointed out that lack of affect, and addition of an incorrect particle to a routine expression, were factors which lowered ratings. For instance, in the following excerpt in which the student asks the teacher if it is all right to submit the homework the following day (Situation 3 in Role-play 1), Ex6 was successful in producing grammatically correct sentences, but not so successful in doing so in an appropriate manner.

Example 1

> 1   J: *Hai, shukudai o dashite kudasai.*
> → 2 Ex6: *E:tto, ashita made yoroshii deshoo: ka?*
> 3   J: *Ashita desu ka? So: desu ne. Wakarimashita.*
> 4 Ex6: *Hai, shitsuree shimasu.*

Example 1 (Translation)

> 1   J: Now, please submit your homework.
> 2 Ex6: Er . . . , may I turn it in tomorrow?
> 3   J: Tomorrow? Let's see. OK.
> 4 Ex6: All right, excuse me.

Rater 1 commented that "A6 said *Ashita made yoroshii deshooka* too smoothly; he should have said it in a more hesitant manner." It is interesting to note that *yoroshii deshoo ka* is a very polite expression to use when asking for permission; despite this, saying it in a very direct manner gives a negative impression to the interlocutor in a context such as the one in this example. No apology at the end of the exchange further lowered A6's rating (rating score of 2.5), even though he said *shitsuree shimasu* (excuse me) at the end.

Sometimes, even when a proper routine expression was used, if it was said in an abrupt manner or with the wrong intonation, it also lowered the student's rating score. For instance, Im10 offered an apologetic thanks, *sumimasen*, when he declined an invitation by his senior to go to a movie (Situation 4 in Role-play 2). Despite the fact that Im10 used *sumimasen* appropriately, Rater 1 remarked that the manner in which Im10 said it did not sound as if he was actually apologizing. Rater 2 also commented that the abrupt manner of speaking lowered Im10's rating (rating score of 2.5). When looking at the transcripts alone, what he said seems most appropriate:

Example 2

> 1   J: *Hai, ano kinyoobi no yoru issho ni eiga o mimasen ka?*
> → 2 Im10: *Ah, sumimasen. Pa:ti: e ikimasu.*
> 3   J: *Ah, so: desu ka? Ja: doyoobi no ban wa?*
> → 4 Im10: *Ah, sumimasen. Arubaito ga aru n desu.*

5   J: *Ah, so: desu ka? Arubaito desu ka. Un, ja mata hima na toki ni mimashoo: ka.*
6 Im10: *Hai.*

Example 2 (Translation)

1   J: OK, would you like to see a movie with me on Friday evening?
2 Im10: Oh, I'm sorry. I will go to a party.
3   J: Oh, is that right? Then, how about Saturday evening?
4 Im10: Oh, I'm sorry. It is that I have a part-time job.
5   J: Oh, is that right? You have a part-time job. Well, then, shall we see when you are free again?
6 Im10: OK.

Rater 2 said, "To his senior, Im10 should speak in a more apologetic manner. If a hedge such as *chotto* (a bit) or explanation using *-kara* (because) or *n desu kedo* (it is that. . .) had been offered, his performance would have been better. Im10 said *sumimasen,* but did not sound as if he was apologizing." These findings shed light on the importance of teaching how to speak in a pragmatically appropriate way. Furthermore, in terms of research, it is necessary to have raters listen to the actual performance rather than have them simply look at the transcripts when rating in order to take paralinguistic cues into consideration.

There were some instances where proper routine expressions were used but the addition of an inappropriate particle lowered the overall rating scores. The particle which was inappropriately used by some students was the particle *ne*, which is used to index affective common ground between the speaker and the addressee (Cook, 1992). Although Japanese attach a final particle to impart some additional hint of the speaker's attitude toward what they are saying (Martin, 1975, p. 914), improper use of the particle causes a problem, even to the point of being an irritation to the interlocutor. In particular, attaching the particle *ne* to routine expressions when talking to a senior interlocutor is inappropriate. Im14 was observed overusing the particle *ne*, which negatively affected his ratings. In the first role-plays, he added *ne* to almost all the routine expressions he used, even with senior students and teachers. In the second role-plays, he evidenced in the same role-play situation mixed use of proper routine expressions at one time, and incorrect forms with the particle *ne* attached in another. When asked why he used the particle *ne* during the interview after the second role-plays, Im14 said, "I always do that. I don't know why. I think it's because I heard those other people use that. Maybe." He indicated that he worked at a Duty-Free Shop (DFS) for about 8 months. Since there were some Japanese female salesclerks who were much older than he was at DFS, their use of the particle *ne* to younger customers might have served as input to him, and that could have contributed to his frequent use of the particle *ne*.

TABLE 8. COMPARISON OF THE FINAL EXAMINATION SCORES

	Mean	SD
Explicit	82.72	7.10
Implicit	88.68	4.95

24 *df*

$t_{crt} = 2.49$

$t_{obs} = 2.50*$

$p < 0.0167$

In the pilot study, there was a strong correlation between the participants' performance in the MCTs and the role-plays, and this tendency was stronger for the explicit group. However, in the current study such correlations were not observed. In order to explain this discrepancy, it may be worth noting the students' academic performance during the semester they participated in this study. Table 8 shows the mean and standard deviation of the final exam scores of the two groups, indicating that Implicit scored higher than Explicit (88.68 versus 82.72), and this difference was statistically significant at $p < 0.0167$ as indicated by a one-tailed *t*-test.[6] Furthermore, more students in Implicit indicated that they had opportunities to interact with speakers of Japanese outside class, and this could have contributed to better ratings. Im13, who received high scores in both sets of role-plays, indicated that he interacted with Japanese students on a daily basis. Even though he said he spoke English with the Japanese students most of the time, it seems that he successfully acquired Japanese mannerisms while interacting with them, which was also noted by Rater 1. On the other hand, there were some students who were exposed to a Japanese-speaking environment but did not necessarily score high on the MCT or role-plays.

Self-reports

The written self-reports elicited subsequent to the MCT and the retrospective interviews following the role-plays indicated what planning decisions the students made in preparing their responses. For example, the students commented on how they considered context variables in response planning, and on the perceived ease and difficulty of the MCT and role-play scenarios. The self-reports were particularly helpful in

6 Institutional constraints did not permit the administration of a pretest prior to the first treatment session.

understanding why the student chose a certain routine formula over other routine expressions. In addition, the retrospective interviews revealed some interesting aspects in planning and executing speech-act utterances as well as students' evaluation of the teaching approaches. I will discuss here some of the major findings.

Some students did not carefully plan what to say in the role-plays, and that led to poor performance. For instance, Ex7, who received low rating scores in both sets of role-plays (overall rating scores of 1.5 and 1.75, respectively), remarked as follows in regard to his planning for scenario 3 (asking a teacher for permission to leave early) of Role-play 2: "I felt like too fast. I couldn't try before you told me to start because, I don't know. I tried to get it out straight, but then I thought just try it. Because I had the first one aloud, so I thought let's try and wing it." This is reminiscent of Cohen's (1996, p. 256) observation that "learners who do a minimal assessment of a situation before starting to speak might be more prone to violate certain sociocultural and sociolinguistic conventions than those of similar ability who do more careful pre-planning." However, careful planning is not always a guarantee of successful performance. There were instances when students had planned well but what they actually said differed from what they had planned. For instance, Ex4 commented on his performance in scenario 2 (an upperclassman helping you move) of Role-play 1 that "I just really plan much. That's why I got messed up, but I forgot the words for chair and desk, but that was the only thing I was thinking of telling about putting it over there. I was supposed to say, I was thinking of saying *mooshiwake arimasen*, but I think I said *sumimasen*. I wanted to say the other one. I don't know why I said that." Trying to recall a forgotten word or expression negatively affected some students when they were called upon to do a new task (cf. Cohen & Olshtain, 1993). For instance, Ex1 indicated that because she concentrated on trying to recall the proper structure to ask about the location of the school cafeteria, she simply forgot to include a routine formula *sumimasen* to get attention. Another participant, Im11, accidentally said *gohyaku doru* (five hundred dollars) when he was supposed to say *gojuu doru* (fifty dollars) for the price of the shoes his customer inquired about. He noted that he had been thinking how to say "an alternative item" in Japanese but he had a hard time figuring it out.

Task familiarity affected ease or difficulty in planning as well as executing a speech act. Eisenstein and Bodman (1993) pointed out that whether or not the participant has encountered a similar situation that she or he is going to enact in a role-play influences the success or failure of the task performance. Ex2, who received relatively high scores for scenario 3 (turning in homework late) of Role-play 1 despite his low rating scores in the other situations, noted that "this was one of the easier ones 'cuz I could relate to it. Like sometimes I have to turn homework in late. I guess this is something I always use." Ex12 attributed the difficulty of closing the dialogue properly in scenario 4 (declining an invitation from an upperclassman) of Role-play 2 to the fact that she had not encountered a similar situation before. Naturally, task familiarity alleviates the demanding process of planning as well. When the student is familiar with the situation, the utterances that she or he is going to produce are more or less routinized and, as a result, it becomes easier for the student to retrieve appropriate expressions.

In planning, most students report thinking in two languages; that is, they read the role-play card (written in English), grasped the context, formulated a response in English, and then translated it into Japanese. Only a few students thought in Japanese from the beginning, such as Ex4, who commented that "I would say each time I was thinking in Japanese. 'Cuz I think the reason is that I'm not kind of reading it, so rather than read it, I'm thinking about what I'm going to say in Japanese." Thinking in Japanese from the beginning was observed in rather easier role-plays; when the role-play became more complicated, the students preferred to plan in English first and then translate into Japanese. Cohen and Olshtain (1993) note that some of their students thought in three languages when planning and executing speech-act utterances. There were two students in the current study whose native language was not English: Ex5 (NS of Chinese) and Im9 (NS of Korean). Interestingly, neither of them reported thinking in their native language while preparing to perform the role-plays. Ex5 thought in English most of the time and then translated from English into Japanese, whereas Im9 thought in Japanese for easier role-plays and in English for more demanding ones. As for a reason for not thinking in Chinese, Ex5 indicated that he had learned Japanese through English. If he had learned it directly from Chinese, he might have thought in Chinese. It could also be argued that since both Ex5 and Im9 were advanced speakers of English, thinking in English had become natural for them.

Most students indicated that they enjoyed participating in this study and that the instruction as well as the materials provided were helpful. Several students commented that the video clips had helped them to understand how routine formulas were used in the actual interaction. For instance, Ex3 remarked that the video was most helpful because it enabled her to better understand the events and the relationship between the interlocutors. It is interesting to note that almost all students in the explicit group indicated that the explicit explanation about the use of routine expressions by the instructor played an important role in their understanding of the use of routine expressions under study. They indicated that the video-only instruction would probably not have been sufficient for them to fully understand the varied usage of these routine expressions. Although some members of the implicit group preferred an explicit explanation, some opted for implicit learning. For instance, when asked whether or not an explanation by the teacher should have been offered, Im12 said, "You could, but I think learning this type of thing is too easy. If you explain, you are telling everybody what they should say at a particular time and they shouldn't, so I think it's better for them to make a mistake and learn by themselves."

Discussion and implications

This study compared the use of explicit and implicit instruction in a number of basic pragmatic routines in Japanese with the aim of determining the effectiveness of each for use in the teaching of Japanese pragmatics. Results on MCTs and role-plays indicated no significant differences between the two groups. It could be argued that four 20-minute treatments over an 8-week period were not sufficient to reveal the effectiveness of different teaching conditions. However, such an explanation is inconsistent with the results of the pilot study (Tateyama et al., 1997), which demonstrated an advantage for the explicit group after a single treatment of only 25 minutes in each group. Therefore, several other factors also need to be considered. One of these is motivation – those who scored higher than others in the role-plays indicated a strong interest in learning Japanese. For instance, Ex11, who received an overall rating score of 4 in Role-play 2, indicated that she would like to learn how to speak Japanese so that she could go to Japan to study textile arts. Im13, who received an overall rating score of 4.5 in Role-play 1, indicated a strong interest in Japanese culture, in particular regional dialects and entertainment. Because those who scored high in the role-plays and/or in the MCTs were highly motivated in the first place, the types of instruction they received may not have caused much of a difference. Interestingly, even among those who responded that they were taking this course to fulfill a language requirement (four students in Explicit and five in Implicit), many commented that they chose Japanese because it was their heritage language and/or they wanted to gain fluency so that they could use the language in the future. Another factor which might have influenced the result is the amount of contact with speakers of Japanese outside of class. Although students in the explicit group had hardly any contact with speakers of Japanese, seven students in the implicit group indicated that they spoke Japanese outside of class on a regular basis. This might have affected their performance in both the MCTs and the role-plays. And finally, the fact that the implicit group academically outperformed the explicit group might have also affected the results. The study should thus be replicated with more comparable groups, as would be achieved by assigning students to the two instructional groups. Despite its limitations, when viewed together with previous research, this study suggests several recommendations for instruction in L2 pragmatics and for further research in this area.

It seems that some aspects of L2 pragmatics are teachable to beginners before they develop analyzed L2 knowledge (Wildner-Bassett, 1994; Tateyama et al., 1997). Unanalyzed chunks and routines play an important role in early L1 and L2 acquisition because they allow learners to participate in communicative interaction early on. Since a great deal of our daily communicative activity consists of using routines (Coulmas, 1981a), and an enormously large amount of natural language is formulaic, automatic, and rehearsed, rather than propositional, creative, or freely generated (Fillmore, 1979), developing the ability to use routines in an appropriate context in L2 early on will lead to fluent and efficient utterance production.

Explicit teaching appears to be more effective than implicit teaching in facilitating the acquisition of L2 pragmatic routines that require a higher formality of the linguistic expressions, as demonstrated by the MCT analysis. Also, the fact that learners in the explicit group used the routine expressions under study more often in authentic situations than implicit learners may suggest the success of consciousness-raising by explicit teaching.[7] However, explicit teaching did not result in higher scores in role-plays, and this seems to suggest that it is necessary to closely examine such factors as motivation, amount of contact with speakers of the target language outside of class, and academic performance, which may affect the effectiveness of such instruction. Regarding different teaching approaches, it may not hurt to take students' learning styles into consideration. More research needs to be done to explore the approaches or activities through which different pragmatic abilities can best be developed.

Previous studies (House & Kasper, 1981b; Wildner-Bassett, 1984; Billmyer, 1990a, 1990b; House, 1996) have demonstrated that communicative practice improves most aspects of learners' pragmatic ability, and although the treatments offered in this study did not include communicative practice, some students indicated that they wanted to have more opportunities to role-play different situations in class. One such student (Ex2) noted that "lots of different situations were given [in the video] but by the fourth time it was kind of same thing. . . . Maybe more role-plays put in situations instead of just watching it make you

7 While the current study was in progress, the author took field notes to see if the routine expressions under study were actually used by the students in authentic situations. Interestingly, those who were observed to use the routine expressions were mostly Explicit students.

think a little more." Another student (Im7) suggested actual simulation in class or creating a video on their own. He indicated that he learned best when actually engaged in communicative activities. As for other activities, Ex1 suggested a video lab, similar to a language lab, where students can go at any time to watch various situations of their choice to help them better understand cultural differences and how actual interactions take place in the target language. In a foreign language setting, where learners have very few opportunities to interact with speakers of the target language outside of class, communicative activities as well as watching videos will allow learners to access and integrate sociopragmatic and pragmalinguistic knowledge more quickly and efficiently (cf. Rose, 1994b).

Results from this study indicate the utility of incorporating retrospective interviews into foreign language teaching on a regular basis. Assessment of learner performance in the target language tends to adopt an exclusive orientation to product, and in so doing neglects process. Although it is time-consuming to administer verbal report sessions, they provide valuable information regarding learners' planning and thought processes, which can help teachers better understand why the learner made a particular error. In this study, many participants indicated that they were thinking about alternatives when they uttered certain phrases or expressions. In particular, selecting an appropriate routine expression out of several similar expressions was difficult for many students. Very often a participant who uttered a routine expression which was not the most appropriate in the given context was actually thinking about the most appropriate one as an alternative. Administering a retrospective verbal report will help teachers better understand why their students perform as they do. Teachers should be aware that L2 learners' utterances are often produced after an internal debate in their minds (Cohen & Olshtain, 1993). Moreover, Ericsson and Simon (1993, pp. xviiiff.) cite evidence demonstrating that verbal report may improve performance. Verbal report is thus not only a useful diagnostic for teachers but also enhances L2 learning.

Finally, the findings from this study may offer research methodological insights as well. For instance, comparing the number of routine formulas used correctly by the learners in disregard of paralinguistic cues may serve to display their knowledge about usage but may not serve as valid data to indicate what they can actually do with the knowledge. In other words, the data collected through the MCTs or DCTs are helpful to assess the participant's metapragmatic knowledge, but they do not reveal whether the student actually has the command of using the expression she or he can produce in the MCT or DCT in face-to-face interaction. The role-plays employed in this study were useful in compensating for this gap and measuring the students' knowledge and control of processing (Bialystok, 1993). Role-plays do not necessarily tell us how students use their pragmatic knowledge in real-life situations, but the task demands of role-play require conversational interaction in real time, making role-plays an effective data collection procedure. Furthermore, the use of verbal reports helps researchers better understand why the students performed as they did in various tasks. In sum, the data elicitation measures used in this study were effective in the sense that they supplemented each other.

11 Explicit instruction and JFL learners' use of interactional discourse markers

Dina Rudolph Yoshimi

Introduction

The development of L2 pragmatic competence entails the ability to use a wide range of conversational routines and discourse strategies to manage one's communicative interactions with others. Since the early 1980s, researchers have established that a foreign language learner's development of various aspects of pragmatic competence may be facilitated by the instruction of pragmatic routines and strategies in the foreign language classroom (Kasper, this volume). House (1996, p. 247) points out that when such instruction is explicit, it appears to be particularly beneficial since it enables learners to develop an awareness and understanding of the differences between L1 and L2 pragmatic preferences, and thereby "counteract negative L1 transfer through 'noticing' (Schmidt, 1993b) and through making attempts to use alternative, more L2 norm-oriented expressions." In a comparison of the relative benefits of implicit and explicit instruction, House (1996) reports on two sections (i.e., implicit and explicit) of a 14-week communication course instructed in the use of everyday, conversational routines. Through lectures, handouts, and explanatory feedback that provided metapragmatic information on the use and function of these routines, the members of the explicit group had additional opportunities to raise their awareness of preferred L2 pragmatic practices and to "notice" differences between L1 and L2 practices. House argues that the greater improvement shown by the explicit group, particularly in areas where the pragmatic preferences of the learners' L1 differed from

This research was supported by a grant from the U.S. Department of Education (CFDA 84.229, P229A60007, administered by the National Foreign Language Resource Center at the University of Hawai'i, Manoa). I am deeply indebted to Tomoko Iwai, Reiko Nishikawa, and Momoyo Shimazu for their work on this project, and to Gabriele Kasper for her support and insight. I also extend my thanks to Kathleen Bardovi-Harlig, John Clark, and James Pusak for their helpful comments on the study design. An earlier version of this work was presented at the 18th Annual Second Language Research Forum at the University of Hawai'i, Manoa (October 15–18, 1998).

223

those of the target L2, is a result of the learners' heightened awareness of L1-L2 pragmatic differences. Focusing on a distinct aspect of pragmatic competence – the use of discourse markers in extended tellings – Yoshimi (1998a, 1998b) was unable to replicate House's (1996) findings. During a 16-week course, advanced English-speaking learners of Japanese were provided with metapragmatic information regarding the use and functions of discourse markers through lectures and discussion of spoken and written texts. However, despite an increase in their use of discourse markers in personal narratives and retellings, this use was more consistent with the pragmatic preferences of the learners' L1 than of the target L2. In discussing her findings, Yoshimi (1998a) identifies the quantity and quality of the practice and feedback components of the instructional treatment as potential deficiencies. In proposing a need to expand these aspects of the instructional approach, she notes Tateyama , Kasper, Mui, Tay, and Thananant's (1997) suggestion that communicative practice and corrective feedback may enhance the "noticing" (Schmidt, 1990, 1993a) afforded by explicit instruction.

This chapter presents a follow-up to Yoshimi (1998a, 1998b) undertaken to determine whether an explicit instructional approach with expanded opportunities for communicative practice and feedback can facilitate learners' development of the targetlike use of Japanese discourse markers in the production of extended tellings. Although a variety of discourse markers were targeted for instruction, I report only on the learners' use of three of these markers: *n desu, n desu kedo,* and *n desu ne.* These markers play important roles in organizing the presentation of an extended telling, and in expressing the speaker's interpersonal orientation in such a telling. Since these functions also render the telling more coherent and engaging for the listener, I will refer to these three items as "interactional markers." The specific functions of each marker will be discussed in conjunction with the analysis of learner use of each item.

Study design and participants

The study used a pretest/posttest, experimental group design. A storytelling task from Tarone and Yule (1989, p. 173) was administered as a pre- and posttest to all participants in the study. In addition, sampling of the extended tellings of the learners in the experimental group was conducted approximately every 2 weeks in conjunction with explicit instructional activities. (See the section titled "Communicative practice" on page 226.) Students from three classes of third-year Japanese at the University of Hawai'i, Manoa, participated in the study. All three classes were instructed by experienced instructors who are NSs of Japanese.

One intact class was designated as the experimental group (n = 5), and twelve volunteer participants from the other two classes (n = 4 and n = 8) were designated as the control group. The participants had studied Japanese for an average of 5 to 8 years, including study in high school and extracurricular Japanese school. With the exception of three NSs of Chinese (one in the experimental and two in the control group), all participants were NSs of English.

Explicit instruction

The explicit instruction component was added on to the regular third-year curriculum (80 contact hours), and accounted for approximately 30% of the total contact hours. The instruction was developed to provide the following: information about the function and use of the target items (explanatory handout); exposure to native models of nonformal, extended discourse and the use of the target items in such discourse (NS model); opportunities for planning the production of nonformal, extended discourse (the planning session); opportunities for communicative practice of the target items in conjunction with extended discourse (communicative practice sessions); and feedback on the use of target items and the production of extended discourse (corrective feedback sessions). A detailed description of each of these components follows.

The explanatory handout

For each target item or set of items, the students were provided with a two- to three-page explanatory handout containing nontechnical descriptions of the function(s) of the item(s) in extended discourse; each handout included sample uses of the item(s) in extended discourse, mostly drawn from natural discourse. The target items presented for explicit instruction on the handouts were selected for their relevance to the organization, coherence, and cohesion of extended discourse and/or the expression of speaker stance, speaker perspective, and/or speaker subjectivity in extended discourse. There were eight handouts in all, approximately one every 2 weeks.

The NS model

The NS model (NSM), conducted as an ad-libbed interaction between two NSs (usually the instructor and another NS), was presented at the beginning of each lesson as an example of the target task for the given lesson (e.g., tell about how you first became interested in studying Japanese, tell a story about your family, retell the story of a favorite book or movie). All efforts were made to preserve the naturalness of the interaction: There were no prepared scripts, and no conscious effort was made to include the items targeted for explicit instruction in the model. Furthermore, an NS (rather than the students) took the role of addressee in order to discourage the speaker from excessive accommodation to the students' speech level. The NSM was videotaped so that, after the initial class discussion of the model, the video could be replayed one or more times to provide the learners with additional opportunities to understand the content and/or to notice the structures used.

The planning session

After the presentation and discussion of the NSM, the class was divided into small groups (two or three students per group) headed by the instructor or a native Japanese-speaking teaching assistant. Each student was then given an opportunity to talk about and/or present her telling in English, and to ask questions about vocabulary and structure for production of the telling in Japanese. The instructor/assistant provided feedback to each student regarding the organization, content, and clarity of the telling. Feedback included suggestions for adding background information about people and places, leaving out tangential material, providing explanations of participants' motives and/or actions, and so on. During the planning session, students often found that their planned telling was "too complicated" or "not very interesting," and would alter the content or nature of the telling.

Communicative practice

For each task, students were provided with three in-class opportunities to perform their planned telling, with a different conversational partner eliciting the telling each time. During these communicative practice (CP) sessions, the student was responsible for fully and effectively communicating her telling to an addressee – the instructor or an assistant – who was not familiar with the content of it. Although the production was elicited as part of a planned classroom activity, the instructor/assistant provided back-channel responses and occasionally asked for clarification or additional background information. More extended interaction often occurred after the student had concluded her telling. The other students in the group acted predominantly as an audience, although follow-up questions and comments by these students were not uncommon. The CP sessions were, on average, spaced 2 class days apart (i.e., days 2, 5, and 8 of a 10-day lesson).

Corrective feedback

Immediately after each CP, the instructor/assistant provided corrective feedback to the student on her production. Feedback focused on the student's use of the target items and on the overall organization and coherence of the telling. Feedback on grammatical and lexical errors was left to the discretion of each instructor/assistant. In addition to these three rounds of immediate feedback, the instructor provided a considerably expanded form of feedback the day after the second CP session (CP2). This expanded feedback was prepared after class by the instructor in collaboration with at least one assistant and the researcher (a nonnative speaker). It included a transcript of the student's telling (with editing of false starts, hesitations, and the like for clarity), feedback on the organization of the telling and the (mis)use of target items therein, and a proposed version of part, or all, of the telling. Revisions in the proposed version addressed inappropriate or missed uses of the target items, awkward or nontarget-like presentation (especially excessive use of monoclausal sentences), and/or lack of coherence or cohesion in the student's telling. Grammatical errors were also edited. On the day after CP2, the instructor/assistant who had been the addressee for that session worked with each of the students in her group to review the expanded feedback. This session constituted an additional opportunity both for supplementary explicit teaching of the target items and for raising student awareness regarding the production of extended tellings.

Control group instructional treatment

The instruction in the control classes did not include any explicit instruction on the production of extended tellings, nor were the target items for the experimental treatment the focal point of any explicit instruction. However, as in the experimental class, the language of instruction in the control classes was predominantly Japanese. Moreover, students in these classes had regular, in-class opportunities for unscripted spoken interaction in small groups with Japanese NSs who visited the class throughout the semester. Both control and experimental classes covered the same textbook as part of the regular course curriculum.

Data and analysis

The data for this study are composed of the experimental and control groups' performances on the pre- and posttest storytelling task, and the experimental group's tellings from the second CP sessions (CP2) of Lessons 2, 4, and 8 (i.e., weeks 3, 7, and 16 of the 16-week course, respectively). The analysis focuses on the learners' use of *n desu, n desu kedo,* and *n desu ne,* a set of linguistic items that were introduced to

TABLE 1.   MEAN FREQUENCY OF USE OF INTERACTIONAL MARKERS BY EXPERIMENTAL
AND CONTROL GROUPS FOR PRETEST AND POSTTEST (CLAUSES WITH INTERACTIONAL
MARKERS/TOTAL CLAUSES)

Group	Pretest	Posttest
Experimental	.02 (1/62)	.39 (25/64)
Control	.02 (2/108)	.00 (0/168)

the experimental group in the third week of the semester, and were the
target of much instruction and feedback throughout the semester.[1] I
will address the following questions in examining the effects of the
explicit instruction on learner production:

1. Does explicit instruction result in increased use of interactional
   markers?
2. Does explicit instruction result in accurate use of interactional
   markers?
3. Are some functions of interactional markers more beneficially
   affected by or resistant to explicit instruction?

In discussing the pretest/posttest data, I will consider only the first two
questions; all three questions will be addressed in the discussion of the
experimental group's CPs.

Frequency and accuracy of learner use of interactional markers

Quantitative analysis of the learners' use of the target interactional
markers in the pretest/posttest storytelling task reveals marked gains by
the experimental group on the posttest. Table 1 shows that the learners
in both groups performed the pretest task with a near-total absence of
interactional markers; for both groups, only two in every hundred
clauses, on average, ended with an interactional marker.[2] In each of the
two groups, only one student produced interactional markers in the
pretest.

The frequency of use changes dramatically for the experimental
group's performance on the posttest, which shows a mean frequency of

1 Although the learners received instruction on five interactional markers (*n desu, n
  desu kedo, n desu ne, n desu yo,* and *n desu yo ne*), they produced only the first
  three markers in the three CPs examined (Lessons 2, 4, and 8).
2 The mean frequency of the occurrence of an interactional marker was calculated
  by dividing the number of clauses ending with an interactional marker by the total
  number of clauses (both dependent and independent).

TABLE 2. SUCCESS RATE FOR INTERACTIONAL MARKER USE (ACCEPTABLE USES/TOTAL USES) ON THE POSTTEST FOR LEARNERS IN THE EXPERIMENTAL GROUP

Marker	A1	A2	A3	A4	A5	Total
n desu	50% (1/2)	33% (2/6)	50% (1/2)	75% (3/4)	67% (2/3)	53% (9/17)
n desu kedo	100% (1/1)	100% (1/1)	NA	50% (1/2)	NA	75% (3/4)
n desu ne	100% (2/2)	NA	100% (1/1)	NA	NA	100% (3/3)
All	80% (4/5)	43% (3/7)	67% (2/3)	67% (4/6)	67% (2/3)	63% (15/24)

nearly four in ten clauses ending with an interactional marker.[3] In contrast, no interactional markers were produced on the posttest by the control group. Notably, all learners in the experimental group contributed to the increased use of interactional markers, with learner use of the markers ranging from three to seven tokens per learner.[4] The relatively small number of interactional markers produced in this task reflects the abbreviated nature of the telling associated with the task. These figures, then, appear to reflect the beneficial effects of explicit instruction on the use of interactional markers in extended tellings.

This increased use of interactional markers in the posttest by the experimental group is also characterized by a reasonably good degree of accuracy. Accuracy was determined by acceptability judgments from two Japanese NSs. The percentage of total uses that were determined to be acceptable constitutes the "success rate" (i.e., total acceptable uses/total attempted uses). The success rate on the posttest task for the learners in the experimental group is presented in Table 2. With one exception (A2), the learners attained at least a 67% success rate in their

3 In a set of NS baseline data (n = 4) where subjects were asked to produce a narrative of personal experience, three of the four narratives showed a frequency of use of interactional markers ranging from 0.4 to 0.45. The fourth narrative reflected a much higher rate of use (0.78.) Notably, in a distinct, but related, genre of spoken discourse, Maynard (1989, pp. 38–39) found that 35% of all sentences in 3-minute segments of casual conversation among Japanese NS pairs ended in final particles of rapport (e.g., *ne, yo, no,* and their various combinations).
4 The mean probability of occurrence for the final authentic performance of the semester, a retelling of a favorite movie or television episode, was 0.38. The fact that the figures for these two highly disparate tasks (i.e., the posttest task and communicative practice) are virtually identical lends strength to the figure as a reliable indication of learner progress in the use of interactional markers in extended tellings.

use of interactional markers. The greatest variability in success rate occurs with the most frequently used interactional marker, *n desu*, where the rate of success ranges from 33% to 75%.[5]

These results demonstrate that the experimental group made significant gains in both the overall frequency and the accuracy of the use of interactional markers in the posttest task. In the subsequent analysis, I will examine the learners' in-class communicative practice sessions. This analysis will provide a clearer picture of how learner use of interactional markers, and learner production of extended discourse in general, benefited (or failed to benefit) from the instructional treatment.

Learner use of interactional markers in the CP2s

Although frequency and accuracy of use of the interactional markers increased over the course of the semester, progress in the use of the items was not consistent across learners. All five learners made use of *n desu*, but only four used *n desu kedo*, and *n desu ne* was used by three learners. Moreover, the patterns of learner production suggest that, by the end of the semester, four of the five learners were generally competent in the use of *n desu*, but that only two or three made progress in the use of *n desu kedo* and *n desu ne*.

LEARNER USE OF N *DESU*

Of the three markers, *n desu* has the least restricted context of use, and consequently occurred most frequently within the tellings. The explicit instruction handout provided the following description of *n desu*:

n desu – provides the "glue" that holds a story together and draws the listener into the story. (Without *n desu* a story may sound like a list of facts and events.)

Following this definition, which highlights the critical role of *n desu* in creating discourse coherence, the interactional function of the marker was explained:

[I]n Japanese, the simplest way to let the listener know you're not yet finished talking is to use *n desu*. Using *n desu* is especially important at points where you are finishing up one part of your story (a particular scene/event, describing an important person in the story) and moving on to the next development.

Illustrative examples of the organizational and interactional functions of *n desu* in extended tellings were also presented. The explicit instruction of *n desu*, then, addressed three facets of the discourse function of

5 In a relatively short telling, when *n desu* appears too frequently, the function of the marker will tend to be anomalous. It is this type of *n desu* overuse that underlies A2's low success rate. Notably, in the more extended tellings of the learners' CPs, the success rate for *n desu* reached 89% in the final lesson of the semester.

the marker: the maintenance of discourse coherence, the segmentation of the story into "parts" (e.g., scenes, events), and the signaling that one's telling is ongoing.

The learners' use of *n desu* reflects attention to all three of these functions, with this use increasing in frequency and accuracy over the semester:

Lesson 2: 10 uses with a 70% success rate (7/10)
Lesson 4: 20 uses with a 70% success rate (14/20)
Lesson 8: 46 uses with an 89% success rate (41/46)[6]

The excerpt in (1), produced for the final CP2 of the semester, provides an example of the learner's progress in the use of the marker:

(1) Effective use of *n desu*

1 *sengetsu ni, ano chikaku no puuru de oboreta no- oboreta*
2 *hito no hanashi o tomodachi kara ki- kiita n desu ne.*
3 *otoko no hito wa, ano daibingu toonamento o, aa renshuu suru*
4 *tame ni, puuru e itta **n desu**.*
5 *sorede, ano hito wa, raifugaado ni, iki o tomete daibingu*
6 *toonamento o renshuu shinakereba naranai to, itte,*
7 *raifugaado wa- raifugaado ga, ii yo to itta n desu. itta n*
8 *da kedo, ano otoko no hito wa, hito wa ano renshuu suru aida*
9 *ni, raifugaado ga, mienakatta **n desu**.*
10 *de, sanjuppun gurai no- de- ato, sanjuppun gurai anoo, onna*
11 *no hito wa, onna no hito ga, raifugaado ni sumimasen, ano*
12 *otoko no hito wa, mizu ni nagai- mizu no naka ni nagai itta*
13 *to itte, raifugaado ga, daijoobu, hito ga, renshuu*
14 *shinakereba naranai to kiita to itta **n desu**.*
15 *soshitara, ano onna no hito wa demo, juppun gurai mizu no*
16 *naka ni ite, mada mada dete konai to itta **n desu**.*
17 *de ano raifugaado ga, mizu ni haitte ano tasuke ni, tasuke*
18 *ni ittara, shinde ita **n desu** . . .* ((continues)) (A2/L8)

Last month I heard a story from my friend about a person who drowned at the pool nearby *n desu ne*. A guy went to the pool to practice for a diving tournament *n desu*. So the guy tells the lifeguard I have to practice for this diving tournament by holding my breath, and the lifeguard said, "All right" *n desu*. *n da kedo*. While the guy was practicing, the lifeguard couldn't see him *n desu*. So about 30 minutes later, a lady says to the lifeguard, "Excuse me, that guy has been in the water for a long time." The lifeguard said,

---

6 The increased use of *n desu* also reflects the production of increasingly longer tellings.

"It's all right, he said he had to practice" *n desu*. Then the lady said, "But he's been in the water for about 10 minutes and he hasn't come up yet" *n desu*. So the lifeguard got into the water and when he went in to save (the guy), (the guy) was dead *n desu* . . . ((continues)) (A2/L8)

In (1), A2's use of *n desu* contributes to both the coherence of his presentation and the structuring of the events within the telling. At several points in the story, A2 uses *n desu* to demarcate scene boundaries or notable developments in the telling events (lines 4, 9, 14, 16, 18). These uses of *n desu* also signal the hearer that the telling will continue. Notably, A2 not only uses *n desu* effectively, but also distinguishes between the use of *n desu*, *n desu kedo* (lines 7–8, where *n desu* is repaired to *n da kedo*), and *n desu ne* (line 2).

Although learner use of *n desu* was, on the whole, highly successful, there were numerous (n = 14) anomalous uses of the marker. Eight of these errors occurred in contexts where a variant of *n desu* (i.e., *n desu kedo* or *n desu ne*) was expected; another four were produced where a conjunctive form (i.e., *-te/-tara*) was anticipated. It is noteworthy that both the *n desu* variants and the conjunctive forms have continuative functions, albeit ones that are distinct from that of *n desu*. Whereas *n desu* is used to indicate continuity between scene or event boundaries, the aforementioned forms all provide continuity within scene or event boundaries.[7] The learners' anomalous use of *n desu*, then, suggests two possible gaps in their understanding of the marker: an overgeneralization of the continuative function of *n desu*, and an underdeveloped awareness of the boundary-marking function of *n desu* (i.e., the segmentation of the story into "parts"). The anomalous use of *n desu* in (2) reflects both of these gaps:

(2) Anomalous use of *n desu*

((A4 is talking about her interest in dance; she has just explained that she studied hula for 6 years as a child.))

1   *demo jyuuissai ni natta toki ni, terebi o mite,* Janet
2   Jackson *to* Paula Abdul *no ongaku no video mita n desu kedo,*
3   *eeto fura wa ammari shitaku nakatta n desu.*
4   *eeto, dakara, okaasan ni, eeto,* Janet Jackson (*to*) Paula
→ 5   Abdul *no dansu o shitai to iimash- itta **n desu**.*
6   *dakara eeto jazu no kurasu ni, eeto, irimash- ireta n desu.*
    (A4/L2)

---

7 The functions of *n desu kedo* and *n desu ne* will be discussed later; *-te* (and), and *-tara* (when), are clause-linking morphemes.

But when I turned 11, I watched TV, and saw Janet Jackson's and Paula Abdul's music videos *n desu kedo*, {after that} I didn't want to do hula much *n desu*. So, I said to my Mom, "I want to dance (like) Janet Jackson and Paula Abdul" ***n desu***. So, (she) enrolled (me) in a jazz class *n desu*.

In (2), A4 explains how her interest in dance shifted from hula to jazz dancing, first telling about her loss of interest in hula (lines 1–3), and then explaining how she came to be enrolled in a jazz dance class (lines 4–6). In (2), then, two scenes or segments of the telling are presented. However, A4's use of *n desu* divides this portion of the telling into three segments, with the use of the marker in line 5 disrupting the flow of the second segment.

The proposed feedback version in (2') illustrates how the second segment (lines 4–6) can be presented as a single scene.

(2') Proposed feedback version of lines 4–6 of (2)

  4 *sore de haha ni Janetto Jakuson to Poora Abudoru no yoo na*
→ 5 *dansu o shitai to **ittara***
  6 *jazu dansu no kurasu ni irete kureta n desu.*

> So when I told my mom, "I want to dance like Janet Jackson and Paula Abdul," she enrolled me in jazz dance class *n desu*.

In line 5, the use of the -tara form (*ittara*, "when I said") renders the daughter's request and the mother's response as a single, connected segment of the telling. Moreover, the cause–effect relationship between request and response is implied by the -*tara* form, obviating A4's use of *dakara* ("so") (line 6 of [2]) to mark the causal relationship between the two events.

Even more prevalent than the anomalous use of *n desu* was the underuse of the marker. Learner underuse is identified by comparing the learner's actual production with the proposed feedback version.[8] Underuse was classified into two types: errors, which are learner utterances without an interactional marker that are edited in the feedback version to include one, and expansions, which are utterances with an interactional marker that do not appear in the learner's CP, but are added in the proposed feedback version to create a clearer or more effective telling. The content of expansions is either implicit in the learner's telling itself, or based on information provided by the student

---

8 In the proposed feedback version, changes to the learner's telling were motivated by awkwardness or unnaturalness of the telling, particularly with regard to the coherence of the telling. However, given the nature of discourse, such awkward or unnatural text may be edited in a number of ways. Since the proposed feedback version constitutes only one possible way of editing a learner's telling, the figures reported for learner underuse must be treated as rough estimates.

during the planning session or the first CP session. There are 41 errors and 5 expansions associated with the learners' underuse of *n desu*. Of the 41 errors, 27 occur when a finite verb form (or, on two occasions, a noun phrase) is used instead of *n desu*. Although one student, whose tellings were characterized by an overall nonproduction of *n desu* throughout the semester, accounted for 40% (11 of 27) of these underuse errors,[9] nearly another 40% (10 of 27) of these errors suggest a pattern of strategic *n desu* avoidance on the part of the other learners. In these errors, the finite verb form occurs either in the final utterance of the telling or at the end of a major segment of the telling. The excerpt in (3) illustrates this type of underuse.

(3) Nonproduction of *n desu* at the end of a telling

    1   *ano chichi wa ano mookaru? okane ga mookattara ano haha to*
    2   *ue no imooto to boku ni okane o moratta- kureta n desu.*
    3   *ano haha wa ano nihyaku doru o, agete, ue no imooto hyakugo*
    4   *doru mo moratte- agete, haha sanbyaku doru moratte, ue no*
    5   *imooto wa hyaku gojuu doru moratte, boku wa nihyaku doru o*
    6   *kureta n desu.*
→ 7   *sorede deta toki yori okanemochi ni **narimashita**.*   (A2/L4)

> When my dad won, he gave my mom and my sister and me money
> *n desu*. He gave my mom $200, he also gave my sister $105, my
> Mom got $300, my sister got $150 and I got $200.00 *n desu*. So,
> compared to when we had left (Hawai'i), we became rich.

(3') Proposed feedback version of line 7 of (3)

    1   *dakara, hawai o deta toki yori kanemochi ni natte kaette*
→ 2   *kita **n desu**.*

> So compared to when we had left Hawai'i, we came home richer
> ***n desu***.

In (3), the learner demonstrates an ability to use *n desu* to structure his telling (lines 2 and 6), yet the marker is not produced in the telling-final turn (line 7). However, as is reflected in (3'), *n desu* is expected in this position, serving to bring the final segment of the telling to a close.

    This pattern of *n desu* underuse is clearly evident among the telling-final turns of the fourteen CPs examined. Eight end with a finite verb (with seven of these being corrected to *n desu* in the feedback version), and four end with a formulaic closing turn (e.g., *owari*, "the end"; *to iu koto desu*, "that's it"). Only two end with *n desu*. Although both

---

9 In the CPs examined, A3 produced only four instances of *n desu* but, notably, all were accurate. This production is the lowest among the learners, constituting less than half of the total for the next lowest in production.

telling-final *n desu* and telling-final formulaic phrases were modeled in the NS models and in the feedback, there was no modeling of telling-final finite verbs. This pattern, then, suggests a strategic nonuse of *n desu,* with learners seeking out a linguistic means of signaling closure to contrast with the continuative function of *n desu.*

This pattern of learner production is consistent with the gaps in the learners' understanding of *n desu* that were shown for the anomalous uses of the marker: an overgeneralization of the continuative function of *n desu,* and an underdeveloped awareness of the boundary-marking function of *n desu* (i.e., the segmentation of the story into "parts"). Notably, this pattern of errors also reflects learner attention to a discourse-level, interactional demand of the task, the closure of the telling. Thus, although this pattern reveals a gap in the instruction of *n desu,* it also demonstrates that the instructional approach itself successfully engaged the learners in managing the interactional demands of producing an extended telling.

LEARNER USE OF *N DESU KEDO*

In comparison with learner use of *n desu,* the use of *n desu kedo* was more limited (n = 19), but, overall, highly successful: 16 of the 19 uses (84%) were accurate. The lower production of this marker may be attributed, at least in part, to the fact that *n desu kedo* has more restricted use than *n desu* in extended tellings, and thus is expected to appear less frequently. However, as with *n desu,* the learners showed a strong tendency to underproduce the marker (n = 31).[10] The more limited use of *n desu kedo* was evident in the explicit instruction, where only one basic discourse function was described for the marker:[11]

n desu kedo – sets up a single point of background information which the listener requires in order to understand the subsequent content of the story.

This definition was augmented by the following explanation:

In telling a story, you may want to mention a single point of information that will provide the listener with the background necessary to understand why someone in your story (re)acted or felt the way she or he did. In such cases, using *n desu kedo* in conjunction with that information signals the listener that what you have just said is background information, rather than a new development in or an important part of the story itself.

---

10 Eleven of the fourteen tellings required the addition of *n desu kedo;* two of the tellings not requiring remediation were extremely short, underdeveloped tellings from Lesson 2.
11 Although *n desu kedo* has other functions in extended tellings, the initial explanation of the marker (provided on the handout in the third week of instruction) was limited to this single function. During the semester, other functions were introduced in conjunction with the feedback sessions.

The high success rate with *n desu kedo* reflects the learners' competence in using the marker to signal this backgrounding function in their tellings: More than 50% (nine of sixteen) of the successful uses of *n desu kedo* present "a single point of background information." Moreover, only five of the thirty instances of underuse of the marker involve this function.[12]

It is noteworthy that the majority of backgrounding clauses marked by *n desu kedo* (five of nine) are used at the opening of the telling to present information about the topic or the setting of the telling, as in (4) and (5), respectively:

(4) Use of *n desu kedo* to introduce background information relevant to the topic of the telling

((The learner talks about his favorite hobby.))

1 *boku wa iroiro na shumi ga aru n desu kedo* . . .
   ((continues)) (A5/L2)

   I have several interests ***n desu kedo*** . . . ((continues))

(5) Use of *n desu kedo* to introduce background information relevant to the setting of the telling

((The learner tells the story of *Beauty and the Beast*.))

1 *ee aru hi, ano, hitori no hatsumeika ga, ano: jibun no uma*
2 *de hatsumei taikai ni itta **n desu kedo*** . . . ((continues)) (A1/L8)

   One day, an inventor went to an inventors' convention on his horse ***n desu kedo*** . . . ((continues))

There was no instruction on the handout regarding the use of *n desu kedo* to present the topic or setting of a telling, nor did the examples on the handout reflect this telling-initial positioning of the marker. Thus, the learners' use of *n desu kedo* to mark background information reflected an uninstructed preference for the positioning (telling-initial) and function (introduce topic or setting) of the marker. This pattern of learner use again suggests learner attention to the discourse-level interactional demands of the extended telling task, in this case, the communicative need to orient the hearer to the teller's frame of reference (i.e., topic or setting) at the outset of a telling.

Learner underproduction of *n desu kedo* (19 errors and 11 expansions) also reflected a clear pattern: More than 73% (22 of 30) of the instances of underproduction (12 of 19 errors and 11 of 12 expansions)

---

12 The second-most common function of *n desu kedo* (n = 5) was marking a contrastive relationship between states or events in the telling; this reflects the learners' familiarity with the semantic meaning of *kedo* ("but").

were associated with the introduction of a new segment in the telling.[13] In an extended telling, *n desu kedo* may be used to signal the hearer that a new segment – a change of perspective, a change of scene, a shift to a subtopic, a reopening of a story ending, and so on – is being introduced. Missed uses of *n desu kedo* in these contexts may lessen the salience of a scene or perspective shift, which may, in turn, reduce the hearer's ability to follow the development of and/or understand the point of a telling. An example of this missed use of the segment-introducing function of *n desu kedo* is provided in (6):

(6) Use of *n desu kedo* to introduce a new segment in the telling

((The learner, retelling the story of the movie *Beauty and the Beast*, explains that, because the Beast had fallen in love with Beauty, he allowed her to leave the castle to rescue her father.))

1 *de naze ano:, yajuu san ga ano Belle chan o nante yuu shaku-*
2 *shakuhoo kureta ka to iu to, ano:, (.) kare ga, ano Belle*
3 *chan no koto, (.) koi ni ochite* ((material deleted)) *suki ni*
4 *natchatta. sugoi tsuyoi ai datta.*
→ 5 *sore de, kekkyoku, ano ato kanojo oshiro ni **modotte**,*
6 *( ), ee yajuu kara, mahoo, tokete, de ningen ni*
7 *modotta. ta n desu.*

> So why um:, did the Beast what's it called? Relea- release Beauty? um:, (.) he, fell in love, (.) with Beauty ((material deleted)) he fell in love with her. It was an extremely strong love. Then, finally, after that she went back to the castle **and**, ( ), um the spell was removed from the beast, and he became human again *n desu*.

In lines 1–4, there is a suspension in the story development as the learner explains the Beast's motivation for his release of Beauty. In line 5, the learner initiates the next segment of his telling in which he reports three events: Beauty's return to the castle, the removal of the spell on the Beast, and the Beast's return to human form. The continuity of these three events, and of the segment overall, is maintained by use of two *-te* forms (lines 5 and 6), which effectively mark the segment as a temporally ordered reporting of the next sequence of events in the movie. This presentation of the segment, however, is problematic since it fails to convey to the hearer that the events reported, more than merely being "the next thing that happens," actually constitute the final resolution of

13 The remaining 7 errors and 1 expansion either constitute borderline cases of "introducing a new segment" or are instances (n = 5) where the contrastive function of the *kedo* ("but") in *n desu kedo* is most salient. Notably, in the latter cases, the use of *n desu kedo* rather than *kedo* alone maintains the flow of the ongoing story segment.

the story (i.e., the Beast, having found true love with Beauty, breaks the spell and returns to human form).

The proposed feedback version in (6') reflects the learner's missed use of *n desu kedo* to introduce this segment:

(6') Proposed feedback version of lines 5–7 of (6)

   5 *sore de, kekkyoku, sono ato kanojo ga oshiro ni*
→ 6 *modoru **n desu kedo**,*
   7 *soshitara* ( ), *ee yajuu wa, mahoo ga, tokete, de ningen ni*
   8 *modotta. ta n desu.*[14]

The use of *n desu kedo* in line 6 signals that Beauty's return to the castle is an event that introduces the next segment; in other words, this event provides a frame within which to interpret the subsequent events. When *n desu kedo* is used in this way, the content of lines 7–8 becomes the focus of the telling. In (6'), then, the use of *n desu kedo* (line 6) communicates the salience of the scene shift (i.e., Beauty's return to the castle), thereby addressing the teller's interactional need to prepare the hearer for the culminating events that will bring this segment, and the telling itself, to a close.

The near-total nonuse of *n desu kedo* for this segment-introducing function is, no doubt, attributable in part to the fact that this function was not introduced on the explicit instruction handout.[15] However, it is important to note that learners were at least as likely to exclude segment-introducing information as they were to include it: Expansions account for nearly half (11 of 23) of the cases of underuse of segment-introducing *n desu kedo*. This suggests that, with respect to the introduction of story segments, the learners were having at least as much trouble providing the relevant segment-introducing information as they were using *n desu kedo* to do so. In sum, the pervasive underuse (both errors and expansions) of segment-introducing *n desu kedo* would seem to indicate that the learners were not able to manage (and, given the absence of explicit instruction, were possibly not even aware of) the marking of salient segment boundaries in their extended tellings. It remains to be seen in future studies whether learner awareness of these demands, and the role of *n desu kedo* in addressing them, can be beneficially influenced by explicit instruction.

14 The gloss for (6') is equivalent to that for lines 5–7 of (6), except that *then* (i.e., *soshitara*) replaces the first *and* (i.e., *-te*).
15 The segment-introducing function of *n desu kedo* was, however, incorporated into the expanded feedback provided after CP2.

LEARNER USE OF N *DESU NE*

As with *n desu kedo*, the discourse function of *n desu ne* is more restricted than that of *n desu* and therefore is expected to occur with less frequency than *n desu* in extended tellings. In fact, *n desu ne* was the least frequently produced marker (n = 10), with only three learners producing one, three, and six tokens of the marker, respectively. Although *n desu ne* was used with a high success rate (seven of ten uses), there was also a strong tendency for underuse (eighteen errors and four expansions). When the function of *n desu ne* was presented, the importance of the marker for managing teller–hearer interaction and for conveying the point of the telling was highlighted in the abbreviated description of the function of the marker:

n desu ne – invites the listener to pay attention to the next piece of the story, often a piece that is central to the point or meaning of the story itself.

and in the more extended prose explanation:

[T]he speaker uses *n desu ne* to make sure that the listener is following before she or he (i.e., the storyteller) moves on to the next part of the story.

These functions were illustrated on the handout in examples where the marker was used in telling-initial position to present components of the setting that were directly relevant to the point of the telling.

Consistent with the examples on the handout, three of the seven successful uses of *n desu ne* occur in telling-initial position with the function of presenting salient components of the setting. Moreover, two errors of underuse, where *ne* is produced without *n desu*, also occur in telling-initial position with this function. An example of the successful use of *n desu ne* to mark a salient component of the setting is presented in (7):

(7) Telling-initial use of *n desu ne* to mark a salient component(s) of the setting

   1 *kono mae no kanshasai yasumi de ano chichi to haha to ue no*
→ 2 *imooto to isshoni, ano* Las Vegas *e itta **n desu ne**?*
   3 *eeto ano chichi to haha wa, boku no tanjoobi tanjoobi no*
   4 *purezento ni, ano boku to, ue no imooto ano* Las Vegas *e*
   5 *tsurete itta n desu* . . . ((continues)) (A2/L4)

> This past Thanksgiving break, I went to Las Vegas with my mother, father, and sister **n desu ne**? My mother and father took me and my sister to Las Vegas for my birthday present *n desu* . . . . ((continues))

The learner's use of *n desu ne* (line 2) establishes the location of the telling and the main participants, highlighting this information as essential to the hearer's understanding of the point of the telling. As the learner's subsequent telling recounts his experience watching his father gamble in Las Vegas, and the way in which the father shared his earnings with each member of the family, it is clear that the information marked by *n desu ne* is indeed important to the point of the telling.

Although this telling-initial use of *n desu ne* was the only one modeled on the handout, the description of *n desu ne* on the handout did not entail any such limitation; moreover, through the feedback sessions, the learners were exposed to other positionings and uses of the marker. The influence of this aspect of the instructional treatment is evident in the fact that the remaining seven attempts with *n desu ne* (four of seven successful) all occur in conjunction with salient events at noninitial positions in the tellings. The most common function that *n desu ne* serves in such noninitial positions is the highlighting of an action or event that immediately precedes or, often, leads to a culminating point in the telling.[16] This function was evident in six of the seven remaining uses of *n desu ne* (three of them successful). Also, two thirds (twelve of eighteen) of the instances of underuse of the marker occurred in conjunction with this function. Notably, both the use and the underuse of *n desu ne* for this action/event-highlighting function tend to occur in tellings with a relatively elaborated plot. Thus, it is not surprising that A1, the learner who told the most extended and elaborated tellings, accounts for four of the six attempted uses and seven of the twelve underuses of *n desu ne* for this function. A1 also accounts for all three successful uses of the marker for this action/event-highlighting function.

Examples of A1's successful use and his underuse of the marker are provided in (8):

(8) Successful use and underuse of *n desu ne* to signal an important
    development in a telling

((Retelling of the movie *Beauty and the Beast*: Beauty's father, an inventor, gets lost on his way home.))

    1 *tochuu ni ano michi ni mayotte, ano:, soshitara ame ga futte*
→ 2 *kita n- futte kite*
    3 *ano chikaku no, oshiro? ga atta node, ano oshiro- oshiro- ni*
→ 4 *hai- haitta **n desu ne**?*
    5 *demo ano oshiro ni sunderu hitori no yajuu? yajuu ga, ano*
    6 *hatsumeika to atte, ee oshiro ni hairu no wa, dame (da)kara,*
    7 *ano, hatsumeika no hitojichi o totta n desu.* (A1/L8)

> On the way, he got lost and then it began to rain and, since there was a nearby castle, he entered the castle *n desu ne*. But the beast

---

16 Often this use of *n desu ne* creates a sense of suspense in the telling, a signal
   that something significant is about to happen in the telling.

that lived in the castle met the inventor and, since it was forbidden to enter the castle, he took the inventor hostage *n desu*.

In (8), the learner relates a significant development in the story: Beauty's father's being taken hostage by the Beast. In line 4, the learner's use of *n desu ne* marks the father's entry into the castle as significant to the plot development; the dire consequences of the father's action are reported in the subsequent text (lines 5–7). This effective use of *n desu ne* reflects the functions described in the explicit instruction: drawing the hearer into the story, and marking an event as central to the plot development (i.e., the point of the story). The learner's underuse of *n desu ne* (line 2) is evident from a comparison of his text with the proposed feedback version, provided in (8'):

(8') Proposed feedback version of lines 1–4 of (8)

   1 *tochuu de ano michi ni mayotte, ano:, soshitara ame ga futte*
→ 2 *kita **n desu ne**?*
   3 *ano chikaku ni, oshiro? ga atta node, sono oshiro- oshiro-*
   4 *ni hai- haitta **n desu ne**?*[17]

In (8'), in contrast with the learner's version, both the change in weather (line 2) and the father's entering the castle (line 4) are marked as salient to the plot development. The additional use of *n desu ne* reflects the fact that the rainfall is, in fact, a key event since it causes the father to seek refuge in the castle. The learner's underuse of the marker here results in a failure to convey this information to the hearer.[18] Instead, in the learner's version, the onset of the rainfall (line 2) is reported with a conjoining *-te* form, which effectively presents the rainfall as one of a series of undifferentiated, temporally ordered events.

Five of A1's seven instances of underuse for this function of *n desu ne* occur with a conjoining *-te* form, suggesting that he may not always attend to the significance of a given action or event vis-à-vis the plot development. This aspect of A1's pattern of underuse, then, reflects a second critical component of the successful use of the action or event-highlighting function of *n desu ne*: Not only must a teller present a telling with elaborated plot development, but he must also be aware of

---

17 The gloss for (8') is equivalent to that for lines 1–4 of (8), except that the second *and* (*-te*) is best glossed by an intonational pattern that marks an impending, ominous development.

18 It is important to note that this sequence of events may be related in a variety of ways that do not employ *n desu ne*. The critical point here is that, regardless of how the events are related, the causal effect of the rainfall and the highlighting of the father's entering the castle as an action that will have serious consequences must be marked by the teller. Given the organization of the learner's original version in (8), it was determined that this marking could be most economically and effectively accomplished by the addition of *n desu ne*.

which actions or events are salient in the plot development. As is evident from the relatively low production of *n desu ne* in general, and in conjunction with the action or event-highlighting function in particular, the task of producing a coherent, extended telling with even minimal plot development proved to be a significant challenge for most of the learners in the experimental group.

The beneficial effects of explicit instruction

As I have demonstrated, the experimental instructional approach had an overall beneficial effect on the learners' use of the interactional markers *n desu, n desu kedo,* and *n desu ne* in conjunction with the production of nonformal, extended tellings. Learner success in the use of these interactional markers was evident in the learners' handling of both the organizational and the interactional demands of the task. On the whole, the learners made effective use of *n desu* to maintain the flow of a telling and to structure the action or event sequences of the telling (i.e., the boundary-marking function of *n desu*) in a coherent way. Learner production also reflected general success in the use of *n desu kedo* for the introduction of background information into the telling. The instructional approach also seemed to increase learner attention to the interactional demands of the task even in areas where no explicit instruction was provided. The uninstructed patterns of learner usage of *n desu kedo* and *n desu ne* to manage the openings of tellings addressed the interactional need to establish the topic of the telling and/or provide the hearer with information about the setting. Similarly, the uninstructed (and in most cases with finite verb forms, anomalous) use of finite verb forms and formulaic phrases in telling-final position preferred by the learners reflects learner attention to the interactional demand of bringing a telling to a close (i.e., signaling an end to the telling). These results support House's (1996) findings that an instructional approach that includes explicit instruction (combined with communicative practice and feedback) heightens learners' ability to attend to the interactional needs of the addressee.

In contrast to the learners' success with these aspects of their tellings, learner production showed considerably less success with the management of organizational and interactional demands relevant to the internal structuring of the telling. Specifically, there was little progress in the learners' ability to mark shifts in scene or perspective or to build up or highlight the point of a telling through the effective use of interactional markers. Although both the explicit instruction and the corrective feedback were directed at these functions, learner production did not reflect an overall benefit from this focus. With regard to this result, the possibility of inadequacies in the instruction, feedback, and/or practice components of the instructional approach cannot be discounted. For example, gaps in the explicit instruction handout were noted earlier, but even though these gaps were addressed in the feedback sessions, the amount of instruction each learner received on these points was, effectively, proportional to his or her production of incorrect or missed uses of the interactional markers for these functions. Thus, learners who produced tellings with numerous scene shifts or extensive topic or plot development tended to receive more feedback than those who did not. If feedback is indeed a critical factor in the success of explicit instruction, then this differential in the amount and nature of feedback provided may account, at least in part, for the variability in the learners' use of and success with *n desu kedo* and *n desu ne* for functions related to the internal organization and presentation of the telling. It should be pointed out, though, that since both the immediate and the extended feedback sessions were conducted as small-group activities, there were opportunities for learners to benefit from the feedback provided to fellow learners. Both Schmidt's noticing hypothesis (1990, 1993a) and Sharwood Smith's auto-input hypothesis (1988, cited in House 1996, p. 246) propose that linguistic development derives from comparing one's own output with native production and recognizing the differences, rather than simply being exposed to instruction that highlights these differences. Receiving feedback on one's own production would be expected to have a beneficial effect on the learner, whereas overhearing feedback to another learner would not necessarily be expected to have this effect.

The question of time must also be considered. The explicit instruction comprised approximately one third of the 80 instructional hours for the course – since all learners showed some development in their ability to use the interactional markers in managing the demands of the task, it is unclear whether more practice time, or a longer period of instruction, would have resulted in greater overall gains. Until these aspects of the experimental treatment are more fully explored, it is premature to suggest that the telling-internal functions of the interactional markers are in some way resistant to the beneficial effects of explicit instruction. In addition to possible inadequacies in the instructional treatment, there are two learner variables that may also be relevant to the results: the learner's ability to perform an extended telling in his or her native language, and learner fluency. With respect to the former, it is clear that the ability to tell a "good story" or provide a clear explanation is not one that all speakers of a language share equally. Any extended telling is, effectively, a performance that may be accomplished with greater or lesser interactional and organizational skill. Since there was no independent measure of this ability, it is not clear whether the learners' lack of progress in using interactional markers to develop the internal structure of their tellings reflects a general inability to do so (regardless of language), or whether it reflects a more limited proficiency in the use of the markers in conjunction with the production of extended tellings in Japanese. As for fluency, although no independent measure was taken, there were two learners with extensive prior contact with Japanese NSs who clearly were the most fluent learners in the experimental group. These two learners consistently produced longer, more elaborated tellings, used *n desu* in a highly accurate and effective way, and made the most extensive use of *n desu kedo* and *n desu ne* for the internal structuring of their tellings. Their extensive prior interaction with Japanese NSs may have provided these learners with a heightened awareness of the interactional and organizational demands of extended tellings and may, therefore, have made them more receptive to the instruction and feedback. Further consideration of both of these variables should be addressed in future studies.

In sum, although there are a number of outstanding issues regarding the variables underlying learner success with this course of experimental instruction, it appears that the instructional approach enabled the learners to improve their ability to manage in targetlike ways the most fundamental aspects of the task: openings, presentation of content, and closings. The tellings were clearly recognizable as such, and, in the words of the instructor, the students definitely "sounded like they were speaking Japanese." From this perspective, then, the claims for the beneficial effects of explicit instruction combined with communicative practice and feedback have been shown to be supported for the production of nonformal, extended tellings. At the same time, the gaps in the learners' production reflect the need to further explore the organizational and interactional demands of extended tellings in order to develop more effective materials and approaches for the explicit instruction of this genre. Based on the positive outcomes and general effectiveness of the approach used in this study, the value of pursuing these efforts is evident.

PART IV:
THE ASSESSMENT OF PRAGMATIC ABILITY

Despite the fact that communicative language teaching has now been with us for more than 3 decades, and a considerable amount of attention has been focused on developing ways to teach learners to use language for communication, far less effort has been expended in developing methods for assessing learners' ability to communicate in a second language. This has begun to change, particularly with work on the assessment of interlanguage pragmatics being carried out by established researchers in language testing.

One of the most frequently used formats for assessing oral proficiency is the oral proficiency interview or the simulated oral proficiency interview (SOPI). In the SOPI, candidates have to address a variety of communicative acts to interlocutors in different constellations of social relationships. Whether or not the SOPI elicits samples of candidates' performance that allow valid interpretations of their L2 sociolinguistic and pragmatic abilities is a central problem of construct validity. John Norris examines this issue in Chapter 12 by analyzing the use of address terms by American high school and university learners of German as a foreign language on the German Speaking Test (GST). For English-speaking learners of German, developing control over the address system involves the acquisition of complex interactions between sociopragmatic and pragmalinguistic aspects of the L2. Six tasks from the GST were identified (asking questions, giving directions, explaining a process, apologizing, requesting, and giving advice) which elicited substantial use of direct address forms and shared similar contextual constraints which likely encouraged the use of direct address. Norris found that although choice of appropriate address register seemed straightforward for all tasks, wide variability was noted both among examinees and across tasks in terms of the frequency with which contexts for direct address were produced and the sociopragmatic accuracy with which pronominal forms were supplied. In general, examinees produced much higher frequencies of address behavior for those tasks requiring familiar forms of address than for those tasks requiring formal address register. However, when examinees chose to produce address forms on tasks requiring formal registers, they did so with very high degrees of sociopragmatic accuracy. It was also noted that such high levels of accuracy came on tasks which called for linguistic contexts in which such behavior may have been facilitated. It would seem, then, that linguistic demands as well as knowledge of sociopragmatic norms played a role in determining address behavior on the GST, especially among examinees rated at the lower ACTFL proficiency levels. Norris concludes that although examinees tend to increase in their abilities to make sociopragmatically accurate address register selections under performance conditions as their overall proficiency level increases, this is by no means a categorical or implicational relationship, as has often been implied by proponents of the ACTFL Guidelines.

In Chapter 13, Thom Hudson notes that an important issue in developing instruments that assess interlanguage pragmatic competence is associated with the variability of speaker behavior in discourse. That is, the study of pragmatic ability inherently involves addressing two contributors to variability in performance: variability associated with the social properties of the speech event, and the speaker's strategic, actional, and linguistic choices for achieving communicative goals; and variability resulting from the particular types of data collection procedures and associated instruments. His chapter describes a project aimed at developing a multiple methods approach to the assessment of interlanguage pragmatics. The test instruments are designed to provide information about both of the sources of variability inherent in this enterprise. Tests were classified into three types – indirect measures, semidirect measures, and self-assessment measures. Additionally, each type of measure involved two test formats that vary along a scale of cued or free examinee response. Hudson discusses the quantitative and qualitative approaches that were applied in the development of the instruments, and then examines the results of the assessments in terms of instructional implications focusing on requests, refusals, and apologies, with specific attention to inherent power relationships and relative social distance between the interlocutors, as well as the degree of imposition in carrying out the speech act.

In Chapter 14, James Dean Brown describes the variety of testing instruments available for testing interlanguage pragmatics, then analyzes what is known about each, and finally recommends which types of tests should be used for each testing purpose. The tests he considers are the Written Discourse Completion Task, which requires the students to read a written description of a situation and write what they would say in that situation; the Multiple-Choice Discourse Completion Task, which requires students to read a written description of a situation and select what would be best to say in that situation; the Oral Discourse Completion Task, which requires students to listen to a description of a situation and to say aloud what they would say in that situation; the

Role-Play, which provides a description of a situation and asks students to play a role with another person in that situation; the Self-Assessment, which provides a description of a situation and asks the students to rate their own ability to perform in that situation; and the Role-Play Self-Assessment, which requires students to rate their own pragmatic performance in a previously performed role-play. Following a detailed description of these six instruments, Brown compiles insights gained from studies done so far on the development of these tests, mainly carried out with students learning English and Japanese. Each test is examined for testing characteristics as well as practicality characteristics, and recommendations are made for which tests would be most suitable for the purposes of aptitude, proficiency, and placement testing on the one hand, and diagnostic, progress, and achievement testing on the other.

12 Use of address terms on the German Speaking Test

John M. Norris

Introduction

The measurement of sociolinguistic competence has proved problematic since Hymes's (1967, 1972) seminal discussions of Chomsky's (1965) distinction between competence and performance, especially given persistent uncertainties regarding how sociolinguistic knowledge interacts with other competencies (e.g., grammatical) and how these interactions are instantiated in learner L2 performance (McNamara, 1996). Nevertheless, that L2 learners need to acquire knowledge of sociocultural norms or rules of language behavior, as well as the ability to appropriately employ these rules in communication, is beyond dispute, as evidenced by their abiding presence in competence or ability models (e.g., Canale & Swain, 1980; Canale, 1983). Most recently, Bachman and Palmer (1996) located knowledge of sociocultural rules within their L2 "ability for use" framework:

Sociolinguistic knowledge enables us to create or interpret language that is
appropriate to a particular language use setting. This includes knowledge
of the conventions that determine the appropriate use of dialects or varieties,
registers, natural or idiomatic expressions, cultural references, and figures
of speech. When we use different registers . . . sociolinguistic knowledge
is involved. (p. 70)

Given this fundamental role for sociolinguistic competence within notions of language competence and ability, it follows that language assessment which purports to measure such global constructs as L2 proficiency must necessarily include the measurement of learners' command of sociocultural rules and corresponding L2 forms. Voices within the language testing literature have thus insisted that any measure of general L2 proficiency carefully elicit examinee performance on tasks which require the application of sociolinguistic knowledge under a variety of contextual constraints, and employ analytic scales in scoring and reporting examinee performances, so as to enable the interpretation of particular components of L2 ability such as command over appropriate L2 registers (e.g., Bachman & Palmer, 1982b, 1996; Bachman & Savignon, 1986; Shohamy, 1988, 1994).

248

Within second and foreign language education contexts in the United States, recent assessment research, development, and policy have acknowledged the importance of incorporating sociolinguistic competence into the measurement of language ability. The National Standards in Foreign Language Education Project (1996) emphasized that it is "acquisition of the ability to communicate in meaningful and appropriate ways with users of other languages that is the ultimate goal of today's foreign language classroom" (p. 3). Accordingly, it recommended the use of context-specific performance assessment in lieu of global proficiency standards for most assessment purposes within foreign language (FL) education (p. 17). In addition, alternatives in language assessment have begun to be investigated which explicitly address the interaction of sociocultural context and learner L2 ability, including measures of pragmatic competence (e.g., Hudson, Detmer, & Brown, 1995; Yamashita, 1996a, 1996b) and task-based performance measures of classroom-, program-, or occupation-related ability (e.g., McNamara, 1996; Norris, Brown, Hudson, & Yoshioka, 1998; Long & Norris, in press). Common to such measures is the use of criteria for scoring, reporting, and interpreting examinee performances according to degree of sociolinguistic appropriateness exhibited, in light of the particular contextual constraints represented within assessment tasks. Thus, for example, although an examinee may exhibit high levels of fluency and grammatical accuracy in making an L2 request, the task would not be considered accomplished if the examinee violated sociocultural norms of request behavior (cf. Blum-Kulka, House, & Kasper, 1989).

Despite the ongoing development of such assessment alternatives, global language proficiency assessment continues to enjoy widespread use. The influence of the ACTFL (1986, 1999) Proficiency Guidelines is evident in the continued use of live and simulated oral proficiency interviews (OPIs and SOPIs) for a variety of decision-making purposes, including among others, fulfillment of university FL requirements, placement into FL courses, teacher certification, and curriculum development and evaluation (e.g., ACTFL, 1986; Stansfield & Kenyon, 1991, 1992a, 1992b; Manley, 1995; Tschirner, 1996; Kuo & Jiang, 1997). Unlike the performance assessments mentioned above, which utilize analytic or task-specific scoring and score reporting, OPIs and SOPIs utilize the ACTFL Proficiency Guidelines as a criterion for assigning a single global proficiency level rating to examinees as well as for the reporting and interpretation of test outcomes. According to ACTFL (1986), the Proficiency Guidelines "allow assessment of what an individual can and cannot do, regardless of where, when, or how the language has been learned or acquired" (p. 1), and they present an integrated and holistic set of descriptors based on purported relationships among various components of language competence at four major proficiency levels (Novice, Intermediate, Advanced, and Superior). In so doing, any given proficiency level represents a combination of aspects of grammatical accuracy and complexity, fluency, and lexical variety, as well as aspects of pragmatic and strategic competencies (cf. Young, 1995; Norris, 1996b).

Although ACTFL-type proficiency tests continue to be used widely in the United States, the extent to which associated interpretations about examinees' language abilities may be warranted has been repeatedly called into question (e.g., Bachman & Savignon, 1986; Bachman, 1988; Lantolf & Frawley, 1988; Shohamy, 1988; van Lier, 1989). The fundamental validity question (cf. Messick, 1989; Shepard, 1993) asks whether examinee performances on OPIs and SOPIs, and the scoring and interpretation of these performances according to the ACTFL Proficiency Guidelines, provide an accurate depiction of what individuals are actually able to do with the target L2. Findings from a number of recent investigations have suggested that, since a rating at a given proficiency level subsumes a wide variety of L2 competencies, interpretations based on global ACTFL levels may not be entirely warranted and may lead to erroneous representations of foreign language learners' complex and developing L2 abilities (e.g., Ross, 1995; Young, 1995; Fulcher, 1996; Norris, 1996a, 1996b, 1997a, 1997b).

Aspects of sociolinguistic competence obviously play some role in ACTFL-type proficiency assessment (see Marisi, 1994), within test tasks as well as in the bases for rater judgments of examinee performances (discussed in the next section). However, given the validity concerns discussed above, what remains to be empirically verified is the extent to which interpretations about examinees' sociolinguistic abilities (among others) may be based on the kinds of tasks examinees are asked to perform within such assessment, the performance attributes on which trained raters assign ACTFL-level scores, and the ways in which scores are reported to examinees and other test-score users. The purpose of the current study was to examine L2 performance on one ACTFL-type proficiency assessment, the German Speaking Test (Center for Applied Linguistics, 1995a), in order to investigate the extent to which associated interpretations about particular sociolinguistic abilities may be warranted.

Sociolinguistic competence and the German Speaking Test

The German Speaking Test (GST) is one of a number of simulated oral proficiency interviews (SOPIs) which have been developed since the late 1980s (see also Stansfield & Kenyon, 1992a, 1992b, 1993). These tape-based SOPIs were originally designed to simulate and serve as surrogates for oral proficiency interviews (OPIs) in the less commonly taught languages, although they have recently been developed for use with more commonly taught languages as well, such as Spanish, French, and German. On the GST, tasks are designed to cover a range of target-language situations and elicit various language functions, as well as to present differing levels of difficulty to examinees, such that oral proficiency in German may be probed. Performance on the GST is tape-recorded and subsequently scored by trained raters, who assign a global rating according to the ACTFL (1986) Guidelines.[1] Results are reported to examinees and other score users in the form of a single ACTFL Proficiency Guidelines rating at one of nine different sublevels (i.e., Novice-Low through Superior), and this rating is accompanied by a copy of the guidelines. Although each of the fifteen GST tasks is rated individually, these task-specific scores are not reported.

Global ratings on SOPIs have generally been found comparable with ratings on standard OPIs (Stansfield & Kenyon, 1992b), although the live versus tape-based formats have also been observed to elicit different types of L2 behavior from examinees. For example, Shohamy (1994) found that SOPIs elicit a greater range and number of register shifts than OPIs, because of the fact that OPIs engage the examinee in conversation with a single interlocutor (the interviewer) whereas SOPIs simulate interactions with a wide variety of interlocutors. Indeed, OPIs have been criticized for presenting the examinee with only a single type of interaction (essentially, a formal interview), which may have little to do with the range of target L2 interactions about which interpretations are often made (Spolsky, 1985; Stevenson, 1985; Lazaraton, 1992; Young, 1995). Furthermore, interviewer behavior has been observed to affect the language elicited in interviews and eventual ACTFL-level ratings (e.g., Ross & Berwick, 1992; Shohamy, 1994; Ross, 1995; Young & He, 1998). Such problems have prompted test developers to posit one advantage for SOPIs over OPIs, in that the influence of contextual variables may be controlled (e.g., Shohamy, 1994). Stansfield and Kenyon (1992b) suggest that "in the SOPI, the sociolinguistic circumstances of the task are carefully contrived" (p. 363) and should therefore provide a useful format for assessing examinees' abilities with respect to this aspect of communicative competence.

A cursory examination of GST tasks reveals that examinees are indeed faced with a variety of sociolinguistic circumstances. For all fifteen tasks, contextual variables are presented to examinees in the form of situational descriptions, wherein the social context of the simulated interaction is

1 ACTFL (1999) recently revised the Guidelines to include ten sublevels of proficiency; future SOPI administrations will be rated according to the revised and expanded descriptors.

explained (e.g., talking with an unknown person on the street). The examinee is asked on all tasks to imagine a direct interaction with a monolingual native speaker (NS), and these speakers are described as having a range of sociocultural relationships with the examinee (e.g., the daughter of a host family, the director of a study abroad program). Finally, other potentially determinant sociolinguistic cues are provided to examinees in the specific instructions for task goals (e.g., accomplishing speech acts such as requests and apologies). In light of such a range of simulated social circumstances, it would seem that the GST should elicit several aspects of the sociolinguistic competencies of German L2 learners, in particular the ability of examinees to produce contextually appropriate language which demonstrates sensitivity to differences in register associated with characteristics of the interlocutor as well as demands of the task.

Examinee performances on each GST task are assigned ratings according to the ACTFL Guidelines. However, given the general nature of descriptors within the Guidelines, more concrete directions for scoring examinee performances are provided by the Center for Applied Linguistics (1995b) in the form of training materials in the German Speaking Test Rater Training Kit (RTK). In the RTK, with respect to sociolinguistic competence, raters are directed to pay careful attention to an examinee's command over formal and familiar registers in German, and appropriate and inappropriate uses for pronouns of address (you: familiar *du* versus you: formal *Sie*) are provided as examples. In describing an Intermediate-Mid rating assigned to an examinee on an Intermediate-level task, the RTK remarks: "His basic vocabulary and use of appropriate register (*du*) allow him to fulfill the task at the intended level" (p. 5.11). In another example, an examinee is rated Intermediate-High on an Advanced-level task because of lack of control over register in selecting pronominal forms of address: "The speaker switches between the formal and familiar forms of address, demonstrating a lack of control over register. This causes his response to sound inappropriate and somewhat comical" (p. 6.13). At the upper proficiency levels, command over register can prove deterministic: For an examinee to receive an Advanced-level rating, the RTK suggests that there must be evidence of command over at least one register and emergence of a second; for an examinee to receive a Superior-level rating, there must be evidence of command over both formal and familiar registers.

In short, command (or the lack thereof) over the register and associated forms of address which are sociolinguistically appropriate in light of contextual constraints found on different GST tasks is one factor contributing to the assignment of ACTFL proficiency ratings. In order to investigate the extent to which interpretations about such sociolinguistic aspects of examinees' proficiencies may be consistently associated with performances and ratings on the GST, the current investigation thus took as its focus an analysis of the subsystem of address behavior within a range of GST performances rated at widely varying ACTFL proficiency levels.

Address behavior in L2 German

Braun, Kohz, and Schubert (1986) define address behavior as a speaker's means of referring to an interlocutor, and they maintain that the selection of particular nominal, pronominal, or verbal forms represents a deliberate marking of the social relationship between speaker and addressee (p. xvii). However, the manner in which such marking is realized is a variable factor among languages. Some languages, like English, have only one currently functional pronoun of address for designating a single addressee, the second person singular *you*. Other languages offer a variety of possibilities for address pronominalization, from the Western European T/V distinctions, to languages with three or more levels of address (e.g., Chinese, Japanese, and Turkish; see Braun, 1984). Sociocultural relationships may also be marked in many languages via the choice of nominal forms (e.g., first name, title plus last name) and in verb conjugation.

For learners of L2 German, or any other L2, developing control over the address system involves acquisition of the pragmalinguistic forms available, the sociopragmatic rules linking particular forms with contextual variables, and an ability to marshal both types of knowledge in language use. One problem faced by learners of German is that the application of L1 sociopragmatic or pragmalinguistic rules may lead to unintended violations of the interlocutor's norms of address behavior (see also Thomas, 1983; Pieper, 1984; Odlin, 1989; Riley, 1989). Of course, whether or not pragmatic transfer or other developmental "errors" such as nonstandard address behavior actually lead to communication problems with NS interlocutors is a matter in need of empirical investigation (Edmondson, 1982; Dittmar & Stutterheim, 1984; Kasper, 1992; Wildner-Bassett, 1994).

In addition, the extent to which sociopragmatic norms may be defined for L1 German address behavior is a matter of debate. Pieper (1984) summarized parameters for understanding norms of address behavior with the question, "Who speaks in what ways to whom in which situations?" (p. 9, my translation). According to such parameters, early sociolinguistic work by Brown and Gilman (1960) and Brown and Ford (1964) established general address norms among NSs of Western European languages. However, answers to Pieper's question may not be as unambiguous as once thought, as original systemic representations of

T/V address behavior, which posited a clear distinction between familiarity/solidarity/intimacy and distance/formality/power-inequality, have since been challenged (e.g., Winter, 1984; Braun, 1988; Tannen, 1993b; Martiny, 1996). With respect to German, Delisle (1993) has pointed out that, in addition to posited systemic sociocultural variables such as formality, social distance, authority, respect, intimacy, and solidarity, other variables may contribute to NSs' selections of address forms, including language variety differences, physical appearance of the interlocutor, location and duration of interaction, age of participants, political ideology, emotional solidarity, occupation, educational level, likability of interlocutor, and simple reciprocity with respect to the address forms selected by an interlocutor (see also Kohz, 1984; Delisle, 1986; Braun, 1988; Martiny, 1996). Such variability notwithstanding, it is generally acknowledged that NSs of German tend to adhere to certain norms of address behavior based on common sociocultural parameters, especially age, degree of intimacy, situational formality, and the principle of reciprocity (Delisle, 1986, 1993). German address behavior is therefore typically based on a distinction between two available address registers: formal, respectful, socially distant (characterized for the remainder of this chapter as "you:formal"); and informal, familiar, socially proximate (characterized for the remainder of this chapter as "you:familiar").

For the purposes of the current study, address behavior was treated as a rule-governed subsystem of the sociolinguistic competence which serves as a common target for L2 acquisition of German among U.S. foreign language learners. However, given the concerns mentioned earlier, care was taken to establish the extent to which sociopragmatic norms could be associated with the tasks and simulated interactions occurring on the GST. The current study therefore examined the elicitation of address behavior on GST tasks, the sociopragmatic norms which might be associated with these tasks, and evidence of examinee control over sociopragmatic norms and pragmalinguistic representations within their test performances.

Microanalysis of address behavior on the GST

A variety of microanalytic techniques have been utilized for the study of oral proficiency assessment (e.g., van Lier, 1989; Riggenbach, 1991; Lazaraton, 1992; Ross & Berwick, 1992; Young & Milanovic, 1992; Douglas, 1994; Marisi, 1994; Ross, 1995; Young, 1995; Young & He, 1998). Common to these techniques is analysis of language produced during test performance (e.g., participation structures) as a function of contextual variables found within the assessment (e.g., interlocutor identities, social setting, examinee objectives). For the current study, microanalytic techniques provided the most appropriate means for investigating aspects of examinee L2 performances as a function of social and contextual variables simulated within tasks on the German Speaking Test. The primary analytic approach involved coding and quantification of forms of address behavior within examinee L2 speech production. However, following cautions by Schegloff (1993) and others (e.g., Hillocks, 1994), confirmation of quantified group patterns was also sought within individual performance samples. Finally, codings of examinee address behavior were grounded in a careful analysis of those contextual variables found on GST tasks which might have influenced examinees' L2 performances.

The following research questions were addressed in the current study:

1. Can norms for address behavior be established for GST tasks?
2. To what extent is address behavior elicited from examinees on GST tasks?
3. With what frequency is pronominal address behavior exhibited by examinees rated at differing ACTFL proficiency levels?
4. What is the sociopragmatic accuracy (according to NS norms) exhibited by examinees rated at differing ACTFL proficiency levels?
5. What is the pragmalinguistic range of address forms exhibited by examinees rated at differing ACTFL proficiency levels?
6. To what extent are interpretations about an examinee's command over address registers warranted, in light of patterns of address behavior found on the GST?

Method

The current investigation proceeded in three stages. Assessment tasks on the GST were first analyzed for contextual cues in order to determine which tasks would be the most likely to elicit direct address behavior, and whether or not available cues were sufficient to establish norms on which address register selections could be based. In the second stage, GST examinee performances were transcribed, coded, and analyzed for frequency, range, and accuracy of German address behavior. Finally, in the third stage, comparisons were made at both the group and the individual examinee levels between these observations of address behavior and corresponding performance ratings according to the ACTFL Proficiency Guidelines.

Contextual cues on the GST

All items on the GST ask examinees to imagine themselves having a conversation with a German NS. However, several tasks seem to elicit greater frequencies of address behavior than do the others. Initial review of forty-four examinee performances on the GST revealed six tasks in particular which elicited extensive use of forms of address. A number of issues may account for the increased address behavior noted on these six tasks, including the identity of the interlocutors (established in item instructions and tape-recorded prompts), the speech functions to be accomplished, and other salient situational cues provided in instructions and task realia (such as pictures). In general, all six of these tasks require the examinee to accomplish clear and contained speech acts within a short amount of time and in interaction with a single interlocutor who is clearly defined within task instructions. By contrast, other tasks on the GST present examinees with more extended objectives which have less apparent parameters for their accomplishment and in which direct address with a single interlocutor does not play a crucial role in accomplishing the task (e.g., describing a displaced series of events or a place, talking about personal activities, hypothesizing about an impersonal topic). In order to examine the contextual cues and likely constraints on register selection, the six tasks eliciting more extensive address behavior are analyzed here in some detail.

Task 1 (asking questions). Directions for this task require the examinee to ask questions directly to Helmut, who is described as an "exchange student" and an L1 speaker of German. Important in the identity of this interlocutor are three factors: He is given a first name, which is suggestive to the examinee of a degree of familiarity in the simulated relationship; his social status is that of a student, which is likely to be similar to that of the examinee (see the next section on examinee data, and note that the GST was designed with U.S. high school and university FL learners in mind); and because he is a student, he is likely to be close in age to the examinee (assuming, of course, common patterns in student populations in Germany and the United States). Task 1 is the only GST task which is not followed by an aural prompt delivered by the simulated interlocutor. However, additional information for Helmut's identity is provided within a set of picture realia that accompanies the task (where he is portrayed as a young man engaging in sports and school activities). Based on these contextual cues, examinee choice of pronominal *du* (you:familiar) and related forms of address would seem appropriate.

Task 2 (giving directions). Directions for this task require the examinee to speak directly to an unknown interlocutor, who is described only as "a woman," in explaining how to get from one location to another. Characteristics relevant for choice of forms of address are: The interlocutor is completely unfamiliar to the examinee, and the interlocutor is an adult. The situation and the identifiable characteristics of the interlocutor would seem to call for the use of *Sie* (you:formal) and related forms of address. This choice should be further influenced by the aural prompt question from the woman, who asks in an adult voice: *Entschuldigen Sie. Können Sie mir sagen, wie ich zum Museum komme?* (Excuse me. Can you:formal tell me how to get to the museum?). Thus, the formal second person pronominal form *Sie* is precedented by the interlocutor, and this precedent should strongly indicate the sociopragmatic need for reciprocity on the part of the examinee.

Task 3 (explaining a process). Similar to Task 1, this task requires the examinee to speak directly to a student (explaining how to make a dental appointment), whose address-determinant characteristics include: She is given a first name (*Sonja*), indicating familiarity between the examinee and interlocutor; she is an exchange student; and she is likely to be close in age to the population of GST examinees. Sensitivity to such factors should result in the rather unambiguous choice of *du* (you:familiar) and related address forms for this interlocutor. This choice may also be influenced by the youthful female voice asking: *Wie kann ich denn einen Termin beim Zahnarzt bekommen?* (How can I get an appointment with the dentist?).

Task 4 (apologizing with tact). This task requires the examinee to make an apology to a host-family "daughter" named Erika. Distinguishing characteristics of the interlocutor include: familiarity is established through provision of her first name and via situational characteristics, and she is likely to be relatively young in age. These characteristics would seem to call for the choice of *du* (you:familiar) and related forms of address. The aural prompt from Erika corroborates this choice, delivered in a young female voice: *Hast du denn den Regenschirm gebraucht?* (Did you:familiar use the umbrella?). Although examinees should be led to reciprocate on the basis of this precedent, the sensitive nature of the apology speech act required by this task may serve as a point of confusion for some examinees, leading them to strategic selection of the more formal register (i.e., *Sie*).

Task 5 (requesting). This item requires the examinee to make a direct request for a refund from a trip organizer, "Mrs. Schneider." Identifying characteristics of this interlocutor include: She is named with title and a family name, but not with a first name, delimiting the familiarity in her relationship with the examinee; and, as the organizer, she is in control of the refund decision, and she is thus provided with unequal power status over the examinee. These conditions would seem to necessitate a choice of formal address register (i.e., *Sie*). In addition, the sensitive nature of the issue and the imposition of the request would likely underscore such a choice. Of course, this kind of sensitivity may also demand a high degree of cultural convergence on the part of the examinee (not to mention sociopragmatic competence), and the request could certainly be realized in divergent ways (e.g., conflict and frustration could inspire divergent choices of address register). The aural prompt from the interlocutor is delivered in an adult female voice: *Es tut mir wirklich sehr leid, aber ich kann Ihnen Ihr Geld nicht zurückerstatten* (I'm really very sorry, but I cannot refund to you:formal your:formal money). The choice of formal address is thus precedented by the interlocutor, although only in the dative and genitive pronominal forms, and not in the perhaps more readily interpretable nominative form (*Sie*).

Task 6 (giving advice). This item requires the examinee to give advice to a friend named Horst. Address-defining characteristics include: The interlocutor is given a first name, he is referred to as a friend, and he is a student and thus likely to be close in age to GST examinees. These cues would seem to definitively call for familiar address behavior (*du*). Horst also precedents the use of the second person familiar pronominal address form: *Was glaubst du sollte ich tun, sofort eine Stelle suchen oder für einige Zeit ins Ausland gehen?* (What do you:familiar think I should do, look for a job right away or travel abroad for a while?).

In addition to contextual cues found in instructions for these six tasks, general test instructions remind examinees that they should emulate NS linguistic norms, as in the following statement: "Remember to use the type and style of language that a native German speaker would use in each situation." Examinees are thus provided a rationale for converging with norms of address behavior identifiable within each task, as it is apparent from instructions that they will be evaluated accordingly.

In order to verify whether the contextual cues provided by these six GST tasks were sufficient for indicating target address norms, baseline data were gathered from ten NSs of German. Informants consisted of five students and five faculty members at two U.S. universities. Each informant was provided with the directions for each of the six tasks as seen by examinees (but not the aural prompts, so as to eliminate the influence of reciprocity on their decisions). After reading the directions, they were then asked to select one of four possible choices as representative of the appropriate form of address for each task: *(a) Sie* (the formal second person nominative pronoun), *(b) du* (the familiar second person nominative pronoun), *(c)* "Either is OK," and *(d)* "Unsure based on the information provided." Options *(c)* and *(d)* were included to ensure that NSs provided accurate information regarding their intuitions about address norms and in response to the adequacy of cues available on the GST tasks. All ten informants exhibited exact agreement (100%) in selecting address forms for all six GST task descriptions. Informants did not seem to find any of the tasks ambiguous for selecting the appropriate address register, as none selected options *(c)* or *(d)* for any of the tasks. Informants agreed exactly with the address norms surmised.

GST examinee data

Examinee data for the current study consisted of forty-four tapes of responses to Form A of the GST.[2] Form A is the disclosed version of the GST which is used by CAL for rater training, institutional administrations, and research purposes. The forty-four tapes were collected from volunteers at high schools and universities during the pilot-testing phase of GST development. Although specific background information for each examinee was not available, the fact that all were high school or college students at the time of testing provided sufficient evidence for establishing likely social distance and age relationships with simulated interlocutors. Of the total sample of forty-four examinee tapes, twenty-seven included performances on all fifteen tasks on the GST, and the remaining seventeen included performances on only the first seven tasks on the GST. For examinees with limited knowledge of German, the "short form" of the GST (the first seven tasks) can be administered, as the final eight tasks represent language topics, functions, and situations which are considered beyond the probable ability of beginning language learners. As such, only a truncated sample of the tapes included performance data on all tasks of interest for the current study. Tasks 1 through 3 were attempted by all forty-four sample examinees, and Tasks 4 through 6 were attempted by only those twenty-seven examinees completing the long form of the GST. Examinee response tapes were transcribed by the researcher, and an NS of German subsequently checked the accuracy of transcriptions against audiotape recordings.

The forty-four sample tapes were assigned provisional proficiency ratings according to the ACTFL Guidelines by staff at the Center for Applied Linguistics. Global ratings were assigned by a single rater for research purposes and therefore do not constitute official GST ratings, although the ratings and tape samples are used within rater training materials and should therefore be considered relatively trustworthy. Table 1 shows the breakdown of global proficiency levels for samples in the current study.

Microanalysis of address behavior

The forty-four GST examinee samples were coded for all pronominal forms of address used on Tasks 1 through 6. Although address behavior is also manifested in German in both nominal (e.g., calling the addressee by first name or title plus last name) and verbal forms (in imperatives or any finite verb forms which conjugate for person) as well as pronominal forms, nominal and verbal forms were not included in the current study. Initial review of the data revealed that only occasional use of nominal

2 Thanks to Dorry Kenyon at the Center for Applied Linguistics for making these data available.

TABLE 1. GST SAMPLE DATA

ACTFL level	n
Superior	2
Advanced-High	4
Advanced	11
Intermediate-High	10
Intermediate-Mid	3
Intermediate-Low	6
Novice-High	7
Novice-Mid	1
TOTAL	44

forms was evident on any of the six tasks, even though names are provided for each of the simulated interlocutors in test instructions. Verb forms were not coded because of their redundancy (in terms of sociopragmatic information) with the use of pronominal forms. Finite verbs were also noted to be subject to substantial variation in form because of levels of examinee control over other linguistic subsystems (e.g., subject-verb agreement, tense marking; see Norris, 1996b).

Each examinee performance on each task was first coded for frequency of pronominal address behavior by identification within the transcripts of all second person pronominal forms used. These forms were then further categorized according to eight morphosyntactic possibilities: nominative singular/plural, accusative singular/plural, dative singular/plural, or genitive singular/plural. Thus, for example, *Ich kaufe dir einen neuen Regenschirm* (I'll buy you:familiar a new umbrella) contains a single token of the second person singular dative pronoun. The results of this round of coding provided frequency data for the number of contexts created by examinees for each of eight possible pronominal types.

In order to investigate the accuracy with which examinees supplied address registers, each context was then further categorized as having either a sociopragmatically appropriate or inappropriate suppliance, according to the pronominal form produced by the examinee. Decisions regarding sociopragmatic appropriateness were based on the contextual cues and NS baseline data reported above. Thus, for Task 1, the sociopragmatically appropriate choice of register would result in the use of familiar second person pronominal forms (*du*, etc.). For example, the statement, *Was machst du mit der Freizeit?* (What do you:familiar do with spare time?) would be coded as containing one context and one appropriate suppliance. However, the statement, *Was machen Sie mit der Freizeit?* (What do you:formal do with spare time?),

TABLE 2. GERMAN PRONOMINAL FORMS OF ADDRESS

| | Nominative | | Accusative | | Dative | | Genitive | |
	Singular	Plural	Singular	Plural	Singular	Plural	Singular	Plural
Register								
You:formal	*Sie*	*Sie*	*Sie*	*Sie*	*Ihnen*	*Ihnen*	*Ihr*	*Ihr*
You:familiar	*du*	*Ihr*	*dich*	*Euch*	*dir*	*Euch*	*dein*	*Euer*

would be coded as containing one context and no appropriate suppliances. Samples were coded in this manner for contexts and suppliances of all sixteen possible second person pronominal address forms shown in Table 2. The results of this stage of coding provided information regarding the frequency with which examinees engaged in pronominal address behavior, the sociopragmatic accuracy of this behavior, and the pragmalinguistic range of address behavior across all possible morphosyntactic categories of pronominal production.

Comparison of address behavior with ACTFL ratings

Finally, in order to investigate the relationship between global ACTFL Guidelines proficiency ratings and examinee address behavior on the GST, three types of comparisons were made in the current study. The first comparison looked at differences in address behavior noted among the six GST tasks, focusing in particular on the differences between tasks requiring formal versus those requiring familiar registers. The second comparison examined the central tendencies of group address behavior, with group determined by ACTFL level rating. Thus, trends in the frequency, sociopragmatic accuracy, and pragmalinguistic range of address behavior at different ACTFL levels were investigated. Finally, individual patterns in address behavior were also examined, in order to clarify the extent to which interpretations about an individual examinee's control over address registers could be validly based on the GST and ACTFL proficiency level ratings. All comparisons were made using descriptive statistics, graphic comparisons, and observations of individual performance segments. Inferential statistical procedures were not warranted, given the low sample sizes at each of the ACTFL proficiency levels.

Results

Results of the microanalysis of pronominal address behavior on the GST are presented in three sections. The first section examines overall frequency and accuracy of pronominal address behavior exhibited by examinees on each of the six GST tasks. The second section examines in more detail the frequency, accuracy, and range of pronominal address behavior exhibited by the total sample of forty-four examinees on Tasks 1 through 3 (from the short form of the GST). Apparent patterns in address behavior are noted for ACTFL proficiency level groupings from Novice-High through Superior. Finally, the third section examines the frequency, accuracy, and range of pronominal address behavior exhibited by the twenty-seven examinees who took the long form of the GST and who therefore completed all six tasks of interest in the current study. Again, patterns in address behavior are noted for ACTFL proficiency level groupings from Intermediate-High to Superior. For all three results sections, transcripts are excerpted to demonstrate observed group tendencies. Patterns in individual address behavior are explored in more detail in the discussion section.

Elicitation of address behavior

Table 3 shows basic descriptive statistics for pronominal address behavior on Tasks 1 through 6. As noted earlier, NS baseline data indicated consistent register preferences for each of the six tasks, resulting in four tasks requiring the use of familiar pronominal address forms (*du* Tasks 1, 3, 4, 6) and two tasks requiring the use of formal pronominal address forms (*Sie* Tasks 2, 5). In general, all tasks elicited direct address forms from the majority of examinees. However, it can be seen in Table 3 that, on the short form of the GST, not all examinees produced pronominal forms of address for each of the three sample tasks. Especially Task 2 (giving directions to an unknown person) elicited pronominal address forms from fewer examinees.

Through review of the GST transcripts it was noted that, in lieu of direct address forms, several examinees utilized alternative means for accomplishing Task 2, as in the following use of *man* (one) by a speaker rated at the ACTFL Advanced level:

T2(A): *Ja, das ist ganz einfach. Man muß einfach vom Post hier vorbei der Bank und dann links um die Ecke auf Schloß, Schloßalleestraße, oder Schloßallee. Und da bei den Restaurant muß man links gehen, und man muß die, bei die Wohnungen vorbei laufen, und bis zum Linzerstraße, wo das Hotel ist. Und da muß man rechts gehen. Und da sieht man links eine Polizei Station, und dann daneben ist das Museum.*

T2(A): Yes, that's really easy. One has to just go from the post office here past the bank and then left around the corner into Schloss, Schlossallee Street, or Schlossallee. And then at the restaurant one has to go left, and then one has to walk by the apartment buildings and up to Linzer Street, where the hotel is. And then one has to go right. And there one sees a police station on the left, and next to it is the museum.

TABLE 3. ADDRESS BEHAVIOR ON TASKS 1–6

	Task 1	Task 2	Task 3	Task 4	Task 5	Task 6
	du	*Sie*	*du*	*du*	*Sie*	*du*
NS baseline						
GST short form ($n = 44$)						
n producing F of A	41	37	42			
frequency (mean, SD)	7.00, 4.02	3.25, 2.40	5.55, 3.25			
accuracy (mean, SD)	0.71, 0.37	0.96, 0.17	0.65, 0.40			
GST long form ($n = 27$)						
n producing F of A	27	24	26	24	22	27
frequency (mean, SD)	9.00, 3.46	4.11, 2.56	7.10, 3.04	2.10, 1.34	2.33, 1.84	8.93, 3.59
accuracy (mean, SD)	0.73, 0.37	0.94, 0.21	0.69, 0.40	0.76, 0.38	0.93, 0.23	0.87, 0.24

Note: Tasks 4 through 6 appear on the long form of the GST only.

Although such use of *man* (one) sidesteps direct address of the interlocutor, it is nevertheless a commonly occurring form in L1 German discourse.

The pattern of fewer examinees producing pronominal forms of address on Task 2 was also observed among the subset of twenty-seven examinees who took the long form of the GST (i.e., more proficient examinees). By contrast, Tasks 1 and 3 elicited pronominal address forms from virtually all examinees, as did Task 6 (with examinees who took the long form). However, Tasks 4 and 5 elicited forms of address from fewer examinees, similar to Task 2. Each of these tasks required the performance of face-threatening and impositional speech acts (apologizing for losing an umbrella, requesting a refund from a trip organizer who has already denied the request). It may therefore have been the case that examinees chose to avoid direct address to some extent as a strategic means for ameliorating the social tensions implied within each speech act. For example, in responding to Task 5, the following examinee (rated at the ACTFL Advanced level) shifted the focus away from a direct request (and associated address forms), and focused instead on providing a rationale for the return of his money:

T5(A): *Aber ich muß es zurück kriegen. Denn ich, ich habe nicht so viel Geld, und es war nicht mein Schuld, daß, daß meine Gastschwester ihre Hochzeit hat an dem Tag. Ich, ich kann wirklich nicht teilnehmen an diesem Program. Ich würde gerne mitgehen, aber ich kann gar nicht. Ich, ich muß wirklich dabei sein, wenn meine Gastschwester heiratet. Bitte, ich, ich, ich habe kein andere Wahl. Ich kann nicht gehen.*

T5(A): But I have to get it back. Because I, I don't have so much money, and it really wasn't my fault that my host sister has her wedding on that day. I, I really can't participate in this program. I would like to come along, but I just can't. I, I really must be there if my host sister is getting married. Please, I, I, I don't have any other choice. I can't go.

Overall means and standard deviations for both frequency and sociopragmatic accuracy of pronominal address behavior on each task are also shown in Table 3. It can be seen that Tasks 1, 3, and 6 elicited on average more frequent use of pronominal address forms than Tasks 2, 4, and 5. However, standard deviations show substantial variability among examinees in frequency of address forms for all tasks, and especially for Tasks 1, 3, and 6. Interestingly, these three tasks all involve conversations with simulated interlocutors who are described as students and who are young in age. Furthermore, these tasks present examinees with relatively low-stakes objectives (asking questions about some photos, explaining how to make a dental appointment, and recommending a course of action to a friend). The other three tasks involve either high-stakes speech acts (apologizing, requesting) or require the use of formal address forms.

Overall, address register accuracy patterns shown in Table 3 indicate that, although tasks requiring the use of formal address forms elicited less frequent address behavior, they also resulted in high levels of sociopragmatic accuracy (i.e., examinees tended to choose second person formal pronouns for these tasks). However, for those tasks requiring familiar address forms, much lower average levels of accuracy were observed. These patterns were observed among all examinees on the first three tasks as well as among the subset of higher-proficiency examinees on all six tasks. Overall, the highest levels of accuracy in address register selection were noted for Task 2, in which examinees gave directions to an unknown interlocutor. It is possible that contextual cues combined with the principle of address reciprocity made this task the least ambiguous, although other tasks wherein a pronominal form was precedented by interlocutor statements did not show such high levels of sociopragmatic accuracy. It is also plausible that the linguistic functions called for by Task 2 tended to enable use of the appropriate address form. Thus, for example, even speakers rated at the Novice-High proficiency level utilized the second person formal address pronoun in responding to Task 2:

T2(NH): *Ja, machen Sie, machen Sie links, vor das Restaurant. Gehen, Gehen Sie auf Schloßalleestraße, und dann machen Sie rechts, vor das Hotel. Und dann.*

T2(NH): Yes, you:formal make, you:formal make a left in front of the restaurant. Go, you:formal go to Schlossallee Street, and then you:formal make a right in front of the hotel. And then.

The majority of examinees similarly utilized the imperative verb plus pronoun pattern for this task. It is possible that high levels of sociopragmatic accuracy in address behavior on this task may have been attributable to "chunked" use of imperative forms with the second person formal pronoun, a pattern that is typically encountered early in German L2 instruction.

The lowest levels of address register accuracy were noted for Task 3, which required the examinee to explain to a young exchange student how to make an appointment with a dentist. Although the choice of address register for this task seems quite unambiguous, producing sociopragmatically accurate address forms proved to be difficult for both lower- and higher-proficiency examinees (see Table 3). Interestingly, this task also elicited the greatest use of modal verbs (e.g., *sollen, müssen, können*) among the six sample tasks in the current study. For example, the following examinee, rated at the ACTFL Advanced level, selected the second person formal address form for all address behavior in the task, and a number of the finite verb forms associated with pronouns of address were modals:

TABLE 4. FREQUENCY AND ACCURACY OF PRONOUNS OF ADDRESS ON TASKS 1–3

ACTFL rating	Frequency (per task)		Accuracy	
	Mean	SD	Mean	SD
Advanced-High/Superior ($n = 6$)	6.67	1.86	0.81	0.18
Advanced ($n = 11$)	7.06	1.52	0.79	0.18
Intermediate-High ($n = 10$)	6.43	1.88	0.73	0.16
Intermediate-Mid/Intermediate-Low ($n = 9$)	3.00	1.39	0.64	0.12
Novice-High ($n = 8$)	2.83	1.33	0.67	0.14

T3(A): *Ja, Sie müssen, Sie haben diese Zahnschmerz. Sie müssen zuerst ein Zahnearzt finden. Wir benutzen immer Doktor soundso. Und Sie müssen nur diese, diese Zahnearzt anrufen und sagen, dass Sie will ein, ein Termin verabreden. Und so, ja vielleicht können Sie es nächste Freitag machen. Dann sagen Sie ja, um drei Uhr will ich ein Termin machen. So, es ist ziemlich einfach. Sie nur sagen, dass was los ist, dass Sie ein, eine Problem haben.*

T3(A): Well, you:formal have to, you:formal have this toothache. First you:formal have to find a dentist. We always use Dr. so-and-so. And you:formal just have to call this, this dentist and say that you:formal want to make an appointment. And so, well perhaps you:formal can make it for next Friday. Then you:formal say yes, I would like to make an appointment at three o'clock. So it is rather simple. You:formal just say that something is wrong, that you:formal have a, a problem.

It may have been the case with this task that irregular conjugation rules associated with modal verbs led some examinees to the selection of a sociopragmatically incorrect register, given the fact that the infinitive forms of modal verbs and the forms utilized with the second person formal pronoun are exactly the same; that is, the simple pattern of *Sie* plus infinitive form may have enabled examinees to utilize modal verbs, whereas the more complex irregular verbal conjugations necessary for utilizing the same verbs with the second person familiar form made the selection of *du* less frequent. For similar reasons, a prioritization of grammatical accuracy by examinees might also account for the selection of *Sie* forms, given the relative ease with which corresponding modal verbs may be supplied.

Group-level analyses for Tasks 1–3

Table 4 shows group means and standard deviations for frequency in production (in words) and sociopragmatic accuracy of pronominal address behavior (proportion of correct address pronouns per total address pronouns) on the first three sample tasks. These descriptive statistics show the central tendency and dispersion of pronominal address behavior for five ACTFL proficiency level groupings: Advanced-High and Superior together (given small samples in each group and overall similarities in performance), Advanced, Intermediate-High, Intermediate-Mid and Intermediate-Low together (given small sample sizes in the Intermediate-Mid group and overall similarities in performance), and Novice-High (with a single Novice-Mid examinee included in this group).

It can be seen in Table 4 that there is a marked difference (more than three address pronouns per task) in the frequency with which address forms were produced by examinees rated at the Intermediate-Mid level and below compared with examinees rated at the Intermediate-High level and above, although variability among individuals rated at each level was similar across the groups. These observed frequency differences were likely related to differences in the overall amount of speech produced by examinees at the different levels (see Norris, 1996b), although there was marked consistency in frequency of address pronouns among examinees rated at Intermediate-High and above as well as among examinees rated at Intermediate-Mid and below. The following two examples demonstrate these overall differences in observed frequencies of address behavior, with the Advanced speaker producing twelve pronominal address forms and the Novice-High speaker producing only four pronominal address forms in a briefer response:

T3(A): *Du, das ist kein Problem. Wenn du Zahnschmerzen hast, mußt du unbedingt ein Termin machen. Ich gebe dir die Nummer von meinem Zahnarzt. Der heißt Doktor W. Und da kannst du einfach anrufen, bestens morgens, und sagen, daß du Zahnschmerzen hast. Da finden sie unbedingt ein Termin für dich da, wahrscheinlich schon an dem Tag, wo du anrufst. Und dann gehst du hin, und der ist ein ganz netter Typ. Er hilft dir bestimmt. Es könnte sein, daß das etwas ernstes ist, also du solltest unbedingt mal anrufen. Sonst verlierst du ein Zahn.*

T3(A): You:familiar, that's no problem. If you:familiar have a toothache, you:familiar definitely have to make an appointment. I'll give you:familiar my dentist's number. His name is Dr. W. And you:familiar can just call there, preferably in the morning, and say that you:familiar have a toothache. They'll definitely find you:familiar an appointment, probably for the day you:familiar call. And then you:familiar go there, and he's a really nice guy. He'll help you:familiar for sure. It could be that it is something serious, so you:familiar should definitely call. Otherwise you:familiar might lose a tooth.

T3(NH): *Das ist sehr schlecht Sonja. Du mußte, mußtest eine, eine dentist gesehen. Und du mußt, mußtest die dentist anrufen, und du mußt mit der nurse sprechen, und die nurse will ein appointment machen. Und du mußt gehen nach der dentist und habe, habe eine schlechtes Zeit.*

T3(NH): That's very bad Sonja. You:familiar have to, have to, see a dentist. And you:familiar have to, have to call the dentist, and you:familiar have to talk with the nurse, and the nurse wants to make an appointment. And you:familiar have to go to the dentist and have, have a bad time.

Mean sociopragmatic accuracy levels on Tasks 1–3 reveal a general decrease in the accuracy of address register selections from the upper-through the lower-proficiency groups, and it should be noted that even for the highest-proficiency examinees, average accuracy levels were only around 80%. Individual variability in accuracy of address register was higher among the three upper proficiency levels, as shown by higher standard deviations, possibly associated in part with the larger frequencies of address forms produced by examinees at these levels. The following two excerpts exemplify these trends in sociopragmatic accuracy. In the first example, the Intermediate-Mid examinee produces eight contexts for pronominal address, four of which she correctly supplies with you:familiar forms (all nominatives) and four of which she incorrectly supplies with you:formal forms (for chance levels of accuracy). In the second example, the Advanced examinee correctly adopts the familiar address register, and she supplies a number of direct address contexts and corresponding correct suppliances across a range of linguistic contexts.

T3(IM): *Ah Sonja, du hast ein Zahneweh. Ich will helfen Sie. Du mußt rufen ein Zahneärzt an. In die gelb, die yellow pages haben wir viele Zahneärzt für Sie. Du kann choose any one you like. Rufen ein an, und dann die, ein, ein assistant will helfen, will fragen Sie viele Fragen. Du mußt antworten Sie diese Fragen, und dann.*

T3(IM): Ah Sonja, you:familiar have a toothache. I want to help you:formal. You:familiar have to call a dentist. In the yellow, the yellow pages we have many dentists for you:formal. You:familiar can choose any one you like. Call one, and then the, a, an assistant wants to help, wants to ask you:formal a lot of questions. You:familiar have to answer (you:formal) these questions, and then.

T3(A): *Ja, schlag mal in den Gelbe Seiten im Telefonbuch nach, und schau da unter Dentist nach. Und da sollst du den Namen M. finden. Und Doktor M. ist unserer Zahnarzt. Und der würde dich wahrscheinlich behandeln. Und seine Telefonnummer steht da. Da kannst du einfach anrufen und fragen, ob sie heute noch Zeit hätten, dich zu behandeln. Und ja, wenn du Glück hast, dann haben sie heute noch Zeit, aber, wenn nicht, dann kannst du es morgen machen.*

T3(A): Well, check the yellow pages in the telephone book, and look there under dentist. And there you:familiar should find the name M. And Dr. M. is our dentist. And he would probably see you:familiar. And his telephone number is there. You:familiar can simply call and ask whether they would have time to see you:familiar today. And well, if you:familiar are lucky, then they still have time today, but if not, then you:familiar can do it tomorrow.

In general, then, examinees rated at lower ACTFL proficiency levels exhibited lower levels of sociopragmatic accuracy in address register than examinees rated at higher levels. For all three tasks from the short form of the GST, the lowest two proficiency level groupings (examinees rated at Intermediate-Mid and below) exhibited sociopragmatic accuracy levels only slightly greater than chance.

TABLE 5. FREQUENCY AND ACCURACY OF *DU* (YOU:FAMILIAR) VERSUS
SIE (YOU:FORMAL) ON TASKS 1–3

	du				Sie			
	Frequency (per task)		*Accuracy*		*Frequency (per task)*		*Accuracy*	
ACTFL rating	*Mean*	*SD*	*Mean*	*SD*	*Mean*	*SD*	*Mean*	*SD*
Advanced-High/Superior (*n* = 6)	7.83	2.21	0.81	0.36	4.33	2.16	1.00	0.00
Advanced (*n* = 11)	8.64	2.09	0.75	0.38	3.91	2.63	0.93	0.17
Intermediate-High (*n* = 10)	7.55	2.37	0.67	0.32	4.20	2.94	0.87	0.33
Intermediate-Mid/								
Intermediate-Low (*n* = 9)	3.44	1.89	0.49	0.33	2.11	1.45	1.00	0.00
Novice-High (*n* = 8)	3.44	1.70	0.53	0.39	1.63	1.41	1.00	0.00

In order to examine the extent to which accuracy differences might be associated with tasks requiring familiar versus formal address forms, means and standard deviations were also calculated by proficiency level grouping for these two subsets of tasks. Table 5 shows that, on Tasks 1 through 3, the single task requiring formal address (Task 2) elicited much lower frequencies of pronominal forms than the two tasks requiring familiar address, although the frequency differences between upper-level and lower-level examinees were maintained. Variability in frequency of address was also similar at the Intermediate-High level and above and at the Intermediate-Mid level and below, for both task types.

Average sociopragmatic accuracy levels on the *Sie* (you:formal) task were high across all proficiency levels; thus, when examinees chose to use forms of address on this task, they generally did so according to sociopragmatic norms. Average accuracy levels on *du* (you:familiar) tasks were much lower than for *Sie* tasks, with especially low accuracy noted for examinees rated at Intermediate-Mid and below. Interestingly, standard deviations for address accuracy were similar and high across proficiency levels for *du* tasks, indicating substantial individual variation from observed group norms, regardless of proficiency rating. In contrast, low variability was noted for most proficiency groups on the *Sie* task, indicating homogeneous behavior on this task, although examinees at the Intermediate-High level were less accurate and more variable. It should be noted that Intermediate-High examinees exhibited a marked increase in frequency of address forms produced on this task, when compared with examinees at lower proficiency levels. A plausible explanation for lower accuracy may be that examinees at lower levels either avoided using direct address forms or produced only the *Sie* pronoun plus an imperative verbal construction, whereas examinees at the Intermediate-High level and above used address forms in more frequent and linguistically extended ways and therefore exhibited less

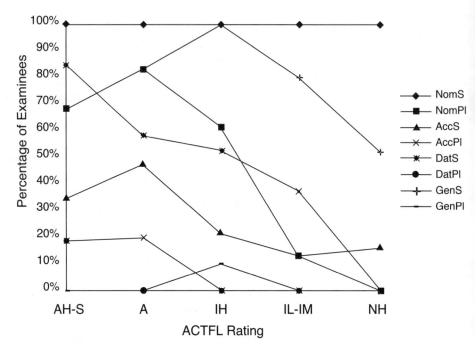

Figure 1   Range of pronoun types produced on Tasks 1–3.

sociopragmatic control, which gradually improved at the higher proficiency levels. The following example of an Intermediate-High examinee
reveals such a pattern of extended linguistic contexts for address forms
(i.e., beyond imperatives) accompanied by variable sociopragmatic accuracy (also note the corresponding low levels of accuracy in verbal agreement with pronominal forms):

T2(IH): *Ja natürlich. Wenn Sie heraus von der Postamt kommt, dann dreht
links und gehe auf Schloß, auf Straße Schloßallee, und es ist nur ja ein bißchen
nach links. Und dann, wenn du auf der Schloßalleestrafle kommt, dann biegen
Sie auch dann links noch mal. Dann gehen Sie nach der Linzerstrafle, und
auf der Linzerstraße dann biegen Sie nach rechts ab, und dann ist es auf der
linken Seite.*

T2(IH): Yes, of course. If you:formal exit from the post office here, then turn
left and go on Schloss, Schlossallee Street, and it is just a little to the left. And
then, when you:familiar come to Schlossallee Street, then you:formal turn once
more to the left. Then you:formal go to Linzer Street, and then you:formal
turn to the right on Linzer Street, and then it is on the left-hand side.

In order to investigate the range of morphosyntactic categories across
which examinees at different proficiency levels produced pronominal
address forms, frequency levels for the eight possible pronominal cate-

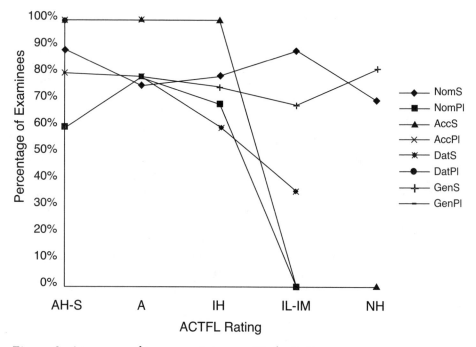

Figure 2 Accuracy of pronoun types on Tasks 1–3.

gories were calculated. Figure 1 shows the percentages of examinees at different proficiency levels producing contexts for each pronoun type on Tasks 1 through 3 combined. It can be seen that both nominative singular (*du* and *Sie*) and genitive singular (typically the possessive *dein*) address forms were produced by relatively high frequencies (50% or more) of examinees at all proficiency level groupings. For all other pronominal categories, generally consistent decreases in frequency of examinees producing the corresponding forms were noted from upper to lower proficiency levels. Especially marked and consistent decreases could be observed in the production of nominative plural (*Ihr* and *Sie*) and dative singular (*dir* and *Ihnen*) forms, with more than 80% of the examinees at the highest proficiency level grouping producing contexts for these forms followed by decreasing percentages of examinees producing contexts through near zero levels at the lowest proficiency level grouping. Similar trends were noted for other pronominal categories, although with much lower overall numbers of examinees producing forms. Virtually no examinees produced linguistic contexts on Tasks 1 through 3 for the genitive plural pronouns (*euer* and *ihr*).

Figure 2 shows percentages of examinees producing sociopragmatically accurate forms for different pronominal categories on Tasks 1 through 3 combined. The two categories noted to be produced with the most frequency, nominative singular and genitive singular forms, were consistently produced with sociopragmatic accuracy across all proficiency level groupings by between 70% and 85% of examinees. For all other pronominal categories, high levels of accuracy were noted among the upper three proficiency level groupings, followed by dramatic decreases in sociopragmatic accuracy levels among examinees rated at the Intermediate-Mid level or lower. It should be noted in Figure 2 that accuracy levels are not represented for groups where no contexts were supplied. Thus, the genitive plural form does not appear on the graph (except for at the Intermediate-High level), and other categorical lines are interrupted. Zero production of contexts should not be confused with zero levels of accuracy. For example, at the Intermediate-Low–Intermediate-High proficiency level, contexts for nominative plural and accusative singular pronominal forms were produced (hence, they are represented on the graph), but sociopragmatic accuracy for the corresponding pronominal forms was zero.

The following two examples give some indication of general patterns in sociopragmatic accuracy and frequency in the production of pronominal forms across a range of morphosyntactic categories. In the four question responses on this single task, the first speaker, rated at the Superior proficiency level, produces sociopragmatically accurate pronominal forms in six of the eight possible morphosyntactic categories:

T1(S):
(q1) *Das ist dein Freund Karl-Heinz. Ist er auch in deinem Alter? Hat, hat er auch deine Schule in Deutschland, in Frankfurt besucht? Seit wie.*
(q2) *Wo liegt denn deine Schule? Wieviele Schüler gibt es dort in der, an deiner Schule? Gefällt dir deine Schule? Gibt es auch Freizeitsbeschäftigungen an deiner Schule?*
(q3) *Naja, es sieht so aus, als ob du Sport treibst, als ob du gerne Sport treibst mit den Freunden. Was macht ihr denn noch? Was für Freizeitsbeschäftigungen gibt's noch bei euch?*
(q4) *Na, Bettina ist sehr schön. Wie lange seid ihr schon zusammen? Wie habt ihr euch kennengelernt? Liebst du sie? Kommst, kommt sie zu.*

T1(S):
(q1) That's your:familiar friend Karl-Heinz. Is he your:familiar age? Did he also go to your:familiar school in Germany, in Frankfurt? For how.
(q2) Where is your:familiar school? How many students are there in your:familiar school? Do you:familiar like your:familiar school? Are there also extracurricular activities at your:familiar school?
(q3) So, it looks like you:familiar participate in sports, like you:familiar like to participate in sports with friends. What else do you:familiar do? What other kinds of activities do you:familiar have?
(q4) Well, Bettina is very pretty. How long have you:familiar been together? How did you:familiar meet? Do you:familiar love her? Does she come to.

The second speaker, rated at the Intermediate-Mid proficiency level, produces fewer address contexts and only utilizes two of the eight possible morphosyntactic categories (nominative singular and genitive singular):

T1(IM):
(q1) *Wer ist dieser Kind in mit die Ball? Wo sind sie?*
(q2) *Magst du deine, deine Schule? Ist das ein Uni oder ein highschool?*
      Wer, wo ist das Schule?
(q3) *Helmut, was machst du in deiner Freizeit? Spielst du gern football?*
      Hast du viel Freunden?
(q4) *Wie alt is Bettina? Wo wohnen sie? Gehen sie in deine Schule?*

T1(IM):
(q1) Who is this child with the ball? Where are they?
(q2) Do you:familiar like your:familiar school? Is it a university or high
      school? Who, where is the school?
(q3) Helmut, what do you:familiar do in your free time? Do you:familiar
      like to play soccer? Do you:familiar have many friends?
(q4) How old is Bettina? Where does she live? Does she go to your:familiar
      school?

In summary, based on the central tendencies of group address behavior observed on the first three sample tasks, it seems that, on average, the higher an examinee's global proficiency rating, the greater the range of morphosyntactic contexts in which the examinee produces pronominal address forms, the higher the frequency of pronominal address forms, and the more sociopragmatically accurate the selection of address register. Particularly marked differences in all three aspects (frequency, sociopragmatic accuracy, and morphosyntactic range) were noted between examinees rated at the Intermediate-Mid proficiency level and lower, and those rated at the Intermediate-High proficiency level and higher. Finally, it should be underscored that variability in frequency, accuracy, and range was noted for all proficiency levels, indicating that the pronominal address behavior of any individual examinee may have differed substantially from the central tendency of examinees with the same global proficiency rating.

Group-level analyses for Tasks 1–6

Table 6 shows descriptive statistics for the frequency and sociopragmatic accuracy of pronominal address behavior for the twenty-seven examinees who completed the long form of the GST (and who therefore completed all of the sample Tasks 1 through 6). It should be recalled that these examinees were all rated at the ACTFL Intermediate-High level or above. As shown in Table 6, examinees at the three proficiency level groupings produced very similar mean frequencies of address pronouns per task, and individual variability in amount of pronominal address behavior was consistent across the three

TABLE 6. FREQUENCY AND ACCURACY OF PRONOUNS OF ADDRESS ON TASKS 1–3

ACTFL rating	Frequency (per task)		Accuracy	
	Mean	SD	Mean	SD
Advanced-High/Superior (n = 6)	5.72	1.21	0.86	0.23
Advanced (n = 11)	5.76	1.03	0.82	0.29
Intermediate-High (n = 10)	5.35	1.32	0.62	0.30

groups. As was noted among the first three sample tasks, average levels of sociopragmatic accuracy in address register selection (i.e., sociopragmatically correct address pronouns per total address pronouns) displayed a continual decrease from the higher through lower proficiency levels for these six tasks. The mean accuracy level for examinees rated at the Intermediate-High proficiency level was much lower (20 percentage points) than that for examinees rated at Advanced or above, although none of the groups showed perfect levels of sociopragmatic accuracy. Standard deviations indicate substantial individual variability within all proficiency level groups.

In order to examine potential differences among those tasks calling for formal versus familiar address, descriptive statistics were calculated for group behavior on these two subsets of tasks for the twenty-seven examinees completing the long form of the GST. Table 7 shows the central tendency and dispersion of scores for these subsets of tasks by proficiency level grouping. Table 7 shows once again that, even among higher proficiency examinees, frequency of pronominal address behavior was substantially different between *du* tasks and *Sie* tasks, with examinees across all proficiency groupings producing twice as many pronominal address forms on the *du* tasks. The two *Sie* tasks called for the examinee to give directions to an unknown person and to make an impositional request from a trip organizer. As noted earlier, Task 2 primarily involved the use of imperative structures, and the task elicited relatively short responses. The second task, Task 5, elicited much longer responses from examinees, yet with consistently fewer examples of direct address (see Table 3). A number of examinees avoided direct address altogether or focused primarily on explanations as opposed to the direct request required by Task 5. For example, the following examinee, rated at the Advanced-High proficiency level, produced a lengthy response without making a request and without producing any address forms:

T5(AH): *Wirklich? Ich meine, ja, daß ich kann schon verstehen, wenn ich das freiwillig machen würde, aber ich muß. Das, das mit der, der Hochzeit, mit der Hochzeit habe ich wirklich total vergessen. Ich bin nicht schuld daran. Es ist keine, es ist keine Frage, es ist gar nichts um Schuld. Aber daß, daß ich das Geld bezahlen muß und dann dafür nichts bekommen. Ich gehe*

TABLE 7. FREQUENCY AND ACCURACY OF *DU* (YOU:FAMILIAR) VERSUS *SIE* (YOU:FORMAL) ON TASKS 1–6

	du				*Sie*			
	Frequency (per task)		*Accuracy*		*Frequency (per task)*		*Accuracy*	
ACTFL rating	*Mean*	*SD*	*Mean*	*SD*	*Mean*	*SD*	*Mean*	*SD*
Advanced-High/ Superior (*n* = 6)	7.00	1.72	0.85	0.26	3.17	1.66	1.00	0.00
Advanced (*n* = 11)	6.91	1.52	0.81	0.30	3.45	1.77	0.87	0.30
Intermediate-High (*n* = 10)	6.53	1.68	0.60	0.31	3.00	1.55	0.92	0.21

nicht hin, ich muß also für die Reise, ich. Warum soll ich für eine Reise bezahlen, wenn ich nicht mehr hingehe, und auch für das Essen, und für alles für den Ausflug? Es, es ist nicht, daß ich einfach nicht will. Es ist, daß ich nicht kann. Also, ich finde das wirklich unfair, wenn ich das Geld nicht zurück komme.

T5(AH): Really? I mean, yes, I can understand it, if I were to do that by choice, but I have to. I totally forgot that, that with the wedding, with the wedding. It's not my fault. It's not, it's not a question of, it doesn't have anything to do with fault. But that, that I should pay money and not receive anything in return. I'm not going, I have to for the trip, I. Why should I pay for the trip, if I'm not going along, and also for the dinner, and for everything for the trip? It's, it's not that I don't want to. It is that I can't. So, I think it is really unfair, if I don't get the money back.

On average, sociopragmatic accuracy levels were noted to be higher for the *Sie* (you:formal) tasks than for the *du* (you:familiar) tasks. Thus, examinees at all of the upper proficiency levels tended to select the appropriate forms for the two tasks requiring formal pronominal address, whereas continual decreases in accuracy were noted for the *du* tasks. Once again, examinees rated at the Intermediate-High level were noted to show only slightly better than chance levels of accuracy when selecting the pronominal address register for those tasks requiring familiar forms. Variability in address accuracy was also noted to be uniformly high for all proficiency level groupings on the *du* tasks, indicating substantial differences among individual examinees within each group. The following examples show performances by the same examinee, rated at the Intermediate-High proficiency level, on two tasks, the first a *Sie* task and the second a *du* task. The difference in sociopragmatic accuracy of pronominal address forms is readily apparent between the two tasks:

T2(IH): *Ja, wenn Sie aus der Tür von Post kommen, gehen Sie am links und danach gerade aus in der Mozartstraße, bis zu der Schloßallee. In der Schloßallee, gehen Sie am links bis zu der Linzerstraße, und Sie sehen einen*

Hotel an der Ecke. Gehen Sie am recht in der Linzerstraße, und das Museum ist am links.

T2(IH): Sure, if you:formal come out the door from the post office, you:formal go left and then straight on Mozart Street, until Schlossallee. On Schlossallee, you:formal go left to Linzer Street, and you:formal see a hotel on the corner. You:formal go right on Linzer Street, and the museum is on the left.

T3(IH): *Zuerst mußt du zu ein Telefonbuch suchen. Sie müssen ein Zahnarzt finden. Wenn Sie die Nummer finden, Sie müssen die Zahnarzt anrufen. Du mußt ihn erzählen, was ist los, was tut, weh tut, wo tut weh, und was, was ist los. Dann er, er, er werde fragen, um wann Sie gehen kann. Und du mußt ihm erzählen, wann du gehen kann um ihn zu sehen.*

T3(IH): First, you:familiar have to look in the telephone book. You:formal have to find a dentist. If you:formal find the number, you:formal have to call the dentist. You:familiar have to explain to him what is wrong, what hurts, where it hurts, and what, what is wrong. The he, he will ask, at when you:formal can go. And you:familiar have to tell him when you:familiar can go to see him.

In order to investigate differences among the upper three proficiency level groupings in terms of the range of morphosyntactic address forms produced, the percentages of examinees at each level producing contexts for each of the eight possible pronominal types were calculated. Figure 3 shows frequency percentages for each pronominal type by each of the three proficiency level groupings. It can be noted that most examinees at all three levels produced contexts for nominative singular and genitive singular (possessive) forms, and that very few examinees at all three levels produced contexts for accusative plural, dative plural, or genitive plural. This phenomenon may be in part attributable to task constraints, as all of the tasks involve the examinee in conversation with a single interlocutor. Nevertheless, it is interesting to note that substantially higher numbers of examinees (between 60% and 80%) produced contexts for nominative plural address forms.

Somewhat unexpected trends can be noted in Figure 3 for examinees rated at the Advanced proficiency level versus the other two proficiency groupings. More examinees in the Advanced level produced contexts for both nominative plural and accusative singular forms than in either the higher or the lower proficiency levels. Only dative singular showed consistent decreases in percentages of examinees producing contexts, from Superior through Intermediate-High levels.

Figure 4 shows the sociopragmatic accuracy levels for each of the eight pronominal types by proficiency level grouping. Generally predictable patterns can be observed for all pronominal types, with the exception of nominative plural forms, which show lower accuracy levels for the highest proficiency level grouping than for the other two groups.

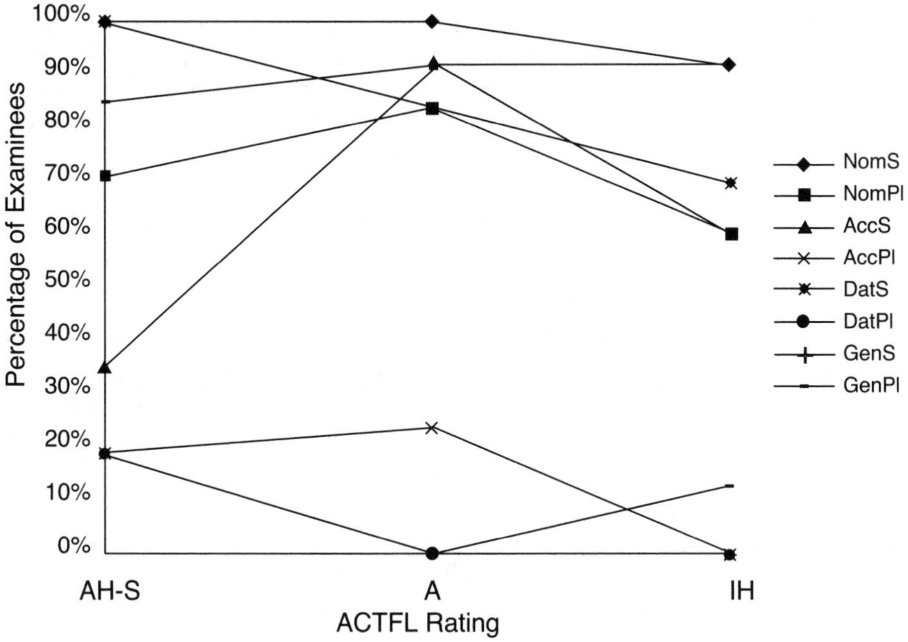

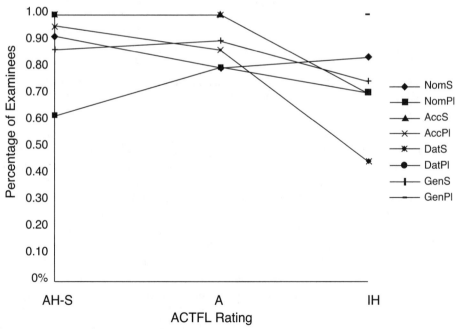

Figure 3 Range of pronoun types attempted on Tasks 1–6.

Figure 4 Accuracy of pronoun types on Tasks 1–6.

Otherwise, sociopragmatic accuracy levels are substantially lower for the Intermediate-High level examinees for all morphosyntactic categories (except for the lone production by one Intermediate-High examinee of the genitive plural form *euer*). Only the dative singular forms seem to show a consistent decrease in accuracy across the three proficiency level groupings.

The following two examples both show brief performances by two examinees on Task 4, which asked the examinee to apologize for losing a host family member's umbrella. In the first example, an examinee rated at the Intermediate-High level produces only a single category of pronominal forms, and he supplies the sociopragmatically incorrect register in doing so (as well as grammatically incorrect forms). In the second example, the Superior-level examinee produces three morphosyntactic categories (featuring one vocative pronoun/nominal form), and he correctly supplies the appropriate sociopragmatic register.

T4(IH): *Ja, es hat viel geregnet. Aber es tut mir sehr leid. Ich habe, ich habe es verloren, und, und ich kann Sie eine andere kaufen. Es, es hat so viel geregnet, und plötzlich eine grosse Winde ist gekommen, und es ist, es ist weggeflogen. Und, aber, Verzeihung. Ich, ich werde Sie eine andere kaufen.*

T4(IH): Yes, it rained a lot. But I'm really sorry. I, I lost it, and, and, I can buy you:formal another one. It, it rained so much, and suddenly there was a big wind, and it, it flew away. And, but, pardon. I, I'll buy you:formal another one.

T4(S): *Ach du lieber Himmel Erika, ich habe den Regenschirm verloren. Es tut mir schrecklich leid. Aber sicher werde ich ihn für dich wieder ersetzen, in ich werde dir einen neuen kaufen. Es tut mir schrecklich leid.*

T4(S): Oh you:familiar, heavens Erika, I lost the umbrella. I'm really terribly sorry. But I will certainly replace it for you:familiar, in I will buy you:familiar a new one. I'm really terribly sorry.

In general, then, examinees rated at the upper ACTFL proficiency levels exhibited similar overall frequencies of address behavior and a consistent decrease in average sociopragmatic accuracy of pronominal address, from the higher to the lower proficiency levels. *Sie* (you:formal) tasks elicited fewer tokens of address but were generally accompanied by appropriate address forms. *Du* (you:familiar) tasks elicited more address tokens and proved more problematic in terms of sociopragmatic accuracy, especially for examinees rated at the Intermediate-High proficiency level. Examinees rated at the Advanced proficiency level and above produced pronominal address forms across more morphosyntactic categories than examinees rated at the Intermediate-High levels, and they generally did so with greater sociopragmatic accuracy.

Discussion

The current study examined patterns in address behavior on the GST in order to investigate the extent to which interpretations about this particular sociolinguistic subsystem may be associated with test performance. From a total of fifteen tasks on the GST, six were identified which seemed to consistently elicit address behavior via simulated interactions. These tasks were noted to share similar contextual constraints which likely encouraged the use of direct address, whereas contexts for the other tasks on the GST did not seem as conducive for eliciting address behavior. It is possible that characteristics of the speech acts and other task objectives associated with these six tasks also contributed to the elicitation of address behavior. The address registers associated with the six tasks were posited to be sufficiently established within task instructions, simulated interlocutor prompts, and other test instructions and item realia. Further corroboration for the sociopragmatically appropriate register for each task was sought from a group of ten German NS informants, who agreed completely with each other and with the posited registers.

Although choice of appropriate address register seemed straightforward for all tasks, variability was noted both among examinees and across tasks in terms of the frequency with which contexts for direct address were produced and the sociopragmatic accuracy with which pronominal forms were supplied. In general, in tasks from both the short and the long forms of the GST, examinees produced higher frequencies of address forms for those tasks requiring a familiar versus a formal address register. However, when examinees produced address forms on tasks requiring a formal register, they consistently did so with high degrees of sociopragmatic accuracy. It was also noted that such accuracy may have been facilitated by the linguistic functions and contexts associated with the tasks. Thus, on Task 2, the majority of address pronouns were found to be nominative singular forms within imperative verbal constructions, a pattern typically encountered quite early by learners of L2 German. Both *Sie* (you:formal) tasks examined in the current study were also noted to elicit apparent avoidance of direct address from some examinees, even in contexts where the pronoun is grammatically required. A final possible explanation for apparent high levels of sociopragmatic accuracy for selected tasks was observable in several examinees who utilized formal address forms as the default register for most or all tasks on the GST. Even at the upper proficiency levels, several examinees utilized only *Sie* forms for addressing all interlocutors. Such address behavior on the part of upper-level examinees stands in contrast to the assumption that examinees rated at the ACTFL Advanced level or above should show command over one register and emergence of control over the other.

Variability in control over appropriate address registers was primarily evident on the four GST tasks requiring familiar address. Overall, the higher the global proficiency rating, the more frequent the use of address forms, the more consistent the selection of accurate address register, and the broader the range of morphosyntactic forms via which address behavior was manifested. This pattern was consistently observed on the short form of the GST, between those examinees rated at the Intermediate-Mid proficiency level and below and those examinees rated at the Intermediate-High proficiency level and above. Within each of these general groupings, less variability was noted between proficiency levels, although a decrease in sociopragmatic accuracy and pragmalinguistic range of address forms seemed to be associated with decreasing levels of proficiency. Consistent patterns were also observed on the long form of the GST, when comparisons were drawn between the group of examinees rated at the Intermediate-High level and examinees rated at the Advanced level and above, especially in terms of sociopragmatic accuracy and range of address forms.

Although such patterns in group behavior apparently associate proficiency level with an examinee's level of ability to engage in sociopragmatically accurate address behavior, these group data should be interpreted with caution. By far the greatest frequencies of address forms produced on the GST were of two pronominal types: nominative singular and genitive singular (possessives). Other categories were produced far less frequently, and sociopragmatic accuracy levels for these categories may therefore be unstable. In general, GST tasks did not seem to consistently elicit a wide morphosyntactic range of address forms across address registers and contextual variables; that is, in order to make accurate interpretations about examinee control over both the sociopragmatic and the pragmalinguistic aspects of address behavior, a careful balance in task design would be necessary, such that equal representation of a variety of contextual and linguistic variables would elicit examinee performances with a range of address forms. Only careful control of such variables would enable interpretations about examinee abilities within this subsystem of sociolinguistic competence. It may also be the case that linguistic factors played a larger role in determining the sociopragmatic accuracy of address forms than did other contextual variables. Thus, it was noted that particular functions or grammatical contexts within certain tasks seemed to cause a breakdown in selection of appropriate address forms. For example, several examinees selected generally correct address registers, but seemed to lack control over their selections when the linguistic context changed. Careful consideration of associated linguistic factors would also therefore need to be introduced into GST tasks before consistent interpretations about examinees' control over address registers would be warranted. Although general patterns were observed for frequency, sociopragmatic accuracy, and pragmalinguistic range of address behavior for different proficiency level groupings, interpretations about an individual examinee's abilities with this subsystem may not necessarily be consistently associated with a given ACTFL Guidelines proficiency rating; that is, it was also observed in the current study that high levels of individual variability were apparent across proficiency levels, and especially in terms of sociopragmatic accuracy of address forms.

In light of such individual variation from group tendencies, then, it may not be the case that interpretations about an individual examinee's abilities with address behavior can be consistently associated with global ratings according to the ACTFL Proficiency Guidelines. Furthermore, although the GST elicits address behavior on a number of tasks, these tasks may not be designed with enough control over a range of linguistic and contextual variables to enable accurate interpretations to be made. Interestingly, the most convincing evidence for an examinee's control over this particular subsystem of sociolinguistic competence can be found in what might otherwise be considered anomalous performances; that is, truly warranted conclusions about whether or not an examinee has knowledge of the sociopragmatic norms affecting address register selection may be drawn with certainty only from those circumstances where examinees self-correct their original selections, thereby revealing explicit knowledge as well as performance ability.

Conclusion

This study has attempted to shed light on the relationship between a simulated oral proficiency interview, the German Speaking Test, and one aspect of sociolinguistic competence, that of address behavior. A number of tasks on the GST were observed to elicit address behavior from examinees at varying proficiency levels, and these tasks were found to present sufficient contextual information to determine the sociopragmatic norms for address register selections. Based on average group-level findings in the current study, it was observed that GST examinees do tend to increase in their abilities to produce sociopragmatically accurate pronominal address forms across increasing pragmalinguistic contexts as their global ACTFL proficiency levels increase. However, based on the variability of examinee performances observed at any given ACTFL level, it was also found that this is by no means a categorical or implicational relationship. Although the probability is apparently greater that examinees rated at higher proficiency levels will engage in address behavior that increasingly approximates NS norms, interpretations about an individual examinee's abilities with this particular sociolinguistic subsystem may not be consistently associated with the examinee's global ACTFL level rating.

These findings may or may not prove problematic for the use of GST scores within foreign language education contexts. As with any other educational assessment, the validity of the GST depends in large part on the ways in which test scores are interpreted and on the decisions and other actions which are in turn based on these interpretations (see Messick, 1989; Shepard, 1993; Norris, 2000). Given the fact that results on the GST are reported to examinees and other score users in the form of a single global ACTFL level rating, and the finding that such a rating may not necessarily reflect particular language competencies, interpretations about an examinee's ability to engage in sociolinguistically appropriate communication should probably be limited. Indeed, it was observed in the current study that examinees who performed in otherwise very proficient ways (and were rated accordingly) did not necessarily exhibit knowledge of or control over norms of address behavior.

It is possible that more individualized interpretations about particular sociolinguistic, as well as other, competencies could be based on GST performances. As I have observed elsewhere (Norris, 1997b), the GST could provide a wealth of information useful for informing pedagogy or for making a range of diagnostic and related decisions about individual examinees. In order to do so, current rating and score-reporting practices would need to be revised such that, in addition to reporting global ACTFL proficiency ratings, *(a)* test performances were scored analytically, according to a range of contributing competencies; *(b)* raters provided rationales for these analytic scores; and *(c)* analytic scores and rater rationales were reported to test score users in an explicit and thorough manner. Such changes would enable teachers and other score users to identify particular strengths as well as problem areas in the developing German abilities of GST examinees, and, for example, could inform focused instruction on the relationship between available German pragmalinguistic forms and associated sociopragmatic variables (see, e.g., Lyster, 1994). Such changes would only serve to enhance our capabilities to accurately assess and interpret "what learners can and cannot do" (ACTFL, 1986, p. 1) with the German language.

13 Indicators for pragmatic instruction

Some quantitative tools

Thom Hudson

Introduction

With ever-increasing attention to the study of the development and use of pragmatics in a second language, there has arisen a concomitant interest in developing appropriate and valid means for the assessment of pragmatic competence. Although there are established methods for assessing other factors of language production, similar instruments have not yet been developed for the assessment of pragmatics. This chapter will discuss three methods of assessing pragmatic production by Japanese learners of English as a second language. Although the full study involved developing a number of different instruments for assessing pragmatics, only three instruments will be examined here: the written discourse completion test, language lab discourse completion test tape recordings, and role-play of scenarios. These were the instruments that required language production by the examinees, and it was felt that these would provide the most information regarding pedagogical applications of language samples obtained through pragmatic assessment.[1]

A brief review of the project

The initial stage of this project (Hudson, Detmer, & Brown, 1992) involved identifying the nature of the instruments to be used and then determining the variables to be examined. A primary purpose of the study was to examine whether the variables could be used to explain variation in pragmatic performance. The processes of determining the variables were iterative in nature, involving literature reviews and pilot testing of the instruments on small samples of informants. In order to utilize the speech acts most generally researched to date, the speech acts of requests, refusals, and apologies were selected as the speech acts to be investigated. These speech acts have been seen in the literature as

1 The original study also included two forms of self-assessment and a multiple-choice DCT.

appropriate for contrasting speech-act realization across a number of languages (see Hudson, Detmer, & Brown, 1992 for a discussion).

The process of determining which variables to include in the tests resulted in the selection of power (P), social distance (D), and degree of imposition (R) as the sociopragmatic variables of interest. These variables were selected because, within the research on pragmatics, they are identified as the three independent and culturally sensitive variables that subsume all other variables and play a principled role in speech-act behavior (Brown & Levinson, 1987; also see Fraser, 1990). It was thus assumed that these would also be important areas in a pedagogical context such as the classroom. The definitions and descriptions of the variables used here in the development of the assessment instruments are as follows (Hudson, Detmer, & Brown, 1995):

Relative power (P): This involves the power of the speaker with respect to the hearer. In effect, it is the degree to which the speaker can impose his or her will on the hearer because of a higher rank within an organization, professional status, or as the result of the hearer's need to have a particular duty or job performed. This, then, relates to the relative rank, title, or social position between the two interactants.

Social distance (D): This represents the distance between the speaker and the hearer and is, in effect, the degree of familiarity and solidarity they share as represented through in-group or out-group membership. This is reflective of the degree to which the two interactants identify with each other or share some affiliation and solidarity.

Absolute ranking of imposition (R): This is the potential imposition of carrying out the speech act, in terms of the expenditure of goods and/or services by the hearer, or the obligation of the speaker to perform the act. This will vary depending on whether the speech act is a request, a refusal, or an apology, and has to do with the extent to which the expenditure of goods, services, or energy is involved in carrying out a request or a refusal, or how severe the offense was that requires an apology.

The pragmalinguistic components of correctness of linguistic expressions, amount of information, formality, directness, and politeness were the categories adopted for evaluating the speakers' actual responses. The first two of these (correctness of linguistic expressions and amount of information) represent variables more related to language correctness, whereas the remaining three (formality, directness, and politeness) represent more social aspects of language, although they, too, are certainly expressed through linguistic conventions. In short, these five variables, along with whether the speaker provides the correct speech act, represent the categories of the dependent variable being used to evaluate the language production. They thus provide the basis for a scale measuring pragmatic competence.

The sociopragmatic and pragmalinguistic variables were incorporated into the assessment strategies employed in the present study. The rationale

TABLE 1. VARIABLE DISTRIBUTION ACROSS ITEMS

Speech Act								
Request	1	2	3	4	5	6	7	8
Refusal	9	10	11	12	13	14	15	16
Apology	17	18	19	20	21	22	23	24
Variables								
Power	+	+	+	+	-	-	-	-
Distance	+	+	-	-	+	+	-	-
Imposition	+	-	+	-	+	-	+	-

for developing assessment instruments of different types for application across different social variables and speech acts evolved from an interest in determining the potential differential effectiveness and utility of the instruments. For example, certain speech acts may be effectively assessed better by one method than by another. Requests may be effectively assessed through a discourse completion test, whereas apologies may not. Further, apologies that involve such power relationships as a worker apologizing to an employer may be more effectively evaluated through role-play than when the power relationships are different. In addition, the different types of instruments were developed in recognition of the fact that different types of research into crosscultural pragmatics will require different levels of detail. An examination of the formulaic structure of apologies may be adequately served by an open-ended indirect discourse completion test (DCT). On the other hand, research into the effects of interpersonal interaction on apologies may be better served by direct observation in a role-play situation. Finally, classroom teachers may use a DCT in order to point out varying social distances between interlocutors and then have the students carry out a role-play to emulate a real-world situation. Likewise, a teacher may have some students working on a language laboratory DCT while involving a smaller number of students in a role-play activity.

A matrix was developed to generate items for the assessment forms such that each speech act was represented in the eight possible configurations of power, social distance, and degree of imposition (all binary). This distribution is represented in Table 1. Thus, for example, the first item generated would be a request that was plus power with the speaker being of a higher rank, plus social distance in which the speaker and hearer do not know or identify with each other, and plus degree of imposition on the part of the hearer to carry out the request. Likewise, the last item would be an apology in which the speaker was of a lower rank, with little social distance between the interlocutors, in which the apology was rather minor in its imposition.

The specific research questions for the study were the following:

1. To what extent do the different test methods affect performance ratings?
2. To what extent would the different speech acts differ in terms of the mean score?
3. What are the correlations between the DCT, language lab, and role-play?
4. To what extent would the different aspects of speech act, expressions, amount, formality, directness, or politeness be rated differently?
5. What is the effect for power, distance, and degree of imposition on scores across the different test types?

Development of instruments

The development of the final version of the three instruments discussed here involved several stages. These stages included the writing, piloting, and revising of item specifications, the writing of DCT items, and then development of three alternate forms of the DCT. After the variable distributions in Table 1 were established, item specifications were developed. These item specifications generally follow the guidelines provided by Popham (1978), and included a general description, sample item, prompt attributes, and response attributes. Following this, test items were generated based on the specifications, and were piloted in several stages. In order to restrict the range of situations and to reduce variability resulting from factors other than the ones under study here, it became apparent that several constraints needed to be put on the generation of situations and items. These constraints came out of the pilot-testing project described in Hudson, Detmer, and Brown (1995). The factors identified in the constraints potentially introduced error into the scenarios. These are:

1. Neither interlocutor has gender specified in the task description.
2. The situation must be face to face. No situation could be over the telephone or written.
3. For requests, the explicit statement beginning with either "You want" or "You need" must be used in the prompt.
4. The situation is context-internal to the roles. For example, if the roles of the interlocutors are "project leader" to "project worker," the context of the speech event is at work and has to do with work-related activities.
5. No explicit money is to be involved in the contexts.
6. No contexts for apologies are the result of physical contact, injury, or violating social norms.

7. No socially stigmatized roles should be included (e.g., rich patron, famous star).
8. Professionally defined or formulaic interactional patterns (e.g., doctor-patient, lawyer-client) were avoided.
9. No relationships with family, close friends, enemies, or intimates were used.
10. Situations were familiar to the examinees.

As noted, these constraints were placed on the generation of situations in order to reduce the variability that their inclusion might have caused. However, in the classroom context, a teacher might choose to intentionally include these elements. For example, the teacher might have doctor–patient roles as the teaching point precisely because of a need to present formulaic interactional patterns. Further, the teacher might want to contrast the pragmatics appropriate between close friends and those used between people of different statuses.

After the three forms of the instruments were developed, they were given to small numbers of native speakers (NSs) and to nonnative speakers (NNSs). An in-depth study of the differences between the two groups was done to look at different strategies used by the groups (Hudson, Detmer, & Brown, 1995). Although the distribution of strategies differed somewhat between NSs and NNSs, the two groups fundamentally used the same strategies. The primary exception to this was that in low imposition (-R) apologies the NNSs tended to use more expressions of regret and concern than did the NS informants. An example of a DCT scene is as follows:

You are the manager in an office that is now hiring new employees. Last week an applicant came into the office and scheduled an interview for tomorrow. Now, that same person is in the office asking to reschedule the interview because of a family funeral. You cannot reschedule because you are about to leave the country for 2 weeks; your schedule is completely full.

You: _____

_____

The NSs were also asked to categorize each scenario according to its speech act, the power relationships, the distance relationship, and the degree of imposition. The changes in the items as a result of the piloting of the instruments are presented in detail in Hudson, Detmer, and Brown (1995). In brief, however, the pilot testing pointed out several problematic areas. First, it became apparent that a scenario might actually require more than one speech act. For example, a request scenario might require an initial apology as the rationale for the actual request. Such scenarios were either adapted or eliminated from the test. A second problem area was that the elicitation of the wrong speech act occurred. For example, for one apology item, the situation itself required so much processing that many of the participants' responses did not include an apology. The participants appeared to be reacting to parts of the described situation other than the apology elicitation. A further apology item appeared to be acting as a request item. A third problem area appeared when participants opted out of responding to the speech act. Opting out generally occurred with refusal items that involved an extremely low degree of imposition and participants felt no need to actually apologize. A final problematic area resulted from participants' misinterpretations of the P, D, and R relationships in certain items. For example, in some situations requiring the examinee to interact with office personnel, it was not clear to the participants that the office staff was actually in the position of power. The problematic items were rewritten to repair the difficulties in these items.

The development of the listening lab instrument involved the direct transfer of situations from written open-ended DCTs. Whereas in the paper and pencil DCT versions participants read the situations and wrote their responses on the paper, in the listening lab version participants read silently along with a provided oral reading of the situations and then responded to the situations orally. Participant responses were audiotaped.

The seventy-two DCT situations, twenty-four each on Forms A, B, and C, were rewritten into a role-play format. Through this process, a number of considerations based mainly on concerns to keep the scenarios focused on language in context rather than general interaction became apparent. First, the individual situations should not place too much of a burden on the test taker in terms of conceptualization and actualization of the scenario. Second, although the test taker is assuming a role, the test is not an acting test. Thus, the scenarios should keep the action involved in the role-play to a minimum and not include highly dramatic elements. Third, it is necessary to consider how much of the role-play involves action, such as handing someone something, and how much involves actual language use. Finally, the use of props, such as paper, pencils, or other small items involved in the situation, is helpful to the test taker if not used in excess. These issues, in addition to those raised in the literature reviews, were taken into consideration when transforming the original DCT situations into role-play scenarios.

Although the situations from the DCT forms were converted into the role-play format, an interview containing twenty-four separate role-play situations, as in the DCT, would clearly take far too long and place too much of a burden on the test taker. Thus, eight representative scenes were written, each involving a request, a refusal, and an apology. By balancing the level of power and the degree of distance and imposition across the eight scenes, all twenty-four cells were covered in the role-plays. In developing these eight scenes, care was taken to follow the considerations discussed in the literature review. For example, in order to limit the degree of burden in terms of conceptualization and actualization on the part of the test taker, none of the scenes contained more than two speech acts with a high degree of imposition. The initial scenes were piloted with five NSs. Revisions were made after each NS piloting, so that some items went through a number of revisions, and others remained unchanged. The examinee was provided a card with the situation written on it. An example of one of the scenes used is the following:

You go to apply for a new job in a small company at 11:30. You see
and greet the personnel manager but accidentally startle him and he drops
some papers on the floor. You need to schedule an interview in the morning
because you currently work in the afternoon. After arranging the morning
interview, the personnel manager asks you to go on a tour of the company
now. But you have to get back to work by 1 today.

Method

Participants

The participants in the study were twenty-five Japanese students studying in intensive English language programs in Honolulu. There were seven males and eighteen females ranging in age from 21 to 42 years, with a mean age of 27.2. The participants were all pre-university-level students studying in intensive English-language programs. In the University of Hawai'i context this would mean that all had a TOEFL below 500. Further, no extremely low-language-ability participants were selected. This decision was made based on an assumption that pragmatics are less important at low-language-ability levels. As will be seen later, this homogeneity of language ability among the participants proved problematic.

Materials and procedures

Each of the participants took all three tests. The order of administration of the three instruments reported here was language lab DCT, open-ended DCT, and the role-play. It was felt that this order would lead to the lowest effect of one test on the subsequent test. There would inevitably be some order effect. However, it was felt that a face-to-face role-play would have the largest effect on subsequent measures, particularly any self-assessment measures. Further, it was felt that the open-ended DCT could provide a practice effect for the language lab DCT and it was therefore placed after the language lab DCT. The students took the open-ended DCT home to complete, and were instructed not to spend too much time on it and not to consult with others. The listening lab DCT responses were tape-recorded. The role-play was a one-on-one interaction which was videotaped. All administrations took place within 2 weeks of each other. Examples of the three instruments are presented in Appendixes A, B, and C.

The evaluation of the open-ended written DCT and the language lab DCT involved the ratings of the examinee responses by three trained raters on six aspects of pragmatic competence using a rating scale ranging from 1 (very unsatisfactory) to 5 (completely appropriate). The intermediate points, 2–4, did not include verbal labels. The ratings were on the following aspects of pragmatic competence:

1. Ability to use the correct speech act
2. Typicality of expressions
3. Amount of speech and information given
4. Level of formality
5. Directness
6. Politeness

A training manual was written for the raters. This manual defined and explained the six aspects of pragmatic competence included in the evaluation form. It provided criteria for rating and tips on troubleshooting, and concluded with examples and a sample rating sheet. The three raters were graduate students in a master's program in ESL. The role-play videotapes were rated by three raters on a scale from 1 (very unsatisfactory) to 5 (completely appropriate). These role-play performances were not rated on the six aspects of pragmatic competence used with the DCTs. Rather, the raters holistically rated the three speech acts in each of the eight scenarios. The results are presented in Table 2. The interrater reliability across the three instruments was modest. The reliability for the role-play ratings was .75, .86 for the DCT ratings, and .78 for the language lab ratings across the three raters, using Fischer's z-transformation on the interrater correlations. This is moderately acceptable given that there were only twenty-five examinees. Further, the reliability may be a reflection of the low variability among the examinees.

Results

There was little variation across the participants, and the data were generally negatively skewed. This relative lack of variance is problematic throughout the present study, and is the result of the general homogeneity of the participants. The participants appear to be at a rather

TABLE 2. MEAN SCORES ON DIFFERENT TEST TYPES BY TOTAL AND SPEECH ACT

	Mean	*SD*
DCT total	4.15	0.43
DCT requests	4.09	0.49
DCT refusals	4.17	0.53
DCT apologies	4.19	0.45
Role-play total	4.20	0.30
Role-play requests	4.26	0.33
Role-play refusals	3.63	0.35
Role-play apologies	4.11	0.40
Language lab total	3.86	0.40
Language lab requests	3.70	0.47
Language lab refusals	3.91	0.61
Language lab apologies	3.96	0.43

high ability level, and may have thus already accommodated to many of the variables included here. In general, the language lab DCT appears to be slightly more difficult than either the role-play or the DCT. It is interesting to note that performance on the role-play was rated the highest of the three language samples and also had the smallest standard deviation. A repeated-measures analysis of variance (ANOVA) indicates a significant effect for test type ($F(2,21) = 13.83$, $p < .05$). Tukey's (HSD) post hoc test comparing means indicates that there is a significant difference between the open-ended DCT and the language lab DCT, as well as between language lab and role-play. Two potential explanations for this relationship between ratings on the language lab performance and the role-play result. First, the raters may have been more lenient in their ratings when they could both see and hear the examinee than when simply listening to recorded tapes. Second, the participants may have more successfully accommodated to the face-to-face interaction than they did with the language lab noninteractional context. The difference between the written DCT and the language lab DCT may be the result of there having been more planning time in the written DCT than in the language lab version.

In terms of the different speech acts, there is also little variation. However, a repeated-measures ANOVA shows a significant effect ($F(2,21) = 5.29$, $p < .05$). Tukey's HSD shows that there is a significant effect between refusals and apologies, but that none of the other contrasts are significant. Apologies are generally rated slightly higher than the other speech acts. This may be in part because apologies are frequently formulaic and thus require less online processing than either requests or refusals. In the role-play context, refusals received the lowest mean rating. Given that the role-play is the most integrated of the three

TABLE 3. CORRELATION FOR THE DIFFERENT METHODS

	DCT	LL	Role-play
DCT	1.000		
LL	.749	1.000	
Role-play	.307	.447	1.000

Note: LL = language lab.

TABLE 4. CORRELATION FOR SPEECH ACTS IN EACH TESTING METHOD

	Requests	Refusals	Apologies
DCT			
Requests	1.000		
Refusals	.690	1.000	
Apologies	.799	.631	1.000
Language lab			
Requests	1.000		
Refusals	.832	1.000	
Apologies	.461	.487	1.000
Role-play			
Requests	1.000		
Refusals	.528	1.000	
Apologies	.598	.483	1.000

assessment formats, this finding may indicate that more indirect measures of pragmatic ability, such as the DCTs, are less effective in assessing this particular speech act.[2] Refusals may be more difficult to negotiate than either requests or apologies.

The correlations between the assessment procedures indicate a relatively high correlation between the written DCT and the language lab DCT, as indicated in Table 3. This may indicate that there is a method effect with the DCT format in general. There was a higher correlation, although still small, between the role-play and the language lab. This appears to indicate that the two tests tap some overlap in the speaking component.

Table 4 shows the correlations between the different speech acts in each of the different testing methods. No overall pattern of relationships between the speech acts emerges across the three testing methods.

2 "Most integrated" here means that the role-plays involved continual interactions with an interlocutor with a relatively common thread across the different speech acts.

TABLE 5. CORRELATIONS AMONG THE SPEECH ACTS BY TEST METHOD

	1	2	3	4	5	6	7	8	9
1. DCT-request	1.000								
2. DCT-refusal	.692	1.000							
3. DCT-apology	.800	.631	1.000						
4. LL-request	.630	.648	.439	1.000					
5. LL-refusal	.751	.701	.648	.832	1.000				
6. LL-apology	.381	.507	.368	.461	.487	1.000			
7. RP-request	.329	.177	.120	.293	.251	.241	1.000		
8. RP-refusal	.572	.184	.000	.157	.280	.108	.528	1.000	
9. RP-apology	.413	.453	.283	.467	.510	.506	.598	.483	1.000

Note: LL = language lab; RP = role-play.

In the written DCT, the three speech acts appear to correlate with one another fairly highly. However, in the language lab DCT, only requests and refusals have a high relationship, and in the role-play all three speech acts have a weak relationship to one another. These findings, particularly in the role-play setting, appear to be a function of the small amount of variance in the test results. This said, the fact that reduced variance affects correlations does not rule out instrument effects or how scenarios might have been perceived differently across the different instruments.

Table 5 shows the correlations between the different speech acts across the three testing procedures. There appears to be a test method effect that indicates that the two DCT formats are operating differently than the role-play. The speech acts of request and refusal correlate highly in the written DCT and the language lab DCT. However, they do not correlate well with the same speech acts on the role-play. In general, the DCT format has the highest correlations with speech acts within its method.

The fourth research question is concerned with whether there are differences in the ratings of the pragmatic components within each rating on the written DCT and the language laboratory DCT. The role-play results were not analyzed using this scale. Repeated-measures ANOVA on both the DCT ($F = (49.365, df = 4,21)$, $p < .025$) and language lab ($F = (55.94, df = 4,19)$, $p < .025$) results, for comparisons of the five pragmatic components, showed a significant effect.[3] However, Tukey's HSD post hoc contrasts do not show any significant differences between distinct pairs of the pragmatic components.[4] Table 6 indicates

3 The probability level of .05 was divided by 2 to indicate the multiple comparisons, resulting in a probability level of .025.
4 This lack of pairwise findings is largely owing to the number of contrasts needed and the conservative nature of Tukey's HSD in spreading the probability level across all comparisons.

TABLE 6. MEANS FOR RATING COMPONENTS

		DCT	LLT
Total	Mean	4.15	3.86
	SD	0.43	0.40
Speech act	Mean	4.56	4.33
	SD	0.41	0.40
Expressions	Mean	3.77	3.41
	SD	0.53	0.49
Amount	Mean	3.96	3.60
	SD	0.50	0.51
Formality	Mean	4.31	4.03
	SD	0.41	0.45
Directness	Mean	4.14	3.86
	SD	0.45	0.45
Politeness	Mean	4.17	3.92
	SD	0.41	0.40

Note: LLT = Language Lab Test.

TABLE 7. MEANS ACROSS RATINGS FOR SOCIAL VARIABLES

		DCT	Language lab	Role-play
Power	+	4.183	3.949	4.157
Power	−	4.114	3.762	4.229
Distance	+	4.121	3.781	4.131
Distance	−	4.176	3.931	4.213
Imposition	+	3.899	3.588	4.190
Imposition	−	4.399	4.124	4.167

that although the differences are small, the rank order on both tests was the same. First, it should be noted that on both tests *speech acts* was rated high. This indicates that very few of the participants did not recognize what speech act was called for. For the pragmatic components, the rankings, in descending order, were *formality, politeness, directness, amount,* and *expressions.* Interestingly, the two lowest pragmatic components were *amount* and *expressions.* Thus, the two components most closely linked to the grammatical and lexical areas were apparently the two most difficult, as defined by the ratings in this study. This finding further supports the conclusion that the particular informants in this study had accommodated to many of the pragmatic differences and the variance in their rating resulted from the linguistic aspects of their production.

The final research question relates to the role of the social variables in perceptions of performance. Table 7 provides the means for each variable. The differences are slight, again owing to the relative homogeneity of the participants in the study. However, in six out of nine comparisons, when the variable was coded as a minus (-), the rating was higher than when coded as a plus (+). The three exceptions were written DCT and language lab DCT *power* and role-play *imposition*. Thus, there is some apparent effect for a plus designation across these variables. Paired *t*-tests show a significant effect for *imposition* with the DCT (t = -8.259, p < .006) and the language lab (t = -7.369, p < .006).[5] It thus appears that degree of imposition does create a burden for the speakers in negotiating an acceptable answer, at least as perceived by the NS raters.

Of additional interest with the relationship of the social variables is the pattern of intercorrelations within the data. Table 8 shows the correlations across the three test methods and the plus or minus designations of *power, distance,* and *imposition*. There are relatively high correlations within each of the methods, as well as a fairly strong relationship between the ratings on the written DCT and the language lab DCT. However, the role-play has very low correlations with the other measures. This further supports the evidence presented in Tables 3 to 5 that the role-play is measuring the construct of pragmatics differently than the other two methods. However, this may also result from the fact that the written DCT and the language lab DCT had a much more similar format with one another than either had with the role-play.

Discussion

As already noted, the current study suffers from a lack of variability among the informants. However, there are several tentative trends in the results. First, the role-play resulted in somewhat higher ratings than the language lab taped responses. Further, the role-play performed differently from the other two methods, indicating that there may be a method effect. This effect indicates that, from a pedagogical standpoint, both the DCT and the role-play formats should be used. They provide different types of language training. Second, there is some evidence that apologies are less demanding than are refusals. As already noted, this may result from apologies being more formulaic, as well as from refusals involving more socially demanding interaction. Refusals are apparently complex interactions involving a great deal of face-saving moves. A third, and somewhat surprising, trend was that the *amount* of language and *appropriateness expressions* were rated more harshly than *formality, directness,* or *politeness*. These two variables are the more grammatical and lexical of all of the variables studied.

5 The probability level of .05 was divided by 9 to reflect the multiple *t*-tests, leaving a probability level of .006.

TABLE 8. CORRELATIONS OF SOCIAL VARIABLES WITHIN AND ACROSS THE METHODS

	d+P	d-P	d+D	d-D	d+R	d-R	l+p	l-P	l+D	l-D	l+R	l-R	r+P	r-P	r+D	r-D	r+R	r-R
d+P	1.00																	
d-P	.85	1.00																
d+D	.93	.93	1.00															
d-D	.90	.92	.83	1.00														
d+R	.92	.91	.94	.87	1.00													
d-R	.89	.92	.88	.92	.79	1.00												
l+p	.68	.75	.69	.75	.75	.67	1.00											
l-P	.59	.56	.52	.63	.53	.61	.52	1.00										
l+D	.70	.68	.61	.77	.66	.70	.73	.89	1.00									
l-D	.60	.65	.61	.63	.63	.61	.76	.82	.72	1.00								
l+R	.54	.62	.55	.62	.61	.55	.78	.84	.86	.88	1.00							
l-R	.77	.72	.68	.80	.70	.78	.71	.88	.90	.81	.72	1.00						
r+P	.32	.16	.23	.24	.21	.26	.19	.59	.40	.54	.39	.53	1.00					
r-P	.38	.17	.30	.21	.27	.25	.17	.39	.28	.36	.26	.39	.63	1.00				
r+D	.35	.18	.26	.25	.23	.28	.17	.50	.33	.48	.30	.49	.88	.87	1.00			
r-D	.38	.23	.32	.26	.28	.31	.20	.57	.36	.57	.42	.49	.83	.85	.85	1.00		
r+R	.46	.34	.41	.37	.34	.45	.20	.63	.39	.60	.42	.55	.71	.78	.82	.88	1.00	
r-R	.21	.02	.11	.09	.12	.08	.13	.34	.22	.34	.23	.32	.87	.80	.88	.83	.57	1.00

Note: d = DCT, l = Language Lab, r = role-play, P = Power, D = Distance, R = Imposition

More research needs to be done in this area. Finally, there was a finding of a significant effect for degree of imposition on both the written DCT and the language lab. When there was a high degree of imposition in the scenes, the speakers had more difficulty. This is not the case for power status relationships or social distance, at least on the present methods of assessment. More research is needed in order to determine whether this is an artifact of the particular instruments utilized here or the result of the lack of variability in the scores overall.

Obviously, several issues remain to be resolved in the assessment of pragmatics. First, the role played by the NS as the standard against which performance is judged is far from resolved. Much more research will need to be conducted to address the variability of NS performance. Second, this study should be carried out on a more heterogeneous group of examinees. Yamashita (1996a, 1996b), in her study of English speakers learning Japanese at beginning, intermediate, and advanced levels, found that the three test types in Japanese differentiated between lower-level students and higher-level students. Third, the decisions made on the basis of assessment through the prototypic instruments must be carefully scrutinized. The instruments developed thus far in this project are preliminary suggestions for the forms that assessment might take. At this time, the instruments should be used for research purposes only, and no examinee level decisions should be made in pedagogical settings. Further validation studies are needed before we can have any certainty about what the results of the tests mean.

Appendix A

Directions: Read each of the following scenarios. In the space provided, write what you would say in the situation in a normal conversation.

Situation 1. You live in a large house. You hold the lease to the house and rent out the other rooms. You are in the room of one of your housemates collecting the rent. You reach to take the rent check when you accidentally knock over a small, empty vase on the desk. It doesn't break.

You:

Situation 2. You work in a small jewelry repair shop. A valued customer comes into the shop to pick up an antique watch that you know is to be a present. It is not ready yet, even though you promised it would be.

You:

Situation 3. You are applying for a new job in a small company and want to make an appointment for an interview. You know that the manager is very busy and schedules interviews only in the afternoon from 1 to 4 o'clock. However, you currently work in the afternoon. You want to schedule an interview in the morning. When you go to the office this morning to turn in your application, you see the manager.

You:

Appendix B

Directions: You will hear descriptions of 24 different situations. Each description will be repeated once. After the repetition, write what would you say if you were in the situation described.

Situation 1. You work in a small department of a large firm. You have worked here for a number of years and are the head of the department. You are attending a meeting in the office of another member of the department. You accidentally knock over a framed picture on the desk. It doesn't break.

You say:

Situation 2. You are applying for a job. You go to the office to turn in your application form to the manager. You talk to the manager for a few minutes. When you move to give the manager your form, you accidentally knock over a vase on the desk and spill water over a pile of papers.

You say:

Situation 3. You are applying for a student loan at a small bank and are meeting with the loan officer. The loan officer is the only person who reviews the applications at this bank. The loan officer tells you that there are many other applicants and that it will take 2 weeks to review your application. However, you want the loan to be processed as soon as possible in order to pay your tuition on time.

You say:

Appendix C

Directions: There are eight role-plays. You will be given a role card before each role-play begins. The role card will describe the situation and your role. If you have questions about the situation or your role, please ask before the role-play starts. During some of the role-plays, you will be given another role card with further instructions.

Situation 1.

Background One: Last week you had trouble with your company van and took it to the company mechanic. The mechanic promised to have it ready by tomorrow at noon. However, you just found out that you have to go on a business trip tomorrow morning and have lots of display materials and samples to bring with you. So, *you need your van to be ready early tomorrow morning.*

Now: You go to the shop and walk over to the head mechanic who is eating lunch.

Background Two: When the mechanic stepped away, you accidentally knocked over his coffee, which spilled all over some paperwork on the table.

Now: The mechanic comes back.

Situation 2.

Background One: You have a gift certificate for one of your favorite gift shops. The gift certificate expires next week, but because you are leaving for a three-week vacation tomorrow, you *must use the gift certificate today.*

Now: You are looking at some items in a case. You see something nice, a vase, and would like to get a better look at it. The salesclerk walks by.

Background Two: You decided to buy this item. The salesperson rings up the sale.

Now: You take out the gift certificate, which you notice is very dirty, and hand it to the salesperson.

14 *Pragmatics tests*

Different purposes, different tests

James Dean Brown

Introduction

Although the assessment of pragmatic proficiency has only recently begun to be explored, so far researchers have tested pragmatics using at least six types of instruments: the written discourse completion tasks, multiple-choice discourse completion tasks, oral discourse completion tasks, discourse role-play tasks, discourse self-assessment tasks, and role-play self-assessments. This paper will begin by defining each of the six types of pragmatics tests and listing pertinent references to the literature in each case. Readers interested in more details about the literature on all six of these measures are referred to Yoshitake (1997) and Yamashita (1996a, 1996b), each of which offers a more comprehensive review of that literature than would be appropriate for this chapter.

A *written discourse completion task* (WDCT) is any pragmatics instrument that requires the students to read a written description of a situation (including such factors as setting, participant roles, and degree of imposition) and asks them to write what they would say in that situation. (For research on WDCT, readers are referred to Blum-Kulka, 1982, 1983; Blum-Kulka & Olshtain, 1986; Cohen, Olshtain, & Rosenstein, 1986; House & Kasper, 1987; Olshtain & Weinbach, 1987; Takahashi & Beebe, 1987, 1993; Blum-Kulka, House, & Kasper, 1989; Færch & Kasper, 1989; House, 1989; Kasper, 1989b; Rintell & Mitchell, 1989; Wolfson, Marmor, & Jones, 1989; Beebe, Takahashi, & Uliss-Weltz, 1990; Edmondson & House, 1991; Hudson, Detmer, & Brown, 1992, 1995; Rose, 1992, 1994a; Bergman & Kasper, 1993; Ikoma, 1993; Takahashi & Beebe, 1993; Rose & Ono, 1995; Johnston, Kasper, & Ross, 1998)

A *multiple-choice discourse completion task* (MDCT) is also a pragmatics instrument that requires students to read a written description of a situation, but, unlike the WDCT, an MDCT requires the students to select what would be best to say in that situation. (For research on MDCT, readers are referred to Tanaka & Kawade, 1982; Hudson, Detmer, & Brown, 1992, 1995; Rose, 1992, 1994a.)

Unlike a WDCT or an MDCT, an *oral discourse completion task* (ODCT) is a pragmatics instrument that requires students to listen to a description of a situation (usually on a tape recorder) and to say aloud what they would say in that situation (typically into another tape recorder). (For research on ODCT, readers are referred to Rintell & Mitchell, 1989; Hudson, Detmer, & Brown, 1992, 1995; Eisenstein & Bodman, 1993; Rose, 2000.)

A *discourse role-play task* (DRPT) is any pragmatics instrument that provides a description of a situation and asks students to play a particular role with another person in that situation. (For research on DRPT, readers are referred to Fraser, Rintell, & Walters, 1980; Cohen & Olshtain, 1981, 1993, 1994; Scarcella & Brunak, 1981; Olshtain, 1983; Edmondson, House, Kasper, & Stemmer, 1984; Kasper, 1984; Trosborg, 1987; Tanaka, 1988; Fiksdal, 1989; Rintell & Mitchell, 1989; Kasper & Dahl, 1991; Hudson, Detmer, & Brown, 1992, 1995; Eisenstein & Bodman, 1993.)

A *discourse self-assessment task* (DSAT) is any pragmatics instrument that provides a written description of a situation and asks the students to rate their own ability to perform the pragmatics necessary in that situation. (For research on DSAT, readers are referred to Hudson, Detmer, & Brown, 1992, 1995; Bergman & Kasper, 1993; Shimamura, 1993; Rose & Ng, this volume.)

A *role-play self-assessment* (RPSA) is any pragmatics instrument that combines the DRPT with the DSAT by requiring students to rate their own pragmatics performance in a previously performed role-play that was recorded on a video recorder. (For research on RPSA, readers are referred to Hudson, Detmer, & Brown, 1992, 1995.)

Purpose

The purpose of this chapter is to compare the six types of measures in actual practice in two different settings: an English as a foreign language (EFL) setting and a Japanese as a second language (JSL) setting. The data for the EFL setting were gathered by Sonia Yoshitake-Strain, and those for the JSL setting were gathered by Sayoko Yamashita. The Yoshitake-Strain project will hereafter be referred to as the EFL study, and Yamashita's work as the JSL study. In both cases, they were gathering data for their doctoral dissertations under the supervision of the author of this report. Yoshitake-Strain's EFL research was reported in Yoshitake and Enochs (1996) and Yoshitake (1997). She directly used the prototype tests previously developed by Hudson, Detmer, and Brown (1992, 1995) and administered them to EFL students at International Christian University. Yamashita's JSL research was reported in Yamashita (1996a, 1996b). She first translated the prototype tests (previously developed by Hudson, Detmer, & Brown, 1992, 1995) into Japanese; then she administered them to JSL students at four different universities in Tokyo and Yokohama.[1] In a sense, these two doctoral studies were mirror images of each other. Comparing the data for these two studies allowed the opportunity to examine what happens when a variety of different pragmatics test types are developed to be more or less parallel in two different languages and then administered to appropriate contrasting groups of students. All of the analyses presented here are based on data graciously supplied by Yoshitake-Strain and Yamashita. In most cases, these analyses are entirely new; that is, they were not done in the original projects, or at least were not done in a way that made the two studies comparable.

The overall goal of these analyses was to compare the data provided in the EFL and JSL studies in order to better understand the differences and similarities between the two studies as well as among the six types of pragmatics tests. To those ends, the following research questions were posed:

1. Are there significant differences between the EFL and JSL groups in the mean performances on the six types of pragmatics tests?
2. Are there significant differences between the EFL and JSL groups in the dispersion of scores on the six types of pragmatics tests?
3. Are there differences between the EFL and JSL groups in the reliability of the six types of pragmatics tests?
4. Are there differences between the EFL and JSL groups in the degree of relationship among the six types of pragmatics tests?
5. Are there differences between the EFL and JSL studies in the underlying variance structure of the six types of pragmatics tests?
6. Are there differences in practicality among the six types of pragmatics tests?

Method

Participants

The participants in the EFL study included twenty-five volunteers from the English language program at International Christian University (ICU), a prestigious private university in the western part of Tokyo.

---

1 It is important to note at this point that Yamashita did not simply translate the words describing the situations and tasks in these tests from English into Japanese; she also translated the situations themselves as appropriate from American situations to Japanese situations. For example, because Japanese universities do not have student body officers as American universities do, she built situations around university club officers (common in Japanese universities) where the original English-language versions referred to student body officers.

They were 28% male and 72% female, and they ranged in English-language proficiency from 423 to 577 on the TOEFL. Their ages ranged from 18 to 26 with an average of 19.16 years. They were in a variety of academic majors, including education (8%), international studies (24%), languages (8%), natural sciences (32%), and social sciences (28%). They were paid 3,000 yen to participate in the study, and it took them about 3 hours to complete all six sets of tasks. The participants in the JSL study included forty-seven North American learners of Japanese at three different prestigious universities in the Tokyo area and one in Yokohama. They were 53% male and 47% female, and ranged in Japanese proficiency from beginning level (25.5%) to intermediate (42.5%) to advanced (32%) based on Japanese-language cloze test scores. Their ages ranged from 18 to 49 with an average of 26.21 years. They were from a variety of academic majors, including Asian history (8.5%), economics (10.64%), international studies (8.5%), Japanese language (19.15%), literature/communication (8.5%), political science/law (6.38%), science (15%), TESOL (4.25%), and other (19%). These participants were also rewarded, but instead of money they were given phone cards and dictionaries worth altogether about 3,000 yen. The tests in the JSL study turned out to be even more time-consuming than those administered in the EFL study.

Materials and procedures

The six types of instruments defined in the introduction to this chapter were used in exactly the same way in both the EFL and JSL studies. Since each of these was defined earlier, I will briefly focus here on the details of how the six measures were constructed in the EFL and JSL studies. Items on the six measures were all designed to measure three speech acts (requests, refusals, and apologies) after Hudson, Detmer, and Brown (1992, 1995). These speech acts were chosen by Hudson, Detmer, and Brown (1992) based on their prominence in the literature. The researchers decided to test power, distance, and imposition for each of the three speech acts because of the prominent position they have been accorded in work on pragmatics such as Brown and Levinson's (1987) politeness theory, leading Hudson, Detmer, and Brown (1995, p. 4) to note that "within the research on cross-cultural pragmatics, they are identified as the three independent and culturally sensitive variables that subsume all other variables and play a principled role in speech act behavior." These three variables were defined as follows in Hudson, Detmer, and Brown (1992, 1995), Yoshitake and Enochs (1996), Yamashita (1996a, 1996b), and Yoshitake (1997):

1. *Power:* the relative power difference between the listener and speaker based on rank, professional status, etc.

2. *Distance:* the relative social distance between the listener and speaker based on familiarity or shared solidarity due to presence or absence of group membership
3. *Imposition:* the degree of imposition of the speech act within the cultural context in terms of expenditure or obligation

In order to measure all possible combinations of power, distance, and imposition, eight items were created for each of the three speech acts for a total of twenty-four items for all tests except the DRPT and RPSA, which (for reasons explained later in this section) had only eight items, each of which included occasions for requests, refusals, and apologies.

Written discourse completion tasks. The WDCT contained twenty-four items, each of which consisted of a description of a situation requiring a request, refusal, or apology in one of the possible combinations of power, distance, and imposition. The WDCT required the students to read twenty-four descriptions of situations and write their responses in the spaces provided after each description. The responses were scored by three raters on a 5-point Likert scale (ranging from 1 for *very unsatisfactory* to 5 for *completely appropriate*). The sum of the average ratings for each item was the score on the WDCT.

Multiple-choice discourse completion tasks. The MDCT contained twenty-four items, each of which consisted of a description of a situation requiring a request, refusal, or apology in one of the possible combinations of power, distance, and imposition. The MDCT required the students to the read twenty-four descriptions of situations and, after each situation, select the response they would make from three options. The responses were scored right or wrong. The number of correct answers was multiplied times 5 in order to maintain a scale similar to the other instruments, and the result became each student's score on the MDCT.

Oral discourse completion tasks. The ODCT contained twenty-four items, each of which consisted of a description of a situation requiring a request, refusal, or apology in one of the possible combinations of power, distance, and imposition. The ODCT was administered in an audiotape format that required the students to listen to the twenty-four descriptions of situations on Tape A and record their responses orally on Tape B. The responses were scored by three raters on a 5-point Likert scale (ranging from 1 for *very unsatisfactory* to 5 for *completely appropriate*). The sum of the average ratings for each item was the score on the ODCT.

Discourse role-play tasks. Because twenty-four role-plays would be extraordinarily punishing to students in terms of the time and energy required, the DRPT was designed in eight scenes, each of which contained a request, a refusal, and an apology with power, distance, and imposition balanced across the eight role-plays (Hudson, Detmer, &

Brown, 1995, p. 60). The DRPT required students to read each scene description (they spent about 2 to 3 minutes doing this on average), and then perform the role-play with a native speaker of the target language. It took about 30 minutes on average for students to complete all eight scenes. The responses were scored by three raters on a five-point Likert scale (ranging from 1 for *very unsatisfactory* to 5 for *completely appropriate*). The sum of the average ratings for each item was the score on the DRPT.

Discourse self-assessment tasks. The DSAT contained twenty-four items, each of which consisted of a description of a situation requiring a request, refusal, or apology in one of the possible combinations of power, distance, and imposition. The DSAT required the students to first read twenty-four descriptions of situations, then think about how they would respond in each situation, and finally rate their own ability to perform in that situation on a 5-point Likert scale (ranging from 1 for *very unsatisfactory* to 5 for *completely appropriate*). The sum of each student's ratings was his or her score on the DSAT.

Role-play self-assessments. The RPSA necessarily contained only eight items because it was based on the eight items in the DRPT, each of which consisted of a request, a refusal, and an apology with power, distance, and imposition balanced across the eight situations (Hudson, Detmer, & Brown, 1995, p. 60). The RPSA required the students to view the videotape of their performance in the DRPT scenes and rate their own performance in each scene on a 5-point Likert scale (ranging from 1 for *very unsatisfactory* to 5 for *completely appropriate*). The sum of each student's ratings was his or her score on the RPSA.

Results

The vast majority of the analyses in this chapter are new; that is, they were not done in the original projects written up by Yoshitake-Strain and Yamashita, certainly not in a way that made the two studies comparable. Indeed, new information is presented in every single table. Recall that the overall purpose of these analyses was to compare the data provided in the EFL and JSL studies in order to better understand the differences and similarities between the studies as well as the differences and similarities among the six types of instruments for measuring pragmatics. To those ends, each of the six types of tests was examined for statistical test characteristics (i.e., task difficulty, score distributions, reliability, and validity) as well as practical test characteristics (i.e., the relative difficulty of administering and scoring the tests as well as the amount of oral language and self-reflection required, and the adequacy of the test for making high-stakes decisions). The relative merits of each

TABLE 1. MEANS AND *t*-TEST FOR THE EFL AND JSL DATA

Measure	EFL M	JSL M	t	p	df	eta²	%
WDCT	92.48	92.31	0.06	0.950	70	.0000	.00
MDCT	70.00	57.80	*3.58	0.001	70	.1548	15.48
ODCT	77.05	93.57	*4.73	0.000	70	.2422	24.22
DRPT	78.88	72.78	1.44	0.156	70	.0288	2.88
DSAT	86.08	79.43	1.70	0.094	70	.0396	3.96
RPSA	78.88	73.53	1.29	0.201	70	.0232	2.32

* $p < .008$

of the six tests were analyzed and compared in terms of these statistical and practical testing characteristics within and between the EFL and JSL studies. The results of the analyses of the statistical characteristics will be presented here in the "Results" section; the analyses of the practical testing characteristics will be presented in the "Discussion" section.

Task difficulty

Table 1 shows the means for each of the six measures in both studies as well as *t*-tests for the differences in means between the EFL and JSL results. These statistics resulted from reanalysis of data supplied by the original authors. The comparison-wise alpha level for the *t*-tests was adjusted using the Bonferroni procedure in order to hold the experiment-wise alpha at .05. Thus, the overall alpha level of .05 was divided across six comparisons as follows: .05/6 = .008 (for the comparison-wise statistical decisions). Notice that only the EFL/JSL mean differences for the MDCT and ODCT were statistically significant at $p < .008$ (see the asterisks in the table). It was therefore concluded that any other observed differences between the two studies (i.e., for the WDCT, DRPT, DSAT, and RPSA) were chance fluctuations. Notice also that the significant mean difference for the MDCT favors the EFL group of Japanese EFL students, while the significant mean difference for the ODCT favors the JSL group of North American JSL students (more about this in the "Discussion" section below).

To put the information in the preceding paragraph in perspective, eta squared analysis (eta²) was conducted. Eta² indicates the proportion of variance accounted for by the observed differences between groups. Thus the eta² value of .1548 shown in the second to last column of Table 1 for the MDCT indicates that 15.48% (shown in the last column) of the total variance in MDCT scores was accounted for by the difference between

TABLE 2A. DESCRIPTIVE STATISTICS FOR THE EFL DATA

EFL	WDCT	MDCT	ODCT	DRPT	DSAT	RPSA
M	92.48	70.00	77.05	78.88	86.08	78.88
SD	6.46	14.43	8.49	10.53	14.59	14.31
MAX	110.09	95.00	97.67	101.67	116.00	111.00
MIN	77.83	30.00	61.00	61.00	60.00	61.00
RANGE	33.26	66.00	37.67	41.67	57.00	51.00
N	25.00	25.00	25.00	25.00	25.00	25.00
KURTOSIS	1.74	1.20	0.98	-0.77	-0.28	-0.22
SKEW	0.36	-0.81	0.53	0.40	0.19	0.76

TABLE 2B. DESCRIPTIVE STATISTICS FOR THE JSL DATA

EFL	WDCT	MDCT	ODCT	DRPT	DSAT	RPSA
M	92.31	57.80	93.57	72.78	79.43	73.53
SD	12.67	13.42	16.30	19.76	16.45	17.85
MAX	114.09	87.50	116.53	113.67	119.00	120.00
MIN	66.95	16.67	55.13	36.67	42.00	38.00
RANGE	48.14	75.00	62.40	78.00	78.00	83.00
N	47.00	47.00	47.00	47.00	47.00	47.00
KURTOSIS	-0.70	0.80	-0.87	-0.63	-0.16	0.09
SKEW	-0.15	-0.38	-0.41	0.32	0.12	0.18

TABLE 3. F_{MAX} TEST FOR SIGNIFICANT DIFFERENCES BETWEEN VARIANCES FOR THE EFL AND JSL DATA

	WDCT	MDCT	ODCT	DRPT	DSAT	RPSA
EFL SD	6.46	14.43	8.49	10.53	14.59	14.31
JSL SD	12.67	13.42	16.30	19.76	16.45	17.85
EFL SD^2	41.73	208.22	72.08	110.88	212.87	204.78
JSL SD^2	160.53	180.10	265.69	390.46	270.60	318.62
F_{MAX}	*3.85	1.16	*3.69	*3.52	1.27	1.56

$* p < .01$

the EFL and JSL groups. Similarly, the eta^2 value of .2422 for the ODCT indicates that 24.22% of the ODCT variance was accounted for by the difference between the groups. The other measures were not significantly different, and their eta^2 values were commensurately small.

Score distributions

Tables 2a and 2b show the mean (M), standard deviation (SD), maximum score (MAX), minimum score (MIN), range, number of students (N), kurtosis, and skew statistics for each of the six measures. Table 2a gives those statistics for the EFL project, and Table 2b does the same for the JSL study. Notice that in all cases except the MDCT, the dispersion as estimated by the standard deviation and range is much smaller for the EFL data than for the JSL results. Just as clearly, on the MDCT, the opposite is true. Note also that two of the kurtosis statistics in the EFL study (for the WDCT and MDCT) exceed 1.00, with values of 1.74 and 1.20, respectively, indicating that these two distributions may be slightly leptokurtic (or too tall), and that none of the kurtosis statistics for the JSL study are above 1.00. In addition, the fact that none of the skew statistics exceeds 1.00 in Table 2a or 2b indicates that the distributions are reasonably well centered and symmetrically distributed about the mean. In short, careful examination of the distributions indicates that all twelve are reasonably normal.

Table 3 shows the standard deviations of the six measures in the EFL and JSL studies in the first two rows. The next two rows show the variances (i.e., the standard deviations squared). The last row provides F_{MAX} statistics for each instrument. The F_{MAX} statistic tests whether the variances of the two groups are significantly different for any of the six tests. The asterisks indicate that significant differences were indeed found between the variances of the two groups for the WDCT, ODCT, and DRPT. In all three cases, the JSL group produced considerably more dispersed scores than the EFL group. The observed differences for the variances of the two groups on the MDCT, DSAT, and RPSA can only be interpreted as chance fluctuations. This will become important information for interpreting the reliability and correlation results later on (more about this in the "Discussion" section).

Reliability

Table 4 shows reliability statistics for the six measures in the JSL and EFL studies. The EFL reliability statistics are presented in the first two rows in the table, and the JSL statistics are in the last three rows. The original JSL study (Yamashita, 1996a, 1996b) included a variety of reliability estimates, including internal consistency reliabilities, interrater reliabilities, intraclass correlations, and standard errors of estimate, while the original EFL study (Yoshitake, 1997) presented no reliability estimates. Since item-level and rater-level data were not available from the EFL study, comparisons between Cronbach alpha internal consistency estimates or interrater reliabilities could not be made. However, K-R21 estimates of internal consistency reliability based on the total

TABLE 4. RELIABILITY ESTIMATES FOR THE EFL AND JSL DATA

Study reliability	WDCT	MDCT	ODCT	DRPT	DSAT	RPSA
EFL						
K-R21	0.4960	0.6050	0.6226	0.7626	0.8931	0.8753
SEM	4.5863	9.0692	8.8647	4.1368	3.4422	5.1522
JSL						
K-R21	0.8746	0.4546	0.9302	0.9344	0.9083	0.9183
Alpha	0.9851	0.4652	0.9920	0.9901	0.9359	0.9459
SEM	4.4867	9.9106	3.5459	4.1736	5.9827	4.7024

score means and variances were possible and, since at least some comparisons of reliability across tests and studies were desirable, K-R21 statistics were calculated as a common reliability statistic that could be reported for all six tests in both studies.

Previous studies (e.g., Brown, 1983) indicated that K-R21 estimates can represent serious underestimates of the true state of affairs for certain types of tests, and sometimes can even result in overestimates (Brown, 1993). To check these possibilities, the Cronbach alpha statistics that were available from the original JSL study were compared to the K-R21 estimates for the same tests. These reliability statistics are presented in Table 4 in the third and fourth rows. Notice that in all cases the K-R21 estimates do underestimate the alpha estimates, but also that both K-R21 and Cronbach alpha are respectably high for all measures except for the MDCT, which had similarly low K-R21 and Cronbach alpha estimates at .4546 and .4652, respectively. Thus, in the JSL study, all measures except the MDCT appear to have been very reliable. In addition, although underestimation does appear to occur with the K-R21 estimates, overestimation does not appear to be a problem, and, in any case, the K-R21 estimates provide similar patterns of high and low reliabilities to those in the alpha statistics.

In the first two rows inside Table 4, it is clear that the EFL study produced consistently lower K-R21 reliability estimates than the JSL study. Note also, in the EFL study, that the WDCT was relatively unreliable at .4960, that the MDCT and ODCT were also fairly low in reliability at .6050 and .6226, respectively, and that the DRPT, DSAT, and RPSA all produced relatively high levels of reliability at .7626, .8931, and .8753, respectively.

The SEM is another approach to reliability estimation, one that expresses the unreliability of a test in terms of the number of points on the test that students' scores can be expected to vary by chance alone (plus or minus one SEM at 68% confidence, plus or minus two SEMs at 95% confidence, and so forth). Thus a small SEM is better than a large one. Notice in Table 4 that the MDCT has a very large SEM in both studies (at 9.9106 and 9.0692, respectively), indicating that, like the K-R21 estimates, the MDCT was very unreliable in both studies. The other SEMs are respectable, as would be expected commensurate with their corresponding reliability estimates.

Validity

Traditionally, the validity of a test has been examined in three ways: content validity, criterion-related validity, and construct validity. The *content validity* of the six tests in the EFL and JSL studies was essentially argued in Hudson, Detmer, and Brown (1992, 1995) in that the tests were carefully planned (on the basis of all available literature) to include three speech acts (requests, refusals, and apologies) with systematically varying degrees of power, distance, and imposition. To the degree that the literature is right about the components of pragmatic competence and the degree that the tests in Hudson, Detmer, and Brown (1992, 1995) do indeed match those components (as judged by those three experts), the tests in the EFL and JSL studies should also be content valid.

The *criterion-related validity* of a test can be argued from the correlation of that test with other measures designed to measure the same thing. Since all six of the tests in this study were designed to measure the same thing, pragmatic abilities, the degree of correlation of any two of these measures would provide an estimate of the degree to which both measures were measuring what they were designed to measure. Table 5a presents all possible intercorrelations among the six measures in the EFL study below the diagonal (the 1.00 values running diagonally across the table) and the squared values of those same correlation coefficients (also known as *coefficients of determination*) above the diagonal. The squared values can be directly interpreted as the proportion of overlapping variance between whatever two tests are involved. For example, in Table 5a, the correlation coefficient for the relationship between the WDCT and the MDCT is shown to be .2254. The squared value of that coefficient is .0508. Thus, the proportion of overlapping variance between the WDCT and MDCT is .0508, or 5.08%.

Notice in Table 5a that the EFL study had only three significant correlation coefficients out of fifteen, indicating there was very little systematically shared variance owing to pragmatic ability among these measures. The coefficients of determination indicate that the percent of overlapping variance for those three significant correlations in the EFL study ranged from a low of 21.72% to 28.77%, indicating a few significant, but not very interesting, degrees of relationship in support of the validity of these measures. The relatively low reliability in the EFL data for the WDCT, MDCT, and ODCT (see Table 4) may have

TABLE 5A. CORRELATION COEFFICIENTS (BELOW THE DIAGONAL) AND
COEFFICIENTS OF DETERMINATION (ABOVE THE DIAGONAL) FOR THE EFL DATA

EFL	WDCT	MDCT	ODCT	DRPT	DSAT	RPSA
WDCT	1.0000	.0508	.2877	.1556	.0084	.1135
MDCT	.2254	1.0000	.0283	.0008	.1098	.0501
ODCT	.5364*	.1683	1.0000	.2856	.0217	.0013
DRPT	.3945	-.0283	.5344*	1.0000	.0000	.0499
DSAT	.0916	-.3314	.1473	.0035	1.0000	.2172
RPSA	-.3369	-.2239	.0366	.2234	.4661*	1.0000

$* p < .01$

TABLE 5B. CORRELATION COEFFICIENTS (BELOW THE DIAGONAL) AND
COEFFICIENTS OF DETERMINATION (ABOVE THE DIAGONAL) FOR THE JSL DATA

JFL	WDCT	MDCT	ODCT	DRPT	DSAT	RPSA
WDCT	1.0000	.1526	.4496	.3421	.2427	.1636
MDCT	.3907*	1.0000	.1393	.0575	.0130	.0309
ODCT	.6705*	.3732*	1.0000	.6162	.3110	.2393
DRPT	.5849*	.2398	.7850*	1.0000	.3668	.2773
DSAT	.4926*	.1139	.5577*	.6056*	1.0000	.4669
RPSA	.4045*	.1759	.4893*	.5266*	.6833*	1.0000

$* p < .01$

something to do with the general lack of correlation shown in Table 5a. Unreliable measures lack systematic variance; hence it is unlikely that they will be systematically related to any other measures.

In contrast, in the JSL study shown in Table 5b, twelve out of fifteen correlation coefficients were significant, indicating a fair amount of systematically shared variance owing to pragmatics ability going on among these measures. The coefficients of determination show that the percent of overlapping variance for those significant correlations in the JSL study ranged from 15.26% to 61.62%, indicating some significant and interesting degrees of relationship in support of the validity of these measures. Notice further that all of the correlation coefficients in Table 5b are significant except those involving the MDCT. The tendency of the MDCT not to correlate with the other measures could be explained by the fact that it is the one measure with low reliability (see Table 4). Again, unreliable measures lack systematic variance; hence it is unlikely that the MDCT will be systematically related to any other measures, regardless of how reliable those other measures may be.

The *construct validity* was examined on the basis of two factor analysis procedures. Examination of the eigenvalues (with 1.00 as the cut-point) and scree plots led to the conclusion that two-factor solutions were appropriate for both the EFL and the JSL data. VARIMAX rotations indicated fairly clear patterns of loadings for both sets of data, despite the fact that the sample sizes would generally be considered far too small for this form of analysis with six variables. Table 6a shows the results for the EFL data. Notice first that the highest loadings (those with bold-faced type) and all loadings above .30 (those with asterisks) are exactly the same. This will not prove to be the case with the JSL data. Examining the highest loadings in Table 6a for each variable (in bold), notice that the WDCT, ODCT, and DRPT load most heavily on Factor 1, while the MDCT, DSAT, and RPSA load most heavily on Factor 2 (though the minus sign indicates that the high MDCT loading is in the opposite direction from the DSAT and RPSA). Since the WDCT, ODCT, and DRPT all use productive item types (i.e., they require students to actually produce written or oral language), Factor 1 might be labeled a productive-language factor, while the other three variables (MDCT, DSAT, and RPSA) can all be considered receptive item types in the sense that the students need only select answers and are not required to produce any language, so Factor 2 might appropriately be labeled a receptive-language factor. The productive and receptive language categories can be considered test method factors, and the pattern is very clear in the EFL data because there are no cases wherein variables load to any interpretable degree on both factors. Notice that the proportion of variance (given in the last row of Table 6a) indicates that the first factor accounts for 34% of the variance in the design, the second factor accounts for 30%, and the two together account for about 64%. The communalities (h^2) in the column furthest to the right also provide useful information about the proportion of variance in each variable that is accounted for by the two factors in this analysis. For instance, the two factors account for as little as 45% of the variance in the MDCT, and as much as 75% in the ODCT.

An entirely different pattern was found for the JSL data as shown in Table 6b. Examining first the highest loadings for each variable (in bold), notice that ODCT, DRPT, DSAT, and RPSA load most heavily on Factor 1, while the WDCT and MDCT load most heavily on Factor 2. Since the ODCT, DRPT, DSAT, and RPSA can all be classified as oral (especially the ODCT and DRPT) or self-assessment of oral abilities (especially the DSAT and RPSA), Factor 1 might be labeled an oral test factor. In contrast, the other two variables (the WDCT and MDCT) can both be considered purely paper-and-pencil tests, so Factor 2 might appropriately be labeled a paper-and-pencil factor. The oral and paper-and-pencil categories are probably test method factors – test method

TABLE 6A. FACTOR ANALYSIS OF EFL DATA (AFTER VARIMAX ROTATION)

Variable	Factor 1	Factor 2	h^2
WDCT	*.79	-.29	.71
MDCT	.20	*-.64	.45
ODCT	*.87	.03	.75
DRPT	*.76	.18	.61
DSAT	.18	*.75	.60
RPSA	.02	*.82	.68
Proportion of variance	.34	.30	.64

Note: Bold-faced type indicates highest loading for each variable. Asterisks show all loadings over .30.

TABLE 6B. FACTOR ANALYSIS OF JSL DATA (AFTER VARIMAX ROTATION)

Variable	Factor 1	Factor 2	h^2
WDCT	*.56	*.61	.68
MDCT	.02	*.90	.82
ODCT	*.70	.54	.78
DRPT	*.78	.36	.74
DSAT	*.89	.03	.79
RPSA	*.82	.04	.68
Proportion of variance	.48	.27	.75

Note: Bold-faced type indicates highest loading for each variable. Asterisks show all loadings over .30.

factors different from those found in the EFL factor analysis. Note also, however, that examination of all loadings above .30 (those with asterisks) indicates that the picture is not quite as clear as it might at first seem because three variables (the WDCT, ODCT, and DRPT) load at least to some interpretable degree on both factors. Once again, the proportion of variance is given in the last row of Table 6b. These proportions indicate that the first factor accounts for about 48% of the variance, while the second factor accounts for 27%, and the two together account for about 75%. Again, the communalities (h^2) in the column furthest to the right also provide useful information about the proportion of variance in each variable that is accounted for by the two factors. For instance, it appears that the two factors in this analysis account for as little as 68% of the variance in the WDCT or in the RPSA, and as much as 82% in the MDCT.

Discussion

This section will provide direct answers to the six research questions posed at the top of this study. To help organize those answers, the questions themselves will be used as headings.

1. *Are there significant differences between the EFL and JSL groups in the mean performances on the six types of pragmatics tests?*

Recall that the mean differences between the EFL and JSL studies for the WDCT, DRPT, DSAT, and RPSA were not significant and that they could therefore only be interpreted as chance fluctuations. Thus these four tests appear to have been about equal in difficulty for the two groups. However, the mean differences between the two studies for the MDCT and ODCT were significant. If such mean differences had been significant across the board and in the same direction, I might have concluded that one group was simply higher in overall proficiency than the other, but that was not the case. Indeed, on the MDCT, the EFL group was higher, whereas on the ODCT, the JSL group was higher. What possible explanations could account for the observed patterns of significant mean differences between these two studies?

The mean difference shown in Table 1 for the MDCT was not only significant but also large. In more detail, the difference for the MDCT was 12.20 points (70.00 − 57.80 = 12.20), with the Japanese EFL students scoring higher. It is tempting to speculate that Japanese students may have done better on the multiple-choice version of the test because of their educational background. Japanese university students may have superior test-taking training and abilities, especially on multiple-choice items, because of the pervasiveness and importance in Japan of the university entrance examinations, which also tend to have high percentages of multiple-choice questions (see Brown & Yamashita, 1995a, 1995b). Thus Japanese students might tend to do better than North American students on that one multiple-choice test format, even though these Japanese students were studying English as a foreign language in Japan (i.e., isolated from exposure to nativelike pragmatics). However, all of this is just speculation. Similarly, the mean difference shown in Table 1 for the ODCT was not only significant but also large. In more detail, the relationship was opposite from that found for the MDCT. For the ODCT, an even bigger difference of 16.52 points (93.57 − 77.05 = 16.52) was found, and that difference favored the North American JSL students. Again, it is tempting to speculate. Perhaps these JSL students who were studying in Japan were exposed to in-country native-speaker pragmatics, which may be reflected more on the ODCT than on any of the other tests, particularly the MDCT. However, one would expect any such differences to be similar in the DRPT results, but that is not the case (indeed, the difference was in the opposite direction from what might be expected). An alternative explanation for the significant difference found for the ODCT could be that the two different sets of raters might have applied different standards in the two studies; that is, they might have been more severe in their ratings in the EFL study and less severe in the JSL study. However, if that were true, it would be reasonable to expect the same pattern to appear in the WDCT and DRPT (also rated by the same raters), but such was not the case.

2. Are there significant differences between the EFL and JSL groups in the dispersion of scores on the six types of pragmatics tests?

Recall that F_{MAX} statistics were used to compare the variances in the EFL and JSL data and that F_{MAX} was not significant for the MDCT, DSAT, and RPSA, so the observed differences were probably chance fluctuations (see Table 3). These three tests appear to be about equal in dispersion for the two groups, or, put another way, there is no basis for concluding that they are systematically different for any reasons other than chance. However, the differences in variances between the two studies for the WDCT, ODCT, and DRPT were significant. In all three cases, the JSL group produced considerably higher variances than the EFL group. Thus the dispersion of the scores for these three tests was probably different for the two groups for reasons other than chance. What might those reasons be?

If the differences in dispersion were significant across the board, it might be reasonable to conclude that one group of subjects simply had a wider range of overall pragmatic abilities than the other, but that is not the case here. The fact that the scores on the WDCT, ODCT, and DRPT were consistently and significantly more dispersed in the JSL data than in the EFL data and the fact that those three tests are all made up of productive language tasks (requiring writing in the WDCT and speaking in both the ODCT and DRPT) suggest that the students in the second language setting (JSL) are significantly more diverse in their oral pragmatics abilities than the students in the foreign language setting (EFL). The same is not consistently true on the other three tests, the MDCT, DSAT, and RPSA, which appear to have variances that fluctuate owing to chance alone. Thus the distributions of scores appear to be more similar between the groups on these three tests, where students are simply required to select an answer. In the case of the MDCT, that might mean that their passive knowledge of the pragmatics of requests, refusals, and apologies are similarly dispersed, though recall that the EFL group had a significantly higher mean on this test. As mentioned earlier, the dispersion of scores is important to consider in interpreting the reliability and correlation statistics, so this issue will be revisited in the sections that follow.

3. *Are there differences between the EFL and JSL groups in the reliability of the six types of pragmatics tests?*

The reliability estimates and standard errors of measurement presented in Table 4 indicate that all of the measures in the JSL data were highly reliable except for the MDCT. Careful examination of the distributions offered no clue as to why the MDCT might be less reliable than the other measures. Yamashita, the author of the JSL study, indicated in personal communication that she thought the items themselves were problematic. She found that it was very difficult to create multiple-choice distractors that were not themselves correct or very close to correct to at least some native speakers of Japanese. Similar problems arose in developing the original English prototypes that were used in the EFL study. And indeed, the MDCT was relatively unreliable in the EFL study at .6050. The WDCT and ODCT were also fairly unreliable in the EFL study at .4960 and .6226, respectively. Indeed, the EFL study generally produced lower K-R21 reliability estimates than did the JSL study. Such a pattern might be accounted for by the fact that the dispersion (as indicated by the standard deviation, variances, and ranges) was consistently lower for the EFL distributions of scores on five of the six tests than the dispersion for the EFL distributions. The one exception was the MDCT, which had a standard deviation of 13.42 in the JSL study and 14.43 in the EFL study. Indeed, that difference in standard deviations and its direction might account for the fact that the reliability estimate for the EFL MDCT was the only one that was higher for the EFL group than for the JSL group.

4. *Are there differences between the EFL and JSL groups in the degree of relationship among the six types of pragmatics tests?*

Recall that the EFL study had only three significant correlations out of fifteen (as shown in Table 5a), suggesting that there was much less systematically shared variance owing to pragmatics ability going on among these measures. The coefficients of determination indicated that the percent of overlapping variance ranged from a low of 21.72% to 28.77%, which means that there were three significant, but not very interesting, relationships. This lack of significant correlations in the EFL data could be accounted for by the generally lower standard deviations for the six measures in that study. As I showed in Brown (1984), the reliability estimates and any correlation coefficients used to argue for the validity of tests are very sensitive to the degree of dispersion (as indicated by the standard deviations) in those tests. Nonetheless, it is clear that this line of correlational analysis cannot be used to convincingly support the validity of these measures for use with EFL students. In contrast, twelve out of fifteen correlation coefficients in the JSL study were significant (as shown in Table 5b), indicating that there probably was considerable shared variance owing to pragmatics ability among these measures. The coefficients of determination also showed that the percent of overlapping variance for correlations ranged from 15.26% to 61.62%. Hence, there appear to have been a number of significant and interesting relationships in support of the validity of these measures. Note that the variance that was not accounted for; that is, the variance that was not shown to be shared between measures in both the EFL and JSL data could be the result of test method effects or other forms of error. In the next section, the role of test method effects will be examined.

5. Are there differences between the EFL and JSL studies in the underlying variance structure of the six types of pragmatics tests?

The test method effects became considerably clearer when factor analyses were performed. Recall that the factor analysis for the EFL data (see Table 6a) indicated that Factor 1 (with heavy loadings for the WDCT, ODCT, and DRPT) appeared to be a productive language factor, while Factor 2 (with heavy loadings for the MDCT, DSAT, and RPSA) seemed to be a receptive language factor. This pattern of loadings on one productive and another receptive factor indicates a strong method effect for this difference in test characteristics – a very clear pattern wherein no variables loaded to any interpretable degree on both factors. An entirely different pattern was found in the factor analysis for the JSL data (see Table 6b), which showed that Factor 1 (with heavy loadings for the ODCT, DRPT, DSAT, and RPSA) might be called an *oral factor*, whereas Factor 2 (with heavy loadings for the WDCT and MDCT) could be labeled a *paper-and-pencil factor*. This pattern of loadings on one oral factor and another paper-and-pencil factor seems to point to a method effect for this difference in test characteristics. However, further examination of the loadings indicated that the WDCT, ODCT, and DRPT all load above .30 on both factors. Therefore, the apparent method effect for differences between oral and paper-and-pencil pragmatics tests is not as clear as the pattern found in the EFL data. Interpreting these results can be tricky because it is tempting to focus entirely on the differences in factor loadings within and between the two studies and ignore the similarities across tests and studies. One fact must be kept in mind while examining those differences: These tests were all designed to measure pragmatics abilities, and they appear to do so to a fairly high degree in the JSL study (as indicated by the number of significant correlations reported in Table 5b and their magnitude) and to a lesser degree in the EFL study (see Table 5a). Thus, if differences surface in these factor analyses, they are likely to be subcategories within pragmatics abilities – subcategories such as test methods. All of that said, what could explain the different method effects for the EFL and JSL data? The EFL factor analysis reflected a strong method effect based on differences between oral tasks and paper-and-pencil tasks. Thus, in the EFL group, it appears that the abilities to handle oral pragmatics tasks may be somewhat different in nature from the abilities to handle paper-and-pencil pragmatics tasks.

In contrast, the JSL factor analysis reflected some method effect for the differences between productive and receptive language tasks. Thus, in the JSL group, it appears that the abilities to handle productive language pragmatics tasks are somewhat different from the abilities to handle receptive language pragmatics tasks. In addition, there were differences in the factor analyses in the amounts of variance accounted for by the two factors. In the EFL data, the first factor accounted for 34% of the variance, the second factor accounted for 30%, and the two together accounted for about 64%. In the JSL analysis, the first factor accounted for about 48% of the variance, while the second factor accounted for 27%, and the two together accounted for a fairly high 75%. These differences in the percentages of explained variance can probably be accounted for, at least in part, by the differences in the magnitudes of the standard deviations between the two studies, and/or by chance fluctuations.

6. Are there differences in practicality among the six types of pragmatics tests?

In addition to the statistical characteristics shown in the "Results" section and discussed subsequently, the six tests used in both studies had certain practical characteristics, which may have considerable influence on which of these types of tests teachers and researchers might choose to use in the future. These characteristics have to do with the relative ease of administering the six types of tests, the relative ease of scoring and interpreting the six instruments, the relative value of the six types of tests for measuring oral language skills, and the relative value of the six tests for making high-stakes decisions. To answer this research question, the relative merits of each of the six types of tests were analyzed in terms of these practical characteristics. The results are in Table 7, and each test type is discussed in the remainder of this section.

WDCTs. As shown in Table 7, one advantage of the written discourse completion tasks is that they are relatively easy to administer because they are in a paper-and-pencil format, which lends itself to large-scale group testing. However, WDCTs also have disadvantages, which are that they require the students only to produce and understand written language and therefore do not encourage oral production. In addition, WDCTs do not promote self-reflection of any kind, and they are difficult to score because they require recruiting, training, scheduling, and paying of raters.

TABLE 7. PRACTICAL CONSIDERATIONS FOR THE SIX TYPES OF TESTS

Test type	Practical advantages	Practical disadvantages
WDCT	Easy to administer because paper-and-pencil	Written receptive and productive language only; does not encourage oral production or self-reflection; difficult to score because it requires recruiting, training, scheduling, and paying raters
MDCT	Easy to administer because paper-and-pencil; easy to score	Written receptive language only; does not encourage oral production or self-reflection
ODCT	Encourages oral production; relatively quick to administer	Relatively difficult to administer because it requires two audiocassette recorders; difficult to score because it requires recruiting, training, scheduling, and paying raters
DRPT	Encourages oral production; relatively quick to administer	Difficult to administer because it must be administered individually using video equipment and an interlocutor; difficult to score because it requires recruiting, training, scheduling, and paying raters
DSAT	Encourages self-reflection; easy to administer because relatively quick and paper-and-pencil; easy to score	Not suitable for high-stakes decisions
RPSA	Encourages self-reflection; easy to score	Relatively difficult to administer because it must be administered individually using video equipment; not suitable for high-stakes decisions

MDCTs. One advantage of the multiple-choice discourse completion tasks is that, like the WDCTs, they are relatively easy to administer because they are in a paper-and-pencil format, which lends itself to large-scale group testing. They are also relatively easy to score; even a machine can do it. However, MDCTs also have disadvantages in that they require only written receptive language and therefore do not encourage oral production. MDCTs also fail to promote self-reflection of any kind.

ODCTs. The advantages of the oral discourse completion tasks are that they encourage oral production (both listening and speaking), and they turn out to be relatively quick to administer. However, ODCTs also have disadvantages in that they are relatively difficult to administer because they require the use of two audiocassette recorders or of elaborate language laboratory equipment. ODCTs are also difficult to score because they require recruiting, training, scheduling, and paying of raters.

DRPTs. The advantages of the discourse role-play tasks are that they encourage oral production (both listening and speaking), and they turn out to be relatively quick to administer. However, DRPTs also have disadvantages in that they are relatively difficult to administer because they must be administered individually using video equipment and an interlocutor, who must be trained and paid. DRPTs are also difficult to score because they require recruiting, training, scheduling, and paying of raters.

DSATs. The advantages of the discourse self-assessment tasks are that they encourage self-reflection on pragmatics ability, and they are relatively easy to administer because they are in a paper-and-pencil format, which is fairly quick and lends itself to large-scale group testing. DSATs are also relatively easy to score. However, one major disadvantage of the DSATs is that, like all self-assessment tests, they are generally not useful for high-stakes decisions (decisions that are very important to the students' futures, progress, etc.).

RPSAs. The advantages of the role-play self-assessments are that they encourage self-reflection on pragmatics ability, and they are relatively easy to score. However, there are also disadvantages: RPSAs are relatively difficult to administer because they must be administered individually using video equipment, and they are also unsuitable for high-stakes decisions (decisions that are very important to the students' futures, progress, etc.).

Conclusion

This comparison of the EFL and ESL results has clearly revealed that the six original English-language versions of the pragmatics tests generally did not work as well as the Japanese translations of those original versions in terms of the amounts of variance they produced, their reliability, and their intercorrelations. In addition, the factor analyses indicated that the EFL tests were probably subject to stronger method effects than the JSL tests. However, that does not mean that the EFL tasks should be abandoned. With different samples of higher or lower pragmatics abilities or wider ranges of abilities, the results might have been more comparable between the two studies or even reversed. In any case, readers who are interested in selecting the best options for testing pragmatics in their teaching or research would be most interested in the comparisons among the six types of measures within each group. To help such readers, Table 8

TABLE 8. RANKINGS FOR THE SIX PRAGMATICS TESTS FOR THE EFL AND JSL STUDIES SEPARATELY

Test characteristics	EFL Study						JSL study					
	WDCT	MDCT	ODCT	DRPT	DSAT	RPSA	WDCT	MDCT	ODCT	DRPT	DSAT	RPSA
Easiness: High to low mean	1	6	5	3.5	2	3.5	2	6	1	5	3	4
High to low variance	6	2	5	4	1	3	6	5	4	1	3	2
High to low reliability	6	5	4	3	1	2	5	6	2	1	4	3
Low to high SEM	3	6	5	2	1	4	3	6	1	2	5	4
Low to high validity	3	6	1	2	4.5	4.5	3	6	1	2	4	5
Easy to difficult to administer	2.5	2.5	4	6	1	5	2.5	2.5	4	6	1	5
Easy to difficult to score	4	1	5	6	2.5	2.5	4	1	5	6	2.5	2.5
Encourages to discourages oral language	4.5	4.5	2	1	4.5	4.5	4.5	4.5	2	1	4.5	4.5
Encourages to discourages self-reflection	4.5	4.5	4.5	4.5	2	1	4.5	4.5	4.5	4.5	2	1
Suitable to unsuitable for high-stakes decisions	2.5	2.5	2.5	2.5	5.5	5.5	2.5	2.5	2.5	2.5	5.5	5.5
TOTAL	37	40	38	34.5	25	35.5	37	44	27	31	34.5	36.5
TOTAL RANK	4	6	5	2	1	3	5	6	1	2	3	4

Note: All rankings are from 1 to 6.

examines the EFL and JSL results separately and ranks the six types of tests for each of the following characteristics: easiness, variance, reliability, validity, ease of administration, ease of scoring, degree of oral language, degree of self-reflection, and suitability for high-stakes decisions.

Degree of *easiness* was judged by comparing the means of the various tests and ranking them 1 to 6 from the easiest (the highest mean) to the hardest (the lowest means). The *variance* was ranked 1 to 6 from the highest standard deviation to the lowest. Similarly, the *reliability* rankings were 1 to 6 from the highest reliability estimate to the lowest. The rankings for the SEM were ordered from 1 to 6 for the lowest SEMs to the highest. Judgments about *validity* were based on the average correlation of each measure with all others, and ranked 1 to 6 from the highest average correlation to lowest. *Ease of administration* was ranked easy to difficult from 1 to 6 based on ease and quickness of administration, with paper-and-pencil tests being viewed as easier to administer than others. *Ease of scoring* was ranked easy to difficult from 1 to 6 based on the notion that mechanical scoring is generally easier than any scoring that requires recruiting, training, scheduling, and paying raters. In addition, within the various rating schemes, scoring written material was considered easier than scoring cassette tapes or videotapes (or first transcribing either before scoring them). The *degree of oral language* was ranked in terms of the amount of oral language encouraged in the various tests based on the notion that the DRPT and ODCT both encourage the use of oral language in that order, whereas the other tests do not (and thus all share the same ranking of 4.5). Similarly, the *degree of self-reflection* was ranked in terms of the amount of self-reflection encouraged by the tests based on the notion that the RPSA and DSAT both encourage self-reflection in that order, whereas the other tests do not (and thus all share the same ranking of 4.5). The reverse is true for the rankings for *suitability for high-stakes decisions.* Self-ratings are not generally felt to be very useful for high-stakes decisions because students who have good reasons to do so will tend to rate themselves very high even if they do not believe that to be a true rating of their abilities. Hence, the DSAT and RPSA share a ranking of 5.5, whereas the other tests are all about equally suitable for high-stakes so they share the ranking of 2.5.

The totals in the second row from the bottom indicate the overall relative standing of the six types of tests within each study with all of the characteristics equally weighted. The total rankings at the bottom show how the six tests in each study compare (with all characteristics equally weighted). Thus it would appear in the EFL study that from best to worst the measures would be ranked overall as follows: DSAT, DRPT, RPSA, WDCT, ODCT, and MDCT. In contrast the overall rankings in the JSL study from best to worst would be as follows: ODCT, DRPT, DSAT, RPSA, WDCT, and MDCT. The only thing the two studies' rankings have in common is the fact that the MDCT is dead last in both.

However, these overall rankings may not be of much use to individual teachers and researchers who do not believe that all of the testing characteristics are of equal interest or importance. Such teachers and researchers may want to just consider the type of study (EFL or JSL) that is appropriate and those testing characteristics that are most germane in their classrooms or research projects. To do so, they need only examine the EFL or JSL results (whichever is most appropriate) and look at only those test characteristics that are of interest to them. They could also add up the rankings of just those test characteristics that are of interest, and use the totals to inform their decisions about which type of test to use.

Implications

This comparison of the results of six parallel tests administered to separate EFL and JSL populations clearly illustrates that a test does not in and of itself have certain characteristics. Rather, testing characteristics will vary depending on the version administered (English or Japanese in this case) or population of students to whom it is given. For example, the fact that the ODCT in the JSL study had a K-R21 reliability estimate of .93 is not a characteristic of that test; rather, it is a characteristic of that test when administered in that version to that particular group of JSL students. If the ODCT were administered to a very similar group, it would be reasonable to expect similar results. However, for different versions and different groups, the results might be quite different. For instance, a quite different estimate of .62 was found for the ODCT in the EFL study. Indeed, if either the Japanese or the English versions of the six tests were given to groups with higher or lower abilities, or narrower or wider bands of abilities, the results would probably have been very different.

That said, the English and Japanese versions of these six tests are available (see Hudson, Detmer, & Brown, 1995; Yamashita, 1996a, 1996b), and they have been piloted as reported in Enochs and Yoshitake (1999), Yoshitake (1997), and Yamashita (1996a, 1996b).

The current comparative study points to the statistical and practical aspects of the six tests that are important to test developers and test users alike, whether they be teachers or researchers. The current study can also serve as a point of comparison for anybody using one or more of these tests in the future.

Suggestions for future research

As is often the case in research, the process of doing this comparative study has raised more questions than it has answered. For anyone interested in pursuing research in this area, the following questions are offered as food for thought:

1. Would similar results be obtained if these six tests were administered at other institutions?
2. Would similar results be obtained if these six tests were administered in other languages?
3. What additional types of pragmatics tests ought to be included in such studies, and what are their testing characteristics?
4. Are pragmatics and pragmatic strategies teachable?
5. What strategies and exercises are most effective for teaching pragmatics?
6. Which types of pragmatics tests are most highly related to those strategies and exercises and therefore most appropriate for diagnostic or achievement testing in a pragmatics curriculum?
7. If pragmatics strategies are teachable, what are the criterion-referenced characteristics of these six test types (necessarily based on a pretest and posttest design)? How large are the gains that are made between the pretest and posttest on each of the types of tests? And, which tests are most sensitive to a pragmatics curriculum?
8. Item by item, how large are the gains that are made between the pretest and posttest on each of the types of tests? And, which items and item types are most sensitive to such a pragmatics curriculum?

References

ACTFL (American Council on the Teaching of Foreign Languages). (1986). *ACTFL proficiency guidelines.* Hastings-on-Hudson, NY: ACTFL.

ACTFL (American Council on the Teaching of Foreign Languages). (1999). *ACTFL proficiency guidelines* (rev. ed.). Hastings-on-Hudson, NY: ACTFL.

Agar, M. (1985). Institutional discourse. *Text, 5,* 147–168.

Alanen, R. (1995). Input enhancement and rule presentation in second language acquisition. In R. Schmidt (Ed.), *Attention and awareness in foreign language learning* (Technical Report #9) (pp. 259–302). Honolulu: University of Hawai'i, Second Language Teaching and Curriculum Center.

Alderson, J. (1988). New procedures for validating proficiency tests of ESP? Theory and practice. *Language Testing, 5,* 220–232.

Allen, P., Fröhlich, M., & Spada, N. (1984). The communicative orientation of language teaching: An observation scheme. In J. Handscombe, R. Orem, & B. Taylor (Eds.), *On TESOL '83* (pp. 231–252). Washington, DC: TESOL.

Allwright, D. (1988). *Observation in the language classroom.* London: Longman.

Allwright, D., & Bailey, K. (1991). *Focus on the language classroom: An introduction to classroom research for language teachers.* Cambridge: Cambridge University Press.

Babbie, E. (1998). *The practice of social research* (8th ed.). Belmont, CA: Wadsworth.

Bachman, L. (1988). Language testing: SLA research interfaces. *Annual Review of Applied Linguistics, 9,* 193–209.

Bachman, L. (1990). *Fundamental considerations in language testing.* Oxford: Oxford University Press.

Bachman, L., & Palmer, A. (1982a). The construct validation of some components of communicative proficiency. *TESOL Quarterly, 16,* 449–465.

Bachman, L., & Palmer, A. (1982b). A scoring format for rating components of communicative proficiency in speaking. Paper presented at the Preconference on Oral Proficiency Assessment, Georgetown University, Washington, DC.

Bachman, L., & Palmer, A. (1996). *Language testing in practice: Designing and developing useful language tests.* Oxford: Oxford University Press.

Bachman, L., & Savignon, S. (1986). The evaluation of communicative language proficiency: A critique of the ACTFL oral interview. *Modern Language Journal, 70,* 380–390.

Bailey, K. (1983). Competitiveness and anxiety in adult second language learning: Looking at and through the diary studies. In H. Seliger & M. Long (Eds.), *Classroom oriented research in second language acquisition* (pp. 67–103). Rowley, MA: Newbury House.

Bardovi-Harlig, K. (1992). Pragmatics as a part of teacher education. *TESOL Journal, 1,* 28–32.

Bardovi-Harlig, K. (1996). Pragmatics and language teaching: Bringing pragmatics and pedagogy together. In L. Bouton (Ed.), *Pragmatics and language learning,* monograph series vol. 7 (pp. 21–39). Urbana-Champaign: Division of English as an International Language, University of Illinois, Urbana-Champaign.

Bardovi-Harlig, K. (1997). The place of second language acquisition theory in language teacher preparation. In K. Bardovi-Harlig & B. Hartford (Eds.), *Beyond methods: Components of language teacher education* (pp. 18–41). New York: McGraw-Hill.

Bardovi-Harlig, K. (1999a). Exploring the interlanguage of interlanguage pragmatics: A research agenda for acquisitional pragmatics. *Language Learning, 49,* 677–713.

Bardovi-Harlig, K. (1999b). Researching method. In L. Bouton (Ed.), *Pragmatics and language learning,* monograph series vol. 9 (pp. 237–264). Urbana-Champaign: Division of English as an International Language, University of Illinois, Urbana-Champaign.

Bardovi-Harlig, K., & Dörnyei, Z. (1998). Do language learners recognize pragmatic violations? Pragmatic versus grammatical awareness in instructed L2 learning. *TESOL Quarterly, 32,* 233–262.

Bardovi-Harlig, K., & Hartford, B. (1990). Congruence in native and nonnative conversations: Status balance in the academic advising session. *Language Learning, 40,* 467–501.

Bardovi-Harlig, K., & Hartford, B. (1991). Saying "no" in English: Native and nonnative rejections. In L. Bouton & Y. Kachru (Eds.), *Pragmatics and language learning,* monograph series vol. 2 (pp. 41–57). Urbana-Champaign: Division of English as an International Language, University of Illinois, Urbana-Champaign.

Bardovi-Harlig, K., & Hartford, B. (1993). Learning the rules of academic talk: A longitudinal study of pragmatic change. *Studies in Second Language Acquisition, 15,* 279–304.

Bardovi-Harlig, K., & Hartford, B. (1996). Input in an institutional setting. *Studies in Second Language Acquisition, 17,* 171–188.

Bardovi-Harlig, K., Hartford, B., Mahan-Taylor, R., Morgan, M., & Reynolds, D. (1991). Developing pragmatic awareness: Closing the conversation. *ELT Journal, 45,* 4–15.

Barnlund, D., & Yoshioka, M. (1990). Apologies: Japanese and American styles. *International Journal of Intercultural Relations, 14,* 193–206.

Béal, C. (1990). It's all in the asking: A perspective on cross-cultural communication between native speakers of French and native speakers of Australian English in the workplace. In A. Pauwels (Ed.), *Cross-cultural communication in the professions in Australia* (pp. 23–52). Melbourne: Applied Linguistics Association of Australia.

Béal, C. (1992). Did you have a good weekend? Or why there is no such thing as a simple question in cross-cultural encounters? *Australian Review of Applied Linguistics, 15,* 23–52.

Beebe, L., & Takahashi, T. (1989a). Do you have a bag? Social status and patterned variation in second language acquisition. In S. Gass, C. Madden, D. Preston, & L. Selinker (Eds.), *Variation in second language acquisition* (pp. 103–125). Clevedon, Avon: Multilingual Matters.

Beebe, L., & Takahashi, T. (1989b). Sociolinguistic variation in face-threatening speech acts: Chastisement and disagreement. In M. Eisenstein (Ed.), *The dynamic interlanguage: Empirical studies in second language variation* (pp. 199–218). New York: Plenum Press.

Beebe, L., Takahashi, T., & Uliss-Weltz, R. (1990). Pragmatic transfer in ESL refusals. In R. Scarcella, E. Andersen, & S. Krashen (Eds.), *Developing communicative competence in a second language* (pp. 55–73). New York: Newbury House.

Bergman, M., & Kasper, G. (1993). Perception and performance in native and nonnative apology. In G. Kasper & S. Blum-Kulka (Eds.), *Interlanguage pragmatics* (pp. 82–107). Oxford: Oxford University Press.

Bialystok, E. (1991). Achieving proficiency in a second language: A processing description. In R. Phillipson, E. Kellerman, L. Selinker, M. Sharwood Smith, & M. Swain (Eds.), *Foreign/second language pedagogy research: A commemorative volume for Claus Færch* (pp. 63–78). Philadelphia: Multilingual Matters.

Bialystok, E. (1993). Symbolic representation and attentional control in pragmatic competence. In G. Kasper & S. Blum-Kulka (Eds.), *Interlanguage pragmatics* (pp. 43–57). New York: Oxford University Press.

Bilbow, G., & Yeung, S. (1998). Learning the pragmatics of 'successful' impression management. *Pragmatics, 8,* 405–417.

Billmyer, K. (1990a). The effect of formal instruction on the development of sociolinguistic competence: The performance of compliments. Unpublished doctoral dissertation, University of Pennsylvania, Philadelphia.

Billmyer, K. (1990b). "I really like your lifestyle": ESL learners learning how to compliment. *Penn Working Papers in Educational Linguistics, 6,* 31–48.

Billmyer, K., Jakar, V., & Lee, M. (1989). The representation of sociolinguistic features in TESOL materials. Paper presented at the 23rd Annual TESOL Conference, San Antonio, Texas, March.

Blum-Kulka, S. (1982). Learning to say what you mean in a second language: A study of speech act performance of learners of Hebrew as a second language. *Applied Linguistics, 3,* 29–59.

Blum-Kulka, S. (1983). Interpreting and performing speech acts in a second language: A cross-cultural study of Hebrew and English. In N. Wolfson & E. Judd (Eds.), *Sociolinguistics and language acquisition* (pp. 36–55). New York: Newbury House.

Blum-Kulka, S. (1987). Indirectness and politeness in requests: Same or different? *Journal of Pragmatics, 11,* 131–146.

Blum-Kulka, S. (1991). Interlanguage pragmatics: The case of requests. In R. Phillipson, E. Kellerman, L. Selinker, M. Sharwood Smith, & M. Swain (Eds.), *Foreign/second language pedagogy research: A commemorative volume for Claus Færch* (pp. 255–272). Clevedon, Avon: Multilingual Matters.

Blum-Kulka, S., & House, J. (1989). Cross-cultural and situational variation in requesting behavior. In S. Blum-Kulka, J. House, & G. Kasper (Eds.), *Cross-cultural pragmatics: Requests and apologies* (pp. 123–154). Norwood, NJ: Ablex.

Blum-Kulka, S., House, J., & Kasper, G. (Eds.). (1989). *Cross-cultural pragmatics: Requests and apologies.* Norwood, NJ: Ablex.

Blum-Kulka, S., & Olshtain, E. (1986). Too many words: Length of utterance and pragmatic failure. *Studies in Second Language Acquisition, 8,* 165–180.

Bodman, J., & Eisenstein, M. (1988). May God increase your bounty: The expression of gratitude in English by native and nonnative speakers. *Cross Currents, 15,* 1–21.

Bolten, J. (1993). Interaktiv-interkulturelles Fremdsprachlernen [Interactive-intercultural foreign language teaching]. In H. Kelz (Ed.), *Internationale kommunikation und Sprachkomptenz* [International communication and language competence] (pp. 124–132). Bonn: Dümmler.

Bonikowska, M. (1988). The choice of opting out. *Applied Linguistics, 9,* 169–181.

Bouton, L. (1988). A cross-cultural study of the ability to interpret implicatures in English. *World Englishes, 7,* 183–197.

Bouton, L. (1990). The effective use of implicature in English: Why and how it should be taught in the ESL classroom. In L. Bouton & Y. Kachru (Eds.), *Pragmatics and language learning,* monograph series vol. 1 (pp. 43–51). Urbana-Champaign: Division of English as an International Language, University of Illinois, Urbana-Champaign.

Bouton, L. (1992). The interpretation of implicature in English by NNS: Does it come automatically – without being explicitly taught? In L. Bouton & Y. Kachru (Eds.), *Pragmatics and language learning,* monograph series vol. 3 (pp. 53–65). Urbana-Champaign: Division of English as an International Language, University of Illinois, Urbana-Champaign.

Bouton, L. (1994a). Can NNS skill in interpreting implicatures in American English be improved through explicit instruction? A pilot study. In L. Bouton & Y. Kachru (Eds.), *Pragmatics and language learning,* monograph series vol. 5 (pp. 88–109). Urbana-Champaign: Division of English as an International Language, University of Illinois, Urbana-Champaign.

Bouton, L. (1994b). Conversational implicature in the second language: Learned slowly when not deliberately taught. *Journal of Pragmatics, 22,* 157–167.

Bouton, L. (1996). Pragmatics and language learning. In L. Bouton (Ed.), *Pragmatics and language learning,* monograph series vol. 7 (pp. 1–20). Urbana-Champaign: Division of English as an International Language, University of Illinois, Urbana-Champaign.

Boxer, D. (1993). Complaints as positive strategies: What the learner needs to know. *TESOL Quarterly, 27,* 277–299.

Boxer, D., & Pickering, L. (1995). Problems in the presentation of speech acts in ELT materials: The case of complaints. *ELT Journal, 49,* 44–58.

Braun, F. (1984). *Die Leistungsfähigkeit der von Brown/Gilman und Brown/Ford eingeführten anredetheoretischen Kategorien bei der praktischen Analyse von Anredesystemen* [The adequacy of theoretical categories of address introduced by Brown/Gilman and Brown/Ford for the practical analysis of address systems]. In W. Winter (Ed.), *Anredeverhalten* [Address behavior] (pp. 41–72). Tübingen: Narr.

Braun, F., Kohz, A., & Schuber, K. (1986). *Anredeforschung: Kommentierte Bibliographie zur Soziolinguistik der Anrede* [Address research: Annotated bibliography on the sociolinguistics of address]. Tübingen: Narr.

Braun, R. (1988). *Terms of address: Problems of patterns and usage in various language and cultures.* New York: Mouton de Gruyter.

Brown, J. (1983). A closer look at cloze: Validity and reliability. In J. Oller (Ed.), *Issues in language testing research* (pp. 237–250). Rowley, MA: Newbury House.

Brown, J. (1984). A cloze is a cloze is a cloze? In J. Handscombe, R. Orem, & B. Taylor (Eds.), *On TESOL '83* (pp. 109–119). Washington, DC: TESOL.

Brown, J. (1993). What are the characteristics of natural cloze tests? *Language Testing, 10,* 93–116.

Brown, J., & Yamashita, S. (1995a). English language entrance examinations at Japanese universities: 1993 and 1994. In J. Brown & S. Yamashita (Eds.), *Language testing in Japan* (pp. 86–100). Tokyo: Japan Association for Language Teaching.

Brown, J., & Yamashita, S. (1995b). English language entrance examinations at Japanese universities: What do we know about them? *JALT Journal, 17,* 7–30.

Brown, P., & Levinson, S. (1987). *Politeness: Some universals in language use.* Cambridge: Cambridge University Press.

Brown, R., & Ford, M. (1964). Address in American English. In D. Hymes (Ed.), *Language in culture and society* (pp. 234–244). New York: Harper and Row.

Brown, R., & Gilman, A. (1960). The pronouns of power and solidarity. In T. Sebeok (Ed.), *Style in language* (pp. 253–276). Cambridge: MIT Press.

Brown, R., & Gilman, A. (1989). Politeness theory and Shakespeare's four major tragedies. *Language in Society, 18,* 159–212.

Buttjes, D., & Byram, M. (1990). *Mediating languages and cultures.* Clevedon: Multilingual Matters.

Byram, M., & Zarate, G. (1994). *Définitions, objectifs et évaluation de la compétence socio-culturelle* [Definitions, objectives, and evaluation of sociocultural competence]. Strasbourg: Report for the Council of Europe.

Campbell, C. (1996). Socializing with the teachers and prior language learning experience: A diary study. In K. Bailey & D. Nunan (Eds.), *Voices from the classroom* (pp. 201–223). Cambridge: Cambridge University Press.

Campbell, R., & Wales, R. (1970). The study of language acquisition. In J. Lyons (Ed.), *New horizons in linguistics* (pp. 242–260). Harmondsworth: Penguin.

Canale, M. (1983). From communicative competence to language pedagogy. In J. Richards & R. Schmidt (Eds.), *Language and communication* (pp. 2–27). London: Longman.

Canale, M., & Swain, M. (1980). Theoretical bases of communicative approaches to second language teaching and testing. *Applied Linguistics, 1,* 1–47.

Carrell, P. (1979). Indirect speech acts in ESL: Indirect answers. In C. Yorio, K. Perkins, & J. Schachter (Eds.), *On TESOL '79: The learner in focus* (pp. 297–307). Washington, DC: TESOL.

Carrell, P. (1981). Relative difficulty of request forms in L1/L2 comprehension. In M. Hines & W. Rutherford (Eds.), *On TESOL '81* (pp. 141–152). Washington, DC: TESOL.

Carrell, P., & Konneker, B. (1981). Politeness: Comparing native and non-native judgments. *Language Learning, 31,* 17–30.

Carroll, S., Swain, M., & Roberge, Y. (1992). The role of feedback in adult second language acquisition: Error correction and morphological generalizations. *Applied Psycholinguistics, 13,* 173–198.

Cazden, C. (1986). Classroom discourse. In M. Wittrock (Ed.), *Handbook of research on teaching* (3rd ed., pp. 433–463). New York: Macmillan.

Center for Applied Linguistics. (1995a). *German speaking test.* Washington, DC: Center for Applied Linguistics.

Center for Applied Linguistics. (1995b). *Rater training kit for the German speaking test.* Washington, DC: Center for Applied Linguistics.

Chaudron, C. (1988). *Second language classrooms.* Cambridge: Cambridge University Press.

Chaudron, C. (1998). Contrasting approaches to classroom research: Qualitative and quantitative analysis of language use and learning. Plenary address, 16th Congreso nacional de la Asociación Española de Lingüística Aplicada, Logroño, April.

Chen, R. (1993). Responding to compliments: A contrastive study of politeness strategies between American English and Chinese speakers. *Journal of Pragmatics, 20,* 49–75.

Chomsky, N. (1965). *Aspects of the theory of syntax.* Cambridge: MIT Press.

Chomsky, N. (1980). *Rules and representations.* New York: Columbia University Press.

Clancy, P. (1985). The acquisition of Japanese. In D. Slobin (Ed.), *The crosslinguistic study of language acquisition,* vol. 1: *The data* (pp. 373–524). Hillsdale, NJ: Lawrence Erlbaum.

Clark, H. (1979). Responding to indirect speech acts. *Cognitive Psychology, 11,* 430–477.

Clark, J., & Clifford, R. (1988). The FSI/ACTFL proficiency scales and testing techniques: Development, current status, and needed research. *Studies in Second Language Acquisition, 10,* 129–147.

Clément, R., Dörnyei, Z., & Noels, K. (1994). Motivation, self-confidence, and group cohesion in the foreign language classroom. *Language Learning, 44,* 417–448.

Cohen, A. (1996). Developing the ability to perform speech acts. *Studies in Second Language Acquisition, 18,* 253–267.

Cohen, A. (1997). Developing pragmatic ability: Insights from the accelerated study of Japanese. In H. Cook, K. Hijirida, & M. Tahara (Eds.), *New trends and issues in teaching Japanese language and culture* (Technical Report #15) (pp. 133–159). Honolulu: University of Hawai'i, Second Language Teaching and Curriculum Center.

Cohen, A. (1998). *Strategies in learning and using a second language.* London: Longman.

Cohen, A., & Olshtain, E. (1981). Developing a measure of sociocultural competence: The case of apology. *Language Learning, 31,* 113–134.

Cohen, A., & Olshtain, E. (1993). The production of speech acts by EFL learners. *TESOL Quarterly, 27,* 33–56.

Cohen, A., & Olshtain, E. (1994). Researching the production of second-language speech acts. In E. Tarone, S. Gass, & A. Cohen (Eds.), *Research methodology in second language acquisition* (pp. 143–156). Hillsdale, NJ: Lawrence Erlbaum.

Cohen, A., Olshtain, E., & Rosenstein, D. (1986). Advanced EFL apologies: What remains to be learned? *International Journal of the Sociology of Language, 62,* 51–74.

Cook, H. (1991). The Japanese sentence-final particle *yo* as a non-referential indexical. Paper presented at the Second International Cognitive Linguistics Conference, University of California, Santa Cruz, July.

Cook, H. (1992). Meanings of non-referential indexes: A case study of Japanese sentence-final particle *ne. Text, 12,* 507–539.

Cook, H. (1999). Situational meaning of the Japanese social deixis: The mixed use of the *masu* and plain forms. *Journal of Linguistic Anthropology, 8,* 1–24.

Cook, V. (1999). Going beyond the native speaker in language teaching. *TESOL Quarterly, 33,* 185–209.

Coulmas, F. (Ed.). (1981a). *Conversational routine: Explorations in standardized communication situations and prepatterned speech.* The Hague: Mouton.

Coulmas, F. (1981b). 'Poison to your soul': Thanks and apologies contrastively viewed. In F. Coulmas (Ed.), *Conversational routine: Explorations in standardized communication situations and prepatterned speech* (pp. 69–91). The Hague: Mouton.

Crozet, C. (1996). Teaching verbal interaction and culture in the language classroom. *Australian Review of Applied Linguistics, 19,* 37–58.

Crozet, C., & Liddicoat, A. (1998). Reconnaissance et ajustement dans l'interaction française [Acknowledgment and affiliation in French interaction]. In B. Caron (Ed.), *Proceedings of the 16th International Congress of Linguists.* Oxford: Pergamon.

Crozet, C., & Liddicoat, A. (1999). The challenge of intercultural language teaching: Engaging with culture in the classroom. In J. Lo Bianco, A. Liddicoat, & C. Crozet (Eds.), *Striving for the third place intercultural competence through language education* (pp. 113–126). Canberra: Language Australia.

Crozet, C., Liddicoat, A., & Lo Bianco, J. (1999). Intercultural competence: From language policy to language education. In J. Lo Bianco, A. Liddicoat, & C. Crozet (Eds.), *Striving for the third place intercultural competence through language education* (pp. 1–20). Canberra: Language Australia.

Crystal, D. (Ed.). (1997). *The Cambridge encyclopedia of language* (2nd ed.). New York: Cambridge University Press.

Decoo, W. (1996). The induction–deduction opposition: Ambiguities and complexities of the didactic reality. *IRAL, 34,* 95–118.

Delisle, H. (1986). Intimacy, solidarity and distance: The pronouns of address in German. *Die Unterrichtspraxis, 19,* 4–15.

Delisle, H. (1993). Forms of address in academic settings: A contrastive analysis. *Die Unterrichtspraxis, 26,* 22–26.

Dittmar, N., & Stutterheim, C. (1984). Communication strategies of migrants in interethnic interaction. In P. Auer & A. DiLuzio (Eds.), *Interpretive Sociolinguistics* (pp. 179–214). Tübingen: Narr.

Doughty, C. (1991). Second language instruction does make a difference: Evidence from an empirical study of SL relativization. *Studies in Second Language Acquisition, 13,* 431–469.

Doughty, C., & Varela, E. (1998). Communicative focus on form. In C. Doughty & J. Williams (Eds.), *Focus on form in classroom second language acquisition* (pp. 114–138). Cambridge: Cambridge University Press.

Doughty, C., & Williams, J. (Eds.). (1998). *Focus on form in classroom second language acquisition.* Cambridge: Cambridge University Press.

Douglas, D. (1994). Quantity and quality in speaking test performance. *Language Testing, 11,* 125–144.

Duranti, A. (1997). *Linguistic Anthropology.* Cambridge: Cambridge University Press.

Duranti, A., & Goodwin, C. (Eds.). (1992). *Rethinking context.* Cambridge: Cambridge University Press.

Edmondson, W. (1982). On the determination of meaning in discourse. *Linguistische Berichte, 78,* 33–42.

Edmondson, W., & House, J. (1981). *Let's talk and talk about it: A pedagogic-interactive grammar of English.* Munich: Urban and Schwarzenberg.

Edmondson, W., & House, J. (1991). Do learners talk too much? The waffle phenomenon in interlanguage pragmatics. In R. Phillipson, E. Kellerman, L. Selinker, M. Sharwood Smith, & M. Swain (Eds.), *Foreign/second language pedagogy research: A commemorative volume for Claus Færch* (pp. 273–287). Clevedon, Avon: Multilingual Matters.

Edmondson, W., House, J., Kasper, G., & Stemmer, B. (1984). Learning the pragmatics of discourse: A project report. *Applied Linguistics, 5,* 113–127.

Ehlich, K., & Rehbein, J. (1979). Sprachliche Handlungsmuster [Linguistic action patterns]. In H. Soeffner (Ed.), *Interpretative Verfahren in den Sozial-und Textwissenschaften* [Interpretive methods in the social and text sciences] (pp. 243–274). Stuttgart: Metzler.

Eisenstein, M., & Bodman, J. (1986). "I very appreciate": Expressions of gratitude by native and nonnative speakers of American English. *Applied Linguistics, 7,* 167–185.

Eisenstein, M., & Bodman, J. (1993). Expressing gratitude in American English. In G. Kasper & S. Blum-Kulka (Eds.), *Interlanguage pragmatics* (pp. 64–81). Oxford: Oxford University Press.

Ellis, N. (1996). Sequencing in SLA: Phonological memory, chunking, and points of order. *Studies in Second Language Acquisition, 18,* 91–126.

Ellis, R. (1990). *Instructed second language acquisition.* Oxford: Blackwell.

Ellis, R. (1992). Learning to communicate in the classroom: A study of two learners' requests. *Studies in Second Language Acquisition, 14,* 1–23.

Ellis, R. (1994). *The study of second language acquisition.* Oxford: Oxford University Press.

Ellis, R. (1995). Interpretation tasks for grammar teaching. *TESOL Quarterly, 29,* 87–105.

Ellis, R. (1997). *SLA research and language teaching.* Oxford: Oxford University Press.

Enochs, K., & Yoshitake-Strain, S. (1999). Evaluating six measures of EFL learners' pragmatic competence. *JALT Journal, 21,* 29–50.

Erickson, F., & Shultz, J. (1982). *The counselor as gatekeeper.* New York: Academic Press.

Ericsson, K., & Simon, H. (1993). *Protocol analysis: Verbal reports as data* (rev. ed.). Cambridge: MIT Press.

Erikson, F. (1975). Gatekeeping and the melting pot: Interaction in counseling encounters. *Harvard Educational Review, 45,* 44–70.

Færch, C., & Kasper, G. (1989). Internal and external modification in interlanguage request realization. In S. Blum-Kulka, J. House, & G. Kasper (Eds.), *Cross-cultural pragmatics: Requests and apologies* (pp. 221–247). Norwood, NJ: Ablex.

Falsgraf, C., & Majors, D. (1995). Implicit culture in Japanese immersion classroom discourse. *Journal of the Association of Teachers of Japanese, 29,* 1–21.

Fanselow, J. (1977). Beyond Rashomon: Conceptualizing and describing the teaching act. *TESOL Quarterly, 11,* 17–39.

Fantini, A. (Ed.). (1997). *New ways of teaching culture.* Washington, DC: TESOL.

Fiksdal, S. (1989). Framing uncomfortable moments in cross-cultural gatekeeping interviews. In S. Gass, C. Madden, D. Preston, & L. Selinker (Eds.), *Variation in second language acquisition: Discourse and pragmatics* (pp. 190–207). Clevedon, Avon: Multilingual Matters.

Fillmore, C. (1976). Pragmatics and the description of discourse. In S. Schmidt (Ed.), *Pragmatik/Pragmatics 2* (pp. 83–104). Munich: Fink.

Fillmore, C. (1979). On fluency. In C. Fillmore, D. Kempler, & W. Wang (Eds.), *Individual differences in language ability and language behavior* (pp. 85–101). New York: Academic Press.

Fotos, S. (1993). Consciousness raising and noticing through focus on form: Grammar task performance versus formal instruction. *Applied Linguistics, 14,* 385–407.

Fowler, F. (1993). *Survey research methods* (2nd ed.). Newbury Park, CA: Sage.

Fraser, B. (1981). On apologizing. In F. Coulmas (Ed.), *Conversational routine: Explorations in standardized communication situations and prepatterned speech* (pp. 259–271). The Hague: Mouton.

Fraser, B. (1990). Perspectives on politeness. *Journal of Pragmatics, 14,* 219–236.

Fraser, B., Rintell, E., & Walters, J. (1980). An approach to conducting research on the acquisition of pragmatic competence in a second language. In D. Larsen-Freeman (Ed.), *Discourse analysis in second language research* (pp. 75–91). Rowley, MA: Newbury House.

Freed, A. (1994). The forms and functions of questions in informal dyadic conversation. *Journal of Pragmatics, 21,* 621–644.

Frölich, M., Spada, N., & Allen, P. (1985). Differences in the communicative orientation of L2 classrooms. *TESOL Quarterly, 19,* 27–57.

Fukushima, S. (1990). Offers and requests: Performance by Japanese learners of English. *World Englishes, 9,* 317–325.

Fukuya, Y. (1998). Consciousness-raising of downgraders in requests. Paper presented at Second Language Research Forum, University of Hawai'i, Manoa, October.

Fukuya, Y., & Clark, M. (in press). Input enhancement of mitigators. In L. Bouton (Ed.), *Pragmatics and language learning,* monograph series vol. 10. Urbana-Champaign: Division of English as an International Language, University of Illinois, Urbana-Champaign.

Fukuya, Y., Reeve, M., Gisi, J., & Christianson, M. (1998). Does focus on form work for sociopragmatics? Paper presented at the 12th Annual International Conference on Pragmatics and Language Learning, University of Illinois, Urbana-Champaign, April.

Fulcher, G. (1996). Invalidating validity claims for the ACTFL oral rating scale. *System, 24,* 163–172.

Gall, S. (1992). Children's instrumental help-seeking: Its role in the social acquisition and construction of knowledge. In R. Hertz-Lazarowitz & N. Miller (Eds.), *Interaction in cooperative groups: The theoretical anatomy of group learning* (pp. 49–68). Cambridge: Cambridge University Press.

García, C. (1989). Apologizing in English: Politeness strategies used by native and nonnative speakers. *Multilingua, 8,* 3–20.

Grice, P. (1975). Logic and conversation. In P. Cole & J. Morgan (Eds.), *Syntax and Semantics,* vol. 3: *Speech acts* (pp. 41–58). New York: Academic Press.

Grotjahn, R. (1991). The research program subjective theories: A new approach in second language research. *Studies in Second Language Acquisition, 13,* 187–214.

Groves, R. (1996). How do we know what we think they think is really what they think? In N. Schwarz & S. Sudman (Eds.), *Answering questions: Methodology for determining cognitive and communicative processes in survey research* (pp. 389–402). San Francisco: Jossey-Bass.

Gudykunst, W., & Kim, Y. (1992). *Communicating with strangers: An approach to intercultural communication.* New York: McGraw-Hill.

Gumperz, J. (1982a). *Discourse strategies.* Cambridge: Cambridge University Press.

Gumperz, J. (1982b). *Language and social identity.* Cambridge: Cambridge University Press.

Gumperz, J. (1992). Contextualization and understanding. In A. Duranti & C. Goodwin (Eds.), *Rethinking context* (pp. 229–252). Cambridge: Cambridge University Press.

Gumperz, J. (1996). The linguistic and cultural relativity of conversational inference. In J. Gumperz & S. Levinson (Eds.), *Rethinking linguistic relativity* (pp. 374–406). Cambridge: Cambridge University Press.

Gumperz, J., Judd, T., & Roberts, C. (1979). *Crosstalk: A study of cross-cultural communication. Background materials and notes to accompany the BBC film.* Southall: National Centre for Industrial Language Training.

Gumperz, J., & Levinson, S. (1996). Introduction: Linguistic relativity re-examined. In J. Gumperz & S. Levinson (Eds.), *Rethinking linguistic relativity* (pp. 1–18). Cambridge: Cambridge University Press.

Habermas, J. (1984). *The theory of communicative action,* vol. 1. London: Heinemann.

Hadley, A. (1993). *Teaching language in context.* Boston: Heinle and Heinle.

Hakuta, K. (1974). Prefabricated patterns and the emergence of structure in second language acquisition. *Language Learning, 24,* 287–297.

Hall, J. (1995a). 'Aw, man, where you goin'?': Classroom interaction and the development of L2 interactional competence. *Issues in Applied Linguistics, 6,* 37–62.

Hall, J. (1995b). (Re)creating our worlds with words: A sociohistorical perspective of face-to-face interaction. *Applied Linguistics, 16,* 206–232.

Hall, J. (1998). Differential teacher attention to student utterances: The construction of different opportunities for learning in the IRF. *Linguistics and Education, 9,* 287–311.

Hall, J., & Verplaets, L. (Eds.). (2000). *Second and foreign language learning through classroom interaction.* Mahwah, NJ: Erlbaum.

Harley, B., Allen, P., Cummins, J., & Swain, M. (Eds.). (1990a). *The development of second language proficiency*. Cambridge: Cambridge University Press.

Harley, B., Allen, P., Cummins, J., & Swain, M. (1990b). The nature of language proficiency. In B. Harley, P. Allen, J. Cummins, & M. Swain (Eds.), *The development of second language proficiency* (pp. 7–25). Cambridge: Cambridge University Press.

Hartford, B., & Bardovi-Harlig, K. (1992). Experimental and observational data in the study of interlanguage pragmatics. In L. Bouton & Y. Kachru (Eds.), *Pragmatics and language learning,* monograph series vol. 3 (pp. 33–52). Urbana-Champaign: Division of English as an International Language, University of Illinois, Urbana-Champaign.

Hartford, B., & Bardovi-Harlig, K. (1996). "At your earliest convenience": A study of written requests to faculty. In L. Bouton (Ed.), *Pragmatics and language learning,* monograph series vol. 7 (pp. 55–69). Urbana-Champaign: Division of English as an International Language, University of Illinois, Urbana-Champaign.

Hassall, T. (1997). Requests by Australian learners of Indonesian. Unpublished doctoral dissertation, Australian National University, Canberra, Australia.

Hatch, E., & Lazaraton, A. (1991). *The research manual: Design and statistics for applied linguistics*. New York: Newbury House.

He, A. (1997). Learning and being: Identity construction in the classroom. In L. Bouton (Ed.), *Pragmatics and language learning,* monograph series vol. 8 (pp. 201–222). Urbana-Champaign: Division of English as an International Language, University of Illinois, Urbana-Champaign.

Herbert, R. (1986). Say 'thank you' – or something. *American Speech, 61,* 76–88.

Herbert, R. (1989). The ethnography of English compliments and compliment responses: A contrastive sketch. In W. Olesky (Ed.), *Contrastive pragmatics* (pp. 3–35). Amsterdam: John Benjamins.

Herrenkohl, L., & Guerra, M. (1997). Participant structure, scientific discourse, and student engagement in fourth grade. Unpublished manuscript.

Hill, T. (1997). The development of pragmatic competence in an EFL context. Unpublished doctoral dissertation, Temple University, Tokyo, Japan.

Hillocks, G. (1994). Interpreting and counting: Objectivity in discourse analysis. In P. Smagorinsky (Ed.), *Speaking about writing* (pp. 185–204). London: Sage.

Hoffman-Hicks, S. (2000). The development of pragmatic competence: Evidence from French program study abroad participants. Unpublished doctoral dissertation, Indiana University, Bloomington.

Holmes, J. (1986). Compliments and compliment responses in New Zealand English. *Anthropological Linguistics, 28,* 485–508.

Holmes, J. (1988). Doubt and certainty in ESL textbooks. *Applied Linguistics, 9,* 21–44.

Holmes, J., & Brown, D. (1987). Teachers and students learning about compliments. *TESOL Quarterly, 21,* 523–546.

Horiguchi, S. (1990). *Jookyuu nihongo gakushuusha no taiwa ni okeru kikite toshite no gengo koodoo.* [Listening behavior in the conversations of advanced learners of Japanese]. *Nihongo Kyooiku, 71,* 16–32.

House, J. (1986). Learning to talk: Talking to learn. An investigation of learner performance in two types of discourse. In G. Kasper (Ed.), *Learning, teaching and communication in the foreign language classroom* (pp. 43–57). Aarhus: Aarhus University Press.

House, J. (1989). Politeness in English and German: The functions of *please* and *bitte*. In S. Blum-Kulka, J. House, & G. Kasper (Eds.), *Cross-cultural pragmatics: Requests and apologies* (pp. 96–119). Norwood, NJ: Ablex.

House, J. (1996). Developing pragmatic fluency in English as a foreign language: Routines and metapragmatic awareness. *Studies in Second Language Acquisition, 18,* 225–252.

House, J., & Kasper, G. (1981a). Politeness markers in English and German. In F. Coulmas (Ed.), *Conversational routine: Explorations in standardized communication situations and prepatterned speech* (pp. 157–185). The Hague: Mouton.

House, J., & Kasper, G. (1981b). *Zur Rolle der Kognition in Kommunikationskursen* [The role of cognition in communication courses.] *Die Neueren Sprachen, 80,* 42–55.

House, J., & Kasper, G. (1987). Interlanguage pragmatics: Requesting in a foreign language. In W. Lörscher & R. Schulze (Eds.), *Perspectives on language in performance,* vol. 2 (pp. 1250–1288). Tübingen: Narr.

Hudson, T., Detmer, E., & Brown, J. (1992). *A framework for testing cross-cultural pragmatics* (Technical Report #2). Honolulu: University of Hawai'i, Second Language Teaching and Curriculum Center.

Hudson, T., Detmer, E., & Brown, J. (1995). *Developing prototypic measures of cross-cultural pragmatics* (Technical Report #7). Honolulu: University of Hawai'i, Second Language Teaching and Curriculum Center.

Hulstijn, J. (1989). Implicit and incidental second language learning: Experiments in the processing of natural and partly artificial input. In H. Dechert & M. Raupach (Eds.), *Interlingual processes* (pp. 49–73). Tübingen: Narr.

Hymes, D. (1967). Models of the interaction of language and social setting. *Journal of Social Issues, 23,* 8–28.

Hymes, D. (1971). *On communicative competence.* Philadelphia: University of Pennsylvania Press.

Hymes, D. (1972). On communicative competence. In J. Pride & J. Holmes (Eds.), *Sociolinguistics: Selected readings* (pp. 269–293). Harmondsworth: Penguin.

Ide, R. (1998). "Sorry for your kindness": Japanese interactional ritual in public discourse. *Journal of Pragmatics, 29,* 509–529.

Ikoma, T. (1993). "Sorry for giving me a ride": The use of apologetic expressions to show gratitude in Japanese. Unpublished doctoral dissertation, University of Hawai'i at Manoa, Honolulu.

Japan Broadcasting Corporation. (1991). *Standard Japanese course.* Tokyo: Japan Broadcasting Corporation.

Japan Broadcasting Corporation. (1996). *Yasashii nihongo* [Easy Japanese]. Tokyo: Japan Broadcasting Corporation.

Johnston, B., Kasper, G., & Ross, S. (1998). Effect of rejoinders in production questionnaires. *Applied Linguistics, 19,* 157–182.

Jourdenais, R., Ota, M., Stauffer, S., Boyson, B., & Doughty, C. (1995). Does textual enhancement promote noticing: A think-aloud protocol analysis. In R. Schmidt (Ed.), *Attention and awareness in foreign language learning.*

(Technical Report #9) (pp. 183–216). Honolulu: University of Hawai'i, Second Language Teaching and Curriculum Center.

Kamio, A. (1990). *Joohoo no nawabari-riron: Gengo no kinooteki bunseki* [The theory of territory of information: A functional analysis of language]. Tokyo: Taishuukan Shoten.

Kamio, A. (1997). *Territory of information*. Amsterdam: John Benjamins.

Kanagy, R. (1999). Interactional routines as a mechanism for L2 acquisition and socialization in an immersion context. *Journal of Pragmatics, 31,* 1467–1492.

Kanagy, R., & Igarashi, K. (1997). Acquisition of pragmatics competence in a Japanese immersion kindergarten. In L. Bouton (Ed.), *Pragmatics and language learning,* monograph series vol. 8 (pp. 243–265). Urbana-Champaign: Division of English as an International Language, University of Illinois, Urbana-Champaign.

Kasper, G. (1981). *Pragmatische Aspekte in der Interimsprache* [Pragmatic aspects of interlanguage]. Tübingen: Narr.

Kasper, G. (1984). Pragmatic comprehension in learner-native speaker discourse. *Language Learning, 34,* 1–20.

Kasper, G. (1985). Repair in foreign language teaching. *Studies in Second Language Acquisition, 7,* 200–215.

Kasper, G. (1989a). Interactive procedures in interlanguage discourse. In W. Olesky (Ed.), *Contrastive pragmatics* (pp. 189–229). Amsterdam: John Benjamins.

Kasper, G. (1989b). Variation in interlanguage speech act realization. In S. Gass, C. Madden, D. Preston, & L. Selinker (Eds.), *Variation in second language acquisition,* vol. 1: *Discourse and pragmatics* (pp. 37–58). Clevedon, Avon: Multilingual Matters.

Kasper, G. (1992). Pragmatic transfer. *Second Language Research, 8,* 203–231.

Kasper, G. (1995). Routine and indirection in interlanguage pragmatics. In L. Bouton (Ed.), *Pragmatics and language learning,* monograph series vol. 6 (pp. 59–78). Urbana-Champaign: Division of English as an International Language, University of Illinois, Urbana-Champaign.

Kasper, G. (1996). Introduction: Pragmatics in SLA. *Studies in Second Language Acquisition, 18,* 145–148.

Kasper, G. (1997a). Can pragmatic competence be taught? (Net Work #6) [HTML document]. Honolulu: University of Hawai'i, Second Language Teaching & Curriculum Center. http://www.lll.hawaii.edu/nflrc/NetWorks/NW6/[access: May 2, 1997].

Kasper, G. (1997b). The role of pragmatics in language teacher education. In K. Bardovi-Harlig & B. Hartford (Eds.), *Beyond methods: Components of second language teacher education* (pp. 113–136). New York: McGraw-Hill.

Kasper, G. (2000). Four perspectives on L2 pragmatic development. Plenary address, Annual Meeting of the American Association of Applied Linguistics, Vancouver, British Columbia, March.

Kasper, G., & Blum-Kulka, S. (Eds.). (1993). *Interlanguage pragmatics.* Oxford: Oxford University Press.

Kasper, G., & Dahl, M. (1991). Research methods in interlanguage pragmatics. *Studies in Second Language Acquisition, 13,* 215–247.

Kasper, G., & Rose, K. (1999). Pragmatics and second language acquisition. *Annual Review of Applied Linguistics, 19,* 81–104.

Kasper, G., & Rose, K. (in press). *Research methods in pragmatics.* Mahwah, NJ: Lawrence Erlbaum.

Kasper, G., & Schmidt, R. (1996). Developmental issues in interlanguage pragmatics. *Studies in Second Language Acquisition, 18,* 149–169.

Kempf, R. (1985). Pronouns and terms of address in Neues Deutschland. *Language in Society, 14,* 223–237.

Kendall, M. (1981). Toward a semantic approach to terms of address: A critique of deterministic models in sociolinguistics. *Language and Communication, 1,* 237–254.

Kerbrat-Orecchioni, C. (1993). Variations culturelles et universaux dans les systèmes conversationnels [Cultural variation and universals in conversational systems]. In J. Halté (Ed.), *Inter-actions: L'interaction, actualités de la recherche et enjeux didactiques* [Interactions: Interaction, current research, and pedagogical challenges] (pp. 61–90). Metz: Centre d'Analyse Syntaxique de l'Université de Metz.

Kitao, K. (1990). A study of Japanese and American perceptions of politeness in requests. *Doshida Studies in English, 50,* 178–210.

Kohz, A. (1984). *Markiertheit, Normalität und Natürlichkeit von Anredeformen* [Markedness, normality, and naturalness of address forms]. In W. Winter (Ed.), *Anredeverhalten* [Address behavior] (pp. 25–40). Tübingen: Narr.

Koike, D. (1996). Transfer of pragmatic competence and suggestions in Spanish foreign language learning. In S. Gass & J. Neu (Eds.), *Speech acts across cultures* (pp. 257–281). Berlin: Mouton de Gruyter.

Kotthoff, H., & Auer, P. (1987). *Lernersprachliche und interkulturelle Ursachen für Mißverständnisse* [Interlanguage and intercultural causes for misunderstandings]. *Englisch-Amerikanische Studien, 2,* 239–250.

Kramsch, C. (1993). *Context and culture in language education.* Oxford: Oxford University Press.

Kramsch, C. (1995). *Redefining the boundaries of language study.* Boston: Heinle and Heinle.

Krashen, S. (1982). *Principles and practice in second language acquisition.* Oxford: Pergamon.

Krashen, S. (1985). *The Input Hypothesis: Issues and implications.* London: Longman.

Kubota, M. (1995). Teachability of conversational implicature to Japanese EFL learners. *IRLT Bulletin, 9,* 35–67.

Kumatoridani, T. (1994). *Hatsuwa kooi to shite no kansha: Tekisetsu-sei jooken, hyoogen sutorateji, danwa kinoo* [Expressing gratitude as speech acts: Proper conditions, strategies for expressions, and discourse functions]. *Nihongogaku, 13,* 63–72.

Kuo, J., & Jiang, X. (1997). Assessing the assessments: The OPI and the SOPI. *Foreign Language Annals, 30,* 503–512.

Lantolf, J. (Ed.). (2000). *Sociocultural theory and second language learning.* Oxford: Oxford University Press.

Lantolf, J., & Frawley, W. (1988). Proficiency: Understanding the construct. *Studies in Second Language Acquisition, 10,* 181–195.

Larsen Freeman, D., & Long, M. (1991). *An introduction to second language acquisition research.* New York: Longman.

Lave, J., & Wenger, E. (1991). *Situated learning: Legitimate peripheral participation.* New York: Cambridge University Press.

Lazaraton, A. (1992). The structural organization of a language interview: A conversation analytic perspective. *System, 20,* 373–386.

Lebra, T. (1976). *Japanese patterns of behavior.* Honolulu: University of Hawaii Press.

Lee, J., & VanPatten, B. (1995). *Making communicative language teaching happen.* New York: McGraw-Hill.

Leech, G. (1983). *The principles of pragmatics.* London: Longman.

Leeman, J., Arteagoitia, I., Fridman, B., & Doughty, C. (1995). Integrating attention to form with meaning: Focus on form in content based Spanish instruction. In R. Schmidt (Ed.), *Attention and awareness in foreign language learning* (Technical Report #9) (pp. 217–258). Honolulu: University of Hawai'i, Second Language Teaching and Curriculum Center.

Levinson, S. (1983). *Pragmatics.* Cambridge: Cambridge University Press.

Liddicoat, A. (1997a). *Communicating in LOTE: Writing and oral interaction.* Canberra: MLTA.

Liddicoat, A. (1997b). Everyday speech as culture: Implications for language teaching. In A. Liddicoat & C. Crozet (Eds.), *Teaching language, teaching culture* (pp. 55–70). Canberra: Applied Linguistics Association of Australia.

Liddicoat, A., & Crozet, C. (1997). *Teaching language, teaching culture.* Canberra: Applied Linguistics Association of Australia.

Liddicoat, A., Crozet, C., Jansen, L., & Schmidt, G. (1997). The role of language learning in academic education: An overview. *Australian Review of Applied Linguistics, 20,* 19–32.

Lightbown, P., & Spada, N. (1990). Focus-on-form and corrective feedback in communicative language teaching: Effects on second language learning. *Studies in Second Language Acquisition, 12,* 429–448.

Lim, D. (1996). Cross-cultural interaction and classroom discourse: A study of foreign language classroom culture. Unpublished doctoral dissertation, Department of East Asian Languages and Literatures, University of Hawai'i at Manoa.

LoCastro, V., & Netsu, M. (1997). *-to omoimasu* and "I think": A pragmatic mismatch with academic skills consequences. Unpublished manuscript.

Loh, T. (1993). *Responses to compliments across cultures: A comparative study of British and Hong Kong Chinese* (Research Report #30). Hong Kong: Department of English, City Polytechnic of Hong Kong.

Long, M. (1984). Process and product in ESL program evaluation. *TESOL Quarterly, 18,* 409–425.

Long, M. (1996). The role of the linguistic environment in second language acquisition. In W. Ritchie & T. Bhatia (Eds.), *Handbook of second language acquisition* (pp. 413–468). New York: Academic Press.

Long, M., Adams, L., McLean, M., & Castaños, F. (1976). Doing things with words: Verbal interaction in lockstep and small group classroom situations. In J. Fanselow & R. Crymes (Eds.), *On TESOL '76* (pp. 137–153). Washington, DC: TESOL.

Long, M., & Norris, J. (in press). Task-based language teaching and assessment. In M. Byram (Ed.), *Encyclopedia of language teaching.* London: Routledge.

Long, M., & Robinson, P. (1998). Focus on form: Theory, research, and practice. In C. Doughty & J. Williams (Eds.), *Focus on form in classroom second language acquisition* (pp. 15–41). Cambridge: Cambridge University Press.

Lörscher, W. (1986). Conversational structures in the foreign language classroom. In G. Kasper (Ed.), *Learning, teaching and communication in the foreign language classroom* (pp. 11–22). Aarhus: Aarhus University Press.

Lörscher, W., & Schulze, R. (1988). On polite speaking and foreign language classroom discourse. *IRAL, 26,* 183–199.

Lustig, M., & Koester, J. (1993). *Intercultural competence: Interpersonal communication across cultures.* New York: HarperCollins.

Lyons, J. (1977). *Semantics.* Cambridge: Cambridge University Press.

Lyster, R. (1994). The effect of functional-analytic teaching on aspects of French immersion students' sociolinguistic competence. *Applied Linguistics, 15,* 263–287.

Maeshiba, N., Yoshinaga, N., Kasper, G., & Ross, S. (1996). Transfer and proficiency in interlanguage apologizing. In S. Gass & J. Neu (Eds.), *Speech acts across cultures* (pp. 155–187). Berlin: Mouton de Gruyter.

Manes, J. (1983). Compliments: A mirror of cultural values. In N. Wolfson & E. Judd (Eds.), *Sociolinguistics and language acquisition* (pp. 96–102). New York: Newbury House.

Manes, J., & Wolfson, N. (1981). The compliment formula. In F. Coulmas (Ed.), *Conversational routine: Explorations in standardized communication situations and prepatterned speech* (pp. 115–132). The Hague: Mouton.

Manley, J. (1995). Assessing students' oral language: One school district's response. *Foreign Language Annals, 28,* 93–102.

Marisi, P. (1994). Questions of regionalism in native speaker OPI performance: The French-Canadian experience. *Foreign Language Annals, 27,* 505–521.

Markee, N. (1995). Teachers' answers to students' questions: Problematizing the issue of meaning making. *Issues in Applied Linguistics, 6,* 63–92.

Markee, N. (2000). *Conversation analysis.* Mahwah, NJ: Lawrence Erlbaum.

Marriott, H. (1990). Intercultural business negotiations: The problem of norm discrepancy. In A. Pauwels (Ed.), *Cross-cultural communication in the professions in Australia* (pp. 33–65). Melbourne: Applied Linguistics Association of Australia.

Martin, S. (1975). *A reference grammar of Japanese.* New Haven: Yale University Press.

Martiny, T. (1996). Forms of address in French and Dutch: A sociopragmatic approach. *Language Sciences, 18,* 765–775.

Matsuda, Y. (1988). *Taiwa no nihongo kyooiku-aizuchi ni kanrenshite* [Teaching Japanese conversation: *Aizuchi*]. *Nihongogaku, 7,* 59–66.

Maynard, S. (1989). *Japanese conversation: Self-contextualization through structure and interactional management.* Norwood, NJ: Ablex.

McLaughlin, B. (1987). *Theories of second language learning.* London: Edward Arnold.

McNamara, T. (1996). *Measuring second language performance: A new era in language testing.* New York: Longman.

Meisel, J., Clahsen, H., & Pienemann, M. (1981). On determining developmental stages in natural second language acquisition. *Studies in Second Language Acquisition, 3,* 109–135.

Messick, S. (1989). Validity. In R. Linn (Ed.), *Educational measurement* (pp. 13–103). New York: Macmillan.

Miles, P. (1994). Compliments and gender. *University of Hawai'i Occasional Papers Series, 26,* 85–137.

Miller, L. (1995). Verbal listening behavior in conversations between Japanese and Americans. In J. Bommaert & J. Verschueren (Eds.), *The pragmatics of intercultural and international communication* (pp. 111–130). Amsterdam: John Benjamins.

Mir, M. (1992). Do we all apologize the same? An empirical study of the act of apologizing by Spanish speakers learning English. In L. Bouton & Y. Kachru (Eds.), *Pragmatics and language learning,* monograph series vol. 3 (pp. 1–19). Urbana-Champaign: Division of English as an International Language, University of Illinois, Urbana-Champaign.

Mir, M. (1995). The perception of social context in request performance. In L. Bouton (Ed.), *Pragmatics and language learning,* monograph series vol. 6 (pp. 105–120). Urbana-Champaign: Division of English as an International Language, University of Illinois, Urbana-Champaign.

Miyake, K. (1994a). *Kansha no taishoo kenkyuu: nichiei taishoo kenkyuu-bunka shakai o han'ei-suru gengo koodoo* [Expressing gratitude in Japanese and English: Language behaviors which reflect society and culture]. *Nihongogaku, 13,* 10–18.

Miyake, K. (1994b). *'Wabi' igai de tsukawareru wabi hyoogen: Sono tayooka no jittai to uchi, soto, yoso no kankei* [Formulaic apologies in nonapologetic situations: A metaanalysis and its relations with the concept of *uchi-soto-yoso*]. *Nihongo Kyooiku, 82,* 134–146.

Mizutani, O., & Mizutani, N. (1978). *How to be polite in Japanese.* Tokyo: Japan Times.

Morosawa, A. (1990). Intimacy and urgency in request forms in Japanese: A psycholinguistic study. *Sophia Linguistica, 28,* 129–143.

Morrow, C. (1996). The pragmatic effects of instruction on ESL learners' production of complaint and refusal speech acts. Unpublished doctoral dissertation, State University of New York at Buffalo.

Moskowitz, G. (1971). Interaction analysis: A new modern language for supervisors. *Foreign Language Annals, 5,* 211–221.

Murphy, B., & Neu, J. (1996). My grade's too low: The speech act set of complaining. In S. Gass & J. Neu (Eds.), *Speech acts across cultures* (pp. 191–216). Berlin: Mouton de Gruyter.

Myers-Scotton, C. (1993). *Social motivations for code-switching: Evidence from Africa.* Oxford: Oxford University Press.

Myers-Scotton, C., & Bernsten, J. (1988). Natural conversation as a model for textbook dialogue. *Applied Linguistics, 9,* 372–384.

Nakane, C. (1970). *Japanese society.* Berkeley: University of California Press.

National Standards in Foreign Language Education Project. (1996). *Standards for foreign language learning: Preparing for the 21st century.* New York: National Standards in Foreign Language Education Project.

Nattinger, J., & DeCarrico, J. (1992). *Lexical phrases and language teaching.* Oxford: Oxford University Press.

Niki, H., & Tajika, H. (1994). Asking for permission vs. making requests: Strategies chosen by Japanese speakers of English. In L. Bouton & Y. Kachru (Eds.), *Pragmatics and language learning,* monograph series vol. 5 (pp. 110–124). Urbana-Champaign: Division of English as an International Language, University of Illinois, Urbana-Champaign.

Norris, J. (1996a). The Portuguese speaking test and native speaker judgments: Examining the validity of a SOPI. In C. Reves, C. Steele, & S.

Wong (Eds.), *Linguistics and language teaching 1995: Proceedings of the 6th Joint LSH-HATESL Conference* (Technical Report #10). Honolulu: University of Hawai'i, Second Language Teaching and Curriculum Center.

Norris, J. (1996b). A validation study of the ACTFL Guidelines and the German Speaking Test. Unpublished doctoral dissertation, University of Hawai'i at Manoa.

Norris, J. (1997a). The German speaking test: Utility and caveats. *Die Unterrichtspraxis, 30,* 148–158.

Norris, J. (1997b). Native speaker judgments as indicators of L2 oral proficiency: Redefining the role of the native speaker in proficiency guidelines. *University of Hawai'i Working Papers in English as a Second Language, 16,* 47–95.

Norris, J. (2000). Purposeful language assessment: Selecting the right alternative test. *English Teaching Forum, 38,* 18–23.

Norris, J., Brown, J., Hudson, T., & Yoshioka, J. (1998). *Designing second language performance assessments* (Technical Report #18). Honolulu: University of Hawai'i, Second Language Teaching and Curriculum Center.

Norris, J., & Ortega, L. (2000). Effectiveness of L2 instruction: A research synthesis and quantitative meta-analysis. *Language Learning, 50,* 417–528.

Nunan, D. (1991). Methods in second language classroom-oriented research: A critical review. *Studies in Second Language Acquisition, 13,* 249–274.

Norton, B. (2000). *Identity and language learning.* Harlow: Pearson Education.

Ochs, E. (1988). *Culture and language development.* Cambridge: Cambridge University Press.

Ochs, E. (1996). Linguistic resources for socializing humanity. In J. Gumperz & S. Levinson (Eds.), *Rethinking linguistic relativity* (pp. 407–437). Cambridge: Cambridge University Press.

Odlin, T. (1989). *Language transfer.* Cambridge: Cambridge University Press.

Ogawa, H. (1995). *Kansha to wabi no teishiki hyoogen: Bogo washa no shiyoo jittai kara no bunseki* [A study of Japanese formulaic thanks and apologies: A data analysis of the use by Japanese native speakers]. *Nihongo Kyooiku, 85,* 38–52.

Ohsugi, K. (1982). *Eigo no keii hyougen* [Referential English: For better international communication]. Tokyo: Taishukan.

Ohta, A. (1993). Activity, affect and stance: Sentential particles in the discourse of the Japanese as a foreign language classroom. Unpublished doctoral dissertation, Department of Applied Linguistics, University of California, Los Angeles.

Ohta, A. (1994). Socializing the expression of affect: An overview of affective particle use in the Japanese as a foreign language classroom. *Issues in Applied Linguistics, 5,* 303–325.

Ohta, A. (1995). Applying sociocultural theory to an analysis of learner discourse: Learner-learner collaborative interaction in the zone of proximal development. *Issues in Applied Linguistics, 6,* 93–121.

Ohta, A. (1997). The development of pragmatic competence in learner-learner classroom interaction. In L. Bouton (Ed.), *Pragmatics and language learning,* monograph series vol. 8 (pp. 223–242). Urbana-Champaign: Division of English as an International Language, University of Illinois, Urbana-Champaign.

Ohta, A. (1999). Interactional routines and the socialization of interactional style in adult learners of Japanese. *Journal of Pragmatics, 31,* 1493–1512.

Ohta, A. (2000a). Re-thinking interaction in SLA: Developmentally appropriate assistance in the zone of proximal development and the acquisition of L2 grammar. In J. Lantolf (Ed.), *Sociocultural theory and second language learning* (pp. 53–80). Oxford: Oxford University Press.

Ohta, A. (2000b). Re-thinking recasts: A learner-centered examination of corrective feedback in the Japanese language classroom. In J. Hall & L. Verplaeste (Eds.), *The construction of second and foreign language learning through classroom interaction* (pp. 47–71). Mahwah, NJ: Lawrence Erlbaum.

Ohta, A. (2001). *Second language acquisition processes in the classroom: Learning Japanese.* Mahwah, NJ: Lawrence Erlbaum.

Ohta, A. (in press). Japanese second language acquisition in the classroom: What the voices of teachers and students tell us about the process of learning Japanese. In H. Nara (Ed.), *Advances in Japanese pedagogy.* Columbus: National Foreign Language Center, Ohio State University.

Okamoto, S. (1998). The use and non-use of honorifics in sales talk in Kyoto and Osaka: Are they rude or friendly? In N. Akatsuka, H. Hoji, S. Iwasaki, S. Sohn, & S. Strauss (Eds.), *Japanese/Korean linguistics 7* (pp. 141–157). Stanford, CA: Center for the Study of Language and Information.

Olshtain, E. (1983). Sociocultural competence and language transfer: The case of apology. In S. Gass & L. Selinker (Eds.), *Language transfer in language learning* (pp. 232–249). Rowley, MA: Newbury House.

Olshtain, E. (1989). Apologies across languages. In S. Blum-Kulka, J. House, & G. Kasper (Eds.), *Cross-cultural pragmatics: Requests and apologies* (pp. 155–173). Norwood, NJ: Ablex.

Olshtain, E., & Blum-Kulka, S. (1985). Degree of approximation: Nonnative reactions to native speech act behavior. In S. Gass & C. Madden (Eds.), *Input in second language acquisition* (pp. 303–325). New York: Newbury House.

Olshtain, E., & Cohen, A. (1983). Apology: A speech act set. In N. Wolfson & E. Judd (Eds.), *Sociolinguistics and second language acquisition* (pp. 18–35). New York: Newbury House.

Olshtain, E., & Cohen, A. (1990). The learning of complex speech act behavior. *TESL Canada Journal, 7,* 45–65.

Olshtain, E., & Weinbach, L. (1987). Complaints: A study of speech act behavior among native and nonnative speakers of Hebrew. In J. Verschueren & M. Bertuccelli-Papi (Eds.), *The pragmatic perspective: Selected papers from the 1985 International Pragmatics Conference* (pp. 195–208). Amsterdam: John Benjamins.

Omar, A. (1991). How learners greet in Kiswahili: A cross-sectional survey. In L. Bouton & Y. Kachru (Eds.), *Pragmatics and language learning,* monograph series vol. 2 (pp. 59–73). Urbana-Champaign: Division of English as an International Language, University of Illinois, Urbana-Champaign.

Omar, A. (1992). Opening and closing conversations in Kiswahili: A study of the performance of native speakers and learners. Unpublished doctoral dissertation, Indiana University, Bloomington.

Oshima-Takane, Y., & MacWhinney, B. (1994). *Japanese CHAT Manual.* Montreal: McGill University.

Ostrom, T., & Gannon, K. (1996). Exemplar generation: Assessing how respondents give meaning to rating scales. In N. Schwarz & S. Sudman (Eds.), *Answering questions: Methodology for determining cognitive and communicative processes in survey research* (pp. 293–318). San Francisco: Jossey-Bass.

Pearson, L. (1998). Spanish L2 pragmatics: The effects of metapragmatic discussion. Paper presented at the Second Language Research Forum, University of Hawai'i, Manoa, October.

Peirce, C. (1955). *Philosophical writings of Peirce.* New York: Dover.

Pennington, M. (1994). *Forces shaping a dual-code society: An interpretive review of the literature on language use and language attitudes in Hong Kong* (Research Report #35). Hong Kong: Department of English, City Polytechnic of Hong Kong.

Peters, A., & Boggs, S. (1986). Interactional routines as cultural influences upon language acquisition. In B. Schieffelin & E. Ochs (Eds.), *Language socialization across cultures* (pp. 80–96). New York: Cambridge University Press.

Pienemann, M. (1989). Is language teachable? Psycholinguistic hypotheses and experiments. *Applied Linguistics, 10,* 52–79.

Pienemann, M., Johnston, M., & Brindley, G. (1988). Constructing an acquisition-based procedure for second language assessment. *Studies in Second Language Acquisition, 10,* 217–243.

Pieper, U. (1984). *Zur Interaktion linguistischer, sozialer und biologischer Variablen im Problemkreis der 'Anrede'* [The interaction of linguistic, social and biological variables in the use of address terms]. In W. Winter (Ed.), *Anredeverhalten* [Address behavior] (pp. 9–24). Tübingen: Narr.

Piirainen-Marsh, A. (1995). *Face in second language conversation.* Jyväskylä: University of Jyväskylä.

Pomerantz, A. (1978). Compliment responses: Notes on the cooperation of multiple constraints. In J. Schenkein (Ed.), *Studies in the organization of conversational interaction* (pp. 79–112). New York: Academic Press.

Pomerantz, A. (1984). Agreeing and disagreeing with assessments: Some features of preferred/dispreferred turn shapes. In J. Atkinson & J. Heritage (Eds.), *Structures of social interaction: Studies in conversation analysis* (pp. 57–101). Cambridge: Cambridge University Press.

Poole, D. (1992). Language socialization in the second language classroom. *Language Learning, 42,* 593–616.

Popham, W. (1978). *Criterion-referenced measurement.* Englewood Cliffs, NJ: Prentice Hall.

Riggenbach, H. (1991). Toward an understanding of fluency: A microanalysis of nonnative speaker conversations. *Discourse Processes, 14,* 423–441.

Riley, P. (1989). 'Well don't blame me': On the interpretation of pragmatic errors. In W. Oleksy (Ed.), *Contrastive pragmatics* (pp. 231–250). Philadelphia: John Benjamins.

Rintell, E., & Mitchell, C. (1989). Studies of requests and apologies: An inquiry into method. In S. Blum-Kulka, J. House, & G. Kasper (Eds.), *Cross-cultural pragmatics: Requests and apologies* (pp. 248–272). Norwood, NJ: Ablex.

Robinson, P. (1996). Learning simple and complex second language rules under implicit, incidental, rule-search and instructed conditions. *Studies in Second Language Acquisition, 18,* 27–67.

Robinson, P. (1997). Individual differences and the fundamental similarity of implicit and explicit adult second language learning. *Language Learning, 47,* 45–99.

Robinson, P. (Ed.). (in press). *Cognition and second language instruction.* Cambridge: Cambridge University Press.

Rose, K. (1992). Speech acts and questionnaires: The effect of hearer response. *Journal of Pragmatics, 17*, 49–62.

Rose, K. (1993). Sociolinguistic consciousness-raising through video. *Language Teacher, 17*, 7–9.

Rose, K. (1994a). On the validity of DCTs in non-Western contexts. *Applied Linguistics, 15*, 1–14.

Rose, K. (1994b). Pragmatic consciousness-raising in an EFL context. In L. Bouton & Y. Kachru (Eds.), *Pragmatics and language learning,* monograph series vol. 5 (pp. 52–63). Urbana-Champaign: Division of English as an International Language, University of Illinois, Urbana-Champaign.

Rose, K. (1997). Pragmatics in the classroom: Theoretical concerns and practical possibilities. In L. Bouton (Ed.), *Pragmatics and language learning,* monograph series vol. 8 (pp. 267–295). Urbana-Champaign: Division of English as an International Language, University of Illinois, Urbana-Champaign.

Rose, K. (1999). Teachers and students learning about requests in Hong Kong. In E. Hinkel (Ed.), *Culture in second language teaching and learning* (pp. 167–180). Cambridge: Cambridge University Press.

Rose, K. (2000). An exploratory cross-sectional study of interlanguage pragmatic development. *Studies in Second Language Acquisition, 22*, 27–67.

Rose, K., & Ono, R. (1995). Eliciting speech act data in Japanese: The effect of questionnaire type. *Language Learning, 45*, 191–223.

Ross, S. (1995). Aspects of communicative accommodation in oral proficiency interview discourse. Unpublished doctoral dissertation, University of Hawai'i at Manoa.

Ross, S., & Berwick, R. (1992). The discourse of accommodation in oral proficiency interviews. *Studies in Second Language Acquisition, 14*, 159–176.

Röver, C. (1996). *Linguistische Routinen: Systematische, psycholinguistische und fremdsprachendidaktische Überlegungen* [Linguistic routines: Systematic, psycholinguistic, and pedadogical considerations]. *Fremdsprachen und Hochschule, 46*, 43–60.

Sakamoto, N., & Naotsuka, R. (1982). *Polite fictions: Why Japanese and Americans seem rude to each other.* Tokyo: Kinseido.

Salsbury, T., & Bardovi-Harlig, K. (in press). "I know your mean, but I don't think so": Disagreements in L2 English. In L. Bouton (Ed.), *Pragmatics and language learning,* monograph series vol. 10. Urbana-Champaign: Division of English as an International Language, University of Illinois, Urbana-Champaign.

Salsbury, T., & Bardovi-Harlig, K. (2000). Opposition talk and the acquisition of modality in L2 English. In B. Swierzbin, F. Morris, M. Anderson, C. Klee, & E. Tarone (Eds.), *Social and cognitive factors in second language acquisition* (pp. 56–76). Somerville, MA: Cascadilla Press.

Sawyer, M. (1992). The development of pragmatics in Japanese as a second language: The particle *ne.* In G. Kasper (Ed.), *Pragmatics of Japanese as a native and target language* (Technical Report #3) (pp. 83–125). Honolulu: University of Hawai'i, Second Language Teaching and Curriculum Center.

Scarcella, R. (1979). On speaking politely in a second language. In C. Yorio, K. Perkins, & J. Schachter (Eds.), *On TESOL '79: The learner in focus* (pp. 274–287). Washington, DC: TESOL.

Scarcella, R., & Brunak, J. (1981). On speaking politely in a second language. *International Journal of the Sociology of Language, 27*, 59–75.

Schegloff, E. (1968). Sequencing in conversational openings. *American Anthropology, 70,* 1075–95.

Schegloff, E. (1986). The routine as achievement. *Human Studies, 9,* 111–51.

Schegloff, E. (1993). Reflections on quantification in the study of conversation. *Research on Language and Social Interaction, 26,* 99–128.

Schieffelin, B., & Ochs, E. (Eds.). (1986). *Language socialization across cultures.* Cambridge: Cambridge University Press.

Schieffelin, D., & Ochs, E. (1986). Language socialization. *Annual Review of Anthropology, 15,* 163–191.

Schmidt, R. (1983). Interaction, acculturation, and the acquisition of communicative competence: A case study of one adult. In N. Wolfson & E. Judd (Eds.), *Sociolinguistics and language acquisition* (pp. 137–174). Rowley, MA: Newbury House.

Schmidt, R. (1990). The role of consciousness in second language learning. *Applied Linguistics, 11,* 17–46.

Schmidt, R. (1992). Psychological mechanisms underlying second language fluency. *Studies in Second Language Acquisition, 14 ,* 357–387.

Schmidt, R. (1993a). Awareness and second language acquisition. *Annual Review of Applied Linguistics, 13,* 206–226.

Schmidt, R. (1993b). Consciousness, learning and interlanguage pragmatics. In G. Kasper & S. Blum-Kulka (Eds.), *Interlanguage pragmatics* (pp. 21–42). Oxford: Oxford University Press.

Schmidt, R. (1994). Deconstructing consciousness in search of useful definitions for applied linguistics. *AILA Review, 11,* 11–26.

Schmidt, R. (1995). Consciousness and foreign language learning: A tutorial on the role of attention and awareness in learning. In R. Schmidt (Ed.), *Attention and awareness in foreign language learning* (Technical Report #9) (pp. 1–63). Honolulu: University of Hawai'i, Second Language Teaching and Curriculum Center.

Schmidt, R. (1998). The centrality of attention in SLA. *University of Hawai'i Working Papers in English as a Second Language, 16,* 1–34.

Schmidt, R., & Frota, S. (1986). Developing basic conversational ability in a second language: A case study of an adult learner of Portuguese. In R. Day (Ed.), *Talking to learn: Conversation in second language acquisition* (pp. 237–326). New York: Newbury House.

Schumann, J. (1978). *The pidginization process: A model for second language acquisition.* Rowley, MA: Newbury House.

Schumann, J. (1979). The acquisition of English negation by speakers of Spanish: A review of the literature. In R. Anderson (Ed.), *The acquisition and use of Spanish and English as first and second languages* (pp. 3–32). Washington, DC: TESOL.

Scotton, C., & Bernsten, J. (1988). Natural conversations as a model for textbook dialogue. *Applied Linguistics, 9,* 213–243.

Searle, J. (1976). A classification of illocutionary acts. *Language in Society, 5,* 1–23.

Sharwood Smith, M. (1988). Consciousness-raising and the second language learner. In W. Rutherford & M. Sharwood Smith (Eds.), *Grammar and second language teaching* (pp. 51–60). New York: Newbury House.

Sharwood Smith, M. (1991). Speaking to many minds: On the relevance of different types of language information for the L2 learner. *Second Language Research, 7,* 118–132.

Sharwood Smith, M. (1993). Input enhancement in instructed SLA: Theoretical bases. *Studies in Second Language Acquisition, 15,* 165–179.

Shepard, L. (1993). Evaluating test validity. In L. Darling-Hammond (Ed.), *Review of research in education* (pp. 405–450). Washington, DC: American Educational Research Association.

Shimamura, K. (1993). *Judgment of request strategies and contextual factors by American and Japanese EFL learners* (Occasional Paper #25). Honolulu: University of Hawai'i at Manoa, Department of English as a Second Language.

Shohamy, E. (1988). A proposed framework for testing the oral language proficiency of second/foreign language learners. *Studies in Second Language Acquisition, 10,* 165–179.

Shohamy, E. (1994). The validity of direct versus semi-direct oral tests. *Language Testing, 11,* 99–123.

Siegal, M. (1994). Looking East: Learning Japanese as a second language in Japan and the interaction of race, gender and social context. Unpublished doctoral dissertation, University of California, Berkeley.

Siegal, M. (1996). The role of learner subjectivity in second language sociolinguistic competency: Western women learning Japanese. *Applied Linguistics, 17,* 356–382.

Silverstein, M. (1976). Shifters, linguistic categories, and cultural description. In K. Basso & H. Selby (Eds.), *Meaning in anthropology* (pp. 11–56). Albuquerque: University of New Mexico Press.

Sinclair, J., & Coulthard, R. (1975). *Towards an analysis of discourse.* Oxford: Oxford University Press.

Spada, N., & Lightbown, P. (1993). Instruction and the development of questions in L2 classrooms. *Studies in Second Language Acquisition, 15,* 205–224.

Spolsky, B. (1985). The limits of authenticity in language testing. *Language Testing, 2,* 31–40.

Stansfield, C., & Kenyon, D. (1991). *Development of the Texas Oral Proficiency Test (TOPT): Final report.* Washington, DC: Center for Applied Linguistics.

Stansfield, C., & Kenyon, D. (1992a). The development and validation of a simulated oral proficiency interview. *Modern Language Journal, 76,* 129–142.

Stansfield, C., & Kenyon, D. (1992b). Research on the comparability of the oral proficiency interview and the simulated oral proficiency interview. *System, 20,* 347–364.

Stansfield, C., & Kenyon, D. (1993). Development and validity of the Hausa Speaking Test with the ACTFL Proficiency Guidelines. *Issues in Applied Linguistics, 4,* 5–31.

Steinberg Du, J. (1995). Performance of face-threatening acts in Chinese: Complaining, giving bad news, and disagreeing. In G. Kasper (Ed.), *Pragmatics of Chinese as a native and target language* (Technical Report #5) (pp. 165–205). Honolulu: University of Hawai'i, Second Language Teaching and Curriculum Center.

Stern, H. (1992). *Issues and options in language teaching.* Oxford: Oxford University Press.

Stevenson, D. (1985). Authenticity, validity and a tea party. *Language Testing, 2,* 41–47.

Strauss, A., & Corbin, J. (1990). *Basics of qualitative research: Grounded theory procedures and techniques.* Newbury Park, CA: Sage.

Strauss, S. (1995). Assessments as a window to sociolinguistic research: The case of Japanese, Korean, and American English. In M. Tokunaga (Ed.), *Gengo-henyoo ni kan-suru taikeiteki kenkyuu oyobi sono nihongo kyooiku e no ooyoo* [Systematic studies of language variation and their application to Japanese language teaching] (pp. 177–191). Tokyo: Kanda University of Foreign Studies.

Svanes, B. (1992). Utviklingen av realisasjonsmønsteret for språkhandlingen 'å be noen om å gjøre noe' hos utenlandske studenter I løpet av 3 år i Norge [Development of realization patterns of the speech act "asking someone to do something" by foreign students during three years in Norway]. *Norsk Lingvistisk Tidsskrift, 1,* 1–50.

Swain, M. (1985). Communicative competence: Some roles of comprehensible input and comprehensible output in its development. In S. Gass & C. Madden (Eds.), *Input in second language acquisition* (pp. 235–253). Rowley, MA: Newbury House.

Swain, M. (1993). The output hypothesis: Just speaking and writing are not enough. *The Canadian Modern Language Review, 50,* 158–164.

Swain, M. (1996). Three functions of output in second language learning. In G. Cook & B. Seidlhofer (Eds.), *Principle and practice in applied linguistics* (pp. 245–256). Oxford: Oxford University Press.

Swain, M. (1998). Focus on form through conscious reflection. In C. Doughty & J. Williams (Eds.), *Focus on form in classroom second language acquisition* (pp. 64–81). Cambridge: Cambridge University Press.

Swain, M., & Lapkin, S. (1995). Problems in output and the cognitive processes they generate: A step towards second language learning. *Applied Linguistics, 16,* 371–391.

Takahashi, S. (1987). A contrastive study of indirectness exemplified in L1 directive speech acts performed by Americans and Japanese. Unpublished master's thesis, University of Illinois at Urbana-Champaign.

Takahashi, S. (1995). Pragmatic transferability of L1 indirect request strategies perceived by Japanese learners of English . Unpublished doctoral dissertation, University of Hawai'i at Manoa, Honolulu.

Takahashi, S. (1996). Pragmatic transferability. *Studies in Second Language Acquisition, 18,* 189–223.

Takahashi, S., & DuFon, M. (1989). Cross-linguistic influence in indirectness: The case of English directives performed by native Japanese speakers. Unpublished manuscript, Department of English as a Second Language, University of Hawai'i at Manoa (ERIC Document Reproduction Service No. ED370439).

Takahashi, T., & Beebe, L. (1987). The development of pragmatic competence by Japanese learners of English. *JALT Journal, 8,* 131–155.

Takahashi, T., & Beebe, L. (1993). Cross-linguistic influence in the speech act of correction. In G. Kasper & S. Blum-Kulka (Eds.), *Interlanguage pragmatics* (pp. 138–157). Oxford: Oxford University Press.

Tanaka, N. (1988). Politeness: Some problems for Japanese speakers of English. *JALT Journal, 9,* 81–102.

Tanaka, S., & Kawade, S. (1982). Politeness strategies and second language acquisition. *Studies in Second Language Acquisition, 5,* 18–33.

Tannen, D. (1984a). *Conversational style: Analyzing talk among friends.* Norwood, NJ: Ablex.

Tannen, D. (1984b). The pragmatics of cross-cultural communication. *Applied Linguistics, 5*, 189–206.

Tannen, D. (1986). *That's not what I meant.* New York: Ballantine.

Tannen, D. (1993a). *Framing in discourse.* Oxford: Oxford University Press.

Tannen, D. (1993b). The relativity of linguistic strategies: Rethinking power and solidarity in gender and dominance. In D. Tannen (Ed.), *Gender and conversational interaction* (pp. 165–188). Oxford: Oxford University Press.

Tarone, E., & Yule, G. (1989). *Focus on the language learner: Approaches to identifying and meeting the needs of second language learners.* Oxford: Oxford University Press.

Tateyama, Y. (1998). Explicit and implicit teaching of pragmatic routines: Japanese *sumimasen.* Unpublished doctoral dissertation, University of Hawai'i at Manoa.

Tateyama, Y., Kasper, G., Mui, L., Tay, H., & Thananart, O. (1997). Explicit and implicit teaching of pragmatic routines. In L. Bouton (Ed.), *Pragmatics and language learning,* monograph series vol. 8 (pp. 163–178). Urbana-Campaign: Division of English as an International Language, University of Illinois, Urbana-Champaign.

Tharp, R., & Gallimore, R. (1988). *Rousing minds to life: Teaching, learning, and schooling in social context.* New York: Cambridge University Press.

Thomas, J. (1983). Cross-cultural pragmatic failure. *Applied Linguistics, 4,* 91–112.

Thomas, J. (1984). Cross-cultural discourse as unequal encounter: Towards a pragmatic analysis. *Applied Linguistics, 5,* 226–235.

Tickoo, M. (Ed.). (1995). *Language and culture in multilingual societies* (Anthology Series 36). Singapore: SEAMEO Regional Language Centre.

Tomlin, R., & Villa, V. (1994). Attention in cognitive science and second language acquisition. *Studies in Second Language Acquisition, 16,* 183–203.

Trahey, M., & White, L. (1993). Positive evidence and preemption in the second language classroom. *Studies in Second Language Acquisition, 15,* 181–204.

Trosborg, A. (1987). Apology strategies in natives/nonnatives. *Journal of Pragmatics, 11,* 147–167.

Trosborg, A. (1995). *Interlanguage pragmatics: Requests, complaints and apologies.* Berlin: Mouton de Gruyter.

Truscott, J. (1998). Noticing in second language acquisition: A critical review. *Second Language Research, 14,* 103–135.

Tschirner, E. (1996). Scope and sequence: Rethinking beginning foreign language instruction. *Modern Language Journal, 80,* 1–14.

Van Ek, J. (Ed.). (1975). *The 'threshold level' in a European unit/credit system for modern language learning by adults.* Strasbourg: Council of Europe.

van Lier, L. (1988). *The classroom and the language learner.* London: Longman.

van Lier, L. (1989). Reeling, writhing, drawling, stretching, and fainting in coils: Oral proficiency interviews as conversation. *TESOL Quarterly, 23,* 489–508.

VanPatten, B. (1994). Evaluating the role of consciousness in second language acquisition: Terms, linguistic features, and research methodology. *AILA Review, 11,* 27–36.

Vygotsky, L. (1978). *Mind in society: The development of higher psychological processes.* Cambridge: Harvard University Press.

Walters, J. (1980). Grammar, meaning, and sociological appropriateness in second language acquisition. *Canadian Journal of Psychology, 34,* 337–345.

Weinert, R. (1995). The role of formulaic language in second language acquisition: A review. *Applied Linguistics, 16,* 180–205.

Wertsch, J. (1991). *Voices of the mind.* Cambridge: Harvard University Press.

Wesche, M. (1987). Second language performance testing: The Ontario test of ESL as an example. *Language Testing, 4,* 28–47.

White, J. (1998). Getting the learners' attention: A typographical input enhancement study. In C. Doughty & J. Williams (Eds.), *Focus on form in classroom second language acquisition* (pp. 85–113). Cambridge: Cambridge University Press.

White, L. (1989). *Universal grammar and second language acquisition.* Amsterdam: John Benjamins.

White, L., Spada, N., Lightbown, P., & Ranta, L. (1991). Input enhancement and L2 question formation. *Applied Linguistics, 12,* 416–432.

White, S. (1989). Backchannels across cultures: A study of Americans and Japanese. *Language in Society, 18,* 59–76.

Wierzbicka, A. (1985). Different cultures, different language, different speech acts. *Journal of Pragmatics, 9,* 145–178.

Wierzbicka, A. (1991). *Cross-cultural pragmatics: The semantics of human interaction.* Berlin: Mouton de Gruyter.

Wildner-Bassett, M. (1984). Improving pragmatic aspects of learners' interlanguage. Tübingen: Narr.

Wildner-Bassett, M. (1986). Teaching and learning 'polite noises': Improving pragmatic aspects of advanced adult learners' interlanguage. In G. Kasper (Ed.), *Learning, teaching and communication in the foreign language classroom* (pp. 163–178). Aarhus: Aarhus University Press.

Wildner-Bassett, M. (1994). Intercultural pragmatics and proficiency: 'Polite' noises for cultural appropriateness. *International Review of Applied Linguistics, 32,* 3–17.

Wilkins, D. (1976). *Notional syllabuses: A taxonomy and its relevance to foreign language curriculum development.* Oxford: Oxford University Press.

Williams, J., & Evans, J. (1998). What kind of focus and on which forms? In C. Doughty & J. Williams (Eds.), *Focus on form in classroom second language acquisition* (pp. 139–155). Cambridge: Cambridge University Press.

Williams, M. (1988). Language taught for meetings and language used in meetings: Is there anything in common? *Applied Linguistics, 9,* 45–58.

Winter, W. (Ed.). (1984). *Anredeverhalten* [Address behavior]. Tübingen: Narr.

Wolfson, N. (1981a). Compliments in cross-cultural perspective. *TESOL Quarterly, 15,* 117–124.

Wolfson, N. (1981b). Invitations, compliments and the competence of the native speaker. *International Journal of Psycholinguistics, 8,* 7–22.

Wolfson, N. (1983). An empirically based analysis of complimenting in American English. In N. Wolfson & E. Judd (Eds.), *Sociolinguistics and language acquisition* (pp. 82–95). New York: Newbury House.

Wolfson, N. (1984). Pretty is as pretty does: A speech act view of sex roles. *Applied Linguistics, 5,* 236–244.

Wolfson, N. (1988). The bulge: A theory of speech behavior and social distance. In J. Fine (Ed.), *Second language research* (pp. 21–38). Norwood, NJ: Ablex.

Wolfson, N. (1989a). The social dynamics of native and nonnative complimenting behavior. In M. Eisenstein (Ed.), *The dynamic interlanguage: Empirical studies in second language variation* (pp. 219–236). New York: Plenum Press.

Wolfson, N. (1989b). *Sociolinguistics and TESOL.* New York: Newbury House.

Wolfson, N., & Manes, J. (1980). The compliment as a social strategy. *Papers in Linguistics, 13,* 389–410.

Wolfson, N., Marmor, T., & Jones, S. (1989). Problems in the comparison of speech acts across cultures. In S. Blum-Kulka, J. House, & G. Kasper (Eds.), *Cross-cultural pragmatics: Requests and apologies* (pp. 174–196). Norwood, NJ: Ablex.

Wong-Fillmore, L. (1976). The second time around: Cognitive and social strategies in second language acquisition. Unpublished doctoral dissertation, Stanford University, California.

Yamashita, S. (1996a). Comparing six cross-cultural pragmatics measures. Unpublished doctoral dissertation, Temple University, Philadelphia.

Yamashita, S. (1996b). *Six measures of JSL pragmatics* (Technical Report #14). Honolulu: University of Hawai'i, Second Language Teaching and Curriculum Center.

Ye, L. (1995). Complimenting in Mandarin Chinese. In G. Kasper (Ed.), *Pragmatics of Chinese as a native and target language* (Technical Report #5) (pp. 207–295). Honolulu: University of Hawai'i, Second Language Teaching and Curriculum Center.

Yoon, K. (1991). Bilingual pragmatic transfer to speech acts: Bi-directional responses to a compliment. In L. Bouton & Y. Kachru (Eds.), *Pragmatics and language learning,* monograph series vol. 2 (pp. 75–100). Urbana-Champaign: Division of English as an International Language, University of Illinois, Urbana-Champaign.

Yoshimi, D. (1998a). The development of communicative competence: Knowledge of the rules of discourse. Paper presented at the Annual Meeting of the American Association for Applied Linguistics, Seattle, Washington, March.

Yoshimi, D. (1998b). The development of discourse competence in a Japanese foreign language classroom. Paper presented at the Pacific Second Language Research Forum, Tokyo, Japan, March.

Yoshimi, D. (1999). L1 socialization as a variable in the use of *ne* by L2 learners of Japanese. *Journal of Pragmatics, 31,* 1513–1525.

Yoshitake, S. (1997). Interlanguage competence of Japanese students of English: A multi-test framework evaluation. Unpublished doctoral dissertation, Columbia Pacific University, San Rafael, California.

Yoshitake, S., & Enochs, K. (1996). Self-assessment and role plays for evaluating appropriateness in speech act realizations. *ICU Language Research Bulletin, 11,* 57–76.

Young, R. (1995). Conversational styles in language proficiency interviews. *Language Learning, 45,* 3–42.

Young, R., & He, A. (1998). *Talking and testing: Discourse approaches to the assessment of oral proficiency.* Philadelphia: John Benjamins.

Young, R., & Milanovic, M. (1992). Discourse variation in oral proficiency interviews. *Studies in Second Language Acquisition, 14,* 403–434.

Yuan, Y. (1998). Sociolinguistic dimensions of the compliment speech event in the southwest Mandarin dialect spoken in Kunming, China. Unpublished doctoral dissertation, Indiana University, Bloomington.

Zarate, G. (1986). *Enseigner une culture étrangère* [Teaching a foreign culture]. Paris: Hachette.

Name index

355

Subject index